PAYING THE PIPER

✤ Paying the Piper ✤

Causes and Consequences of Art Patronage

Edited by

JUDITH HUGGINS BALFE

University of Illinois Press
Urbana and Chicago

© 1993 by the Board of Trustees of the University of Illinois
Manufactured in the United States of America
1 2 3 4 5 C P 5 4 3 2 1

This book is printed on acid-free paper.

Library of Congress Cataloging-in-Publication Data
    Paying the piper : causes and consequences of art patronage / edited by
    Judith Huggins Balfe.
        p. cm.
    Includes bibliographical references and index.
    ISBN 0-252-02005-7 (cloth). — ISBN 0-252-06310-4 (paper)
    1. Art patronage.   2. Cultural policy.   3 Arts.   I. Balfe,
    Judith H. NX700.B44 1993
    306' .2–dc20   92-38280
                                                                        CIP

To Margaret J. Wyszomirski and the rest of our crowd
at Social Theory, Politics, and the Arts Conferences

✤ CONTENTS ✤

✤ INTRODUCTION ✤

JUDITH HUGGINS BALFE

The essays in this collection concern art patronage: the deliberate sponsorship of the creation, production, preservation, and dissemination of the so-called "fine arts." Such patronage is but one segment of a broad category of arts support, a category that includes the immediate audience ("box office") and the more anonymous consumers (buyers of "platinum" records). Patrons distinguish themselves from arts audiences and consumers by their "start-up" financial investment in the arts; focusing on the "supply side," as investors they assume a degree of control over the "product" that the "demand side" of supportive audiences cannot match. As they are paying the piper, they assume that they can call the tune; audiences can only respond to whatever the piper plays.

This distinction between patrons and lesser supporters has a long history, but it has recently been obscured by many advocates of public arts funding, in turn contributing to the current controversies over such programs. Thus many arts *supporters* assume that they are entitled to exercise a control over both the artistic process and product equivalent to that of the *patrons*. (Artists contest both notions of control, of course.)

Collectively, the essays in this volume demonstrate that conflating arts patronage with support obscures what most needs to be revealed. Indeed, as states and even international organizations assume the function of art patron on behalf of the wider taxpaying audiences and consumers, they risk the political and artistic failure of their programs if they respond only to audience demand and forego the trickier issues of artistic supply. Thus we distinguish here between art patrons and audience/supporters in order to illuminate the various and complex relationships between them. In making this distinction we join many other scholars who have long recognized that dissemination of the so-called "fine arts" to an audience beyond any artist's personal circle requires some specific patronage. However, most of these analysts then focus on the artists and the art that they produce, with whatever degree of freedom from their patrons. Instead, we focus on the patrons: What causes them to support the production of art

1

at all, by which artists and arts institutions, with what presumed degree of control, for what intended audiences? What are the consequences, both intended and unintended? In sum: given the risks and costs involved, how are the patrons supposed to benefit?

Patron Interest in Art as Merit Good or Public Good

Today, art is commonly assumed to be a merit good, to be appreciated for its own sake. This has led some critics to view art patronage as an act of pure self-interest on the part of patrons: patrons support the arts because this is how they obtain the art they want for themselves, even if others do not appreciate it. They should not then expect public support and applause for these activities, especially as most patrons have more cultural and financial capital than the population at large.

In contrast is the argument that art is a public good that brings other social benefits. Here, other critics respond that this patronage too is self-interested, as it is merely a means to other ends. From this perspective, those with no necessary love for the arts support them for what they see as the greater economic, political, or cultural good of society—and the security of their own place within it.

However, in both cases more complex motives, including self-disinterest, are surely involved. As for the first instance, patronage can easily be anonymous and the artistic product monopolized. (Such patronage has indeed occurred, in which case by definition we do not know much about it—at least not usually during the lifetime of these "unknown benefactors.") When the source of patronage is identified, moreover, the audience may ridicule rather than applaud the patron if the art itself does not "come off." Some considerations beyond the patron's own aesthetic interests—such as providing an opportunity for others to share in this "merit good," presumably with gratitude for the patron's beneficence—usually prompt the patron to assume the necessary risk and expense.

The second assumption of art patronage on the grounds of public utility, rather than art for art's sake, advances our understanding to a greater degree. From the outset it acknowledges multiple and often conflicting motives and, therefore, the inevitability of pragmatic considerations in any arts sponsorship, whether by private individuals or commercial organizations. But if the first perspective is flawed when it does not try to explain why any patron's nonaesthetic purposes may be useful or even necessary in the advancement of the arts, the second is flawed when it does not consider why the arts are supposed to work toward the attainment of ends other than themselves. When is there an affinity between consummatory art and functional ends—and when not?

Patronage Visibility and Control

Patronage is a risky and inevitably costly business. By definition, the arts are not totally predictable and even less are their interpretation and social effects. Further, patronage always involves issues of both visibility and control. If the sponsored art appears to be too controlled by the patron, it will be recognized as banal advertising or overt propaganda, and regardless of visibility, the patron will be seen as merely manipulative. Yet if little control is exercised, with invisibility patrons win no reflected glory from any successes, and with visibility they are held accountable for any failures. The risk of failure is taken lest a competitor seize the initiative of support and take credit for the successes: without such status competition, even among those who support art "for its own sake," why bother?

Modernization, with its attendant pressures toward social segmentation and bureaucratization (and thus toward new forms of status rivalries), has led to varying structures of arts patronage with different results for both artists and patrons. Without question, art patronage is intended to contribute to the production of cultural meaning through the arts themselves, as well as to the (re)production of social relations and institutional practice. As a by-product, it sets in motion the forces through which individuals and groups act upon and reconstruct those meanings and practices.

Thus while any patron's artistic taste and purpose will surely be appreciated by those in the audience who already share them, such people are usually not the majority of those who take note of the sponsorship, approvingly or not. There is always a wider, diverse public to the particular activities being supported, a public that is to be persuaded of the valorization that is going on, interactively, among patron, artist, artwork, and audience. When patronage has succeeded on both consummatory and functional grounds (that is, when both artist and patron can be said to have attained their purposes among the audience and the wider public), the patronage is often seen as an "art" in itself, somehow beyond rational planning and bureaucratic control. Still, however it must understand the artistic ethos, such patronage is necessarily behind the arts, not coequal with them. When patronage has failed, it is because it has effaced in the public eye the very art it was to promote.

Case Studies of the Problematics of Patronage

How can we assess—and thus anticipate and counteract—the problems inherent in art patronage? This collection of essays provides a number of independently written case studies that allow us to explore the interplay of two key sets of variables: whether the patronage is by *private or public* individuals or institutions, and whether it is *direct or indirect*. The essays are arranged here on these terms, in order of scale: from traditional, direct, private individual patronage, to the mixed forms found at the level of contemporary cities, to either direct or indirect public patronage through national and multinational ministries of culture (and their equivalents or subsidiaries).

Together, these essays allow us to compare the consequences of the various patronage structures. Ironically, despite the dispersal of risk by contemporary public arts agencies, the traditional forms have remained the models by which the successes of contemporary ones are judged by all concerned. Thus the National Endowment for the Arts (NEA) is blamed by both liberals and conservatives for not finding and funding a "new Beethoven," as if any federal agency could operate with the freedom of late eighteenth-century Viennese aristocrats. At the same time, others ask why any would-be "new Beethoven" need bother to curry the favor of such seemingly censorious, bureaucratized patrons when there are so many private and commercial avenues for artistic success.

Although these essays vary in their empirical focus, for the most part their authors remain disengaged from current debates over ideal models of theorizing and interpretation, of deconstruction, semiotics, reflexivity, and the like. Primarily, this is because the authors generally agree that qualitative aesthetic distinctions *can* be made, both between genres (of "high" or more "popular" culture) and within them. They do not regard all "texts" as inherently equal in significance, varying in their artistic rank-ing only because of the status of their respective sponsors or "readers." By accepting the principle that aesthetic hierarchies are determined in large measure by the artworks and not just by the power relations of their patrons and audiences, these authors cast light upon the current theo-retical debates, even if these are not the primary focus here. Rather, in the limited space available to them, in general these analysts have tried to tell the story "straight," historically and phenomenologically as it has apparently been understood by its participants.

The arts and the forms of their patronage are neither identical nor equal. Collectively, these authors allow us to compare the consequences of alternative forms of patronage and the ideological presuppositions that underlie them, consequences that are both obvious and immediate as well as those that are more subtle, far-reaching, and complex. Given competing demands for their time, attention, and money, why do people patronize the arts—and to what effect? The concluding chapter provides a summary and final evaluation of the evidence.

✤ PART ONE ✤

DIRECT PATRONAGE

BY PRIVATE INDIVIDUALS

Traditional art patronage is face-to-face, even if sometimes full of conflict (as between Pope Julius II and Michelangelo). In such cases, the patron benefits from direct experience with the artist and from exercising some control over the final product. At the same time, the artist can respond directly to the patron and negotiate the terms of the relationship to his or her own advantage. Such adjustment is all the more possible when there are rivalries among various individual patrons, actual or potential, even if they are united by social position or even as colleagues in an institution whose primary purpose is arts support.

The following three case studies show how the interacting roles of individual patrons and artists shifted during the eighteenth and nineteenth centuries. Tia DeNora analyzes Beethoven's aristocratic patrons who, by supporting him, promoted as well his assertion of artistic genius. Their standing as art patrons of innate sensitivity required validation if they were to maintain their status among the civilized court circles being threatened by the rising bourgeoisie. Beethoven, in turn, used their support to raise his own status. Accordingly, the new assumption was that art was no longer a matter of craft involving deferential service to the patron; it was inherently "for its own sake." Thus Beethoven established the model of the artist-genius that has resonated in Western culture ever since.

Jaap van der Tas examines the differences between art patronage provided by both aristocratic and gentrified dilettantes (as for Beethoven on an individual basis, or through their involvement in artists' academies in England and Germany) and that of bourgeois dilettantes in the Netherlands during the same period. There, in the absence of courtly or clerical traditions of artistic support, dilettantes and artists formed collegial associations as peers interested in reviving the Golden Age of seventeenth-century Dutch culture. But through these activities, the artists advanced toward professionalization: like the genius Beethoven surpassing his sponsors, Dutch artists went beyond their dilettante associates. Once they were no longer peers, these dilettantes came to be regarded as philistines. But in this case, the artists ended up losing as well; in the nineteenth century, the bourgeois Dutch republic came to be controlled by the same class of business-minded "philistines" who had been left behind, and the state provided almost nothing in art support.

Linda Fritschner discusses those "philistines" who became the first literary agents in late nineteenth-century England. Accepting and enhancing the claims to gentleman-status asserted by many writers, the agents curried their favor by taking on the mundane tasks of marketing their books. In time, having taken over their writers' financial affairs altogether, literary agents carved out a niche in the increasingly complex structure of art patronage. Appealing to the model of artist-genius that their writer-clients hoped to embody and thus enlisting their personal loyalty, the agents advanced their own role and status against those of the publishers, who became increasingly relegated to commercial rather than artistic spheres. But within the present generation, as the field of publishing has expanded even more (in part as a result of the agents' own activities), these individuals themselves have become derided for their skill in manipulating the very market concerns in which they specialized, and are now regarded as nameless and minor functionaries to be switched at will.

In each of these cases, whether the individual patron was an aristocrat, a bourgeois dilettante, or a market-minded "philistine," the immediate cause of the patronage was clearly support for artists who could create work beyond the patron's own capacities. These patrons were directly involved with the artists. Through such personal interaction as well as through the art that was to be created, the patrons expected that the quality of their own lives would be enhanced. But a wider audience was also to benefit, as witness both to the patronage and to the art. In each case, as an unintended consequence, the artist rose in status—both literally and figuratively at the expense of his patron.

❖ 1 ❖

The Social Basis of Beethoven's Style

TIA DENORA

The recognition of Beethoven's music by his contemporaries was neither spontaneous nor uncontested. Almost from the outset of his Viennese career, Beethoven's works were perceived by both his opponents and his advocates as different from other compositions that conformed to conventional Viennese critical standards. When judged according to these criteria of musical worth, Beethoven's works were sometimes described as deficient. During the composer's first decade in Vienna, hostile objections were directed toward what was judged the highly unconventional and arbitrary quality of his music.

Clearly, there were obstacles to be overcome before what Beethoven called the "peculiarities" of his style could be celebrated as exemplifying musical greatness. Explaining Beethoven's reputation by referring to the transcendent quality of his works alone tends to elide some of the more *sociologically* interesting features of his success: first, the extent to which Beethoven's eventual reputation was the result of practical tasks on the part of his patrons; second, the ways in which his style interacted with these activities; and third, how his emergent success was part of a micropolitical struggle over status to be achieved through music consumption.

Beethoven's "new path," as he later came to call it, was anchored to a "new" set of aesthetic criteria and stylistic conventions, and its acceptance entailed a corresponding reorientation of taste. Because of this, we must recognize that the construction of Beethoven as a "great" talent involved aesthetic and music-organizational entrepreneurship. In turn, Beethoven's eventual eminence as Vienna's premier composer during the 1790s and early 1800s (as indicated by what his contemporaries said about him and through concert repertories) had consequences, not only for the late-eighteenth-century Viennese music world, but also for the shape of subsequent international musical and aesthetic practice.

9

Beethoven's eventual success—both within Vienna and internationally—was dependent upon his initial lionization by aristocratic society. For this reason, it is important to examine more closely the "first decade of unbroken triumphs" (Solomon 1977a, 57). Specifically, we must understand the initial basis for elite receptivity to Beethoven and, along with this, follow some of the ways in which these aristocratic patrons assisted Beethoven in his progression from pianist, to pianist-composer, and from around 1800 on, to composer. What follows is an exploration of several topics relating to the social bases of Beethoven's success during his first ten years in Vienna. First, I will provide a sample of the practices by which Beethoven's patrons helped to launch him as a superior musician during the early stages of his career; second, I will briefly discuss some of the practices (and the resources for these practices) through which Beethoven put himself forward to his select public as *a* (if not *the*) Viennese musical "star"; third, I will show how Beethoven's "new path" can be seen as an appropriate line of conduct given his social position and musical strengths and weaknesses (and here, I intend to critique the argument that proposes Beethoven's political outlook as the major motivating force behind his unconventional music); fourth, I will review the controversy over Beethoven's music that occurred between 1795 and 1805; and finally, I will consider the ways in which Beethoven's "difficult" music and the controversy it provoked may have provided a resource for his patrons, a "cultural vehicle" for a "social tenor" (Griswold 1983; 1987) or "work space" (DeNora 1986) in which they could attempt to resolve certain dilemmas of patronage and aristocratic music leadership in the early nineteenth century. Within this last topic, I will allude to the ways in which Beethoven's disregard of Viennese compositional conventions led to the nineteenth-century notion (still with us to some extent today) of the composer as heroic genius.

Beethoven and His Patrons

Shortly before Beethoven's departure from Bonn in 1792, Count Waldstein inscribed the composer's autograph book with this now famous message: "Dear Beethoven. You are going to Vienna in fulfillment of your long-frustrated wishes. The Genius of Mozart is still mourning and weeping the death of her pupil. She found a refuge but no occupation with the inexhaustible Haydn; through him she wishes once more to form a union with another. With the help of assiduous labour you shall receive Mozart's spirit from Haydn's hands. Your true friend, Waldstein" (Solomon 1977a, 57).

That Beethoven's music is the embodiment of "the spirit of Mozart from the hands of Haydn" has become one of the platitudes of music history. Yet the irony of the phrase is great. For one thing, opposition to Beethoven was initially (and throughout the nineteenth century) based on Beethoven's lack of resemblance to Mozart (in fact, the French had to redefine the term "Mozartian" before they could find a way to accept Beethoven's later works [Schrade 1978]). Second, the teacher-pupil relationship between Beethoven and Haydn was far from satisfactory. Haydn was too preoccupied with his own (belated) success to be of much assistance, and Beethoven secretly sought additional help with his counterpoint from Johann Schenk (1753–1836). Moreover, to simply call Waldstein's statement "prophecy," as Beethoven scholars typically have done (Forbes 1964, 1:115; Schindler 1966, 48; Solomon 1977a, 58), is to elide some of the crucial sociological aspects of Beethoven's success. If there were those who mourned the death of the "pupil" of Mozart's "Genius," it is likely to have been a certain number of the aristocratic music patrons themselves. To secure their "lineage" as leaders of musical life, they needed an heir— another special composer to whom, at the initial stages, they could lend their exclusive support. Haydn had recently been pensioned off from Esterhazy and was working in Vienna as an independent composer at the height of his fame; though venerable and feted in Vienna during the 1790s, he was sixty years old—perhaps too senior for the part of "heir."

One can see why Beethoven may have been an attractive candidate. Tested in the provinces, backed by Waldstein (Prince Liechtenstein's brother-in-law) and the Elector of Bonn (uncle to Emperor Franz), and un-sullied by support from Vienna's "second society" (the newly ennobled), Beethoven could be patronized and "launched" as the "exclusive" property of the Viennese aristocrats who had "discovered" him. For these reasons, it is interesting to examine the ways in which Waldstein's so-called prophecy became self-fulfilling as the aristocrats, beginning with Lichnowsky, began to "groom" Beethoven for the job of filling Mozart's shoes.[1]

In his correspondence with the nineteenth-century musicologist Otto John, Carl Czerny (Beethoven's pupil) observed: "It has repeatedly been said in foreign lands that Beethoven was not respected in Vienna and was suppressed. The truth is that already as a youth he received all manner of support from our high aristocracy and enjoyed as much care and respect as ever fell to the lot of a young artist" (Forbes 1964, 1:444). This point has not escaped the notice of conventional music scholars. The foremost of these, Maynard Solomon, has thus described these patrons of Beethoven: "So great was their passion for music and so important was it to their social status that they be known as patrons of an important artist, that they lavished money and gifts upon him" (1977a, 60).

After Beethoven's three-year apprenticeship under Haydn and Schenk, he was taken by Prince Lichnowsky on a concert tour of Prague, Leipzig, Dresden, and Berlin (where Friedrich Wilhelm II was favorably impressed).[2] A survey of Beethoven's letters during these early years reveals a gradually increasing confidence in his powers and future career. We see less of the cagey pianist who, two years before, had sworn enmity against his competitors and had possessively committed to print his extemporaneous piano pieces in order to gain a primitive form of "copyright" over "the peculiarities of my style" (Anderson 1961, 1:9). When Beethoven returned to Vienna after his tour, his reputation was enhanced by his foreign success; he was beginning to possess a history of recognition—an important part of the framework that would increase the probability of his future success. From then on, Beethoven could be introduced as the composer who had experienced wide acclaim abroad and who had particularly pleased the king of Prussia. In these ways, then, we see how Lichnowsky may be said to have served as Beethoven's liaison with royalty and other important arbiters of taste, simultaneously functioning as publicity manager by deliberately placing Beethoven in situations that would flatter his talent.

Lichnowsky also played an important role in facilitating Beethoven's move from the occupation of virtuoso pianist to that of published composer. Here it is important to note that virtuoso playing was a comparatively low-risk, low-status occupation both for the musician (it required relatively little investment in terms of time—the music, if it was not from the pens of other composers, was extemporized) and for the patron (it was relatively cheap to support, a pianist being the only requirement). By offering supportive but strategically limited local forums in which Beethoven's early compositions (as opposed to his improvisations) were aired, Lichnowsky and other aristocratic patrons helped Beethoven to kindle interest in his composed works.

Of equal importance, these patrons helped to condition taste for these works, some of which, even as early as 1793, had caused Haydn to worry that they might not be "quickly and easily understood and so favourably received by the public." By administering his compositions to the wider aristocratic audience in homeopathic doses, Beethoven and his initial patrons were able to guard against premature rejection of his innovative works. In this way they could insure that, as one contemporary observer put it, "hearers not only accustomed themselves to the striking and original qualities of the master but grasped his spirit and strove for the *high privilege* [emphasis mine] of understanding him" (Forbes 1964, 1:164).

In 1795, when Beethoven decided to publish his trios on a subscription basis, Lichnowsky underwrote the venture; on his own, the prince sub-scribed to 20 of the 247 available copies, and members of his family bought another 33. Indeed, it is possible that it was Lichnowsky who provided the initial sum of 122 florins for the printing (and that Beethoven knew this—though he acted as if he did not). By helping to underwrite the publication costs, Lichnowsky helped Beethoven to look like an already successful composer (in other words, not a *mere* pianist). This highly successful first publication was simultaneously a precondition for further success, not just an index of a prior condition.

Here then, we can see the initially modest means through which Bee-thoven and his patrons established a supportive interpretive frame that would flatter and protect the subsequent works offered within it. Indeed, by 1803, Beethoven's name and reputation were secure enough to be able to precede the works. In his memoirs, Beethoven's friend and fellow musi-cian Ferdinand Ries tells how "I was . . . able to observe the fact that for most people the name [Beethoven] alone is sufficient for them to judge everything in a work as either beautiful and perfect or mediocre and bad.[3] One day, tired of playing from memory I played a March just as it came into my head. . . . An old Countess went into raptures of admiration because she imagined it as a new piece by him. In order to have some amusement . . . I hastened to assure [her] that this was so." To Ries's embarrassment, Beethoven soon appeared on the scene, where "he then received extravagant panegyrics on his genius. . . . Later he said to me, 'look here, my dear Ries! Those are the great connoisseurs. . . . Just give them the name of their favorite: that's all they need'" (Robbins Landon 1970, 39).

Beethoven as Social Entrepreneur

Beethoven was hardly a passive object around which his patrons consti-tuted a framework of greatness. From the beginning we see Beethoven actively conditioning his patrons' behavior toward him. Specifically, Bee-thoven worked to construct an image of himself as "autonomous," that is as a self-determining composer. It is worth examining a sampling of the strategies he employed in this task, especially since the ways in which he attempted to renegotiate the traditional composer-patron relationship were used in turn by subsequent generations of composers (for example, Liszt, Berlioz, and Wagner) to professionalize the occupation of composer. Accordingly, the functions of setting the standards of artistic evaluation moved from the patron's to the composer's domain.

Ironically, one key resource here for Beethoven was the traditional conception of privilege, namely, that some individuals (that is, nobles) are more worthy than others. Contrary to the received mythical image of Beethoven's political engagement, he was not engaged in abolishing this conception. Rather, he was involved in hollowing it out—disconnecting the conception of privilege from its traditional content so that it could accommodate or be transferred to other, nonhereditary (yet ascribed) types of nobility: nobility of spirit, of character, or of talent. That Beethoven was more successful than other composers in changing the ways in which privilege was conceived is due, in part, to the peculiar advantage served by what has come to be known as Beethoven's "nobility pretense." It is therefore necessary to look briefly at the history of Beethoven's duplicity with respect to his aristocratic origins (Solomon 1975a).

Among members of Beethoven's public, it was assumed that the prefix "van" in his name was an insignia of nobility like the German prefix "von." This assumption continued—uncorrected by the composer—until 1818, when, during the final litigations over custody of his nephew, Beethoven inadvertently disclosed that his nephew was not of noble birth. This revelation in turn led the court to inquire into Beethoven's own origins and Beethoven was forced to concede that the Dutch prefix *van* was not identical to the German *von*. As Solomon has observed: "There was surely no *economic* necessity [emphasis mine] involved in this deception. Haydn had risen to the rank of a national composer despite his humble origins, and without benefit of a nobility patent. It was not necessary for Beethoven to pretend to nobility in order to gain entree as a musician for these were open to those of less than noble rank" (1977a, 87). Solomon's point is well taken, but the "psychological" reasons he offers for why Beethoven perpetuated the pretense are less convincing. Solomon argues that "central to the nobility pretense [was] the need for acceptance by those in command of society: the leaders and shapers, the royalty and nobility. That Beethoven felt he had to pretend nobility in order to obtain such acceptance may be a poignant indication of the depth of this need in him" (1977a, 5). In addition was fulfillment of what Solomon sees as Beethoven's "family romance"—namely, Beethoven's fantasy that he was the natural son of the king of Prussia: "Through the pretense, he sought transcendence of his parentage and his humble origins; through it he could, perhaps, pursue his quest for a mythical, noble father to replace the mediocre court tenor who had begotten him. The nobility pretense, then, may well have been a fantasy through which Beethoven 'lived out' his Family Romance" (1977a, 89).

From a sociological point of view, the problem with Solomon's explanation is that he has confined his inquiry to the psychological motives or *origins* of Beethoven's duplicity, and in so doing, he has deflected attention from the social effects or *consequences* that the nobility pretense helped make possible. Specifically, the "van"/"von" confusion may have served as a practical resource in Beethoven's attempt to renegotiate his status vis-à-vis his patrons. While Solomon is undoubtedly correct in arguing that the nobility pretense met no economic necessity—that Beethoven did not need to feign nobility to be as successful as Haydn—the point remains that Beethoven did not want to be as successful as Haydn. Rather, Beethoven aimed to be successful in quite another way.

On the strength of Beethoven's nobility pretense, and also because of weakened patronage authority brought about through the diffusion of patronage through other ranks of Viennese society, Beethoven was able to innovate socially and, in so doing, to redefine the quality of the patron-composer relationship. Into this framework we can fit some of the more "bizarre" aspects of Beethoven's comportment and conduct. We can now see them in terms of their function (if not intent): as strategies to "redefine the situation" culminating, eventually, in a shift in the basis of musical-critical authority from an authority predicated on the institution of nobility to that based on the nascent institution of the autonomous music world itself (Moore 1987).

We can see Beethoven's social innovations in his physical contrast to Haydn and Salieri while they were all waiting in the corridor of Lichnowsky's, the latter two dressed in the old way (in silk hose, buckled shoes, and wigs), the former "almost ill-dressed" and wigless (Robbins Landon 1970, 64). Similarly, we may read Beethoven's increasing dislike of performing when requested, and his not uncommon refusals to perform at all (Forbes 1964, 1:2). More than once these refusals seem to have reduced certain of his more enthusiastic aristocratic supporters to begging him to play. Moreover, as his reputation increased, Beethoven became especially strict about the type of attitude with which his audience ought to receive his music. Ries tells of an incident when he and Beethoven were performing at Count Browne's:

> Young Count P, sitting in the doorway leading to the next room, spoke so loudly and so continuously to a pretty woman, that Beethoven, after several efforts had been made to secure quiet [efforts made by other audience members, since Beethoven and Ries seem to have been playing] suddenly took my hands from the keys in the middle of the music, jumped up and said very loudly, "I will not play for such swine!" All efforts to get him to return to the pianoforte were in vain; he would not even allow me to play the sonata. So

the music came to an end in the midst of general ill humor. (Forbes 1964, 1:307)

In these strategies one can see Beethoven's attempt to demarcate his salon performances as special events and, further, to reform the listening etiquette appropriate to such special occasions. In the late eighteenth century, audience members could talk, move about the room or hall, eat and drink, play card games and other games of chance, and (in the privacy of opera boxes) meet with courtesans and paramours. Beethoven was increasing the stakes of music consumption by attempting to specify the listening situation, redefining it as one in which "serious" devotion to the performance was the only "appropriate" form of conduct. In other words, he was setting up his listeners so as to evoke a response quantitatively greater and qualitatively different than the behavior typical of his time.[4]

Beethoven's Music as Resource or "Work Space"

So far, I have briefly noted some of the ways in which Beethoven and his patrons were involved in a reciprocal process of conditioning each other according to their respective projects and the ways in which Beethoven's contribution entailed clearing a conceptual and behavioral space for his middle-period works—a contribution that resulted in a partial renegotiation of the meaning of music patronage (Johnson 1982). I have not made conclusive remarks on these topics but rather have offered a rough sketch of their relation to Beethoven's contemporary reputation.[5] Three tasks remain. The first is to account sociologically for Beethoven's artistic choices—to discuss the social conditions under which Beethoven made these choices and to analyze the social consequences to which they and the resulting "new path" may have contributed (Meyer 1983; Pasler 1987). The second is to review the controversy this music provoked, and the third is to attempt to consider the issue of elite receptivity to this new and controversial style.

The Social Origins of Beethoven's "New Path"

The two most common ways of accounting for Beethoven's style have been to propose either biographical and psychological causes or to point to political motivating factors. The former approach tends to portray the evolution of Beethoven's style as dependent upon his innate psychological and physiological characteristics. The latter mode of explanation assumes, implicitly at least, the opposite: that in some kind of superhuman fashion, Beethoven was capable of writing in *any* style and that the style for which he was to become known was one he rationally *chose* to develop, and that he consciously rejected the lighter, more "polite" Viennese tradition in favor of his own, alternative (and "revolutionary") approach. For instance, Solomon (1977a) points to Beethoven's deafness as the "painful chrysalis within which his 'heroic' style came to maturity" and focuses on Beethoven's "crisis" period during his stay in the country at Heiligenstadt in the autumn of 1802, where he wrote the "testament" to his brothers in which he states that he will end his life. In contrast, Adorno (1976), Knight (1973), and Crabbe (1982) tend to portray Beethoven as "choosing" to break out of eighteenth-century forms in order to dramatize the Rousseauistic-democratic conception of the heroic individual or "natural man," released from the conventions of "polite" society and its hierarchies.[6]

While these psychologically and ideologically grounded accounts may in part capture what Beethoven "thought" he was doing (that is, some of the motives with which he would map and account for his actions), they by no means constitute a complete explanation of Beethoven's artistic choices. Such accounts make unproblematic the issue of why Beethoven framed his decisions within the confines of some ideals and not others and therefore they overlook the possibility that ideals (as promissory lines of conduct) are also resources (Berger 1981; Bourdieu 1984; Swidler 1986). As such, they are congruent with practical and structural situations. Thus, to adhere to idealized explanations for action is also to occlude equally persuasive, if more mundane, accounts.

Beethoven had been trained by Christian Gottlob Neefe (1748–98), a devotee of the expressive, legato style of Emmanuel Bach. Because Beethoven received this training in Germany, he was further removed from the Italianate approach favored in Vienna. Accordingly, for reasons relating to either skill or style (the two are, of course, interdependent) Beethoven may simply have felt uncomfortable trying to adapt to the unfamiliar Viennese criteria of crisp, light playing. For this reason alone, his improvisational style sounded different. This hypothesis is supported by contemporary reports of Beethoven's pianism, wherein his playing is contrasted with the lighter, brighter approach of Wölffl and Gelinek (DeNora 1988).

But what does Beethoven's ability as a pianist have to do with his ability as a composer? One does not need to be able to play all the works one composes, nor to compose as one would play. In Beethoven's case, however, the links between his pianistic ability, his improvisational approach, and the eventual style of the early piano compositions are far from tenuous. Moreover, these early piano works may be viewed as stylistically foreshadowing his later, larger piano and instrumental works. First of all,

Beethoven's method of composition during his first decade in Vienna (he composed at the piano [Forbes 1964, 1:308; Johnson 1982, 17]) suggests that it was through such improvisations that he developed much of his compositional material. Second, it is in the early piano sonatas of 1796–99 that Beethoven began to clarify the radical approach to the sonata form that he developed in depth during the years 1803–5 (Kerman and Tyson 1973, 99). Because piano works required no additional performers and so were not "expensive" to perform, and also since there was a large market for published works for this instrument, piano music could more easily serve as a "practice genre," one in which Beethoven could get "experience in the symphonic style without taking any of the risks" (Johnson 1982, 18). In other words, he could try out his stylistic innovations before an audience in a medium that required few resources and, hence, less of an "investment" for both audience and composer.

Political and social ideals aside, then, Beethoven's "new path" may also have had its origins in what Beethoven did and did not feel comfortable with—in his pianistic strengths and weaknesses. As noted, these were linked, at least in part, to his early training in Germany under Neefe, who, in teaching according to Emmanuel Bach's dictum that the student "play from the heart, not like a trained bird," no doubt encouraged the legato playing, unexpected pauses, surprises, and generally loosely constructed improvisations that later struck Viennese listeners as unusual.[7] Thus, it should not come as a surprise that, as Ringer (1970) and Blom (1958) have persuasively argued, Beethoven was stimulated by the emotionally expressive piano works of Dussek. Certainly he was acquainted with Dussek's music as early as 1798; like Neefe, Dussek had been a pupil of Emmanuel Bach and had certainly learned from his teacher the dominant stylistic value of emotional expression. Around 1799, when Beethoven was pitted against pianists of the rival Viennese style (the aristocracy would occasionally encourage their proteges to take part in pianistic duels), this "dramatization" of Beethoven's differences perhaps served to further his commitment to his own distinctly different approach: he was *not* another Mozart, nor was he another Wolffl, Hummel, or Tomaschek.

That Beethoven's style coincided with the sorts of pianistic techniques with which he felt most at home does not necessarily mean that the development of his peculiar style was unrelated to the motives with which he accounted for it. Nor does it necessarily preclude Beethoven's having consciously attempted to capitalize on the differences between his own approach and that of his opponents. These musical innovations were related to his social innovations discussed above: Beethoven's "strange" and "surprising" music clamored for a qualitatively and quantitatively different form of attention.[8] Thus his unusual style provided a resource with which he could claim previously unoccupied territory in the social space of music production and consumption. To go against the grain of established stylistic conventions was to refuse classification according to these standards (standards that, it should be remembered, were not flattering to Beethoven) and also to refuse to be treated according to the conventional patterns of patron-composer behavior. His ideology furnished him with a line of conduct congruent with his particular strengths and weaknesses as a pianist-composer.

Clearly, Beethoven's stylistic innovations comprised an "alternative" route to Viennese success, and the success of his "alternative" approach was dependent upon his initial patrons' willingness to "buy in" to the alternative criteria that these innovations implied. It is here that we can appreciate the importance of elite receptivity to the success of Beethoven's style. Even while this style became increasingly idiosyncratic, his backers remained willing to invest in it their capital, both material and cultural (in the guise of approval that in turn functioned as propaganda). Without the intermediary link that this elite backing provided, it is questionable whether Beethoven would have been able to achieve the success that even by 1801 set him so far apart from his composing contemporaries. Moreover, it was this initial success that eventually enabled him to "finance" more of the same on a grander scale: the grandiose (and listener-intensive) works of 1801–6 and beyond.

What makes this final issue particularly interesting is that in embracing Beethoven's new style, his patrons also needed to accept a reallocation of the social space of music listening, in which their own part (vis-à-vis that of the musician/composer) was significantly reduced. Why were they willing to condone and back a style that implicitly called for a reform in which they would lose some of their traditional "patronage rights"? To understand why Beethoven's patrons were willing to go along with the sorts of demands that he made through his social and musical innovations requires us to turn again to the social conditions of Viennese patronage at the turn of the nineteenth century. Specifically, we must consider the democratization of patronage that was occurring at the time, and we must look at the dilemma this posed for the traditional heirs to the leadership of Viennese and (at the height of the Austro-Hungarian Empire) Western European taste. Beethoven's success through his symbiotic relationship with his patrons led, in turn, to another sort of symbiotic relationship, one that neither Beethoven nor his patrons could have initially foreseen. In the remainder of this essay I will address, first, the nature of the controversy that Beethoven's music provoked and, second, the ways in which this controversy became a resource for Beethoven's aristocratic patrons whereby they could resolve the dilemma of music leadership facing them.

The Controversy over Beethoven's Music

The pianist Ignaz Moscheles (1794–1870) recalled that sometime around 1804 he had heard of Beethoven, who "wrote the most extraordinary stuff, which no one could either play or understand; a Baroque music in conflict with all the rules" (Robbins Landon 1970, 100). Moscheles brought a copy of opus 13 (the sonata *Pathétique*) to his teacher, F. D. Weber (who thought Beethoven's compositions to be "harebrained"); the teacher, he said, "warned against playing or studying eccentric productions . . . before I had developed a style based on more respectable models" (Robbins Landon 1970, 100). Among musicians, Moscheles's teacher was hardly alone in his opinion. The Abbé Gelinek (musician and house chaplain to Prince Esterhazy) thought Beethoven's compositions were "lacking in internal coherency" (Forbes 1964, 1:240). Kozeluch (during Beethoven's early years the most popular composer in Vienna) reportedly threw a copy of the C minor trio (presumably opus 9, number 3) at the feet of his fellow composer Dolezalek after the latter (a Beethoven enthusiast) attempted to play it for him. Kozeluch and Haydn were of one mind regarding this trio (and presumably most of Beethoven's post-1796 compositions): according to Dolezalek, they agreed that "we would have done that differently" (Forbes 1964, 1:259).

This sort of opposition was by no means restricted to conservatively oriented (and possibly jealous) composers. We hear similar stories from the different musicians called upon to perform Beethoven's works. The string players who first read through opus 59, number 1 (the first of the "Razumovsky" string quartets) were convinced that the repeated note played by the cello in the opening of the second movement was intended as a musical "joke," and they were not amused. (On the whole, it seems Beethoven was not well liked by the musicians of his time, mainly because his music was particularly difficult for them to perform and he did not seem to willingly concede this point.)

Moreover, objections to Beethoven did not originate from musicians and composers alone. There is ample evidence that Beethoven was opposed by a significant contingent of patrons[9] and critics, and I will return to these momentarily. Although it is difficult to know what the "average" audience member thought of Beethoven, Czerny reported that "at this time [around 1800] the general public [i.e., individuals who would have attended his public concerts but who were not part of his close circle] completely condemned Beethoven's works, and all the followers of the old Mozart and Haydn school opposed him bitterly." And at a public performance of the *Eroica* Symphony in 1805, one member of the gallery reportedly shouted out, "I'll give another kreutzer if the thing will but stop!" (Solomon 1977a, 75).

Indeed, conflict over Beethoven's music seems to have begun in 1796, when he first embarked on his career as a full-fledged composer, and it continued throughout the following decade. It was particularly apparent on two occasions: when opposing taste publics clashed in 1801 over Beethoven's ballet *The Creatures of Prometheus,* and again over the *Eroica* Symphony in 1805. In the first case, the public was split into two factions. On the one side Beethoven's supporters hailed *Creatures* (and the junior ballet master's choreography) for its more natural, expressive style while, on the other, the defenders of the older taste (and the more senior ballet master) thought the ballet ungraceful and inharmonious. According to the playwright von Collin (for whose play *Coriolan* Beethoven wrote miscellaneous music), not even the most important affair of state would have aroused "more violent divisions of opinion than the battle did at that time over the respective superiority of the two ballet masters" (Robbins Landon 1970, 139).

Turning to the published criticism that Beethoven received in the years both before and after the *Creatures* controversy, we see that even the reviewers frequently perceived Beethoven's music as perplexing.[10] In 1799, for instance, a writer in the *Allgemeine Musikalische Zeitung* (*AMZ*) described Beethoven's "bizarre" and "singular gait" (style) and compared it to being invited to take a stroll through a forest only to find at "every minute, inimical barriers . . . [returning] at last exhausted without having had any pleasure." In 1805, when the *Eroica* received its public performances, another reviewer in *AMZ* (by this time the journal was pro-Beethoven in stance) still argued: "The symphony would gain immensely . . . if Beethoven would decide to shorten it and introduce into the whole more light, clarity and unity. But if, as now, its coherence escapes the most attentive ear after repeated hearings, it must appear peculiar to the unprejudiced listener [i.e., the listener unfamiliar with the work]. Moreover, there were very few people who liked the symphony" (*AMZ* May 1805).

At this time, when the reality of the "new path" may be said to have been recognized by all concerned, the rift in taste appeared in its most self-conscious form. It is worth quoting at length a passage from a review of the *Eroica* concert that appeared in *Der Freimütige* in April 1805, for the writer (possibly the dramatist von Kotzebue, who collaborated with Beethoven in "The Ruins of Athens") outlined the conflict in detail:

Beethoven's most special friends contend this particular symphony is a masterpiece, that it is exactly the true style for music of the highest type and that if it does not please now it is because the public is not sufficiently cultivated in the arts to comprehend these higher spheres of beauty; but after a couple of thousand years its effect will not be lessened. The other party absolutely denies any artistic merit to this work. They claim that it reveals the symptoms of an evidently unbridled attempt at distinction and peculiarity, but that neither beauty, true sublimity nor power have anywhere been achieved either by means of unusual modulations, by violent transitions or by the juxtaposition of the most heterogeneous elements . . . the creation of something beautiful and sublime, not the production of something merely unusual and fantastic, is the true expression of genius. . . . The third, very small party stand in the middle. They concede that there are many beautiful things in the symphony, but admit that the continuity often appears to be completely confused and that the endless duration of this longest and perhaps most difficult of all symphonies is tiring even for the expert; for a mere amateur it is unbearable. . . . One fears . . . that if Beethoven continues along this road, he and the public will make a bad journey. Music could easily reach a state where everyone who has not been vouchsafed a thorough knowledge of the rules and difficulties of the art will derive absolutely no pleasure from it. (Robbins Landon 1970, 153–54)

Beethoven and His Patrons: The Symbiotic Relationship

Ostensibly, Beethoven's patrons backed him because they thought they had found another Mozart and they explicitly groomed him to take Mozart's place. But Beethoven can be seen as simultaneously grooming his patrons through social and musical strategies in order to gain additional "space" in the composer-patron relationship (Bourdieu 1984). Without the continued approval of these patrons, it is questionable whether Beethoven's "new path" would ever have been perceived as a success in the first place. The question then remains: Why were Beethoven's patrons receptive to his innovations? To answer this, we must turn to the social conditions of Viennese patronage at the turn of the nineteenth century. What is ironic here is that the increased democratization of patronage was unwittingly caused by the aristocrats themselves (Moore 1987).

During the 1780s and 1790s aristocrats began to disband their house musical ensembles (the *Hauskapellen*) and to turn instead to dilettante forums in which they played alongside the quasi-freelance musicians whom they invited to their homes.[11] Inadvertently, this organizational change in the basis of music patronage opened the door to further participation on the part of those who could not afford to maintain a *Hauskapelle*. Now anyone who had the means to partially subsidize a musician could do so, either as a concert goer or as a cosponsor of a private music event. This meant that maintaining the traditional basis for distinction as a music patron—being one of a select group able to monopolize a composer and support a group of musicians—became increasingly difficult. It also became increasingly expensive, as musicians began to assert themselves as free lance professionals. More particularly, the same musicians could be sponsored by patrons of varied social standing, albeit at different times. Thus, this organizational change resulted in the erosion of the means by which aristocrats had traditionally maintained their monopoly over high cultural musical life. It is in this context then that we must understand Beethoven's relationship with his patrons.

Given the revised circumstances in which Vienna's old aristocratic music patrons found themselves, the controversy that Beethoven's increasingly distinctive style provoked could become an unanticipated resource through which such patrons could reassert their status as leaders of musical and social life. Since these patrons were no longer able to distinguish themselves as musical leaders through the sheer quantity of their musical spending (on *Hauskapellen* and the large genres such as opera, oratorio, mass, and symphony) they were forced to compete with—or at least distance themselves from—the money barons and other members of the "second society."

With Beethoven they could maintain their status through qualitative (stylistic) rather than quantitative means, by supporting a distinctive "vanguard" style, thereby redefining the meaning of musical activity so that they would again be at the privileged center of that social space. Beethoven's "vanguard" style could become a resource for his patrons in that their "discovery" of the "superiority" of Beethoven's alternative aesthetic enhanced—even as it was legitimated by—their previous history as leading patrons of music and arbiters of taste. While a writer in *AMZ* described Beethoven's devotees as a "fringe group," a minority taste public, they were a minority who carried a lot of cultural weight. In Loesser's words: "A relatively small group of accomplished amateurs, connoisseurs, snobs and romantically minded devotees of 'the grandiose' as they liked to say, were the carriers of [Beethoven's] repute; they were an official lot that could not be readily opposed. To most people, Beethoven's reputation was an article of superstition" (1954, 146).

Admittedly, it is doubtful that Beethoven's patrons had all this in mind when they began to groom him for the job of Mozart's "heir." On the other hand, it seems plausible that they "discovered" the usefulness of Beethoven's distinctive style in the course of their patronage work. As *they* made this discovery (and encouraged Beethoven to pursue his original line of composition) *he* was able to innovate in ways that secured for him further compositional autonomy. As a composer with an original and unconventional talent, he exploited and expanded an environment that nurtured such originality.

By cushioning Beethoven against the sorts of interpretations that would threaten his reputation, the members of his circle of patrons worked not only as carriers but also as guardians of his repute. They no doubt recognized that one of the mechanisms for Beethoven's continued favorable recognition was control over the contexts in which he was "framed." As Baron Kubeck (not one of his fans) wrote in 1797: "Whoever sees Beethoven for the first time and knows nothing about him would surely take him for a malicious, ill-natured, quarrelsome drunkard who has no feeling for music. . . . On the other hand, he who sees him for the first time surrounded by his fame and his glory, will surely see musical talent in every feature of an ugly face" (Robbins Landon 1970, 71).

Conclusion

The evidence given here supports the argument that at the outset, Beethoven's reputation depended upon his patrons' support, even as their own reputations as leaders of musical life depended upon their "discovery" of a superior talent such as his. Because of changes in the bases of music support and the reciprocal conditioning to which these changes contributed, neither party in this symbiotic relationship got exactly what it might have initially expected or wanted. Beethoven was never able to achieve his dream of becoming a court *Kapellmeister*, and his patrons, in order to retain their dominant position in musical life, were burdened (or "blessed") with the task of espousing one of the first in a long line of self-consciously "difficult" artists and self-consciously "difficult" styles. In sum: in order to maintain their traditional status against democratic threats, the old elite came to foster an artistic avant-garde. Any excavation of the social origins of the bifurcation of musical taste into conservative and avant-garde camps (and, more generally, the social transformation of artistic taste as a whole) would have to include an understanding of how Beethoven's aesthetic contributed to and reflexively helped to condition such a change.

Notes

1. In addition to Prince Lichnowsky, Beethoven's early circle of aristocratic patrons included Baron van Swieten, Baron Zmeskall, and Count Browne-Camus.

2. See Forbes (1964); it is probable that the king was pleased by the inclusion of cello sonatas (op. 5), being a cellist himself. It is also possible that he was even more pleased by Beethoven's choice of theme in the cello variations ("See the conqu'ring hero comes"—Handel). In any case, the king expressed his approval with the gift of a gold snuff box filled with louis d'ors. Beethoven was pleased with this gift since, as he proudly informed his friends, it was no "ordinary" gold snuff box but of the kind offered to visiting diplomats.

3. Ries was employed by Count Browne-Camus to reproduce Beethoven's pieces (pianists here providing the function later served by recordings) for, as Ries put it, "an assembly of rabid Beethovians" (Wegener and Ries 1987).

4. "Appropriate" late eighteenth-century audience conduct (at secular events, at least) included a wide range of behaviors not typically found at modern "high-culture" music events. This range was progressively narrowed during the nineteenth century as the autonomy of the musical field increased. It was given impetus by and was reflected in (for example) seating arrangements, architecture, music programming practices, and, of course, the musical forms themselves. (See Weber 1980, and also specific contemporary accounts too numerous to mention here. For a discussion of the sociological significance of comparable changes that occurred in Boston, see DiMaggio 1982.)

5. Other actions of Beethoven's helped him secure a position of prominence; among these were his shrewd negotiation of an annuity contract in 1809, and his convenient rededication of the *Eroica* to Lobkowitz at the political moment when his allegiance to France (more accurately his allegiance to a Parisian career) became dangerous (see Solomon 1977a, 136, for a balanced account of this). Equally important is Beethoven's concern with—and impact on—musical technological developments, particularly with respect to the piano. Beethoven lobbied for the transformation of the piano from the harplike instrument of the eighteenth century to the louder instrument of the nineteenth. In 1809, it was reported that Streicher, one of Vienna's major piano manufacturers, "at Beethoven's advice has given his instruments a more resisting touch and elastic action so that the virtuoso who executes with strength and meaning has more control of his instrument in sustaining and carrying in striking and releasing" (Robbins Landon 1970, 94). Changes in piano technology played an important role in the transformation of "piano politics" since the new instrument enabled a clearer distinction to be made between experts who would be likely to execute "with strength and meaning" and amateurs whose execution would, of course, be more tentative.

6. See Meyer (1984) for a discussion of how romantic music in general may be said to reflect Rousseauistic ideas. Frequently overlooked in these accounts is the fact that Beethoven was by no means glorifying the "common man" but rather the heroic "leader" who, out of his own "genius," is able to rise above the mundane and achieve sweeping changes by cutting through the constraints posed by conventional authority (social irresponsibility is therefore condoned as a necessary means to achieve social reform). Napoleon was the embodiment of this concep-

tion and Beethoven imagined himself to be a musical equivalent of this (though he did not profess admiration for Napoleon after 1804 when, as his "passport to Viennese citizenship" [Solomon 1977a, 137], Beethoven removed the Bonaparte inscription from the title page of the Third Symphony). According to the violinist Wenzel Krumpholz, Beethoven's comment upon hearing of Napoleon's victory at Jena (1806) was, "It's a pity that I do not understand the art of war as well as I do the art of music. I would conquer him!" (Forbes 1964, 1:403).

In practice, Beethoven's "democratic" ideals had little to do with the common person or with "ordinary" life. His music was written for the extraordinary listener. According to the tenor Rockel (who sang Florestan in the 1806 performances of *Fidelio*), the composer thought he had been cheated when his share of the receipts was low, and the theater manager, Baron Braun, tried to placate him with allusions to increasing ticket sales: "He hoped the receipts would increase with each representation; until now only the first ranks, stalls and pit were occupied; by and by the upper ranks would likewise contribute their shares. 'I don't write for the galleries!' exclaimed Beethoven. 'No?' replied the Baron, 'My dear Sir, even Mozart did not disdain to write for the galleries!' " (Forbes 1964, 1:398).

7. We may assume that Beethoven continued to value the lessons he learned from Emmanuel Bach's piano method; considerably later he dismissed Czerny—then serving as piano teacher to his nephew Karl—because he believed that Czerny was not giving sufficient emphasis to Bach's works. Emmanuel Bach preferred the clavichord (ancestor of the piano) to the harpsichord, mainly because of the former's capacity for delicate dynamic shadings (the clavichord, incidentally, was the instrument of the educated bourgeoisie and was known as the instrument of weeping par excellence). However, the last five sets of his sonatas were written for pianoforte (1780–90). Like Beethoven's later works, Bach's compositions were characterized by abrupt shifts of harmonic modulations, surprising turns of phrase, sudden pauses and sforzandos, all of which his audiences reportedly found deeply moving. Thus, in these respects, Beethoven's own style may be seen as a continuation of German "fantastic" music, which was meant to be improvisatory and composed, literally, of flights of "fancy" (*Phantasie*).

The similarities discussed here between Emmanuel Bach's *empfindsamer Stile* (literally: sentimental style) and Beethoven's "new path" must not be allowed to occlude the differences, which were of musical structure and of scale. For one, Bach's "flights of fancy" were less sustained structurally, more firmly tied to the cadence points that closed them off. Moreover, the clavichord was so soft-toned that it could only be played for an intimate audience or, as Loesser has put it (1954, 59) it was "best played alone and thus became a useful implement for enabling a 'beautiful soul' to make love to itself most privately. One writer called the clavichord, 'the thrilling confident of solitude.' " Beethoven differed from Bach in that he explicitly "amplified" the *empfindsamer Stile*: he brought what was essentially private in intent (and the result of technological limitations) out into a public arena by enlarging its scale.

8. In that its stylistic conventions were less familiar (less easily "placed" by listeners) and that the music was simultaneously louder and more full of contrast, Beethoven's music was likely to jar listeners and in so doing, force the issue of

their attention (they would either have to attend to it more closely or to reject it as unworthy of their attention). Thus we see how Beethoven's music itself played an active role in his attempt to reconstitute the meaning of the listening setting—in Bourdieu's terms (1968), to rearrange the social space of that setting.

9. Esterhazy, for instance, who continued to practice the traditional form of patronage (he continued to keep resident musicians), was never a partisan of Beethoven. The Mass in C, composed for his wife's name day, met with disapproval and Beethoven left Eisenstadt never to return. Similarly, Emperor Franz (who preferred Dittersdorf and Salieri) found Beethoven's music unpleasing; according to Dolezalek, this is because he thought that there was something "revolutionary" about it (Robbins Landon 1970, 107). Just before 1800, as the lines were drawn between absolutists (this would include members of the aspiring upper bourgeoisie) and the older, once-more-powerful nobility, Beethoven's music was more a symbol of the latter than the former.

10. Around 1800, music critics still assumed a quasi-professional status, somewhat akin to the older, nonprofessional role of "connoisseur." After the transformation of the status of critic from knowledgeable amateur to professional, we see critics beginning to value the complications they had previously shunned, perhaps because these musical difficulties tended to legitimate the function of the critic as mediator and guide.

11. The reasons for this are the subject of some debate among music historians. Some (Loesser 1954; Raynor 1978; Solomon 1977a) have argued that because of the effect of the Napoleonic wars upon aristocratic fortunes, most aristocrats were simply unable to afford to maintain their *Hauskapellen*. This position has been recently and rather convincingly critiqued by Moore (1987), who has proposed as an alternative hypothesis that the *Hauskapellen* became less fashionable for higher aristocrats when minor aristocrats began to ape the practice.

References

Adorno, Theodor. 1976. *Introduction to the Sociology of Music.* New York: Seabury.

Allgemeine Musikalische Zeitung. 1798–1806. Berlin: Breitkoph and Hartel.

Anderson, Emily, ed. 1961. *The Letters of Beethoven.* 3 vols. London: Macmillan.

Becker, Howard S. 1982. *Art Worlds.* Berkeley: University of California Press.

Berger, Bennett. 1981. *Survival of a Counter Culture.* Berkeley: University of California Press.

Blom, Eric. 1958. "The Prophecies of Dussek." In *Classics, Major and Minor*, 88–117. London: Macmillan.

———. 1968. *Beethoven's Pianoforte Sonatas Discussed.* New York: De Capo Press.

Bourdieu, Pierre. 1968. "Outline of a Theory of Art Perception." *International Social Science Journal* 20(4): 589–612.

———. 1984. *Distinction.* Cambridge, Mass.: Harvard University Press.

Comini, A. 1987. *The Changing Image of Beethoven: A Study in Mythmaking.* New York: Rizzoli.

Crabbe, J. 1982. *Beethoven's Empire of the Mind.* Newbury, Berkshire, Eng.: Lovell Baines Print, Ltd.

Czerny, Carl. 1956. "Recollections from My Life." *Musical Quarterly* 42: 302–17.

DeNora, Tia. 1986. "How Is Extra-Musical Meaning Possible? Music as a Place and Space for 'Work.'" *Sociological Theory* 4(1): 84–94.

———. 1988. "Piano Politics: Beethoven's Impact on Early Nineteenth-Century Piano Technology." Paper presented to the Society for the History of Technology, Hagley Museum, Wilmington, Delaware, October.

DiMaggio, Paul. 1982. "Cultural Entrepreneurship in Nineteenth-Century Boston: The Creation of an Organizational Base for High Culture in America." *Media, Culture, and Society* 4: 35–50, 303–22.

———. 1987. "Classification in Art." *American Sociological Review* 52: 440–55.

Forbes, Elliot. 1964. *Thayer's Life of Beethoven*. 2 vols. Princeton: Princeton University Press.

Forsyth, D. 1985. *Buildings for Music: The Architect, the Musician and the Listener from the Seventeenth Century to the Present Day*. Cambridge, Mass.: MIT Press.

Griswold, Wendy. 1983. "The Devil's Techniques: Cultural Legitimation and Social Change." *American Sociological Review* 46:668–80.

———. 1987. "The Fabrication of Meaning." *American Journal of Sociology* 96(2): 1077–1118.

Hebdige, Dick. 1979. *Subculture: The Meaning of Style*. London: Methuen.

Henning, Edward S. 1960. "Patronage and Style in the Arts: A Suggestion Concerning Their Relationship." *Journal of Aesthetics and Art Criticism* 18:464–71.

Johnson, Douglas. 1982. "1794–1795: Decisive Years in Beethoven's Early Career." *Beethoven Studies* 3:1–28.

Kanne, R. 1973. "Aristocracy in the Eighteenth-Century Habsburg Empire." *East European Quarterly* 7(1): 1–13.

Kerman, Joseph, and Alan Tyson. 1983. *The New Grove Beethoven*. New York: Norton.

Knight, Frieda. 1973. *Beethoven and the Age of Revolution*. London: Lawrence and Wishart.

Loesser, Arthur. 1954. *Men, Women, and Pianos*. New York: Simon and Schuster.

Meyer, Leonard. 1973. *Explaining Music*. Berkeley: University of California Press.

———. 1983. "Innovation, Choice and the History of Music." *Critical Inquiry* 9(3): 517–44.

———. 1984. "Music and Ideology in the Nineteenth Century." The Tanner Lectures on Human Values, Stanford University, May 17 and 21, 1984.

Moore, Julia. 1987. "Beethoven and Musical Economics." Ph.D. diss., University of Illinois, Urbana-Champaign.

Morrow, Mary S. 1989. *Concert Life in Haydn's Vienna: Aspects of a Developing Musical and Social Institution*. New York: Pendragon Press.

Pasler, Jann. 1987. "Apaches in Paris: The Making of a Turn-of-the-Century Parisian Art World." Paper presented at the Conference of the American Musicological Society, November.

Raynor, H. 1978. *Music and Society since 1815*. London: Schocken.

Ringer, Alexander. 1970. "Beethoven and the London Pianoforte School." *Musical Quarterly* 56:742–59.

Robbins Landon, H. C. 1970. *Beethoven: A Documentary Study*. New York: Macmillan.

Salmen, W. 1985. "Social Obligations of the Emancipated Musician in the Nineteenth Century." In *Sociology of Music*, vol. 1. New York: Pendragon Press.

Schenk, H. 1953. "Austria." In *The European Nobility in the Eighteenth Century*, edited by A. Goodwin. London: Adam and Charles Black.

Schindler, Anton. 1966. *Beethoven as I Knew Him*. Chapel Hill: University of North Carolina Press.

Schrade, Leo. 1978. *Beethoven in France*. New York: Da Capo Press.

Solomon, Maynard. 1974. "Beethoven and the Enlightenment." *Telos* 19:146–54.

———. 1975a. "Beethoven: The Nobility Pretense." *Musical Quarterly* 61:272–94.

———. 1975b. "The Dreams of Beethoven." *American Imago* 32.113–44.

———. 1977a. *Beethoven*. New York: Schirmer Books.

———. 1977b. "Beethoven's Class Position and Outlook." In *Bericht über den Internationalem Beethoven-Kongress in Berlin*, edited by K. Niemann. Berlin.

Swidler, Ann. 1986. "Culture in Action: Symbols and Strategies." *American Sociological Review* 51:273–86.

Wallace, R. 1986. *Beethoven's Critics: Aesthetic Dilemmas and Resolutions in the Composer's Lifetime*. Cambridge: Cambridge University Press.

Weber, William. 1980. "Learned and General Musical Taste in Eighteenth-Century France." *Past and Present* 89:58–85.

———. 1984a. "The Contemporaneity of Eighteenth-Century Musical Taste." *Musical Quarterly* 70:175–94.

———. 1984b. "La Musique Ancien in the Waning of the *Ancien Régime*." *Journal of Modern History* 56:59–88.

Wegeler, Franz, and Ferdinand Ries. 1987 (1838). *Beethoven Remembered: The Biographical Notes of Franz Wegeler and Ferdinand Ries*. Arlington, Va.: Great Ocean Press.

❖ 2 ❖

Dilettantism and Academies of Art: The Netherlands Example

JAAP VAN DER TAS

Private amateur involvement in academies of art—a specific form of dilettantism—has influenced academic discourse on art (the *querelle des anciens et des modernes* that haunted the French Academy at the end of the seventeenth century may serve as an illustration). The professionalization of artists was both stimulated and, at times, checked by dilettante preoccupations and actions. In this paper, I will discuss the two major traditions of dilettantism, aristocratic and bourgeois, and contrast them with the atypical Dutch case that developed in the eighteenth century.

Dilettantism is defined as the cultivation of the arts by amateurs. Although the term "dilettante" currently carries the connotation of a mere "dabbler," originally dilettantism was based on a new humanistic conception of man and on the recognition of the arts (and thus of artistic occupations) as special activities that were not mere crafts and tradesmen's practice but rather something worthwhile in themselves as *artes liberales*. From the start, dilettantism has been connected to a specific definition of the arts and, consequently, to an idealized concept of artists. The arts were considered to have intrinsic value; as transmitters of that value, artists were thus culturally superior beings. This idealization introduced a split between the art of tradesmen, which historically dominated artistic production, and "high" art. This split created a way for dilettante patrons to use their own hierarchical value commitments to treat local art and artists as inferior; such artists did not meet the new and idealized standards set by the classical or academic artists supported by both traditional aristocracies and the nouveaux bourgeois elites.

In dilettante activities themselves, many of these ideological components are hidden. However, if we consider the aims behind these activities and the ideas about art and the relationship between the dilettante patron and artists that they expressed, the specific underlying values become clear. These values have included an assumed moral superiority located in certain persons and groups in society (especially aristocrats), a superiority that was demonstrated through their involvement in typical dilettante activities. Based on a different (if equally hierarchical) concept of man and society, bourgeois values included personal development and the pursuit of high moral standards to oppose aristocratic claims.

But in the Netherlands, private arts patronage was based on the comparatively equal status of the dilettante patrons and the artists. The absence of status competition between artists, and between aristocrats and bourgeois, caused Dutch art academies to differ considerably from those found elsewhere in Europe. Such a difference also existed in the degree and structure of state art patronage when—in the nineteenth century—the government took over the role the dilettantes had previously played.

Patronage and the Art Academy

Seen as a single type of institution, the academy of art has not always served the educational goals we are so familiar with today. For a long time, the education of young people in artistic practice and careers was only a secondary aim of the academy—if it was even an aim at all. In the earliest Italian academies of the sixteenth and seventeenth centuries (at a time when training in the specifics of practice took place largely between artists and apprentices in ateliers), far more important than the training of new artists was the legitimation of artistic production outside the guilds and the institutionalization of power and authority among different artists in the fine arts.[1]

Thus the academy played its part in the development of professional status for artists long before the French Royal Academy (founded in 1648) attained almost complete artistic domination. But as the center of the academic world moved from Rome and Florence to Paris, theoretical discourse on art (based on the rules of classicism) and the artistic ranking of local artists became its primary features. Thus the academy turned into a distinctive institution; while membership of the Royal Academy in Paris bestowed prestige on the academicians, these academic artists made distinctions among themselves as well, and a whole range of titles was formulated for promotions within the institution. The close ties between the Royal Academy and the royal court contributed to the academy's intermediary function in the patronage of artists. Of particular interest here is the fact that a select number of dilettantes were actively involved in the matters of the academy and received the special title of *académicien honoraire*.

Academies of art contributed to the professionalization of the fine arts in different ways, sometimes supporting the arts in general and contributing to the artistic authority and autonomy of the artists, at other times supporting only a select number of artists and distributing among them social prestige based on dependency on the court. *Professionalization* indicates a certain change in the power relationship between the artist and his patrons/clients. Put simply, the more "professional" an artist, the greater his artistic authority over his clients and the smaller his dependence in artistic matters on the clients' needs and demands. (The recognition of artists' quasi-professional authority by patrons in the Renaissance period is well documented.) Another indication of professionalization was the increasing significance of one's authority among colleagues (Gombrich 1985). The academy represents the institutional form of this relationship as the outcome of the negotiations between the power of the client and the authority of the artist.[2] However, the academy was not merely the objective result of these "negotiations"; it has had a productive capacity itself, as can be seen in the German Bauhaus in the 1920s.[3]

Over time, the institution of the art academy has consolidated the social position and the self-esteem of artists in different ways, enhancing their theoretical knowledge and contributing to their control over artistic production. Among these variants, the eighteenth-century bourgeois dilettantes in the Netherlands had specific purposes for their own participation in the academy. Some saw it as an institution to raise the general level of culture, to develop and distribute high moral standards to society as a whole (thus indirectly demonstrating their own moral superiority); others, more simply, saw it as a social club for relaxation. Either way, there was an obvious affinity between these bourgeois values and the professional aspirations of the Dutch artists.

Dilettantism as Activity and as a Complex of Values

As an artistic pursuit by amateurs, dilettantism has been linked to the art academy throughout its history in the context of an idealized conception of man and society. In England, unlike France, the aristocracy and gentry moved beyond the confines of the court, and thus developed dilettantism into something worthy of pursuit in its own right outside of court influence. In turn, from the middle of the eighteenth century dilettantism was taken up by the rising bourgeoisie. As a consequence it came to acquire a different meaning: while the aristocracy used dilettantism to show its "natural" superiority in moral and aesthetic matters, the bourgeoisie used dilettantism as a means of emancipation. In both cases the patronage of artists was affected.

Aristocratic Dilettantism

Aristocratic dilettantism flourished in England in the seventeenth and eighteenth centuries, as art patronage increasingly became the concern of the landed aristocracy at the expense of the central court. Charles II and his court had tried to centralize culture in the manner of Louis XIV, but this policy failed, mainly because the activities and expenses of the court were controlled by Parliament, which did not support the individual pursuits of the king; the interests of Tories and Whigs were of greater weight than the king's prestige.

In this absence of royal patronage, the aristocracy then laid a claim to cultural primacy to legitimate its own position as the ruling elite. This claim became all the more important with the increase of the economic power of the bourgeoisie. The core element in the legitimating strategy of the aristocratic elite was the *gentleman's ideal*. Based on a redefinition of the Renaissance ideal of education and training, young aristocrats went on the Grand Tour to the Continent in order to acquire a socially indispensable knowledge of "high" culture. In time, their reverence toward the ancients and the arts, and the education and activities they undertook to live up to their station, turned them not only into connoisseurs, but into practicing artists as well. Music, fine arts, and especially architecture were practiced by aristocratic amateurs, many of whom were a match for the artists (Foss 1971, 32). Instead of being the artists' patrons, they often became their competitors.[4]

These aristocratic dilettantes thought it their duty to perform on a higher level than "regular" artists. The patron, not the artist, was to be the arbiter of taste. Consequently the artist was to serve mainly as a craftsman, not as an original designer. Those seeking to become recognized as arbiters of taste finally organized the Society of the Dilettanti in 1734, establishing a forum where they could demonstrate their profound erudition in discussion of problems of taste.

The ideology of such aristocratic arbiters of taste combined a notion of a particular formal education along with an assumption of a "natural gift" based on a universal aesthetic disposition. They believed that this precious disposition was lost in most individuals, because it needed cultivation in order to blossom—cultivation that was generally neglected.

Only the aristocratic education allowed this disposition to be developed into an unspoiled intelligence capable of objective judgment (Pears 1988).[5] In the words of Lord Shaftesbury in 1731:

> Nothing is so common as the affectation of, nor anything so seldom found as Taste. Bad principles of education, an ill choice of acquaintance, the ignorance of instructors, and our own prejudices, all contribute to the confirmation of this evil. So much depends on a true Taste, with regards to eloquence, and even morality, that no one can be properly stil'd a gentleman, who does not take every opportunity to enrich his own capacity, and settle the elements of taste, which he may improve at leisure. (Denvir 1983, 63)

For many such dilettantes, to be the better artist was a moral duty. The "regular" artist should be inferior to the gentleman in every respect. John Gwynn (in a contemporary review of Lord Burlington's dilettante architecture) put the matter beyond doubt: "If it is indispensably necessary that an artist should, by unwearied application and unremitted study, make himself a master of the art he professes in order to render his work worthy of the approbation of the great, is it not equally necessary that his employer, who ought to be supposed his superior in every aspect, should be furnished with at least as much knowledge of the art he patronizes as will enable him to form a judgement of the degree of excellence with which it is executed?" (Jenkins 1961, 70).[6]

But as English gentlemen aspired to be arbiters of taste, they gave little attention to the patronage of native painters. Through their knowledge of classical art and their need to express their cultural status, they neglected English artists—a neglect that in turn contributed to the poor state of English art. History painting was recognized as a supreme expression of "noble" values in England as well as on the Continent, requiring as it did knowledge of both history and literature. However, continental history painters were favored over any English artists who offered historical images. Thus the latter tended to restrict themselves to portraiture and landscape painting and did not develop skill in history painting until well into the eighteenth century (Wittkower 1968, 74).

Although English painters as a group longed for the status of gentleman (by then an almost "classical" self-concept of artists), most of them remained uneducated tradesmen and were no match for the gentlemen virtuosi. The aristocracy's fashionable and extensive practice of collecting foreign artworks was facilitated by the comparative cheapness and easy acquisition of such works at the time; financial problems caused many Italian collectors to sell off their famous collections at such low prices that the English aristocrats had even less incentive to patronize English painters (with the exception of a few individual gentlemen-painters of their own class).

The involvement of the aristocracy and gentry with the arts, first formalized in the Society of the Dilettanti, was reinforced in 1751 with the foundation of the Society for the Encouragement of Arts Manufactures and Commerce. Largely ignored by aristocratic patrons, English artists increasingly advocated the establishment of a Royal Academy to support their interests. In 1755 a committee of artists laid the foundation of the academy, but this effort to bring artists nearer to their aristocratic patrons was prevented by these intended patrons, whose insistence that their own Society of Dilettanti have a central influence in the new academy was rejected by the artists. Here the confrontation between artists aspiring for a professional social status and the interests of the established dilettantes is shown clearly. The foundation of the British Royal Academy, delayed until 1768, coincided with the emergence of the rich middle class as patrons. As had first been proposed, the new Royal Academy was run primarily by artists and was committed to the elevation of the status of the artist from craftsman to professional.[7]

The Society for the Encouragement of Art Manufactures and Commerce lost its aristocratic nature when wealthy members of the upper-middle class acquired positions in the society and shared seats with the aristocracy and gentry. Thus new elements of bourgeois dilettantism were inserted into the old ideal of the gentleman. These new patrons of art were less preoccupied with the classical codes, taking an interest instead in the native arts of landscape and portraiture. However, they did not replace the values and practice of aristocratic dilettantism until well into the nineteenth century.

Bourgeois Dilettantism

One of the main themes of eighteenth-century social thought was that reason, knowledge, and education were basic to a sound moral order and to a sound economical system. Some elements of this doctrine could be found in the aristocratic idea of the gentleman's cultural superiority as well as in the bourgeois concept of the cultured individual. However, the aristocratic ideal was dominated by a conservative and elitist conception of man and society, while the bourgeois ideal was more democratic: education for all in order to maintain a free and good society. This latter ideology ultimately led to the emancipation and domination of the bourgeoisie as the elite in modern society.

Bourgeois dilettantism flourished later than did aristocratic dilettantism and involved a different relationship with artists, contributing to the emancipation of the intelligentsia and artists as well. As the *ancien régime* decayed in the second half of the eighteenth century, declining court and aristocratic patronage in both France and England overlapped with the bourgeoisie's growing interest in art. Although some among the bourgeois elite felt obliged to take over the responsibilities inherent in the traditional aristocratic role of the aristocratic patron, the new social conditions forced artists to redefine their own position in society—including their relationship with the large and new body of clients, the bourgeois dilettantes. (The impact of a more general public audience was not felt until well into the nineteenth century.)

By the end of the eighteenth century, a new conception of the artist emerged next to that of the academician, and with it a new interpretation of the artist's relation to the dilettante. On the one hand, academic professionalism as developed in Paris had spread all over the Western world, adapting to the changing forms of patronage. On the other hand a new notion of art and the artist was introduced outside the world of the art academy. This was the concept of the artist-genius and the theory of the artistic personality by which it was supported, which became most fully developed in Austria (see DeNora in this volume) and Germany (for example by Goethe and Schiller). These ideas then affected bourgeois ideas of education as well.

Inverting the English views of an innate aristocratic aesthetic sensitivity, German bourgeois dilettantism was based on recognized differences in mastery (*Meisterschaft*), which artists had and dilettantes did not. Writing at the turn of the nineteenth century, Goethe explained dilettantism using mastery as the central reference (Goethe 1949 [1799]). Although he never finished his study on dilettantism, it contains some elements that are interesting for us; he not only undertook the exercise from his point of view as a literary artist, but also from his perspective as the dilettante he considered himself to be in the fine arts. The dilettante, Goethe writes, is a lover of art who wants not only to enjoy and contemplate works of art but also to practice them. Goethe discriminates between two forms of practical participation: direct participation in drawing and painting (*ausübend*) and participation through the structuring or control of drawing and painting, as maecenas, collector, or critic (*anordnend*). The difference between artist and dilettante is essential, because the artist, the maestro, is born with a creative talent for the arts while the dilettante can only imitate. The dilettante is not an artist: because of his lack of talent he makes serious mistakes, and he should not attempt the first form of participation but rather concentrate on the latter (Vaget 1971).

In Goethe's view, both artists and dilettantes need one another; a symbiotic bond holds them together. The artist should not be on his own and work only for himself. Indeed, the artist takes serious risks when he contacts a public who has no feeling for his arts. He is dependent on the mediation of the dilettante, on the dilettante's susceptibility to art, on his enthusiasm, and on his experience and knowledge. The dilettante's involvement in his art supports the artist and brings him the recognition he wishes. Thus the dilettante is the artist's closest partner among the public, but his lively involvement and his knowledge of the arts are based on experience, not on genius. For his part, however, the dilettante is easily led to self-deceit: Goethe argues that the dilettante might confuse the nature and quality of his motive for pursuing the arts with the artist's drive. Therefore the need to imitate should be strictly distinguished from the drives of original genius (Goethe 1949 [1798]). Later in the nineteenth century, when Goethe's views had become generalized and radicalized, this conception of the dilettante was thought through to its logical conclusion. Nietzsche (1981 [1873]) would treat the dilettante as the outstanding example of the philistine. The cooperation of artists and dilettantes was reduced to the point that the latter had to leave the scene.

Bourgeois Dilettantism and Aristocracy through Culture

As Elias (1981 [1961]) and others have pointed out, the eighteenth-century German concepts of *Zivilisation* and *Kultur* imply quite different views of cultural education. The aristocratic way of life could be viewed as "civilized," whereas that of the bourgeois is "cultured." In a these terms, *Zivilisation* can be understood as refined (if superficial) behavior, while *Kultur* involves the possession of "high" character that touches the soul (Weber 1950 [1935], 402–7). The associated bourgeois ideal of *Bildung* refers to the process of character-building through the acquisition of culture. This ideal, too, goes back to the enlightened secularized concept of man in which man was considered to be a *tabula rasa* who could be developed into a person of high moral standards as a result of a good education. On these grounds, classical education came to be in vogue among the bourgeoisie in France as well as in Germany and the Netherlands.

But *Bildung* meant more than the acquisition of knowledge; as a character-building activity it took on a specific meaning for the German intelligentsia, including the artists. While most French artistic life was centralized in Paris, where the so-called *philosophes* were acclaimed and where artists were known and admired, the German intelligentsia lived isolated in small towns. Their singular social position as learned bourgeois in a still-feudal society pushed them to the cultivation of personality as a possible means of emancipation from their bourgeois background onto some "aristocratic" level. Not members of the aristocracy by birth, they invented the *Geistesaristokratie*, the aristocracy of culture, as their heritage and station. Goethe applied this term to the learned bourgeois elite, to facilitate their (and his own) social integration as intellectuals and artists. In this scenario the dilettante was given the special role noted above, as intermediary between artist and the public to facilitate the social recognition of genius.

Bildung should be distinguished from the ideal of the gentleman because the values governing the transmission of *Kultur* are bourgeois values, while the gentleman virtuoso stands for aristocratic distinction. Basic to the bourgeois values inherent in *Bildung* was the apolitical humanistic ideal of cultivation. This ideal could be used as an ideology by the aspiring elite for their emancipation into central positions, without the need to formulate any (potentially dangerous) specific political ideology or objective. (The importance of this ideal among the apolitical intelligentsia in the twentieth century is demonstrated by the length of time it took Thomas Mann to take a political stand against the Nazi regime.)

As a core element in the aristocracy of culture, *Bildung* should also be distinguished from the ideal of the gentleman because building character and personality required effort. Part of this struggle involved the acquisition of knowledge of the classics in art; another part was the continuing fight against moral decay. In contrast, the gentleman was thought to receive his personality by nature, without any need for effort or constraint. Goethe gives evidence of his admiration of the natural formation of personality, which he saw in his English aristocratic guests, such as Lord Byron.

In sum: while the English aristocracy and gentry believed themselves superior to artists by natural endowment from birth and carried this perspective into their activities as dilettantes, the German bourgeoisie had different views in that they regarded dilettantism as the means to improve the moral and social position of both dilettante and artist, separate but equal. Before long, bourgeois artists reasserted—and inverted—the traditional unequal relationship between artist and dilettante. Now it was the artist who took the role of the aristocrat, and the dilettante was understood as merely the best of the public, trying hard to understand the artist. Thus the idea of aristocratic superiority came to be used against the dilettante by the "innate genius," the new aristocrat of culture: the artist. And so the dilettante sank from patron to supportive client to philistine.

Dutch Art Institutions in the European Context

Both manifestations of dilettantism discussed here found their roots in the traditional hierarchies of aristocratic patronage, either perpetuating or replacing them with bourgeois content. In contrast to both is the case of the northern Netherlands, where in the seventeenth century there was no substantial royal or clerical patronage. Thus no aristocratic ideal could be perpetuated or referred to for comparative purposes. Artists produced primarily for the market, and the main buyers, particularly of landscape and genre paintings, belonged to the same middle levels of society as did the artists themselves.

Protestant iconoclasm after 1566 had marked the end of the production of religious images; the Calvinistic interpretation of Protestantism (which dominated religion in the Netherlands) denied them any efficacy. Further, the secular lords did not constitute a central power strong enough to show its authority by way of an artistic patronage. Thus the traditional forms of patronage of painters and sculptors, which dominated most of the European countries until the end of the ancien regime, did not exist in the "burgher republic" of the Netherlands.

The lack of a strong landed aristocracy in the Netherlands contributed to a different kind of collective bourgeois self-consciousness than in England, where the new rich tried to achieve respectability by relating to the landed aristocracy and gentry through marriage and more generally by copying their social and cultural behavior (Hexter 1978 [1965]; Becket 1986). The English bourgeoisie commonly emulated the aristocracy through artistic patronage and by sending their young men on a Grand Tour (Wiemers 1986). But the Dutch had no aristocracy to marry into and—because of the same lack—had no need for comparable efforts of social mobility.[8] Indeed, they felt no special obligations toward the arts and toward artists because patronage did not belong to their cultural heritage. There was occasional structural patronage of an artist by a rich burgher (Montias 1987), but the ruling elite assumed no special obligation toward artists outside the market. Rather, the burgher class that controlled the government of cities and provinces in the Netherlands saw trade and social security as their primary fields of obligation.

The court of the princes of Orange (the *stadholders*, or governors, of Holland) was small and relatively powerless, and the prince remained dependent on the regents and served at their discretion. These regents and the rich merchants were never patrons of any importance to the artists, and, on the few occasions when a large commission was to be given, native artists were usually neglected because they did not suit classicist taste.[9]

Another group of regents must be acknowledged here as patrons of the Dutch artists: these were the administrators of private institutions, such as the guilds, the *schutterij* (companies of citizen soldiers), and the orphanages. They gave commissions to Dutch artists mainly for collective portraits. The early group portraits in the Netherlands stem from these commissions (Rembrandt's painting *Frans Banning's Company Prepares for Marching*, the so-called *Night Watch*, is a famous example of this kind of private patronage).

Production for the market—primarily a market for painted commodities—affected the form and content of the artworks; paintings were usually small in scale and intentionally made affordable to ordinary burghers. Foreign visitors were astonished to find paintings in every Dutch house, even in the workshops of tradesmen (Wiemers 1986, 154). Paintings were valuable as objects of investment, and they were used by artists to work off debts; they were sold from one person to another, through lotteries and auctions, and by art dealers.

Many features of seventeenth-century Dutch art can be understood by this production for the market and for burgher clients—not only the size of the paintings and their stock production, but also the typical imagery of domestic interiors and local landscapes. The flourishing art market together with a lack of substantial institutional patronage contributed to the genesis of the "free art" (free from religious meaning and aristocratic ideological elements) that the Dutch painters produced in the seventeenth century.

Alpers (1983) contrasts the phenomenon of the descriptive art of the Netherlands with the constructive and narrative art of Italy in the same period. She argues that the art of the European north was part of a culture that valued discriminating perception, a culture that contributed to the knowledge of nature by a detailed examination of the world, followed by a visual report of the details perceived. In the north, the growth of knowledge was primarily empirical and inductive, based on the description of nature observed. On the contrary, the art of the south was more theoretical and deductive, based on traditional narrative, perspective, and an abstract ideal of beauty that hardly existed in Dutch art. Italian art was an art of the mind and centered around the observer who constructed a universe from a predetermined viewpoint outside the picture. The perceiving eye of the northern artist is part of the picture: it is the moving eye that takes in multiple aspects of reality.

Certainly this way of treating reality and accumulating knowledge about the world is closely related to the prevailing system of patronage. In the south, patronage by the church and the aristocracy contributed to the continuation of a hierarchical worldview (though now seen from an individualized standpoint). In the north, Dutch artists painted for an uncertain public of no specific status and with no centralized value system or single viewpoint to defend or be expressed through visual means.

However, about 1680 the great period of landscape painting came to an abrupt end. In trade as well as in art, the so-called "Golden Age" ended as the bourgeoisie came to live on the revenues of their capital more than on the direct profits from trade and industry, the original basis of their entrepreneurial grandfathers' wealth. Under the new conditions, the two main genres through which an artist could earn a living were topographic pictures, especially engravings (views of villages, streets, towns, and countrysides), and decoration. Wall decoration by way of large formulaic paintings became a fashion in the first half of the eighteenth century and provided an important source of artistic employment. However, the mode of producing these works, using typical landscapes filled with a few stock figures, made even contemporary critics (let alone those of later generations) regard this practice as a symptom of artistic decay (Bosma 1987).

Still, there was no general economic decline to account for the decline in artistic standards and production, as Holland kept its position as an important trade country for almost a century. More precisely, the transition from actual trade to administration is seen as the main cause of a changing taste of the elite: like the ruling elite of an earlier period, they became influenced by French aristocratic culture.

At the same time, their inherited collections of seventeenth-century paintings were considered precious possessions. On these accounts the wealthy collected and decorated their walls with pieces of art belonging to this heritage, but they hardly patronized contemporary local artists. A well-to-do merchant usually owned a representative collection of seventeenth-century Dutch art, which was displayed in his picture hall along with a collection of exotic insects and other curiosities. But such a man was also expected to have an interest in the academic discourse on art (Verroen 1987). It is this expectation that helped lay the groundwork for the specific form of Dutch dilettantism. While changing tastes among the elite might have had a minor impact on the contemporary Dutch art scene because so many of the artists' clients were ordinary burghers, by the early eighteenth century the taste of these people also changed.[10] Among ordinary people, decorative wall hangings, topographic drawings, and (foreign) prints came into fashion and replaced the old "picture hall" paintings (Heek 1979).

Artists who did not adjust to this fashion took shelter under foreign classicism, which became the major influence on the new art theory and practice, contributing to the changes in taste of the elite and the more common patrons alike. Classicist influences came from the Royal Academy in Paris, as well as from English and German theories on art (like those of Reynolds and Winckelmann), which were often introduced by learned dilettantes. As history painting rose in prestige in the Netherlands, the cachet of landscape painting declined, as did its contemporary practice.

However, neither the public nor the artists lost all their interest in their cultural heritage; landscape as a genre was revived and acknowledged as an academic specialty in 1760, long before it was accepted by the French Academy. The founding of Dutch dilettante art societies and their pursuit of a revival of cultural hegemony was thus motivated by reminiscences of the Golden Age, and based on popularized "enlightened" ideas on education as well as on the other European art academies.

Dilettantes in the Netherlands

As we have seen, conditions for the institutionalized pursuit of knowledge, artistic refinement, and "sociability" varied among the European countries. In the seventeenth and eighteenth centuries, dilettantism in England was basically an aristocratic affair, somewhat external to the royal court; so well established was this among the aristocracy and the gentry that the bourgeoisie could only emulate it. In France and Germany the learned societies were not only aristocratic in nature but were usually closely aligned with the governing courts as well, whether centralized—as in Paris—or dispersed among smaller principalities as in Germany (Mijnhardt 1987, 32–33). In the Netherlands, however, the search for knowledge was more informal and personal, and more widespread. Education generally reached a high standard, with illiteracy being the lowest in Europe, so special societies of art and learning did not seem to be so necessary.

It was not until the second half of the eighteenth century that members of the Dutch bourgeoisie, trying to regain their lapsed prestige in European high culture, organized into new collectives with social and cultural emancipation as the central aim. In many cases they were able to expand the existing brotherhoods or "academies," which had been founded by artists in the preceding century.

For these brotherhoods, the prior lack of institutionalized (aristocratic) patronage had long contributed to instability and disorganization. They had to struggle to maintain financial solvency, and many did not last very long. But if these societies of art and learning were able to win the protection of the *stadtholder* and the (provincial) state, prestige and continuity followed (Mijnhardt 1987, 91). Such support was eagerly pursued, if not always obtained. When these societies were expanded by the bourgeoisie in the mid-eighteenth century, they usually followed the French model of academic and moral education inspired by Rousseau and Locke. Scientific and cultural knowledge was sought by the bourgeoisie in order to raise the individual in particular and society in general to a higher moral level; by acquiring knowledge one was expected to become a better person, and society as a whole would become a better society. It is not surprising that bourgeois Dutch dilettantes favored a typically bourgeois ideal of moral education such as this, where knowledge and education were seen as distinguishing marks. But unlike dilettante educational societies elsewhere, those in the Netherlands were seldom used as part of a strategy of social and cultural emancipation among the bourgeois elite, as a means to reach and maintain higher positions in society. As noted above, such strategies were unnecessary; these dilettantes already belonged to the social elite. However, for the artists (some of whom were virtually bourgeois themselves, rather than mere craftsmen), the purpose of these societies was professionalization. By increasing their theoretical knowledge and improving their skills, they could raise their social status from the rank of craftsmen, a rank most artists still held. In addition the societies offered them access to wealthy dilettante-collectors.

The tradition of trade and profits in the Netherlands gave dilettantism an additional functional weight; the knowledge and skills transmitted in these societies were also expected to benefit the economy.[11] For the bourgeoisie, the intended improvement in aesthetics was supposed to have practical consequences: "It is a mark of patriotism to bring factories and workshops to prosperity, and to advance the wealth of the burgher, the art of design as a foundation of all art trade should first and foremost be protected, [and] the practitioners should be encouraged, above all in order to be able to employ enough competent designers" (Knolle 1984, 26).

Thus, dilettantism in the Netherlands became institutionalized in the mid-eighteenth century to support the moral standards of society in general and of the bourgeois elite in particular. At the same time, it served as a form of institutionalized private patronage in which artist and bourgeois shared many of the same purposes. The Dutch artists of the period were still primarily tradesmen, whose efforts to professionalize were based both on the moral respectability accorded to history painting by the French Academy and on the fame of the Dutch Golden Age painters. The founding of academies was often explicitly motivated by this aim. Together, the dilettantes and the artists believed they could restore the prestige of Dutch painting and strengthen the moral and economic conditions of Dutch society.

Dutch Art Academies in the Eighteenth Century

The precursors of later art academies in Holland had been founded in the last decades of the seventeenth century as brotherhoods of artists who wished to develop their trade by working together a few evenings a week. These "drawing societies" often depended on the organizational skills, active interest, and financial support of one or two individuals; any larger institutional base was usually nonexistent. At this time the skills necessary for an artist to practice his trade were still taught by a master artist in his atelier or workshop. Such training was not threatened by the institution of the nascent academies, because academy members pursued aims other than the development of practical skills. For artist-members, the main concern was to raise their status as artists by mastering the basic elements of (French) academic art. Academic education was based on the *beau idéal* of classicism, centered around the drawing of the human body and organized along a didactic routine. Thus the first practice adopted by the Dutch societies was the painting and drawing of the human body. A more systematic organization of artistic education followed much later. While the main education concern was to draw several evenings a week, lectures on art theory and general philosophy were also given by the dilettantes, who were valued for their knowledge and rhetorical skills.

The Stadstekenacademie (city drawing academy) in Amsterdam may serve as a model for this mix of proto-professionalism and institutionalized dilettantism. The academy was founded as the Oefenschool der Tekenkunst in 1718 and rebaptized as the Tekenacademie in 1741. The Oefenschool itself had developed from the efforts of a few artists to co-operate in hiring, and drawing from, a live model. Within a few years only a few members were left. The academy revived, but once again it came to an end, this time because of quarrels among the members. Finally, about 1750 the academy made a new start with a combined group of twenty artists and dilettantes. Yet it was not until 1765 that this academy became more than an informal gathering of artists and *liefhebbers* (art lovers, another name for dilettantes). In that year the members agreed upon a formal structure with regulations intended to improve its continuity and stability as the Stadstekenacademie. In these regulations the dilettantes received formal membership to the academy. Jonas Witsen, an important dilettante who was one of the city governors, was even asked to become the head director of the organization. As a rule, from 1765 onward one of the city governors was appointed director of the academy. Such a director could be of great help in obtaining better quarters.

Although formal teaching was not part of the program (there was no specified faculty), students were accepted and placed at one of three levels of skill. The directors gave advice if necessary. Most of the students were young amateurs or artists by occupation. Meetings were only twice a week and in winter the working members were obliged to be present on penalty of a fine. Each of the directors had to supervise the meetings once a month. (These attendance requirements were probably motivated by the hiring of a life model during the winter, who was worth paying only if everyone was present; in the summer, drawing was done from plaster casts.)

An important new rule increased the responsibility of the dilettantes among the six directors. The directors had to pay for the prizes that were presented to the best of the three classes each year. Thus the dilettantes increased their financial contributions to the maintenance of the academy. However, their contribution was not only material; the many prominent honorary members imparted prestige and decorum to the academy as well. One leading dilettante, Cornelis Ploos van Amstel (one of the academy's directors), enrolled as members several other prominent burghers and aristocrats, even from abroad (Ploos van Amstel 1980, 106–7). The status of such men was sometimes sufficient to exempt them from regular dues. In the course of 1766–67, the academy counted as dues-paying members forty-nine "working" members (artists) and twenty-five "honorary" members (dilettantes), an indication that the academy had become a success only a year after its formal organization. The "honorary" members were obliged to contribute seven guilders annually, and they also made considerable donations of necessary material and funds. In addition, they conferred prestige on the academy as they also derived prestige from it. To this end, men like Ploos van Amstel became members of several societies. Trustworthy patronage and a stable academy were seen as mutually beneficial.

Certainly the artists—the "working" members of the academy—benefited from their relationship with the "honorary," dilettante patrons. In addition to the enhanced knowledge and association already discussed, artist members gained a competitive edge because many artists who were not related to academy members were not enrolled. Those admitted were often young amateurs of bourgeois background who had already been socialized into their expected societal and cultural roles. They could readily learn the aesthetic vocabulary that was necessary for their social position, along with improving their craft skills. In addition, they had the opportunity to learn skills in organizational leadership. While the head director was usually a dilettante and a prominent member of local society, a majority of the other directors were practicing artists in daily life who taught youngsters in their ateliers. They recruited appropriate pupils (often their own sons) into academy membership; not surprisingly, these students became frequent prizewinners.

For the honorary members, the academy served their own social interests. They could participate in the drawing sessions, of course, but when the academy was flourishing and had enough extra space, they could use it as a clubhouse for informal gatherings and as a place to receive their foreign visitors in an elegant and "cultivated" environment. This environment was very important; the meeting room in which lectures were given was also the gallery for the display of replicas of ancient sculptures and paintings. These prompted much stimulating discussion in which the members could demonstrate their own cultural erudition and competence. The academy thus served as an important institution to improve the knowledge and the cultural level of both artists and dilettantes and provided in turn the justification for art collection and revaluation (Verroen 1987, 22).

State Involvement in the Art Academy

In the nineteenth century, the dilettante-patrons of the academies and the government became more intertwined than before, as the academies' increasing need for financial support coincided with changes in the government's educational policy, which placed more emphasis upon practical concerns. New schools for technical drawing were set up through combined private and state initiatives to train craftsmen, and many of the existing academies converted their educational programs to this end, if only to sustain themselves economically. Once these new programs were implemented, many members reluctantly accepted the loss of the cherished friendly cooperation of artists and dilettantes. One historian has noted:

> The education of pupils, which used to be of secondary importance in the [Rotterdam Academy], became more and more its main concern, which did not benefit the spirit of brothers-in-art of the members, the number of which did increase because of the Union [of two former art societies], while the harmonious cooperation flagged, and many, who did not know the nature and purport of the Old Art Society, held a different view of it than those who, during so

many times, had witnessed the various vicissitudes of the society, because of which it had become so dear to them. (Bakker 1900, 68, translation mine)

Still, the education at these new schools remained based on the traditional academic principles featuring the drawing of the human figure, a residue from the dilettante academies that did not meet the approval of the proponents of the new practical education: "Most of the schools instituted for the instruction in drawing had a too exclusive tendency towards the fine arts, meanwhile more or less neglecting the useful arts, because of which these schools, in educating future craftsmen, do not deliver the education of the useful skills, [which] we might have expected if the education would have been more suitably arranged" (Derkinderen 1908, 16, translation mine).

Given the predominance of economic issues in both local and state policy initiatives in the nineteenth century, there was no question as to which aspect of the academy structure would survive, but at least two royal decrees were needed to establish a structured training for both artists and craftsmen. While some art societies kept their dilettante members and the associated traditions alive until midcentury by ignoring these decrees, for the most part the era of the dilettante was over. As the dominant interest of the state was to foster the useful, applied arts, a general indifference toward the training of fine artists increased. Any such training was to be left to private initiative: "In many respects the government can and should act only to show the way and make it easier to take that road by encouragement. But only the citizens could, by their knowledge of what is useful and what pleasant, and prompted by their inborn or cultivated taste, provide a kind of extent and breadth to many institutions, which the government is not able to accomplish by its own means" (Martis 1984, 35, translation mine).

A well-documented illustration of the notorious indifference of the state is presented by the history of the Koninklijke Academie (Royal Academy), founded by William I in 1822. Upon its establishment, the aforementioned Amsterdam Stadstekenacademie closed its doors. The governing regulations of the state's Koninklijke Academie show that private support and involvement on the part of dilettante members were no longer welcome; their places were taken by officials who served as public authorities to represent "the prestige and authority of the arts nationwide" (Derkinderen 1908, 14, translation mine). While practicing dilettantes could become sustaining members, they no longer controlled the patronage of the prizes, which now became awards given by the state.

Still, these sustaining members remained influential in matters of art management and art policy until the 1830s. Most of them held seats in the fine art department of the Institute for Science, Literature, and Art (Koninklijk Instituut van Wetenschappen, Letterkunde en Schone Kunsten), which had been founded in 1808, after the French example. Accordingly, they had been influential in the formulation of the 1817 decree that had set up the Royal Academy in the first place, and they held seats on its governing board (Hoogenboom 1985, 49). But with this elevation, before long they shifted their own taste from an appreciation and encouragement of Dutch art toward a higher evaluation of classical art, as had their elite predecessors a century before. Having "sold out" their artistic heritage, they found that the influence of the institute diminished and it rapidly lost all its authority.

The state's general lack of interest in the arts became evident in its sale of prominent private collections that had been bequeathed to it to sustain the national heritage by a number of dilettante collectors, now dying off. Although the main Dutch museums were based on such donated private collections, many of these collections were sold to foreign buyers on the rationale that even the small compensation asked by the heirs and the necessary maintenance costs were too high.[12]

As for the building that housed the Koninklijke Academie, it was in such poor condition that part of the expected instruction could not be carried out and many pupils had to be dismissed. The major state prize, the Prix de Rome, was abolished to save money; the prime minister claimed that talented artists did not need this prize trip to Rome for any additional training, which meant that good money was inevitably being wasted on less talented artists.[13]

In 1851, the supporting Institute of Science, Literature, and Fine Arts itself was closed and replaced by the Koninklijke Academie van Wetenschappen (Royal Academy of Sciences), which had no faculty for the arts. Thus the academies fostering the arts and literature were left to look after themselves. Without state support on any scale, the Koninklijke Academie barely survived, waiting for better days that would arrive only in the last quarter of the century. Then increasing public enthusiasm for the arts led to increasing state patronage and the academy's replacement by the new Rijksacademie in 1870. Founded to teach neoclassical principles, this institution survived through the turbulent modernist times and today provides post-secondary education in fine arts.

By the turn of the twentieth century, government support for the arts increased as industrialization in the Netherlands took off, and as modernization paradoxically increased public awareness of the importance of the national past in sustaining Dutch culture in the present. While a full discussion of this change is beyond the scope of this chapter, it is worth noting that after World War II the Dutch state became a world leader in art patronage. In the case of fine artists, a system of social supports (for example, medical benefits and income subsidy) was at the root of the state policy, which then led to an explosive increase in the number of artists and of art students. Economic conditions again affected the artistic outcome, as in the 1980s these general social supports for artists were reduced and were replaced by far more restricted artistic support—even though the number of artists graduating from the academies and thus entitled to the remaining subsidy remained high.

Conclusion

The distinction made here between aristocratic and bourgeois dilettantism remains analytically useful, because both types of amateur participation in—and patronage of—the arts are found today as specific cultural references for art patrons. The former rationale is based on an assumption of a "natural" aesthetic disposition heightened by a devotion to classical standards; the latter is based on a claim to a democratic sharing of power. For advocates of the first position, their activities in artistic performance legitimate their "natural" dominance of society—including its subordinate artists. For advocates of the second, however, "amateur" art patronage legitimates their claim to a democratic share of high culture and the power associated with it.

As we have seen here, while aristocratic patronage and dilettantism varied considerably among the European countries, in the eighteenth century it became integrated with bourgeois principles of power-sharing, especially in England and Germany. In the Netherlands, however, a third model of dilettantism developed; the small separation between social strata and the absence of an aristocracy precluded the other types of amateur art patronage. As bourgeois-dilettantes and tradesmen-artists united in art academies in a cooperative effort to regenerate Dutch high culture, there were no strong needs for class legitimation. But once the state did provide support for the arts and for professional training for artists, the dilettante art societies fell, having no additional function of status assertion. As they fell, public support for the arts in general declined. Whatever the problems of status rivalry and snobbery associated with aristocratic and bourgeois dilettantism, these forms of patronage appear to have benefited the arts more than those based on egalitarian principles.

Notes

1. There is disagreement concerning the nature and quality of the instruction given at these early Italian academies. Some researchers describe a curriculum based upon such applied subjects as mathematics and figure studies (Barzman 1989), while others follow Pevsner (1940) and doubt the structural implementation of such systematic training. Many of the lectures given at these academies seem to have focused on art as a theoretical discipline and thus demonstrate its inclusion among the *artes liberales*.

2. In the sociological literature, professionalization is defined either as a system of features or as a complex of power relations legitimated by specialized knowledge (Freidson 1986). As used here, professionalization implies both an analysis of the power dynamics and an analysis of specific features. As here detailed, the formal education established in the art academy contributed to the professionalization of the artist and thus to the "amateurization" of the patron.

3. In the Bauhaus the arts faculty tried to develop a professional attitude in young artists based on programmatic points of departure, which were deduced from a specific ideology of artistic professionalism.

4. An interesting example is the influence of aristocratic dilettantism on delaying the professionalization of architects. From the sixteenth century there was a bond between patron and master builder, to the point that in some cases the patron became his own architect, often taking his designs from the many Italian books on architecture available in England (Jenkins 1961, 44). In technical matters, the patron-architect was supported by the practical knowledge of the builder, who in turn learned much about classical ornamentation from the dilettante-architect. The thorough training given by Sir Christopher Wren (1632–1723) to his workmen was well known. Among the aristocracy many such commissions were given and dilettante expertise was widely available. During the eighteenth century educated architects entered the scene, but it was a long time before the hegemony of the dilettante came to an end (Kaye 1960, 40–49).

5. Among the aristocratic moral duties was charity toward the poor, including the education of impoverished children. But such education usually maintained the status quo and the children's illiteracy: the ability to write was often seen as a luxury liable to undermine their "right" direction.

6. Although well articulated by the English, these ideas about the inherently aristocratic nature of "taste" are prominent among the French aristocracy as well. Saint-Evremond distinguished between good and bad taste on the one hand and between taste and no taste on the other: although bad taste could be found among the aristocracy, taste of any kind was essentially considered a court value (Moriarty 1988, 109).

7. The Royal Academy was also open to "colonial" artists; one of its founders was Benjamin West, born near Philadelphia, who became its president in 1791 for a thirty-year tenure. Another American expatriate, John Singleton Copley, was elected an associate in 1776 and full academician in 1779.

8. The political and social elites in the Netherlands showed a certain aristocratization in their habits and cultural attitudes, but no real aristocratic alternative or

competition was offered to the bourgeois culture of which they constituted the upper level.

9. The regents and royalty shared the international taste for classicism and the baroque, while most of the northern Dutch painters lacked the classical knowledge obtained by court-sponsored artists in the southern Netherlands, where the tradition of clerical and aristocratic patronage lived on among such artists as Peter Paul Rubens. Differences in painting between the south and north derived from the outcome of the politically and religiously motivated war against Spain, which brought about the split between the Northern Provinces (now the Netherlands) and the Southern Provinces (now Belgium and northern France). At the war's end in 1648, the Southern Provinces remained Spanish, and consequently clerical and court patronage remained, whereas in the Protestant north these ceased to exist (Geyl 1988 [1932]). With less power at their disposal, the Dutch court remained aware of the superior artists of the south, particularly Rubens, from whom they commissioned works rather than patronize native painters (Rosenberg, Slive, and Ter Kuile 1966, 171).

10. The distance between social strata in Dutch society has always been small and contact among the elite, the burgers, and the artists was frequent. The elite lived among the burghers in the city and took part in its general public life. Besides, the elite itself was differentiated in levels, the lowest reaching down to include the ordinary burgher.

11. This was not entirely new. The aristocratic societies also served very practical goals, particularly concerning the management and development of the aristocrats' lands. In contrast, bourgeois societies were primarily concerned with strengthening their cultural capital through education and intellectual development.

12. The effect of this negligence could be seen in the autumn of 1990 in an exhibition at the Mauritshuis in The Hague featuring Dutch paintings sold to American collectors by the state during the nineteenth century. Recognition of such short-sightedness was not only recent, however. In 1935 a Rotterdam museum borrowed from the Louvre a small Vermeer for a complete show of the artist's work. The painting had once belonged to a collection offered to the city of Rotterdam in 1869, for a compensation of Fl.50,000. The offer was declined, as the money was needed for special projects. When the painting was borrowed in 1935, it alone was insured for Fl.300,000, six times the price of the entire collection only seventy years before (Boekman 1989 [1939], 22–24).

13. It must be admitted that the Dutch artists sent to Rome on these grants were not very successful upon their return.

References

Alpers, Svetlana. 1983. *The Art of Describing: Dutch Art in the Seventeenth Century.* Chicago: University of Chicago Press.

Bakker, A. 1900. *De oorsprong der Academie van Beeldended Kunstenen Technische Weten-*

schappen te Rotterdam, aagetoond in de geschiendenis van het Teekengenootschap "Hierdoor tot Hooger." Rotterdam.

Barzman, K. E. 1989. "The Florentine Accademia del Disegno: Liberal Education and the Renaissance Artist." In *Academies of Art between Renaissance and Romanticism,* edited by A. W. A. Boschloo, E. J. Henrikse, L. C. Smit, and G. J. van der Sman. The Hague: SDU.

Becket J. V. 1986. *The Aristocracy in England, 1660–1914.* Oxford: Oxford University Press.

Boekman, Emanuel. 1989 (1939). *Overheid en Kunst in Nederland.* Amsterdam: Van Gennep.

Bosma, H. 1987. " 'Het verderf van onze kunst in de 18de eeuw, het zoogenaamd behangselschilderen . . . ,' over de Nederlandse behangselschilderkunst, de fabriek voor geschilderd behangsel te Hoorn en enkele kamerdecoraties di daar werden vervaardigd." In *Achttiende eeuwse kunst in de Nederlanden,* edited by Scheffer. Delft: Deltsche Uitgevers Maatschappij.

Denvir, Bernard. 1983. *The Eighteenth Century: Art, Design, and Society, 1689–1789.* London: Longman.

Derkinderen, A. J. 1908. "De Rijks-Academie van Beeldende Kunsten te Amsterdam." *Tijdschrift der XXe eeuw.* Haarlem.

Elias, Norbert. 1981 (1961). *Uber den Prozess der Zivilisation, Sociogenetische und Psychogenetische Untersuchungen.* Frankfurt/Main: Suhrkamp Verlag.

Foss, Michael. 1971. *The Age of Patronage: The Arts in England, 1600–1750.* Ithaca, N.Y.: Cornell University Press.

Freidson, Eliot. 1986. *Professional Powers: A Study in the Institutionalization of Formal Knowledge.* Chicago: University of Chicago Press.

Geyl, Pieter. 1988 (1932). *The Revolt of the Netherlands, 1555–1609.* London: Cassell.

Goethe, Johann Wolfgang von. 1949 (1798). "Einleitung in de Propylaen." *Werke,* vol. 12. Hamburg.

———. 1949 (1799). "Uber den sogenannten Dilettantismus oder Die practische Liebhaberei in den Kunsten." *Weimarer Ausgabe I,* vol. 47: 321–24.

Gombrich, E. H. 1985. "The Renaissance Conception of Artistic Progress and Its Consequences." In *Norm and Form: Studies in the Art of the Renaissance,* vol. 1: 1–10. Oxford: Oxford University Press.

Heek, Frederik van. 1979. "Bloei en ondergang van de Hollandse zeventiende-eeuwse landschapsschilderkunst (1620–1670)." *Mens en Mattschappij* 54.

Hexter J. H. 1978 (1965). "The Myth of the Middle Class in Tudor England." In *European Class: Stability and Change,* edited by B. Barber and E. G. Barber, 334–52. New York: Greenwood Press.

Hoogenboom, A. 1985. "De rijksoverheid en de moderne beeldende kunst in Nederland, 1975–1848." In *Kunst en Beleid in Nederland,* 13–79. Amsterdam: Van Gennep.

Jenkins, Frank. 1961. *Architect and Patron: A Survey of Professional Relations and Practice in England from the Sixteenth Century to the Present Day.* London: University of Durham Publications.

Kaye, Barrington. 1960. *The Development of the Architectural Profession in Britain.* London: Allen and Unwin.

Knolle, P. 1984. "Tekenacademie in de Noordelijke Nederlanden: de 17de en 18de eeuw." In *De Lucaskrater,* edited by M. van der Kamp, P. G. J. Leijendekkers, J. L. Locher, and J. B. H. Vierdag, 19–33. Assen.

Martis, Adi. 1984. "Van 'tekenschool' tot 'kunstvakschool': de Rijksoverheid en het onderwijs in de beeldende kunsten van circa 1820 tot circa 1940." In *De Lucaskrater,* edited by M. van de Kamp, P. G. J. Leijendekkers, J. L. Locher, and J. B. H. Vierdag, 35–50. Assen.

Mijnhardt. 1987. *Tot heil van 't Menschdom: Culturele Gennotschappen in Nederland 1750–1815.* Amsterdam: Rodopi.

Montias, John Michael. 1987. "Vermeer's Clients and Patrons." *Art Bulletin* 19(1): 68–76.

Moriarty, M. 1988. *Taste and Ideology in Seventeenth Century France.* Cambridge: Cambridge University Press.

Nietzsche, Friedrich. 1981 (1873). "David Strauss, der Bekenner und der Schriftsteller." In *Unzeitgemasse Betrachtungen.* Frankfurt/Main: Insel Verlag.

Pears, I. 1988. *The Discovery of Painting: The Growth of Interest in the Arts in England, 1680–1768.* New Haven: Yale University Press.

Pevsner, Anton. 1940. *Academies of Art, Past and Present.* Cambridge: Cambridge University Press.

Ploos van Amstel, G. 1980. *Portret van een koopman en uitvinder, Cornelis Ploos van Amstel.* Assen.

Rosenberg, James, Seymour Slive, and E. H. ter Kuile, eds. 1966. *Dutch Architecture, 1600–1800.* London: Harmondsworth.

Vaget, Hans Rudolf. 1971. *Dilettantismus und Meisterschaft. Zum Problem des Dilettantismus bei Goethe: Praxis, Theorie, Zeitkritik.* Munich: Winkler-Verlag.

Verroen, Th. L. J. 1987. " 'Een verstandig ryk man,' de achttiende eeuwse verzamelaar Adriaan Leonard van Heteren." In *Achttiende eeuwse kunst in de Nederlanden,* 17–62. Delft: Deltsche Uitgerers Maatschappij

Weber, Alfred. 1950 (1935). *Kulturgeschichte als Kultursoziologie.* Munich: Piper.

Wiemers, M. 1986. *Der "Gentleman" und die Kunst, Studien zum Kunsturteil des englischen Publikums in Tagebuchaufzeich-nungen des 17. Jahrhunderts.* Hildesheim.

Wittkower, Rudolf. 1968. "The Artist." In *Man versus Society in Eighteenth-Century Britain,* edited by J. L. Clifford, 70–84. Cambridge: Cambridge University Press.

❖ 3 ❖

Literary Agents and Literary Traditions: The Role of the Philistine

LINDA MARIE FRITSCHNER

In the strictest sense, a work of literature consists of the marks that a writer has put on the sheets of paper before him forming the definitive version of a printed work that finally bears his name.[1] In theory, the greater the genius of the author, the larger the likelihood that the original markings—the manuscript—and printed book will be identical. In practice, the author's words are touched by many hands in the course of a long journey toward publication—if it finally reaches that stage. Among all who have a part in this process, literary agents have increased the length and variety of the journey between the author's pen and the book, even as such agents have increased the variety of books available to the public.

Since literary agents came on the scene in the 1880s, they have gained such a secure foothold in the literary world that it is rare for a writer to be without one. Just how agents and agencies rose to exert such a profound influence on literary life is a complicated story. There are two chronicles of the rise of literary agents, one by William Heinemann (1893), the publisher, and the other an historical analysis and economic interpretation by James Hepburn (1968). Heinemann's account has charm and accuracy. He writes:

> This is the age of the middleman. He is generally a parasite. He always flourishes. I have been forced to give him some little attention lately in my particular business. In it he calls himself the literary agent. May I explain his evolution? . . . You become the literary agent by hiring an office; capital and special qualifications are unnecessary; but *suaviter in modo* must be your policy, combined with a

54

fair amount of self-assertion. You begin by touting among the most popular authors of the moment, *and* by being always at hand and glad of a job, you will soon be able to extract from them testimonials, which, carefully edited, make up a seductive prospectus to send out broadcast. (Nov. 11, 1893)

Heinemann goes on to state that this seductive prospectus is to emphasize how "you the agent have made one author wealthy (You, not his work, oh no, not his work!) who was poor before; another has found you invariably reliable, and a third has tried you two years ago, and has never been anywhere else since" (Nov. 11, 1893). The agent's advertisement is to stress the shameful neglect of publishers and the fact that in exchange for a mere 10 percent commission the author's income can double, treble, increase tenfold.

Heinemann casts the literary agent as an unsympathetic character engaged in feathering his own nest at the expense of the publisher and the author. At the time of Heinemann's writing, he and Henry Holt were the chief spokesmen for their fellow publishers. Indeed, they generally described the agent as a "parasite" who interfered with the "right" relationship between author and publisher, and they blamed the agent for debasing literature by commercializing it (Holt 1905; Heinemann 1901–20). Curtis Brown, one of the early agents, wrote in his memoirs: "In the days of the beginning of literary agents it was held by most publishers that the agent devils were occupied with detaching from tried and true publishing friends, authors who had been created by the publishers, and selling those authors to hasty competitors who had not respect for the good old publishing traditions, for higher prices that were the fruits of the old friends' activities" (1935, 281). In fact, until his death in 1920, Heinemann held to the belief that agents were dishonest and greedy; he called agents "monsters" and "literary leeches"; they were the "grossest abuse of modern innovation," who served neither publisher nor literature.

It is paradoxical that the more helpful forerunners of the literary agents were found in the offices of some of the more reputable publishers. Thomas Hardy and George Gissing remembered that George Meredith, a reader for the publishing house Chapman and Hall, encouraged their literary ambitions. George Gilfillan, the Scots literary critic, took endless trouble with authors. He praised; he criticized; and he found publishers. Even after agents were established, literary readers (such as Edward Garnett) continued to act on behalf of authors. The most notable of the informal agent-precursors was probably John Forster, the journalist and literary critic principally remembered for his biography of Charles Dickens.

Arthur Waugh said that Forster bridged the gap between the patron of the eighteenth century and the agent of the twentieth. Thackeray said of Forster: "Whenever anybody is in a scrape we all fly to him—he is omniscient and works miracles." Tennyson, Landor, Carlyle, and Dickens sought his counsel. Dickens had an enduring and intimate friendship with him. Forster read and commented on most of Dickens's manuscripts and he assumed the job of proofreader. He also advised Dickens on nonliterary matters, notably the breakup of the author's marriage.

In the nineteenth century, there were many figures such as Forster who also served as informal literary agents and as unpaid patrons of writers. What irked Heinemann and Holt was the formal agent who had disassociated himself from the publisher and who began to act as the author's agent rather than on behalf of the publisher. Heinemann's charge that unscrupulous agents threatened to crush life from literature by transforming art to a market enterprise was substantiated by the business practices of some early agents. For example, A. M. Burghes, one of the first nameable agents and one of the first to advertise as an author's agent and accountant, represents this shady side of literary agency at its origins. Little is known of Burghes's work or of his clients, but it is recorded that in 1912 he was prosecuted for the fraudulent conversion of fifty pounds that a woman had given him to pay the publisher John Ousley as a subsidy for her book. The court found Burghes guilty. A short time later, his son was convicted of similar charges and the agency of father and son collapsed (Hepburn 1968). This disreputable side of agency work undoubtedly is as significant as the reputable side. It is not found, however, among the powerful triumvirate—A. P. Watt, J. B. Pinker, and Curtis Brown—who had impeccable business records and who by their actions established the contemporary role of agents and agencies in England, America, and elsewhere.

Because of the obscurity of literary agents, it is difficult to secure information about their work and to assess their influence. The problem is remedied in part by *The Author's Empty Purse*, by James Hepburn (1968), which contains a quantity of interesting and valuable information about literary agents and their precursors. Hepburn demonstrates how literary agency increased the author's bargaining position in the emerging literary marketplace, and he connects the increase in the author's income to the rise and activity of the literary agent.

My work draws on that of Hepburn and on the backgrounds of the early agents, the published correspondence between them and their authors, their memoirs, and the biographies and autobiographies of the authors they served. The agents themselves left their account books but so few other records that their important role not only as businessmen but as creators and promoters—indeed, as patrons—of literary traditions and community must be reconstructed primarily on the basis of these secondary sources.

Early Agents and Their Backgrounds

One thread that connects the early agents is their experience in the publishing world prior to becoming literary agents. A. P. Watt, a self-educated man described as being devoted to books, was for a time a bookseller in Edinburgh. He married the sister of a publisher, Alexander Strahan. A short time later he became Strahan's assistant and (before the firm failed financially) his business partner. Through Strahan, Watt came to know Tennyson, George MacDonald, Thomas Macleon, and other literary and religious figures. After Strahan's failure, Watt's first recourse was to become an advertising agent, and then he became a literary agent (Nicoll 1895b).

The exact date Watt began agency work is unknown. George MacDonald, his first client, set the year as 1882; Watt himself in an interview for *The Bookman* in 1892 put the date at 1878. Whatever the date, for many years he stood alone, until James Brand Pinker opened his London office in 1896. Pinker's background is obscure. Arnold Bennett in his *Letters* (1966) tells us that Pinker had little schooling and that he earned his first wage as a clerk at Tilbury docks. After leaving that position, he was employed by the *Revant Herald* for three years. His next job was as assistant editor of the *Black and White*, an illustrated weekly. While on its staff, Pinker also read for a publishing house and for the editor of *Pearson's Magazine*.

Curtis Brown, the third of the powerful early agents, wrote in his memoirs that he entered agency work accidentally (as had Watt and Pinker). An American, he had planned on finishing his education at Cornell University and embarking on a career in chemistry, but at the suggestion of a friend, he left normal school and his hated job as a cashier to enter newspaper work. His journalistic career began on the *Buffalo Express* in 1884. From 1894 to 1898 he was Sunday editor of the *New York Press*. In 1898 he went to London as the *Press*'s representative and for the next twelve years he continued to represent that newspaper and several other American papers. On one occasion, while he was interviewing the popular novelist Pearl Theresa Craigie (whose pen name was John Oliver Hobbes) for a story about her work, plans, and methods for the *New York Press*, he was asked if he would use his contacts with American and English magazine editors to place a novel she had just finished. As Brown wrote later:

"The very next day I happened to see the editor of the *Pall Mall Magazine*. He said, 'You get around among the authors. Do, for Heaven's Sake, let me know of a smart society serial. I'm in desperate need of just the right kind, and cannot find it!' " Brown obliged, placing Craigie's manuscript, *The Vineyard*, with *Pall Mall*, and soon thereafter arranged to place Egerton Castle's novel *The British Comedy* with an American publishing house. Thus, Brown launched his career as a literary agent (Brown 1935).

Watt, Pinker, and Brown established the model for the agents who followed them. For their job, neither diploma nor much capital was required. Others could do as they did—declare and advertise themselves as authors' agents. What these early agents brought to their work were connections. They had an intimate knowledge of publishers, publishing conditions, and practices, and they entered agency work with knowledge of the literary world. For their 10 percent commission they became first readers and distributors of manuscripts.

These first agents were a developmental phenomenon in the progressive division of literary labor. As first readers of manuscripts, the agents usurped the traditional publisher's function for a fee, just as the publisher at an earlier period had stripped away some of the functions of the booksellers and private patrons (Coser 1970). As the agent bargained for the economic interests of his authors, his role expanded so that in addition to becoming the first reader of an author's manuscript, the agent also became both a legal adviser and author's advocate. In the process, the agent's social allegiance moved from the publisher he once served to the author; increasingly, the author transferred his allegiance comparably as well. Thus when William Heinemann and Henry Holt verbally attacked the literary agent, their target was the agent in the role of author's representative rather than as a publisher's representative. Heinemann possibly had Henry James's agent, Pinker, in mind. Heinemann had published all of James's work, from *The Spoils of Poynton* to *The Awkward Age*, until Pinker negotiated more economically favorable contracts for James with Methuen and Constable (Edel 1969, 338).

Caretakers of Authors' Sensitivity

The early agents had seized a portion of the publisher's role, and by defining themselves as business experts for their authors, they substantially defined business as outside the authors' domain and as destructive to the art of writing. A. P. Watt would approach authors with the suggestion that as they were professional people, they could not indulge in arts and crafts as mere trade. "Yet," he said, "they did have their brokers and bankers in matters financial. Why not have an agent or steward or a factor in things creative . . ." (Doran 1935, 92). In exchange for his commission, the agent was to relieve the author of worry and undignified haggling with publishers. Watt believed that authors should not taint their souls or their art by bargaining. Brown considered it a question of specialty: the author's work is to write. If he is to write, he can't in justice spend the time necessary to gain the business knowledge and experiences of the man whose work it is to buy and sell. It was a question of specialty, not ability: writing is the author's job, selling is the agent's function (Brown 1906, 357).

Of course, there was a group of authors who disagreed both verbally and in practice. Probably the most impressive statement that attests to the author's business acumen came from George Bernard Shaw in 1911. Shaw says that authors think that their interests are protected by their agent; they believe the agent when he says that the author will get more if he employs an agent, that their interests are identical. In the short run, this may be so, but in the long term, things are different. The agent has to bargain with a publisher, and soon he finds out that if he does not try to drive a hard bargain with the publisher, he can place a dozen books at 10 or 15 percent author's royalty in the time it would take to fight out one or two books at 20 percent. And if the author should realize that the royalty offered by the agent is less than it might be, the agent can merely say that for each book his time is limited. Shaw recommends that agents pay authors a percentage of their annual profits and then their interests would align. Still, Shaw is not entirely negative about agents; he finds them useful for the mass of hack writers and for the beginner in need of a quick boost. His final judgement on agents and authors is that "the literary agent is a favorite . . . resort of persons who have not ability enough for either ordinary business or for literature" (Shaw 1911).

H. G. Wells is another author who employed agents from time to time, but who attacked them when they tried to gain control of all of his business. On this matter, he quarreled with Pinker, his first agent, and later with others. In a letter in *The Author* (dated June 1913) he spoke of being plagued by agents who wanted to handle his business. He wrote that he knew of no way to stop the increasing nuisance of agents except by declaring that he employed agents for specific jobs and specific jobs only, such as pressuring publishers for a big advance. As he later told one of his agents: "Always get a big advance, it makes the publisher sweat for his money" (1934, 209).

To argue that authors are capable businessmen is not the main concern. Some are and some are not. But it was with the rise of the possibility of specialized agency that their ineptitude for financial matters was more and more frequently discussed. Indeed, agents wanted authors to be "above" things commercial, for any author without a taste or a talent for business would have to employ an agent. The financially incompetent author then became the irrefutable example to justify agency.

One could offer Joseph Conrad as a prime example. As a seaman he had incurred debts. Once he left the sea and commenced a career in writing, he involved himself in the business of his art. But his chronic inability to write on schedule and to deliver copy when promised entangled him in endless quarrels with publishers. His correspondence in the 1890s reveals a dense mass of arguments with a swarm of book publishers and magazine editors over fees, royalties, dates, advances, rights, serialization, and contractual obligations of one sort or another. However, it was not until 1899, when Pinker appeared on the scene, that Conrad admitted to his unbusinesslike methods. At the outset of their relationship he wrote to Pinker: "My method of writing is so unbusinesslike that I don't think you could have any use for such an unsatisfactory person. I generally sell a work before it is begun, get paid when it is half done and don't do the other half until the spirit moves me. I must add that I have no control whatever over the spirit—neither has the man who paid the money" (Conrad 1935, 86).

After Conrad employed Pinker, his economic incompetence seems to have increased as did his literary temperament. During the years of their association Pinker advanced Conrad money, which at one time or another amounted to more than 1,600 pounds. He also collected his royalties, paid his income taxes, rent, and fixed expenses, and even paid for milk and cigars and gave Jessie Conrad approval to buy a coat (Bennett 1966). The accumulating indebtedness and Conrad's slowness in writing *Under Western Eyes* irked Pinker so much that in 1909 author and agent quarreled. Pinker refused to advance Conrad more money unless more copy was forthcoming (Gurko 1962). Conrad poured out his exasperation in a letter to John Galsworthy: "Does he think I am the sort of man who wouldn't finish a story in a week if he could? Do you? Why? For what reason? Is it my habit to lie about drunk for days instead of working?" He goes on to complain that for two years he hasn't seen a picture or listened to a note of music. Instead he sits at his desk twelve hours, sleeps six, and worries the rest of the time. In his rage he even threatens to burn the manuscript (Coolidge 1972, 175). H. G. Wells commented that he thought Conrad's performance in this and other incidents unbearably pretentious. In his *Experiments in Autobiography*, Wells wrote that he couldn't stand the way Conrad "had gone literary"; he described as ridiculous "Conrad's persona of a romantic adventurous un-mercenary intensely artistic European gentleman carrying an exquisite code of honor through a universe of baseness" (1934, 526, 530).

The case of Joseph Conrad demonstrates that the original agents became caretakers of the artistic temperament which they, at least in part, helped to create. The rhetoric from the agents was that authors needed agents because they were too shy and sensitive to stand rebuffs from blunt and busy editors and publishers. The agent was the buffer to maintain the morale of authors. In 1933 (by which time agents had become an accepted fact in the literary world) John Gallishaw described the caretaking functions of agents in *The Writer*: "He [the agent] deals with and on behalf of people too thin-skinned to be good bargainers; and he has to keep up the morale of people who by temperament flower best under the sunshine of praise" (34). Agents were to know how to nurse, protect, and encourage their sensitive authors. Like the chemist they were to stimulate a writer even when the writer is in what Gallishaw terms "one of those temporary depressions so common to all creative people."

At this time, agents emphasized the fragility of authors, but the fact was that many authors worked quite methodically both before and after they employed agents. Arnold Bennett is, of course, an extreme example. Max Beerbohm traded on Bennett's workhorse image in a series of caricatures depicting the mature Bennett talking to his young self. The paunchy and prosperous Bennett looks at the raw youth and says, "All gone according to plan, you see," and the unawed youth replies, "My plan, you know." Bennett would determine to write 160,000 words of a novel in six months—and then actually do so. One wonders the degree to which acquiring an agent facilitated Bennett's literary productivity; Pinker became Bennett's literary agent in 1901, six years after Bennett had begun writing his first serious novel and before he had finished writing his second. The intervals between subsequent novels were much shorter.

Many authors adhered to a routine work schedule. Henry James and Edith Wharton, for example, always wrote for four, five, or six hours in the morning, leaving afternoons and evenings free. A rejection of a manuscript did not upset their routine. D. H. Lawrence accepted being rebuffed and was prosecuted for obscenity, yet he continued his literary productivity when he was with and without an agent. Despite such evidence, the agents' propaganda had it that if an author's sensitivity were to be hurt, this would reduce his productivity or he might drop a rejected manuscript in the bottom of a drawer and never send it out again.

Between 1890 and 1920 the literary market became increasingly complex. As agents succeeded, they became powerful and potent figures instrumental in increasing the royalties paid to authors. As agents took a 10 percent cut of the authors' royalties, their income was directly correlated with the increases in the authors' income. The irony was that the agent contributed to the cult of the author's sensitivity and the opinion that authors were incompetent to sell their own literary products, a view that assured agents a supply of loyal authors and an income.

Maintaining, Creating, and Destroying Literary Relationships and Traditions

There was a debate over just which authors the agent should serve. Although there was no absolute answer to the question, the organization of an agency as a commercial enterprise seems to have influenced the response. Nicoll described literary agency as a good business to be in; all that was required was a small office, no capital was needed, there were no losses, selling a popular author was easy, and the 10 percent fee provided a continuous income. Nicoll remarked of the literary agent, "It is obvious that as years go on income keeps continually mounting up, because he has not only the gains of new business, but the gradual accumulation of the past, and every popular book of the period which passes through his hands pays toll to him" (1895b, 250). The calling could be quite lucrative.

However, this economic structure of agency work began to put new writers at a disadvantage. As a businessman, an agent couldn't afford to work with small markets. Since the agent's income was derived solely from the fee, it was better business practice to confine his clientele to those authors who commanded higher prices. The fee structure increased the probability that stories from new writers would be rejected by agents and thus never even get to publishers for review.

Although A. P. Watt asserted that his business interests were as much with unknown writers as with known ones, in practice that emphasis shifted. His advertisements in literary yearbooks listed fifty of his famous clients. He used their testimonials to recruit authors to his literary stable. But not all those who read the quotation about tripled incomes and relief from financial worries were equally impressed. Henry James tried Watt and found him wanting. When Joseph Conrad was invited to join Watt, he wrote J. B. Pinker that the book of testimonial letters reminded him of the credentials of his Malayan laundrywoman.

Brown used similar advertising tactics. In reaction, Pinker (with a tone of both snobbery and sour grapes) wrote of his rival in a letter to Arnold Bennett in 1909: "Yes, I think Curtis Brown is losing ground. I like him personally, and think he is an honest, capable man, but he is like all Americans and wants to make a lot of money in a very little time. I could always see that he thought my English way was slow and rather stupid, and I do not think he ever realized that the capacity for snapping up commissions does not make a Literary Agent" (Bennett 1966, 124).

Of the early agents, J. B. Pinker took more risks with unknown writers. In doing so, he acted in contrast to Watt and Brown, whom Ford Madox Ford characterized as patronizing agents for the distinguished. Rather than listing testimonials of the famous, Pinker's own advertisement simply read: "Mr. Pinker has always made a special point of helping young authors in the early stage of their career, when they need most the aid of an advisor with a thorough knowledge of the literary world and the publishing trade" (Bennett 1966, 24). Pinker was the exception in agency work. As Watt and Brown knew so well, the prizes in the writing profession go to those with reputations, with established publics, who will thereby insure revenue for publisher and agent.

Thus like many more widely recognized and applauded patrons, the literary agent functioned like a railroad switchman: he would open the track to increase the literary flow of established writers and only occasionally throw the switch for an unknown. This mode of operation had at least two results. The rejection rate for new authors was high. New writers who did negotiate through agents frequently had their manuscripts sent to second-, third-, and fourth-rate publishers. But for the writer whose work already commanded high prices, the market machinery became increasingly well organized. Concurrently, the method for handling the literary output of newcomers and less established writers became more disorganized. Most new writers were forced to depend on direct marketing of their own work. Working without an agent, they lost time and expended energy they could have spent writing, and they sold their own products at lower prices as well. Arthur Waugh, managing director of Chapman and Hall from 1902 to 1930, reported that authors who dealt with the firm through agents got better terms than those who dealt direct (1930).

As a first reader to the publisher, the literary agent gained control of manuscript traffic, becoming a literary "weeder." A contributor to *The Writer* with the initials W. H. H. described this screening function as early as June 1891:

It helps the well-known editor by keeping from him the manuscripts which it is palpable he could not use, and the less famous editor, also, by turning toward him manuscripts which may be useful to him, and which otherwise he would not get. It helps the writer by saving him the postage he would surely expend in discouraging attempts to get into periodicals which are necessarily closed against him, and by directing him to editors whose doors are open for his entrance, or else advising him frankly to discontinue his work. (1891, 123)

This author described the best service of the agent as that of a literary clearinghouse turning manuscripts in the direction that it is best for them to take.

Just as an agent's position was tied to the career of an author, an author's career was influenced by his selection of an agent. A well-known agent's name on a manuscript was a sign to the publisher and editor that the author had already passed a severe test of eligibility. In part, manuscripts were judged by the character and reputation of their representative (Harris 1929). The imprint of a second-rate agent was of little value, since the best publishers knew from experience who the good agents were. Agents' reputations were made by and became identified with the authors they promoted.

In this way, as the agents took over the role of businessmen for their authors, it was the authors who made their agents more than businessmen. Although agents emerged to increase the royalties paid to authors and to take over the financial aspects of authorship, in the process there were a number of unintended results. To begin with, business was defined as being outside the domain of the writer. In turn, the author who was incompetent in financial matters became the irrefutable evidence to justify the usefulness of literary agents, and this helped assure agents more clients. Accordingly, the social allegiance and loyalty of authors transferred from publisher to agent. Finally, the agent's stable of authors began to stand for his ideas and influence on authors, literature, and literary traditions. Thus, the agent began to acquire the aura of a professional tastemaker and patron; his work was seen as being directed toward intellectual and moral ends.

J. B. Pinker probably provides the best example of how a literary agent affected literary tradition at the time. Ford Madox Ford wrote that in the area of literature, Pinker deserved a page to himself. Various authors have taken Ford literally and devoted a line, a page, or even more to Pinker. Frank Swinnerton described him as "a short sturdy man, clean shaven, with a plump ruddy face, deceptive spectacles, and close-cropped whitening hair" (1936, 198). His calm demeanor, his high old-fashioned handshake, his ability to sit with an interested expression and say nothing but "Oh" and "Yes" while another person blithered his heart out were assets to this genius of an intermediary. He knew the monetary secrets of authors and the weaknesses of publishers; he terrified some of the latter and was refused by others; he dominated editors and he enjoyed much power. And as noted, unlike many of his colleagues, he welcomed young unknown writers as well as mature and established ones.

Yet when Pinker died in New York in 1922, there were only two brief notices, one in the *London Times*, the other in the *New York Times*. A New York correspondent wrote the announcement for the *London Times:* "Mr. J. B. Pinker, the literary and dramatic agent, died of pneumonia at the Hotel Baltimore here, last night. He arrived from England with his daughter in the Aquitania on Friday. He was suffering from influenza. Mr. Pinker was a close friend of Henry James, John Galsworthy, Joseph Conrad, and Compton Mackenzie and many other well known authors for whom he acted" (Death of Mr. J. B. Pinker 1922). *The New York Times* added to this only that Pinker was an agent of Talbot House London and that he was making one of his usual business trips to America. Otherwise, there was no public notice of his death.

But from an author's point of view, Joseph Conrad's letter to Doubleday, written a week after Pinker's death, is most revealing:

> I need not tell you how profoundly I feel the loss of J. B. Pinker, my friend of twenty years standing, whose devotion to my interests and whose affection borne towards myself and all belonging to me were the greatest moral and material support nearly all my writing life. During the years of the war our intimacy had become very close. For the last two years he was frequently staying in our house and I learned more and more to appreciate in him qualities which were not perhaps obvious to the world, which looked at him mainly as a successful man. (Baines 1960, 427)

In a letter dated July 15, 1916, Conrad had written John Quinn of his strong bond with Pinker: "Those books owe their existence to Mr. Pinker as much as to me. For fifteen years of my writing life he has seen me through periods of unproductiveness, through illnesses, through all sorts of troubles. . . . The fact remains that Pinker was the only man who backed his opinion with his money, and that in no grudging manner, to say the least of it" (Baines 1960, 427).

Ford Madox Ford wrote that without Pinker, we "would never have had Conrad and poor Crane could hardly have lived. He smoothed out, too, furrows in the later paths of Henry James. I had mysterious and obscure rows with him myself" (1931, 58). Stephen Crane, Joseph Conrad, John Galsworthy, Frank Swinnerton, Compton Mackenzie, H. G. Wells, D. H. Lawrence, Arnold Bennett, Hugh Walpole, Stephen McKenna, and

A. S. M. Hutchinson all were among the clients of this little Scotsman with a small office at the bottom of Arundel Street in London. Their correspondence to him reveals that he invested faith and money in each of them. At one time or another they all owed Pinker money: Conrad as much as 1,600 pounds, Bennett at one time over 1,150 pounds; Ford and Lawrence troubled Pinker for loans, and Crane's debt just accumulated unpaid.

Crane's correspondence to Pinker represents well the demands that authors typically made on the agent's financial resources. Most of the letters deal with Crane's constant and desperate need for money along with details concerning placement and serialization of his novels. For example, on February 26, 1899, Crane wrote from Brede Place asking for thirty pounds: "If you can stick to your end, all will go finely and I will bombard you so hard with ms that you will think you are living in Paris during the siege." Crane did bombard Pinker—with more letters for more pounds. Finally, on Tuesday, October 24, 1899, Pinker was moved to write Crane from the London office:

> Dear Crane, I have received the two mss today, with your note, and I also acknowledge a letter from Mrs. Crane. I confess that you are becoming most alarming. You telephoned me Friday for twenty pounds; Mrs. Crane, on Monday, makes it fifty pounds; today comes your letter making it 150 pounds, and I very much fear that your agent must be a millionaire if he is to satisfy your necessities a week hence, at this rate. Seriously, you pinch me tightly. Mrs. Crane says that I have probably advanced money to Mr. Crane that I have not myself yet collected. As a matter of fact this sum, at present, is 230 pounds. I mention this to impress you less with an obligation to me than to yourself. . . . (Crane 1960, 236)

Even if we don't know the bases for his choices of clients, Pinker built a specific literary tradition by sponsoring and encouraging particular authors. The evidence that Pinker helped create and promote the direction of early twentieth-century literature rests on the testimonials of these more notable clients. (I have not seen the letters of the more obscure authors.) Yet there is another side to Pinker's dealings with even the reputable authors. Long before D. H. Lawrence broke with Pinker he described him to a friend as "that little parvenu snob of a procurer of books" (Bennett 1966, 26). James Joyce too was disgruntled by Pinker's handling. Oscar Wilde went to him seeking a publisher for *The Ballad of Reading Gaol* and when Pinker didn't find a publisher, Wilde wrote Leonard Smithers that Pinker was not to be trusted. Pinker also failed with Seuman MacManus and H. G. Wells, who had been one of his first clients. Thus not all of his clients would have agreed with Conrad's epithet, "the Pinker of agents."

Even among the authors who generally supported Pinker, quarrels arose over the rate of production of their work—whether too slow or too fast. For example, Pinker thought that Bennett was producing faster than advisable, and he suggested holding up certain work and not publishing in volume form the series of essays that were to start Bennett's pocket philosophies. Bennett responded:

> You would be under a false impression if you imagined that I am working at pressure. I am not. I could do lots more. I have vast leisure. When I think I wrote *The Grand Babylon Hotel* in less than a month and that I am taking over three months with *Hugo*, I ask my-self, Why? You don't yet realize what an engine for the production of fiction you have in me. . . . I am never content unless I am turning out the stuff. . . . You must accustom yourself to these facts and do what you can to meet them. . . . The public and the reviewers always have given way, and always will give way, to the idiosyncrasies of an author who is strong enough to make them. The history of litera-ture is nothing but the performance by authors of feats which the best experience had declared could not be performed. You say, and experience should support you, that the public cannot be made to buy more than an average 2 books a year by one author, I say it can, and I am certain that I shall make it as I am certain, my dear Pinker, that I am yours always,
>
> E. A. Bennett
>
> You think me a blustering person, Pinker, but I am not. The truth is you twist me round your little finger. (Bennett 1966, 50–51)

In 1899, Crane also responded to Pinker on the topic of overloading the market: "Your remark upon the possibility of overloading the market struck me as being extremely wrong. I have been aware for some years that I have been allowing over half of my real market to languish with-out any of Stephen Crane's stories. I mean 'the Century,' 'Scribner's and 'Youth's Companion' and a lot of newspaper syndicates in America which have made me personal requests to help fill their pages" (Crane 1960, letter dated Nov. 4, 1899).

In both cases, Pinker sometimes held back the work, but more often he did indeed develop new markets. For example, he placed two books for Bennett in 1904, three in 1905, three in 1906, four in 1907, and five books and one play in 1908. Among publishers, Pinker was one of the substan-tial agents whose opinion they respected. Arthur Waugh described Pinker particularly as one "whose shrewdness and knowledge of what the public wants were invaluable to his authors, while his lively sense of humour and flow of anecdote, were apt to render his visit to a publisher so beguiling that, before he knew where he was, the man of business (here the publisher) would find that he had suddenly agreed to terms which ten minutes before he had no intention of conceding" (1930, 204–5).

As noted above, Pinker worked just as indefatigably for the undiscovered author, without profit at first, but with the expectation that his perspicacity and confidence would be well rewarded when a market for the author's work had been created. And that Pinker saw as his job. The immediate market was not, however, the public; it was the publisher and the editor—even while it was at the latter's cost.

Transforming Social Relationships between Publisher and Author

Pinker shows us the important role that literary agents played in nurturing a literary tradition. To some degree this was at the publishers' expense, as Heinemann and other publishers feared; the formation of literary circles around publishers was interrupted and to a large extent such circles were destroyed.

Prior to the rise of the agent, it had been the publisher who promoted and pulled groups of authors together. Among such publisher's coteries were those of John Murray II, whose literary circle included Byron, Southey, and Coleridge; the Macmillans with Hare and Kingsley; George P. Putnam with Washington Irving, James Fenimore Cooper, and Bayard Taylor; the Longmans and Macaulay; and James T. Fields with a list of clients (all of them personal friends) including Emerson, Lowell, Holmes, Whittier, and Hawthorne. Publishers prided themselves on the literary groups that became connected with their centers; as George Putnam put it, publishers like "the bringing together into one group, possessing a certain distinctive character of its own," noteworthy writers who expressed some definite publishing policy "and who will themselves find pleasure and advantage in their association with their publisher and with each other" (1897, 142–44).

With the rise of literary agents the center of the literary community moved away from the publishing firms. Because the agent bargained for the best fees for an author, individual writers came to have many publishers. Their loyalty was to their agent, not the publisher. Among other consequences, this made it difficult to assemble a collected edition of an author's writings. Although agents could bring their authors together in a friendly social circle as had publishers, the agent's circle was more loosely knit, in part because of the competition among writers for publishers and in part because agents sought authors and contacted various publishers on their behalf. This undermined personal friendships and peer relations between authors and publishers.

In addition to connecting authors to one another in a new form of social relationship, the agent often took over another of the publisher's functions, that of shaping the writer's work and directing his talents (Putnam 1897). Indeed, the agent became the aesthetic arbiter. Curtis Brown said that the agent was "to be an unprejudiced judge of what is really good." But what did the agent mean by "good"? Watt and Pinker, as far as I am aware, were silent on this issue. However, their successors used *The Writer* (one of the main "how-to" writers' periodicals in the United States, published from 1887) as a vehicle to advise authors on manuscripts that would be acceptable and successful. (The journal ran a special Symposium Series from 1934 to 1936, based on interviews with Curtis Brown, Harold Ober, Paul R. Reynolds, Sydney A. Sanders, and other agents.) One agent advised that the good story was one that attracted the readers to the characters and made them vitally concerned with what they were doing. Another said that it was the beginning of the story that is always crucial. Others advised on endings. These agents mentioned not only what they wanted but also what they did not want.

What emerges is a picture of the kinds of manuscripts and writing that agents were willing to handle. Once a first-class agent accepted a manuscript it usually appeared in print somewhere. Through all of this, the agent had become more than a scout, a sleuth, or a commission merchant; by the 1910s and 1920s, agents were telling authors how to write, basing their counsel on sales data.

Conclusion

It is difficult to assess the full impact of the literary agent on publishers, authors, and literature. The publishing industry is enormously complex and varied. For the most part, literary agents have remained in the background. A. P. Watt, as the first nameable agent, had his difficulties, but dozens of writers came to him in his first ten or fifteen years. Similarly, the careers of J. B. Pinker and Curtis Brown seem never to have been in doubt. For his first two decades in the field, Watt dominated it. Then, without losing in volume of work, he began to share the field with Pinker and Brown as more writers produced more work for an expanding readership and a growing number of publishers. In 1910, Brown employed perhaps a half dozen people, and by 1968, more than fifty (Hepburn 1968). Until his death in 1922, Pinker employed about six people; when his son thereupon assumed the business, the number of employees doubled. It is estimated that in 1926, approximately 50 percent of the annual publication of books in England and America passed through these three agents. By 1968 there were about seventy agents, but 90 percent of agency work was still carried on by five leading agencies. In total, about 75 percent of the books published in 1968 went through agents (Hepburn 1968).

Other figures are instructive: in the 1950s the *Saturday Evening Post* took 80 percent of its material through agents. A 1959 article in the *Economist* says that of a thousand manuscripts, the agent tries to place one hundred and succeeds with three or four. The anonymous writer of this article views agents "as a sieve through which a large proportion of the flood of incoming manuscripts is shortlisted." Whatever the exact figures, the literary agent has gained such a powerful and secure foothold in the literary world today that authors rarely work without one.

As middlemen between publishers and authors, between established institutions and individual creative artists, the literary agents have remained nearly invisible in the publishing trade. Their important role and influence have remained obscure. Yet in the late nineteenth century, these "middlemen" gained control over literary traffic. They not only helped to raise the income of the authors whom they represented, they redefined the social role of the writer and, in turn, the relationship between publishers and authors. They became the patrons and caretakers of the authors who retained them, and by influencing the selection of manuscripts accepted for publication, they played a major role in determining the course of what is recognized as literature.

Note

1. The masculine pronoun is used throughout the text. It is not intended as a sexist reference. The language is framed by those who used it at the end of the nineteenth century and the beginning of the twentieth. At that time, all literary agents were men.

References

The Athenaeum. 1883 (Feb. 3, 10, 17); 1892 (Dec. 3). London.
The Author. 1892 (May 2: on agents); 1893 (Sept. 1: Walter Besant on author-publisher); 1901 (Oct. 1: William Heinemann on agents); 1904 (Apr. 1: G. H. Thring on agents); 1905 (July 1: G. B. Shaw on publishers); 1906 (Nov. 1: on

agents); 1909 (July 1: on agents); 1911 (Mar. 1: on agents); 1911 (Nov. 1: on agents); 1911 (Dec. 1: May Sinclair, G. B. Shaw, and others on agents); 1912 (Mar. 1: on agents); 1913 (June 1–Oct. 1: H. G. Wells, Arnold Bennett, Hall Caine on agents); 1926 (Jan 1: on Curtis Brown); 1926 (Apr. 1: Curtis Brown replies); 1932 (Summer: Hugh Walpole, Marie Belloc Lowndes, and others on agents); 1932 (Winter: Lawrence Housman and others on agents); 1937 (Summer: on agents); 1937 (Autumn: on Curtis Brown; Alec Waugh on agents); 1939 (Christmas: on agents).

Baines, Jocelyn. 1960. *Joseph Conrad: A Critical Biography*. New York: McGraw-Hill.

Bennett, Arnold. 1933. *The Journals of Arnold Bennett*. Vols. 1–3. Edited by Newman Flower. London: Cassell.

———. 1966. *Letters of Arnold Bennett: Letters to J. B. Pinker*. Vol. 1. Edited by James Hepburn. London: Oxford.

Brown, Curtis. 1906. "The Commercialization of Literature and the Literary Agent." *Fortnightly Review* 80 (Aug. 1): 355–63.

———. 1935. *Contacts*. London: Cassell.

Colvert, James B. 1961. "Agent and Author: Ellen Glasgow's Letters to Paul Revere Reynolds." *Studies in Bibliography* 14: 176–96.

Conrad, Jessie. 1935. *Joseph Conrad and His Circle*. New York: E. P. Dutton.

Coolidge, Olivia. 1972. *The Three Lives of Joseph Conrad*. Boston: Houghton Mifflin.

Coser, Lewis. 1970. *Men of Ideas: A Sociologist's Viewpoint*. New York: Free Press.

Crane, Stephen. 1960. *Stephen Crane: Letters*, edited by R. W. Stallman and Lillian Gilkes. New York: New York University Press.

Death of Mr. J. B. Pinker. 1922. *London Times*, Feb. 10, p. 9.

Doran, George H. 1935. *Chronicles of Barabbas: 1884–1934*. New York: Harcourt Brace.

The Economist. 1959. July 25: 202–3.

Edel, Leon. 1972. *Henry James: The Master, 1902–1916*. New York: J. B. Lippincott.

Faber, Geoffrey. 1934. *A Publisher Speaking*. London: Faber and Faber.

Ford, Madox Ford. 1931. *Return to Yesterday*. London: Victor Gollancz.

Gallishaw, John. 1933. "The Literary Agent and the New Writer." *The Writer* (Feb.): 33–37.

Gissing, George. 1908. *New Grub Street: A Novel*. London: Smith, Elder.

Gurko, Leo. 1962. *Joseph Conrad: A Giant in Exile*. New York: Macmillan.

Harris, William E. 1929. "Is It Necessary to Have an Agent?" *The Writer* (Oct.): 267–69.

Heinemann, William, ed. 1893. *The Hardships of Publishing: Letters to "The Athenaeum."* London: Heinemann.

Hepburn, James. 1968. *The Author's Empty Purse and the Rise of the Literary Agent*. London: Oxford.

Holt, Henry. 1905. "The Commercialization of Literature." *Atlantic Monthly* 96 (Nov.): 576–600.

"James B. Pinker dies here." 1922. *New York Times*, Feb. 10, p. 15.

Joseph, Michael. 1925. *The Commercial Side of Literature*. London: Hutchinson.

Lawrence, D. H. 1962. *Collected Letters of D. H. Lawrence*. Edited by Harry T. Moore. New York: Viking.

————. 1943. *The Rainbow*. New York: Viking.

————. 1977. *Women in Love*. London: Penguin.

Nicoll, W. Robertson. 1895a. "Authors and Publishers." *The Bookman* (July): 390–92.

————. 1895b. "The Literary Agent." *The Bookman* (May): 249–51.

————. 1914. "A. P. Watt, the Great Napoleon of the Realm of Print." *British Weekly* 57 (Nov. 12): 127.

Page, Walter Hines. 1905. *A Publisher's Confession*. London: Gay and Bird.

Pound, Reginald. 1953. *Arnold Bennett*. New York: Harcourt Brace.

Putnam, George Haven. 1897. *Authors and Publishers: General Hints for Authors*. New York: G. P. Putnam's Sons.

Shaw, George Bernard. 1911. *The Author*. Dec. 1.

Swinnerton, Frank. 1936. *Swinnerton: An Autobiography*. New York: Doubleday, Doran.

Unwin, Stanley. 1926. *The Truth about Publishing*. New York: Houghton Mifflin.

Warendorf, M. M. E. H. 1936. "Literary Agents." *Publishers Circular* (Sept. 19): 422–24.

Watson, E. H. Lacon. 1902. *Hints to Young Authors*. London. G. Richards.

Waugh, Arthur. 1930. *A Hundred Years of Publishing, Being the Story of Chapman Hall*. London: Chapman Hall.

Wells, H. G. 1934. *Experiments in Autobiography: Discoveries and Conclusions of a Very Ordinary Brain since 1866*. New York: Macmillan.

Woodbury, George E. 1891. "Literature in the Marketplace." *Forum* 11 (Aug.): 652–61.

The Writer. 1887—. 1891 (June: on literary bureaus); 1900 (Mar.: Walter Hines Page on author-publisher); 1906 (Sept.); 1908 (July: on author-publisher); 1910 (Oct: William Heinemann on agents); 1917 (Feb.); 1918 (June, Nov.); 1919 (Mar.); 1926 (Apr., Oct.); 1927 (Mar.); 1929 (Oct.); 1933 (Feb.); 1934 (Mar.–Apr.); 1935 (Apr.); 1936 (Nov.); 1940 (June, Sept.); 1967 (July).

✤ PART TWO ✤

DIRECT PATRONAGE

BY PRIVATE INSTITUTIONS

By the twentieth century, many social reformers had come to share the modern faith that participation in the arts, whether as creator or as audience, would change individual hearts and minds for the better and enhance the quality of life for society as a whole. The origins of this view lie in earlier alliances of political and artistic radicals, which largely fell apart with the general failure of socialist revolutions in Europe in the mid-nineteenth century and the success of the Russian Revolution in the twentieth. Thereafter aesthetes and intellectuals tended to look for salvation outside of structures of governance, and avant-garde art retreated—or advanced—into an apolitical yet quite elitist realm of "art for art's sake." In America—its own revolution long since concluded and with no aristocratic tradition of patronage to emulate or rebel against—a comparably apolitical but populist version of "art for life's sake" was taught by the philosopher John Dewey and came to dominate public arts education, both in schools and in museums. In this view, artistic expression was seen to be "natural" and good for the soul; it could have no specific partisan affiliation.

Accordingly, many American institutions, founded with varying missions of social improvement, have provided direct support to the arts as the means to accomplish their other, primary goals. Institutions like museums that were founded explicitly to patronize the arts have been expected to have social purposes as well. We will consider the role of public agencies in later sections; here the focus is on private institutions. When these have funded the arts directly, without public/governmental involvement and oversight, like private individual patrons they have not needed to answer to any wider constituency. But by definition, they have acted as *institutions*, following institutional agendas rather than those of any single member. This makes their control over artists somewhat more elusive, especially when they have also been committed ideologically to the principle of individual freedom of expression. By promoting artistic freedom for their own ends, they have contributed as well to the unintended consequences. Taking advantage of the complexities of the institution, both the participating patrons and the recipient artists have used that institution to advance often contradictory agendas. Artists who most live up to some of the expectations of the institutional patron are very likely to subvert others.

Two such American cases from the 1920s are presented here. Kenneth Dauber discusses the Indian Art Fund, founded in Santa Fe in 1925, which was overtly dedicated to the revival and preservation of Native American crafts, particularly Pueblo pottery. However, this revival was promoted not for its own sake, but as a means to other ends. Members of the founding board had a diverse set of purposes; their aesthetic, political, economic, and intellectual goals were often at odds with each other even as all focused on enhancing elite tourism in Santa Fe through the promotion of Pueblo pottery. The elitist IAF founders also agreed upon an individualized "art for art's sake" ethos, and rewarded its appearance among the potters. This had unanticipated consequences among the Pueblo Indians, and led as well toward a new market orientation of craftwork, which subverted the IAF's original control.

Clyde W. Barrow provides an analysis of the use of drama by the labor colleges that were founded throughout the United States during the 1920s and 1930s, with the purpose of advancing the cause of labor in particular and populism in general by educating the workers. "Workers' theaters" were developed to help workers communicate their own experiences in a public forum and thus to convey a specific political message. In the process, labor movement patrons lost their ability to determine the theatrical practice or the meanings found in the plays by both the worker-actors and the audience. As the theaters came to achieve their highest artistic success, they failed as radical politics.

Thus even when the institutional patronage of artistic creativity was direct, the purposes overt, the audience recognized, and the effects immediate, the outcome was not always what the patrons intended. This might well be expected when the arts are seen merely as the means to achieve the primary social missions of these institutions, whether they be elitist or populist. But what of the many private institutions whose primary mission *is* the preservation and presentation of the world's artistic and cultural heritage? Here we find universities, of course, but more particularly museums, symphony orchestras, and opera and ballet companies. The overt purpose of all such organizations is "art for art's sake"; for them, any social agendas held by their patrons or staff are merely the means to achieve this end. Given the purity and focus of their direction and the fact that most such institutions deal with artworks of presumably established value and provenance, their patrons take fewer risks than do those who support creative artists in the present en route to other ends. Still, even when the patrons' rewards are more certain, they must deal with issues that they might not have expected.

Judith Huggins Balfe and Thomas A. Cassilly discuss organized "Friends" of art museums and other cultural institutions. Such groups subscribe with fees that are well above those of ordinary membership and are specifically directed toward the collection and preservation of objects rather than to the general maintenance of the parent institution. In this regard, Friends serve more like the founding and succeeding trustees than like the public agencies or even the corporate and foundation donors who provide the bulk of the operating funds for the institution itself. Nonetheless, however comparatively modest are the contributions of most individual Friends, status ranks are evident among them and are based upon the dollar amount of their patronage. Their contributions toward the preservation of "priceless" art of the past enmesh them in—and perpetuate—a very costly game of prestige in the present.

In each of these cases, individual patrons have apparently gained status as they have helped to make aesthetic experience more widely available. However, their role as patron has become "professionalized" through the very institutions they have supported; any possible patronage control is diluted by professionalized artists or by "staff." Indeed, in the half century between these examples, staff control has come to be expected as a guarantee for those patrons who cannot risk large investments, but whose cumulative donations are critical for the survival of all culturally oriented institutions. Through their affiliation with these organizations, artists or their Friends may acquire status, but it is the professional staff members who determine the rewards of its distribution.

❖ 4 ❖

The Indian Arts Fund and the Patronage of Native American Arts

KENNETH DAUBER

Marsden Hartley's 1920 paean to "red man ceremonials," which he subtitled "an American plea for an American esthetics," celebrated the cultural products of Native Americans in the pueblos of New Mexico as constituting the basis for a genuinely American art. Hartley, an important modernist painter, spared no praise for the Indian artist: "Science looks upon him as a phenomenon; esthetics looks upon him as a giant of masterful expression in our midst. The redman is poet and artist of the very first order among the geniuses of time" (1920, 7). Hartley's appreciation was to become part of a more general, though not always so fulsome, interest in Pueblo crafts and ceremonies. This interest took organizational form in 1925, with the founding of the Indian Arts Fund in Santa Fe, dedicated to the revival and preservation of Native American arts, particularly Pueblo pottery.

To understand the Indian Arts Fund, it is necessary to recognize that in the 1920s, Pueblo pottery was an unlikely object of patronage—a sense that is difficult to recapture now. From the perspective of the present, the Indian Arts Fund represents a visionary recognition of the aesthetic quality of Pueblo pottery at a time when the very survival of the art was threatened. In northern New Mexico today, one is constantly told that Pueblo pottery is art: visitors to Santa Fe in the summer and fall of 1990 could visit two major museum shows of contemporary and historic pottery; participate in two seminars bringing together scholars, dealers, potters, and collectors; see the IAF collection in a spectacular vault designed to house it; and purchase pottery in dozens of shops and galleries at prices ranging from twenty dollars to thousands. Native American art is obviously a big and serious business; during the mid-1980s, one event alone—the annual Indian Market held in Santa Fe each August—brought over $134 million each year into the local economy (State of New Mexico Arts Division 1986).

In the 1920s, however, the aesthetic quality of Pueblo pottery was not so clear, nor was there any obvious need for an effort to "revive" it. At that time, the only systematic collections of pottery had been for ethnological purposes (Parezo 1987). Tourists looking for cheap souvenirs of a trip to the Southwest made up the vast bulk of the market. Recasting Pueblo pottery as art and its past as a "tradition" that should be preserved was a creative act, entailing a shift in both attention and evaluation. My goal in this chapter is to explain this shift, and in particular to account for why the IAF's members turned their attention to pottery. I argue that in a variety of distinct ways, Pueblo pottery was introduced into projects in which its patrons were primarily engaged. Its usefulness in advancing other agendas allowed it to serve as a neutral focus for the different and often contradictory interests of the IAF's members, thus producing a remarkable coalition that was able to persuasively assert the cultural and social importance of traditional Pueblo pottery.

An alternative interpretation, one more in keeping with the way the Indian Arts Fund is generally understood today, is to appeal to the inherent aesthetic quality of Pueblo pottery. I eschew such a move, for two reasons. First, my task is to account for the reasons this perceived quality was recognized by a relatively small number of people at a particular point in time; an appeal to intrinsic merit is both too powerful and too diffuse for this purpose. Second, as I have indicated, our willingness today to see Pueblo pottery as having inherent aesthetic value may in large measure be a product of the IAF's efforts, though there is not space here to fully make that argument (for a useful discussion of the social production of value that is relevant to this case, see Smith 1988).

In reality, these approaches are not contradictory. By posing the problem as one of attention—asking what drew these particular people to these objects at this time—it is possible to deny *both* that the aesthetic qualities of art constitute a sufficient explanation for patronage *and* that involvement in artistic production is reducible to interests. Objects, and the repertoire of ways of relating to objects, exert their own influence (Csikszentmihalyi and Rochberg-Halton 1981, 43–44). However, asking why patrons attended to particular classes of objects does provide leverage for understanding the focus of their attention: it is not simply the act of attending to objects that is important, but the *way* in which attention is structured.

At its founding, the IAF framed its purpose as a response to the perceived decline in the aesthetic quality of Pueblo pottery, brought about by tourism and by the replacement of pots with manufactured goods for use in the pueblos. Its efforts to reverse this decline took on a wide variety of forms: it distributed designs to both established and potential potters, bought pottery in order to encourage favored developments, purchased examples of older pottery, established standards for judging pottery at fairs, and mounted traveling exhibitions in order to educate the buying public about Pueblo pottery (for further information on the IAF's activities, and evaluations of its consequences, see Amon Carter Museum 1966; Batkin 1987; Toulouse 1977; Wolf 1978).

Behind all of this effort was a remarkably diverse group of people. The fund's original twenty-five-member board of trustees, on whom I focus, consisted of four distinct groups: modernist painters and avant-garde intellectuals from the Santa Fe and Taos art colonies; ethnologists and archaeologists; politicians from the "Old Guard" faction of the New Mexico Republican party; and reformers from the East.

In order to understand this diversity, I draw on Paul DiMaggio's (1982) account of the founding of several high culture institutions in nineteenth-century Boston. DiMaggio argues that the Boston Brahmins, facing threats to their social and political authority stemming from the growth of Boston and an influx of ethnically conscious immigrants, organized high culture institutions both as a way of asserting a basis for their social authority—their refinement and culture—and as an identification of their own interests with those of the broader community.

What is particularly useful about DiMaggio's analysis is his implicit conception of cultural sponsorship as strategic action, in which the act of patronage asserts claims about the identity and status of patrons. Yet the intended or anticipated consequences of this act need not be enhanced authority or legitimacy. In other words, while we tend to think of patronage as inherently bringing status, this goal does not exhaust the range of possible reasons for cultural sponsorship. Patronage sets up a complex social relation, with multiple layers of possible contents and possible motives. In addition to bringing prestige, its benefits may include the advancement of an aesthetic conception, or the formation of political alliances, or organizational interlocks in a larger field, or combinations of all of these.

A useful theoretical framework for bringing order to this potentially chaotic situation, particularly when multiple groups are involved in patronage, is Chester Barnard's (1938) classic definition of an organization as a "system of consciously coordinated personal activities or forces." In Barnard's conception, actors contribute resources to organizations in order to satisfy individual needs, which may vary among the contributors

(44). While an organizational purpose is required in order to achieve a system of cooperation, there is no need to assume that this purpose constitutes the motivation for individual contributors: "Strictly speaking, an organization's purpose has directly no meaning for the individual. What has meaning for him is the organization's relation to him—what burdens it imposes, what benefits it confers" (88). Taking Barnard's example of a shoe company, the motivations of employees, suppliers, and customers for contributing resources are clearly distinct. For each group the aspects of the organization that are relevant to their purposes are also distinct: for customers, it is the fact that the organization makes shoes which elicits the cooperation, while for the employee, it is the fact that the shoes make a profit sufficient to pay a wage which is critical. A shift in what the organization does may therefore have relevance to one actor and not another: a customer wanting shoes will not support a company making coats, while employees may be indifferent to the product so long as it produces wages. Put another way, the specifics of attention and identity are closely linked, and serve to connect as well as to distinguish the broader social context and the organization.

Translated into the sphere of cultural sponsorship, Barnard's argument implies that we cannot assume that it is the particular nature of the cultural objects that are produced, or even the fact of their production, that motivates any particular contributor. While it is true that some agreement on what the organization is about is necessary in order to sustain cooperative action, the stake of different actors in any particular content to that purpose may vary greatly.

The Indian Arts Fund, by virtue of the diversity of its trustees, constitutes an ideal context in which to examine the usefulness of these arguments. In what follows, the general principle that people are drawn to particular acts of patronage because of the usefulness of those acts to projects in which they are engaged is used in order to explore the appeal of Pueblo pottery to the various groups represented in the IAF's membership. I conclude with some speculations about the consequences of the composition of the IAF for its actions, and hence for potters in the pueblos, who had their own reasons for participation in this system.

The Context

In the 1920s, New Mexico in general and Santa Fe in particular were in a state of social and political flux. New Mexico did not attain statehood until 1912, and basic legal questions regarding land and water rights stemming from Spanish and Mexican rule had not yet been resolved. The political order, built on an alliance between Anglo business interests and the Hispanic elite, was being transformed by factionalism and immigration. Tourism was becoming an increasingly important economic activity, which produced new alignments of economic interest. In more general terms, the increasing integration of New Mexico into the rest of the United States produced tensions and struggles over control that were very much alive in the first half of the twentieth century. Located in the new state capital, Santa Fe, were the dominant cultural institutions: the Museum of New Mexico and the associated Museum of Fine Arts. Both had been founded in the two decades immediately preceding and following statehood. With its art colony, an emerging commercial class, state politicians, and mix of Anglo, Hispano, and Pueblo residents, Santa Fe was the center of these processes of change (Horgan 1956; Meinig 1971).

The Art Colonies and Modernism

Both the Santa Fe and Taos art colonies had become important national artistic centers by the 1920s. The first Anglo artists in the region had settled in Taos in the 1890s, and by the 1910s a dozen painters there represented a stable community with an identifiable style and subject matter. The archetypal Taos-style painting pictured a Pueblo Indian, probably from Taos Pueblo, usually draped in a colorful blanket, with a pot or two nearby as conspicuous markers of place. The subject was handled with a concern for accuracy and realism, although filtered through the conventions of academic and studio painting of the period (Truettner 1986; Coke 1963; Udall 1984). Eight of these painters formed the Taos Society of Artists (TSA) in 1912, with the goal of increasing sales through joint traveling exhibitions. Their marketing strategy was highly successful, producing high prices for Taos paintings and in fact leading to the demise of the TSA in 1927, by which time the artists had access to an assured market for their work (Gibson 1983).

The Taos style was challenged by new developments in the American art world, represented most famously by the 1913 Armory Show in New York. Modernist painters, critics, and dealers, inspired by developments in Europe, criticized the ideal of mimetic representation of the visible world, arguing instead for a more experimental art that would acknowledge explicitly the materials of art itself and search for universal elements of design (Zilczer 1975). While the first generation of artistic immigrants to New Mexico were largely traditionalist painters who centered on Taos, later arrivals (after about 1917) were more likely to be modernists and to choose Santa Fe as their base of operations, setting up a rivalry between the two groups (Schimmel 1986).

The debate between modernist and traditionalist painters was carried out in New Mexico as well as in New York, and the prominence of the art colonies in the life of the community meant that the conflict had a much higher public profile than in New York or the country as a whole. At one point in this dispute, the local Santa Fe newspaper identified modernism with "Bolshevism" and called for the banning of subversive art from the state-funded Museum of Fine Arts. Modernist painters, in turn, took pains to distinguish themselves from the Taos genre (Udall 1984). Marsden Hartley, for example, publicly considered the Taos artists to be hacks (Schimmel 1986).

Not surprisingly, then, the founding board of trustees of the Indian Arts Fund included three Santa Fe artists (Frank Applegate, Andrew Dasburg, and B. J. O. Nordfeldt) and a Taos-based but modernist artist and writer, Mabel Dodge Luhan. Dasburg and Nordfeldt were nationally prominent modernist painters, and Mabel Dodge had run one of the two most important avant-garde salons in New York before moving to New Mexico. These trustees, too, were engaged in the dispute over the relative value of modernist and traditional art. Frank Applegate wrote to a friend in New York that "there are about 20 painters here, some of them moderns and some pot boilers painting romantic Indian subjects."[1] Mabel Dodge Luhan wrote to Alfred Stieglitz about Dorothy Brett, noting that "[s]he is truly painting the Indian life. All the others shut themselves into their studios and hiring complacent models they paint the everlasting American *idea* of indians [sic], crouching with a pot, or shading their eyes from the sun!"[2]

Equally as important as the presence of modernists in the IAF was the absence of traditionalists. This absence is particularly curious given the close association between the Taos artists and Pueblo Indians, who served as the artists' subjects and provided the basis for their commercial success. Pottery in particular played an important iconographic role in Taos-style paintings, as I noted above, as an indicator of cultural identity.

It was precisely the connection between the Pueblo Indians and the Taos artists that made any attempted redefinition of the meaning of Native American culture so important in the struggle between traditionalists and modernists. As the remark by Marsden Hartley with which I began this chapter indicates, modernist painters in New Mexico attempted to draw a connection between what they identified as the aesthetic underlying Native American art (it was nonrepresentational, organic, concerned with elemental aspects of design and form) and the features of their own work that differentiated it from traditional, academic American painting. In making this link, modernist artists traded on more general intellectual and critical developments. The attempt to associate "primitive" art and modern art had begun in New York around the time of the Armory Show: Stieglitz presented the first American exhibitions of African sculpture and archaic Mexican pottery in 1914, and Robert Coady showed European modern art, African sculpture, and children's art together at about the same time, in a show that impressed Mabel Dodge with the possibility of a native American art built upon the work of American blacks (Zilczer 1975). An exhibition of modern art that included Pueblo painters was held in New York in 1922 (Cahill 1922). By the 1930s, with several important exhibitions of Native American art, the possibilities for the use of Indian art as an American primitive art were clear (Rushing 1984).

The modernists' involvement in the Indian Arts Fund was thus an attempt to legitimate their own artistic experimentation by laying claim to the authority of the Pueblo artist—an important cultural icon in both the Santa Fe and Taos art colonies. From the artists' point of view, the most attractive element about the fund was its direct involvement in cultural production. These artists did not seek any general social or professional association with the Pueblo Indians. Rather, through their patronage of the IAF, the modernists sought to criticize the existing associations between the traditionalist artists and Native Americans, associations that did not appear to recognize what the modernists considered to be the meaning of the Indians' aesthetic. In this way, the modernists acted to promote their particular cultural niche (in a process identified by Rosenblum [1985]), but they did so by becoming actively involved in a socially distanced sponsorship of cultural production rather than through more direct conventional marketing strategies.

The Politics of Pueblo Land

The politicians and social reformers who became involved with the IAF were engaged in a conflict equally as intense as that of the modernist painters, a conflict rooted in changes in the economy of New Mexico. An alliance of wealthy Hispanos and Anglo lawyers, ranchers, and businessmen had dominated the Republican party and state politics from the territorial period. The Old Guard's political strength rested in the heavily Hispanic counties of northern New Mexico and the Rio Grande valley. This strength was growing increasingly tenuous in the 1920s and 1930s, as a progressive faction within the Republican party peeled away Hispanic support from the Old Guard and as immigration from southern states boosted the Democratic electorate (Russell 1938; Holmes 1967).

The Old Guard saw an opportunity to turn back these threats with legislation to aid Hispanic farmers in a dispute over conflicting claims to Pueblo lands. The status of the Pueblo land grants was a particularly confused issue, even within the context of New Mexico land rights, and it was brought to a head in the 1920s by attempts by the Pueblo Indians to remove people they viewed as trespassers, many of whom had farmed the disputed lands for generations (Hall 1987). In 1922 Holm Bursum, a Republican U.S. Senator from New Mexico with strong ties to the Old Guard, introduced what became known as the Bursum Bill, which would have confirmed most of the claims of those using Pueblo lands (Philp 1970).

The Bursum Bill ignited both national and local protests. For a national audience, the bill typified the maltreatment of Native Americans.[3] For a section of the local community, centered among the writers and artists but including other elements of the elite (most notably the editor of the *Santa Fe New Mexican*), the bill represented a blatant attempt by the Old Guard to win back its Hispanic support at the cost of Pueblo land rights.[4] Several members of the Indian Arts Fund were involved in the fight against the bill through the New Mexico Association on Indian Affairs (Mayhew 1984). These reformers used the IAF to call attention to the economic value of the pueblos (a result of tourism) and to assert a concern with the welfare of the Pueblo Indians that outweighed that of local conservatives.

Elizabeth Sergeant, a writer, reformer, and original trustee of the fund, explicitly noted the connection between the economic importance of the pueblos and political support in New Mexico in commenting on the effect of national publicity on local residents: "The inhabitants of Santa Fe, having been indifferent if not hostile all these years to the affairs of the Pueblos, are aroused by their success in the East to the suspicion that they may be an asset after all. All this work, time, and money has been given by a very small group, most of them not old inhabitants—and the old inhabitants feel aggrieved—and we want to get their cooperation and their money while they are in the mood!"[5] The *Santa Fe New Mexican* of April 30, 1923, also called attention to this effect, pointing out that the movement against the Bursum Bill "has done Santa Fe a great service by advertising the unique historic, science and ethnological attractions of this region."

The success of the reformers in making the case against the Bursum Bill also accounts for the involvement of Charles Springer, a key figure in the Old Guard, in the Indian Arts Fund. In all likelihood, his participation was a strategic attempt to repair the damage caused by the Bursum Bill to the image of the Old Guard in Santa Fe. Without the support of Hispanos, the sole political base of the Old Guard rested in the older Anglo elite in northern New Mexico, and particularly in Santa Fe. The Bursum Bill was of particular concern to this group since the economic future of Santa Fe, increasingly dependent on tourism, was bound up with the survival of the Pueblo Indians. The IAF provided for both the reformers and the Old Guard a visible alignment with the interests of Native Americans in the pueblos.

Art and Commerce in Santa Fe

The shift in Santa Fe's economic base to tourism produced tensions over control that united artists and writers against the business community's attempt to profit from Santa Fe's reputation. While the artists were happy to benefit financially from tourism, they fiercely resisted attempts by businessmen to capitalize on the artists' colony in ways that removed control from artists. The most visible sign of this opposition came in 1926, when the Chamber of Commerce, in concert with the National Federation of Women's Clubs, proposed the construction of a culture colony that would draw thousands of summer visitors to Santa Fe to take classes and attend lectures. Opponents formed the Old Santa Fe Association, led by Mary Austin, a writer and one of the founders of the Indian Arts Fund.

The artists' principal objection was to what they called an "incorporated army" of tourists that was to be organized by businessmen and produce far more income than had the artists (Chauvenet 1983). This characterization of the proposal reflected the artists' understanding of the consequences of such an invasion for their role as controllers of a scarce and highly prized resource, Santa Fe's reputation as a cultural center. Their ultimate victory over the culture colony was followed by other battles, including an attempt to prevent the Santa Fe Railroad from sponsoring the annual fiesta.[6]

Thus independent of any aesthetic quarrels between modernists and traditionalists, for the artists the Indian Arts Fund represented not only an attempt to revive the production of traditional Pueblo pottery, but also an effort to gain access to —and control of—the marketing structure for Native American arts. The most common means for marketing Pueblo pottery during this period were direct sales by potters to tourists and residents in Santa Fe, at railroad stations and in the pueblos and also through retailers in Santa Fe and Albuquerque. Through its involvement in the annual Indian Fair and the mounting of traveling exhibitions (with accompanying sales of pottery), the IAF inserted artists into the exchange relation between Native Americans and tourists. In the 1930s, artists in the IAF advocated opening a shop to sell "approved" Indian art in Santa Fe. Accordingly, in 1936 the IAF and the New Mexico Association of Indian

Affairs began to hold a weekly fair, at which placards were posted telling tourists what to look for in pottery and other Indian art (Dietrich n.d.). By tying the art colony to promotion of Pueblo pottery and other Native American arts, artists attempted to avoid being rendered irrelevant by the increasingly autonomous economic importance of the pueblos.

Evidence of the importance of this role for the IAF for this particular segment of its membership came in the debate in the early 1930s over a federal bill establishing an agency to promote and market Indian arts (see Schrader 1983 for a history of the resulting organization, the Indian Arts and Crafts Board). Members of the Indian Arts Fund, led by Mary Austin, protested that by virtue of its experience and knowledge, the fund should play a large role in any government effort. They particularly objected to government involvement in marketing, arguing that the new agency should support the fund's educational programs instead.[7] This argument closely paralleled their case against the culture colony: it was not tourism or the commercialization of pueblo arts that they objected to, but the emergence of a competing organization that would dilute the importance of artists and writers in directing and controlling their anticipated benefits.

Archaeologists and the Politics of Institutionalization

The group with the largest representation on the IAF was composed of archaeologists and museum anthropologists, located both in New Mexico and elsewhere. The presence of these anthropologists seems to offer the easiest case for explanation: archaeologists, who were professionally involved in the analysis of prehistoric pottery, were therefore also interested in contemporary production. However, this was true only to a limited extent. Carl Guthe, for example, one of the original IAF trustees, had done a pioneering ethno-archaeological study of pottery making at San Ildefonso Pueblo in connection with excavations at Pecos, near Santa Fe (Guthe 1925). But it is likely that the IAF's appeal to such archaeologists rested less on its involvement with pottery than on its potential as a convenient organizational base in the Southwest in their conflict with institutionalized and professionalized anthropology.

Several institutional developments had begun to threaten the place of archaeology within the broader discipline. The decline of museums and the federal government's Bureau of American Ethnology as the center of anthropological work, and the rise of university departments oriented toward the other social sciences, strengthened ethnology at the expense of archaeology (Stocking 1976). The growing dominance of the Columbia University anthropologist Franz Boas and his students constituted a related threat: Boas did not oppose archaeology per se, but his attack on museums and object-centered ethnology in preference for university-based fieldwork inevitably alienated archaeologists, many of them associated with museums.

A more immediate threat to professional archaeology existed in the Southwest itself, the single most important area for American anthropological research during this period. Archaeologists regarded local scientists (most notably Edgar Hewett of the School of American Research in Santa Fe) as incompetent. This judgment was probably strongly influenced by the desire of archaeologists from national institutions such as Harvard and the Universities of Chicago and California at Berkeley to control southwestern research. The Indian Arts Fund provided an organization (albeit with limited resources and charter) that was independent both of Boasians and of Hewett. This beachhead was quickly transformed into a major institutional presence with the founding in Santa Fe of the new Laboratory of Anthropology, designed to be an archaeological research institution. The key to this transformation was the support of John D. Rockefeller, Jr., who was the first major funder of the IAF and who also provided several hundred thousand dollars for the construction and operation of the new archaeological laboratory (Stocking 1982).

Not surprisingly, the IAF became the focus of these disputes. Hewett accused the laboratory of being a cover for eastern institutions intent on removing artifacts from New Mexico to their own museums, a charge that had some historical precedent. His casting the laboratory in this light threatened both to cause the legislature to restrict its archaeological work and to deprive it of local support and funding. In response, A. V. Kidder, the chairman of the laboratory and an IAF trustee, used the IAF to counter this charge in a letter to J. F. Zimmerman, president of the University of New Mexico:

> You are perhaps not aware that the Museum-Laboratory is, practically speaking, the direct offspring of the Indian Arts Fund, an institution founded and supported by citizens and friends of New Mexico who felt that neither the State Museum nor the School of American Research was making effective efforts to gather and preserve the fast-vanishing pottery, textiles, and other products of the Pueblo Indians. The Indian Arts Fund, which exists for the sole purpose of saving these things for New Mexico, has not only gone on record as heartily endorsing the aims of the Museum-Laboratory, but has offered to deposit its priceless collection of pottery with that institution, "pending the working out of a closer affiliation."[8]

The instrumental relation between the laboratory and the IAF caused continuing ambivalence among the archaeologists about the value of the IAF's work, particularly when funds were tight. A. L. Kroeber, an anthropologist at Berkeley, expressed this ambivalence clearly in a letter to Kidder in the summer of 1929: "The popular-aesthetic-social demand is going to be satisfied anyway because it will be around and insistent. Once it gets the upper hand, it will be damn hard to get any real science started. I think we ought to shoot straight at the latter. There'll be enough sag in the trajectory to take care of the wants of the unscientific."[9] In fact, in 1934 Kidder advocated abolishing the IAF entirely, it having served its purpose as the nucleus of the laboratory.[10]

Organizational Ramifications

In sum, the particular role that participation in the IAF played varied among the trustees. For the modernist painters, the Indian Arts Fund represented an opportunity to claim legitimacy for a new aesthetic, by redefining the cultural symbolism of Native Americans. For both reformers and Old Guard Republicans, the fund represented an opportunity to ally themselves visibly with the interests of Native Americans in the pueblos in the face of political threats. For the cultural community generally, the fund provided a way to assert control over an aspect of cultural life critical to the commercial interests in which they had a stake. For anthropologists, finally, the fund served as an independent organizational base for archaeological research in the Southwest.

Returning to Barnard's classic analysis of organizations, we can now consider the consequences of these differences. It is perhaps most revealing to examine conflict over the organization's activities and goals. The starkest such dispute came in 1933, with a sharp drop in funding for the Indian Arts Fund and the Laboratory of Anthropology, both dependent on continuing gifts from John D. Rockefeller, Jr. A self-described "progressive" wing, composed of the artists, writers, and reformers, opposed a "conservative" wing, composed in part of the trustees whose primary motivation was collecting and study (Kenneth Chapman and Harry Mera), but largely of the archaeologists. Faced with major budget cuts, the progressives prepared a policy statement advocating a large-scale program for educating potters and other artists and setting up a shop to sell Pueblo art in Santa Fe. The conservatives (who were a majority of the trustees) opposed these proposals and advocated an emphasis on collecting and further experimentation with fieldwork techniques.[11]

These positions were a direct consequence of the role of the IAF in the conflicts in which trustees were primarily engaged. For the progressives, the fund's value was in its visible involvement in sponsoring and marketing Pueblo art. In shops, homes, and museums, traditional pottery testified to the involvement of the IAF's members in the pueblos and the success of their efforts. For the conservatives, the usefulness of the fund was served either by its collecting activities, or, for the archaeologists, had already been fulfilled by serving as the nucleus of the lab. The prospect of increasing spending on the Indian Arts Fund's activities was particularly threatening to the archaeologists, struggling to maintain adequate funding for their scientific activities.

Art and Politics in the Pueblos

As important as what was fought over within the fund was what was not. At the time, there was little conflict over what now appear the most problematic issues: the definition of tradition in Pueblo pottery and the nature of the relation between patrons and artists. Most important, regardless of the positions taken by progressives or conservatives, those in the fund paid little attention to the social relations surrounding pottery production in the pueblos. Indeed, the renewed continuity of the form of pottery with that of earlier periods actually masked the radical changes taking place in the way pottery making was organized, and in its economic and social role in pueblo communities.

In the nineteenth century and earlier, pottery production was largely carried out by individual women, who gathered the clay, formed and decorated the vessels, and fired them. Nearly every woman made pots for home use and for some trading, although some women were more skilled than others. Pottery production was integrated into the other activities associated with a subsistence agriculture economy. This pattern of organization dominated the tourist market as well (Bunzel 1929).

The most visible sign of change from this pattern came with the emergence of "name" potters, who became well known and whose pots commanded a premium price. The first of these was the famous Hopi potter Nampeyo in the 1890s, but the phenomenon did not take hold until the 1920s, when—in large part through IAF sponsorship—Maria Martinez of San Ildefonso Pueblo became a national figure. Martinez was featured in numerous magazine and newspaper articles, and a biography was published in 1948 (Marriott 1948). Her pottery brought in over $2,000 per year in the mid-1920s, an extraordinary cash income for pueblo residents (Guthe 1925).

The fame of Maria Martinez and a few others had consequences beyond their personal wealth. San Ildefonso, where the pottery market became highly advanced in the 1920s and 1930s, provides a useful example. Some potters were able to subdivide the labor and employ workers, from both within and outside their families. Maria Martinez relied on the help of three sisters and employed four women from outside her immediate family to aid in the time-consuming polishing of pots. Several other potters hired one or two women for wages to aid in pottery making (Dauber 1990; Office of Indian Affairs 1935, 68). The key element in making this system viable was the value of well-known potters' signatures, the product of encouragement by Anglos who identified individualized expression with art. Today, this identification is so strong that those who study Maria Martinez and her work deny that a division of labor was ever used, or that if it was, it was not a departure from the practice of earlier periods (e.g., Spivey 1989).

The creation of distinctions among potters, implied by market differentiation and the practice of signing pots, had far-reaching implications for stratification within the pueblos. "Name" potters could command high prices for their pots, while other potters—those who did not achieve this kind of commercial success or recognition from Anglo patrons—hired themselves out to more successful potters or struggled along in the low end of the tourist market, where prices were much lower. At San Ildefonso, pottery production was an important element in a long-running dispute that split the village. A faction dominated by Maria Martinez's extended family, held together by credit and subcontracting relations, opposed the dictates of the traditional religious authority (Dauber 1990; Whitman 1947). In other pueblos, such as Santa Clara, disputes emerged over the unwillingness of some families to fulfill their communal labor obligations, particularly involving maintenance of irrigation ditches (Dozier 1966). These disputes may well have resulted from the role of pottery in providing an alternative to agriculture for gaining access to food.

The members of the IAF were clearly aware of these changes. One of the founding members of the fund, Elizabeth Sergeant, wrote what is in many ways an astonishing condemnation of the role of "fine art" pottery production at San Ildefonso, for a broader government study of land use changes in the upper Rio Grande watershed (Office of Indian Affairs 1935, 60–86). Sergeant based her conclusions on a study of the pueblo that she performed for John Collier, the Commissioner of Indian Affairs. Sergeant argued that commercialization of pottery production had failed to revive the traditional role of pottery in pueblo life, instead producing social disorganization as older bases of authority were supplanted by access to cash and as stratification emerged among the potters and their families.

Sergeant's conclusions were clearly influenced by a romantic image of the centrality of pottery to Pueblo cultural life. Yet they also reveal the bounds of the Indian Arts Fund's understanding of what constituted "traditional" Pueblo pottery. Its definition was restricted to the shape and decoration of vessels, and did not extend to the social relations surrounding their production, even when these social relations were radically transformed by the market it helped foster. Ironically, it was in the tourist market, where pottery forms bore the least resemblance to older pots, that the organization of production most closely resembled that of the past.

My purpose in pointing out this lacuna is not to criticize the fund; representations of "tradition" always serve other purposes, and there is little profit in trying to discover an essential past that can serve as a touchstone for the present. Rather, I am concerned to trace the social basis of this representation. The IAF's "neutral" focus on form flowed directly from the differing goals of its members. The broader economic context of pottery making was invisible to the IAF's audience, whose everyday acquaintance with pottery in Santa Fe and other towns far outmatched their contact with potters themselves. Just as fundamentally, the definition of pottery making as "art," an essential part of the redefinition of pottery and its marketing, built in a strong propensity not to investigate too closely its economic and social preconditions, a reluctance integral to modernist conceptions of art and artists.

The greatest challenge to theoretical understanding of patronage is its diversity. Just as the solidity of objects conceals an extraordinary range of possible uses and meanings, the seemingly simple act of supporting and consuming art masks a wide range of possible motives. The value of the Indian Arts Fund to the larger goal of analyzing patronage is the complexity of projects it encompassed and their consequences for transforming the organization of production. Clearly, it was not simply status that motivated the IAF's trustees, nor were the range of its effects implied in its own understanding of its efforts. That Pueblo pottery, formerly the province of ethnologists and tourists, was reclassified as art testifies both to the transformative power of patronage and to the breadth of its reach.

Notes

1. Frank Applegate to Mary Mowbray-Clarke, May 2, 1922. *Archives of American Art*, John and Mary Mowbray-Clarke Papers.

2. Mabel Dodge Luhan to Alfred Stieglitz, June 1926. Yale University, Beinecke Library, Alfred Stieglitz Collection.

3. An article entitled "Terriffic [sic] Barrage Aimed at Pueblo Indian Bill All Over the United States," in the Santa Fe New Mexican of December 6, 1922, contains a useful description of the reaction to the bill: "Seldom has a proposed piece of national legislation or a public man had to bear the brunt of such a universal press fusillade as that now being directed throughout the country against the so-called Bursum Indian Bill and against Secretary of the Interior Fall [another Republican from New Mexico] as its chief sponsor. Newspapers and magazines from San Francisco to New York, organizations ranging from the National Federation of Women's Clubs to the Girls Scouts, and art, archaeological and ethnological associations have united in this barrage, and it is doubtful if any measure so 'purely local,' as Senator Bursum says, in its effect has ever before aroused in this country such an upheaval of popular indignation." The article goes on to cite negative commentary from a wide range of sources.

4. See, for example, Francis Wilson to George Vaux, Nov. 6, 1922: "There is intense bitterness here amongst those who are friendly to the Indians because the Republican party has made the Bill a party measure and is using it in the present campaign as a ground for getting votes amongst the settlers on Indian lands." New Mexico State Records Center and Archives, Santa Fe, Francis C. Wilson Papers.

5. Elizabeth Sergeant to F. W. Hodge, Feb. 9, 1923. Southwest Museum, Los Angeles, Frederick W. Hodge Collection.

6. Paul A. F. Walter to Edgar Hewett, May 24, 1927. Museum of New Mexico, Edgar Hewett Collection.

7. See a series of letters between Mary Austin and John Collier, Jan. 31, 1930–May 26, 1930. John Collier Papers (Microfilm Edition). On April 20, 1930, for example, Austin wrote that "the Indian Arts Foundation [sic] means business, the business of rescuing Indian artists from government futility, of fostering Indian talent, of educating the American public to appreciate it, and of finding a market for high quality Indian products. We have been successful beyond our greatest expectations. We would be very glad to count you in on this work. I think the wisest thing you could do would be to become a member of the Foundation, and avail yourself of its highly specialized aid." Austin made similar points in an exchange of letters with Secretary of the Interior Wilbur in 1930 and 1931 (Mary Austin Collection, Huntington Library).

8. A. V. Kidder to J. F. Zimmerman, Feb. 14, 1928. Hewett Collection.

9. A. L. Kroeber to A. V. Kidder, no date [summer 1929]. Indian Arts Research Center, School of American Research, Santa Fe (SAR). See also Fay-Cooper Cole of the University of Chicago to A. V. Kidder, Dec. 9, 1935: "I am not particularly interested in providing another museum for Santa Fe or the Southwest, neither am I concerned to any extent with the art development described to me by Strong. However valuable both may be, they do not in any way fulfill the ideals we had in mind when the Laboratory was established." SAR.

10. A. V. Kidder to A. L. Kroeber, June 14, 1934. SAR.

11. The progressives' policy statement is in SAR. The conservatives' "Declaration of Principles" is in the Hodge Collection.

References

Amon Carter Museum of Western Art. 1966. *Quiet Triumph: Forty Years with the Indian Arts Fund, Santa Fe*. Fort Worth: Amon Carter Museum.

Barnard, Chester. 1938. *The Functions of the Executive*. Cambridge, Mass.: Harvard University Press.

Batkin, Jonathan. 1987. *Pottery of the Pueblos of New Mexico*. Colorado Springs: Taylor Museum.

Bunzel, Ruth L. 1929. "The Pueblo Potter: A Study of Creative Imagination in Primitive Art." *Columbia University Contributions to Anthropology* 8. New York.

Cahill, E. H. 1922. "America Has Its 'Primitives.'" *International Studio* 68 (Mar.): 80–83.

Chauvenet, Beatrice. 1983. *Hewett and Friends: A Biography of Santa Fe's Vibrant Era*. Santa Fe: Museum of New Mexico Press.

Coke, Van Deren. 1963. *Taos and Santa Fe: The Artist's Environment, 1882–1942*. Albuquerque: University of New Mexico Press.

Csikszentmihalyi, Mihaly, and Eugene Rochberg-Halton. 1981. *The Meaning of Things: Domestic Symbols and the Self*. Cambridge: Cambridge University Press.

Dauber, Kenneth. 1990. "Pottery, Land and Politics in a New Mexico Pueblo." Unpublished paper.

Dietrich, Margretta. n.d. "The History of Indian Markets." Santa Fe: New Mexico State Records Center and Archives, SWAIA Collection.

DiMaggio, Paul. 1982. "Cultural Entrepreneurship in Nineteenth-Century Boston." *Media, Culture and Society* 4:33–50, 303–22.

Dozier, Edward P. 1966. "Factionalism at Santa Clara Pueblo." *Ethnology* 5(2): 172–85.

Gibson, Arrell Morgan. 1983. *The Santa Fe and Taos Colonies: Age of the Muses, 1900–1942*. Norman, Okla.: University of Oklahoma Press.

Guthe, Carl E. 1925. "Pueblo Pottery Making: A Study at the Village of San Ildefonso." *Papers of the Phillips Academy Southwestern Expedition* 2. New Haven: Yale University Press for Phillips Academy.

Hall, G. Emlen. 1987. "The Pueblo Grant Labyrinth." In *Land, Water, and Culture: New Perspectives on Hispanic Land Grants*, edited by C. L. Briggs and J. R. Van Ness, 67–138. Albuquerque: University of New Mexico Press.

Hartley, Marsden. 1920. "Red Man Ceremonials: An American Plea for an American Esthetics." *Art and Archaeology* 9(1): 7–14.

Holmes, Jack E. 1967. *Politics in New Mexico*. Albuquerque: University of New Mexico Press.

Horgan, Paul. 1956. *The Centuries of Santa Fe*. New York: Dutton.

Marriott, Alice. 1948. *Maria: The Potter of San Ildefonso*. Norman, Okla.: University of Oklahoma Press.

Mayhew, Robert William. 1984. "The New Mexico Association on Indian Affairs, 1922–1958." M.A. thesis, University of New Mexico.

Meinig, D. W. 1971. *Southwest: Three Peoples in Geographical Change*. New York: Oxford University Press.

Office of Indian Affairs. 1935. *Tewa Basin Study*. U.S. Department of the Interior, Office of Indian Affairs, Indian Land Research Unit.

Parezo, Nancy J. 1987. "The Formation of Ethnographic Collections: The Smithsonian Institution in the American Southwest." *Advances in Archaeological Theory and Method* 10:1–47.

Philp, Kenneth. 1970. "Albert B. Fall and the Protest from the Pueblos, 1921–1923." *Arizona and the West* 12:237–54.

Rosenblum, Barbara. 1985. "The Artist as Economic Actor in the Art Market." In *Art, Ideology, and Politics,* edited by Judith H. Balfe and Margaret J. Wyszomirski, 63–79. New York: Praeger.

Rushing, William Jackson, III. 1984. "The Influence of American Indian Art on Jackson Pollock and the Early New York School." M.A. thesis, University of Texas at Austin.

Russell, John C. 1938. "State Regionalism in New Mexico." Ph.D. diss., Stanford University.

Schimmel, Julie. 1986. "From Salon to Pueblo: The First Generation." In *Art in New Mexico, 1900–1945: Paths to Taos and Santa Fe,* edited by C. Eldredge, J. Schimmel, and W. Truettner, 43–57. New York: Abbeville.

Schrader, Robert Fay. 1983. *The Indian Arts and Crafts Board: An Aspect of New Deal Indian Policy.* Albuquerque: University of New Mexico Press.

Smith, Barbara Herrnstein. 1988. *Contingencies of Value: Alternative Perspectives for Critical Theory.* Cambridge, Mass.: Harvard University Press.

Spivey, Richard. 1989. *Maria.* Flagstaff: Northland.

State of New Mexico Arts Division. 1986. *The Economic Impact of the Arts in New Mexico.* Santa Fe.

Stocking, George W. 1976. "Ideas and Institutions in American Anthropology: Thoughts toward a History of the Interwar Years." In *Selected Papers from the American Anthropologist, 1921–1945,* edited by G. W. Stocking, 1–50. Washington, D.C.: American Anthropological Association.

————. 1982. "The Santa Fe Style in American Anthropology: Regional Interest, Academic Initiative, and Philanthropic Policy in the First Two Decades of the Laboratory of Anthropology, Inc." *Journal of the History of the Behavioral Sciences* 18:3–19.

Toulouse, Betty. 1977. *Pueblo Pottery of the New Mexico Indians: Ever Constant, Ever Changing.* Santa Fe: Museum of New Mexico Press.

Truettner, William H. 1986. "The Art of Pueblo Life." In *Art in New Mexico, 1900 1945: Paths to Taos and Santa Fe,* edited by C. Eldredge, J. Schimmel, and W. Truettner, 59–99. New York: Abbeville.

Udall, Sharyn Rohlfsen. 1984. *Modernist Painting in New Mexico, 1913–1935.* Albuquerque: University of New Mexico Press.

Whitman, William. 1947. "The Pueblo Indians of San Ildefonso: A Changing Culture." *Columbia University Contributions to Anthropology* 34.

Wolf, Arthur H. 1978. "The Indian Arts Fund Collection at the School of American Research." *American Indian Art Magazine* 4(1): 32–37.

Zilczer, Judith K. 1975. "The Aesthetic Struggle in America, 1913–1918: Abstract Art and Theory in the Stieglitz Circle." Ph.D. diss., University of Delaware.

❖ 5 ❖

Playing Workers: Proletarian Drama in the Curriculum of American Labor Colleges, 1921–37

CLYDE W. BARROW

> Through his job the worker may earn a living, but he must
> seek life elsewhere.
> —Jean Carter, Bryn Mawr Summer School
> for Women Workers, 1935

American trade unions were active participants in a world workers' educational movement that swept across the Western industrial nations during the early decades of the twentieth century. One of the central objectives of this movement was to establish and maintain alternative models of adult education that were known variously as labor colleges, workers' universities, and peoples' institutes (Gleason 1921; Hansome 1931). This chapter examines the use of formal dramatic studies and theatrical performances by labor colleges to illustrate the way in which supporters of "proletarian drama" viewed theater as part of a broadly conceived political strategy. Cultural policies were designed explicitly to advance the interests of labor, not simply as an economic movement, but as an important cultural and intellectual force pushing toward an ever-deeper democratization of society. In pursuing this goal, the chapter explores the theoretical role played by the fine arts in working-class formation, particularly as a medium for institutionalizing the visual symbols, linguistic meanings, and collective patterns of sentiment and feeling that E. P. Thompson calls class culture (1963).

94

Labor Colleges and the American Labor Movement

A "labor college" was a group of workers and educators brought together for the purpose of gathering and distributing educational literature and for conducting educational campaigns among the workers of a local industrial area (Craig 1918). Its basic organizational units were small study classes in which groups of workers met regularly (usually once or twice a week) along with an instructor or discussion leader to investigate a specific subject of interest to its members (Miller 1929). Groups of study classes met in union halls, public school buildings, churches, libraries, and community centers. Where a coherent network of these classes was developed, administered, and financed by an individual union, a local party organization, or a city labor federation, the study classes were called a labor college.[1]

There were at least sixty identifiable labor colleges in the United States when the movement reached its zenith in the mid-1920s. Indeed, one estimate finds that over the entire course of the 1920s, more than three hundred labor colleges were established (Dwyer 1977). As individual units, these colleges sponsored anywhere from one to seventy-five study classes per academic term. Enrollments at the various colleges ranged from a handful in some rural areas to several thousand in major urban centers such as New York City. A conservative estimate, made in 1923, found that nationwide annual labor college enrollment was about thirty thousand students (Maurer 1924, 42).[2]

Most labor colleges were established in urban industrial centers either by local coalitions of university professors, teachers, trade unionists, and other social activists or separately by local labor federations and by socialist and communist parties. The labor colleges were usually guided by two educational missions. One goal was to provide rank and file workers with information and organizational skills that would assist them in their mobilization as active citizens in the unions, the workplace, and the wider political community. A second goal was to offer more advanced and specialized training in the professions and social sciences to adult workers who were expected to remain in the labor movement as public servants of the working class. Thus, labor colleges trained independent journalists, trade union and political party officials, organizers, statisticians, lobbyists, lecturers, and negotiators. In this respect, labor colleges were envisioned as institutional centers for "elaborating" an organic working-class intelligentsia (Barrow 1989; 1990). The colleges constituted, in Gramsci's imagery (1971), an ideological counter-apparatus from which to wage a "war of position" against bourgeois cultural and intellectual hegemony.[3] Indeed, the official policy statement of the Workers' Education Bureau, a national association of U.S. labor colleges, declared that the primary function of the labor college curriculum was to create "an intelligent army of workers conscious of their aims and of the best methods of realizing them" (*American Labor Yearbook* 1922, 217).

Curriculum and Culture in U.S. Labor Colleges

The core curriculum of a comprehensive labor college usually consisted of six departments: English, economics, trade unionism, political science, sociology, and history. The available evidence indicates that at least four-fifths of the courses offered by labor colleges fell within one of these departments (Miller 1929). The full core-curriculum was implemented so far as possible whenever financial resources and faculty were sufficient. The underlying goal of the curriculum was to provide all workers with a liberal education that was practical in the broadest sense of the word; namely, it was designed to promote participatory union membership, individual initiative, rank and file leadership, a sense of class identity and union solidarity, and active citizenship in politics.

However, outside the consensus that supported this core curriculum, there was also a recurring and continuing dispute within the workers' education movement as to whether or not labor colleges should offer cultural subjects such as literature, music, art, and drama (Hanchett 1922). The dispute was fueled in part by an international "proletcult" movement that swept through radical intellectual and political circles during the 1920s and 1930s (Paul and Paul 1921). Proletcultists, in particular, advanced the idea that labor organizations should utilize their workers' education programs to implement cultural policies that would promote the creation of a distinctively "proletarian culture" in opposition to the dominant "bourgeois" and "aristocratic" cultures of capitalist society.

The ensuing debate over cultural policy during the 1920s and 1930s split the workers' education movement into two distinct camps. These camps roughly paralleled the emerging cleavage between business and social unionists, a division that in the 1930s led social unionists to splinter off and form the Congress of Industrial Organizations. In contrast to these social unionists, the American Federation of Labor's dominant craft aristocracy was generally committed to a philosophy of business unionism. From this perspective, the business of trade unions was to bargain in the marketplace for better wages, hours, and working conditions. Auxiliary institutions such as labor colleges were regarded as useful only insofar as they strengthened workers' collective ability to bargain and negotiate for improved economic conditions. However, "politics" and "culture" were regarded as separate spheres of social life where workers respectively exercised their individual rights as equal citizens and developed their individual self-identity through other institutions such as political parties, family, and church. The business unionists who dominated national policy in the American Federation of Labor considered cultural policy outside the AFL's narrowly defined economic program (Carroll 1923; Reed 1930).

Thus support for a cultural curriculum in the labor colleges came primarily from the coalition of self-styled labor progressives who formed the nucleus of the future CIO; namely, industrial unionists, selected city labor federations, liberal-left intellectuals, and left-wing party activists (Morris 1958). During the 1920s, these groups began to coalesce as a movement for social unionism and began challenging the theoretical foundation of business unionism by emphasizing that labor power was not really separable from the laborer. Consequently, the responsibilities and objectives of labor organizations were not exhausted at a fixed point defined by the boundaries of the labor market. Instead, the laborer was to be regarded by labor organizations as a whole person with multiple needs and concerns that extend beyond wages, hours, and working conditions. Thus, in order to better serve their members, labor organizations should actively strive to transform American politics and culture in the image of the working class.

However, social unionists in the workers' education movement did not necessarily agree that "culture" fell within the proper scope of the labor college curriculum, nor did they necessarily agree with each other as to what was meant by a "working-class culture." Simultaneous with the debate over whether labor *should* have a cultural policy, a parallel debate took place among social unionists about *what kind* of cultural policy should be pursued by labor organizations and about whether that policy should be implemented through the labor colleges. This second axis of conflict can be conceptualized as a division rooted in two competing theories of culture: is culture to be understood by the form or by the content of artistic practices?

The formal theory of culture was largely grounded in the assumption that cultural practices and the artworks produced by these practices consist of formal qualities that are recognized as stylistically and qualitatively distinct. These formal qualities, whether those of an Elizabethan drama, a Wagnerian tragedy, or a contemporary sitcom, can be identified, fixed, and thus appreciated by everyone, regardless of time or social distance. As such, art appreciation and cultural literacy consist of understanding the formal qualities that define artistic styles. A knowledge of the historical social origins of an objet d'art may deepen our understanding of particular styles, but this knowledge does not pose an obstacle to our appreciation of specific artistic styles or inhibit our ability to recognize as "great works" those productions that supply the archetypes of a particular style.

From this standpoint, there are no inherently proletarian, bourgeois, or aristocratic cultures. In the context of this debate, for example, Alexander Fichlander, a member of the International Ladies' Garment Workers' Union (ILGWU) Educational Department, argued: "Art knows not of class distinctions. It appeals equally to rich and poor." According to Fichlander, all forms of art—whether painting, sculpture, literature, or drama—"are the same whether taught in a capitalist or a workers' school." In other words, to the degree that the "appreciation of beauty knows no class distinction . . . (t)here is no capitalistic sunset to be tabooed by the proletariat" (1921, 50).

In this regard, the formalists maintained that it was the use and control of particular art forms by dominant classes (that is, as instruments of cultural domination) that determined their social meaning at any particular time. It is not the style or even the content that makes cultural artifacts into class cultures. Instead, the class character of art (to the extent that such a concept is meaningful) lies in its social monopolization by a particular class. Accordingly, the cultural dominance of a ruling elite was constituted solely in its political and economic domination (that is, patronage) of a society's cultural institutions. On this point, Horace Kallen, a psychology instructor at the New School for Social Research, agreed that in present-day capitalist societies "people controlling wealth hold and continue to hold a monopoly of the arts and sciences. . . . They have converted culture and knowledge into a private property. They have harnessed them to the chariot of their class ideals" (1925, 51).

Yet, this also meant that for formalists the key to democratizing art and drama lay in making existing cultural productions available to the working class and to the general public. In other words, great art was inherently great and thus socialization to its appreciation was primarily an issue of price and audience; that is, of democratizing the accessibility of art currently controlled by exclusive museums and theaters. This view implied that the chief cultural objective of the labor movement should be to democratize great art by supporting more extensive government funding for existing cultural institutions in order to make them more accessible to ordinary citizens and to enable those institutions to provide more extensive arts appreciation education.

From the formalist standpoint, once the problem of accessibility was solved, the door was open for ordinary people to lay hold of artistic culture and make it an instrument of their own enjoyment and personal development, rather than the exclusive province of the wealthy. Moreover, it was expected that a widening of the audience for cultural productions would also lead to a shift in the social meaning of art, since cultural productions would then "be interpreted for workers by workers themselves" (Fichlander 1921, 50). Hence, there was no plausible reason in the formalists' view why workers could not enjoy Shakespeare even if they enjoyed it for reasons different from those of a bourgeois audience.

Consequently, while formalists accepted the idea "that workers should have all the beauty that the world has to offer," they doubted the need for separate cultural institutions that were exclusively proletarian. For instance, Fichlander argued that already "in large cities, workers can go to the opera at a comparatively low cost. . . . Similarly, they can hear the best symphonic music played by magnificent orchestras at extremely low prices. . . . Similarly with painting, sculpture, etc." As a result, cultural formalists were convinced that "workers can satisfy their love for beauty in existing institutions" (1921, 49). The democratization of art was simply a matter of promoting and financing educational policies by government that made art and art appreciation available to a mass audience.

On the other hand, the proletcultists argued that artistic cultures were infused with the language, images, characterizations, and moral themes of a specific class at its point of production. Thus the social meaning of dramatic art, for example, was built into the plot, characters, and theme that gave it social force for an audience. Moreover, as Lukács (1971) was arguing in Europe at the same time, this meant that the content of art imposed an inner logic which constrained the development of style within limits that could not be surpassed without a shift in that content. Consequently, for proletcultists, artistic styles were dependent on the content of artistic works and this implied that artistic productions of any type were inextricably class-based in their imagery. In this respect, it was argued, simply democratizing access to bourgeois art would merely strengthen the cultural dominance of capital over labor by constraining working-class tastes within the boundaries of bourgeois convention.

Jean Carter, a drama instructor at the Bryn Mawr Summer School for Women Workers, correctly noted that such a viewpoint implied that the aims of a labor movement cultural policy should be to institutionalize through art "a mode of thinking, feeling, and acting in terms of the problems of labor" (1935, 179). As a result, a specifically proletarian drama would entail far more than simply making good plays available to workers at an affordable price. In Carter's view, labor drama had to be constructed at the point of cultural production so as to give the worker "the opportunity to feel himself a part of the enterprise as a subscriber, as an actor, or as an important part of the audience. His participation goes even farther, for he is able to see plays that deal with the life to which he is accustomed and that treat of problems of his everyday existence" (1935, 179).

Thus, Carter suggested that the sense of ownership must be present not only in the consumption of art, that is, in its appropriation as a commodity in the marketplace. More important, a genuinely proletarian culture must generate a sense of democratic participation and workers' self-ownership in its production and management as well as in its consumption. Otherwise, culture not only reproduces dominant class imagery in its content, but also reproduces and extends the commodity form into the cultural realm through the process of consumption. So long as ownership takes place only through the form of consumption (that is, at the level of distribution), art becomes a way to adjust the cultural needs and demands of labor to the structural economic requirements of capitalist production. Socialization to consumption alone thus merely strengthens the structural constraints of capitalist society within and through the field of art.

The Promise of Proletarian Drama

It should be recognized that both types of cultural policy, as implied respectively by the formal and proletculture theories, were pursued simultaneously in the American labor movement. However, the proletcultists generally prevailed in the labor colleges. A curriculum survey conducted by the Workers' Education Bureau (WEB) in 1927–28 found that courses in "The Arts" (excluding literature) probably never accounted for more than 3 percent of the total number of classes and study courses offered by workers' education programs in the United States. This was roughly half the percentage reported by the Workers' Educational Association in Great Britain (Hansome 1931).

However, reports by labor educators suggest that student interest in artistic courses was increasing throughout the 1920s and that the WEB's measurement of the mere numbers of courses being offered fails to capture the enrollment levels within those courses. For example, Algernon Lee, director of the Socialist Party's Rand School of Social Science, noted that by 1921 literature and drama were for the first time drawing larger enrollments than courses on economics, socialism, and trade unionism (1922). Likewise, Alexander Fichlander complained that at the ILGWU's Workers' University, cultural subjects "attract more students than economics, history of the labor movement and labor problems" (1922, 3). At the New School for Social Research, Kallen also found that "the disciplines to which the worker, in his classes, seems most willingly to subject himself are those in which . . . he finds enhancement and expansion of his personality-feeling, intensification of his sense of personal worth, free play for his sentiment of himself as an individual" (1925, 68). Kallen pointed especially to the popularity of literature, dramatics, and philosophy.

Yet another indication of this trend, especially of the labor drama's growing importance in the workers' education movement, was the steady increase of working-class dramatic troupes and theaters throughout the country. As early as 1920, the United Labor Education Committee (ULEC) was established in New York City to coordinate the educational activities of the Rand School, the ILGWU Workers' University, the Active Workers' School of the Amalgamated Clothing Workers, and several other union-sponsored educational enterprises. A special section on drama was established with the mandate "to provide a theater for the people, giving productions of modern art at reasonable rates" (Sweeney 1920). ULEC members attempted to institutionalize the labor drama by establishing "The Workmen's Theatre." Its players were billed as "heralds for the pageant of the New" who would "play a triumphant march over the body of the old order as it is being carried to the funeral pyre" (Koven 1919, 3). A year later, however, the Workmen's Theatre was defunct. As one participant observed, "A great deal of effort was devoted to this attempt which proved to be somewhat premature" (Budish 1921, 24).

Nevertheless, experiments in labor drama began to proliferate from coast to coast. In 1921, students from the Amalgamated Clothing Workers' Rochester Labor College began performing labor plays as part of that union's annual May Day celebrations (Blanshard 1921). In the same year, the Seattle Labor College organized a student dramatic section within the college and an amateur dramatic society to arrange performances in the local labor community (Gleason 1921). Similarly, in 1922, the Portland Labor College established a troupe known as the Labor College Players (Lembcke 1984). By the middle of the decade, dramatics was listed as one of Portland's three major course offerings alongside labor history and labor economics. The Rand School institutionalized its burgeoning enrollments in labor drama by forming the Young Circle Dramatic Studio, a theater troupe described by one its actors as "a workers' group combatting capitalism thru [sic] drama" (Beder 1931). Early experiments in the development of labor drama were followed by similar efforts elsewhere. Brookwood Labor College, located in Katonah, New York, began offering dramatic instruction in 1923 under the direction of Hazel MacKaye. Soon thereafter student dramatists were organized into the Brookwood Labor

Players. When MacKaye left Brookwood in 1926 to develop a similar program for the United Mine Workers, she was replaced by Jasper Deeter,
an anarchist actor/director previously associated with Eugene O'Neill's
Provincetown Players.

MacKaye and Deeter were also important in two other vignettes in
the promotion of labor drama. When MacKaye left Brookwood, it was at
the invitation of Tom Tippett, educational director for Subdistrict 5, District 12, of the Illinois United Mine Workers, and a former Brookwood
student. Soon after leaving Brookwood himself, Tippett had organized a
series of small study classes in the rural mining communities of southern
Illinois. He then recruited MacKaye to teach a small class on labor drama
and assist the students in producing several plays throughout the district.
The crude plays met with such success among mineworkers that the class
in labor drama became a traveling players' troupe with a regular circuit
among the mining communities (Tippett 1926).

As MacKaye's successor at Brookwood, Jasper Deeter extended the
reach of the Brookwood Labor Players by directing the first performances
of a new Workers' Theater that had been formally established in December 1925. The Workers' Theater was founded by three hundred delegates
from Jewish unions and workers' study circles in New York City at the call
of *Freiheit* (the Jewish Communist daily). The Workers' Theatre adopted as
its model the Russian agit-prop and German proletcult theaters by maintaining a policy of performing only "plays dealing with problems of the
workers' daily life" (Ball 1931; Mareg 1931; Raugh and Hartman, 1931).[4]

By the mid-1920s, most major urban centers were reporting some level
of activity in the field of labor drama. The Boston Trade Union College
offered a regular drama class that produced a number of plays at the
closing exercises of the college each year (Saposs 1926). The Denver Labor
College developed a Labor College Theater that performed one-act plays
throughout the year. Once or twice a year, the Denver drama classes
would also present what were billed as "major industrial plays" (Holwell
1927). In Duluth, the IWW Work Peoples' College was offering a class
in playwriting.[5] Other workers' education programs were offering drama
courses to black workers in Atlanta, Georgia; to textile workers in Mobile,
Alabama; to silkweavers in Pawtucket, Rhode Island; to clothing workers
in Louisville, Kentucky; and to members of the Central Labor Union in
Nashville, Tennessee.

For proletcultists, the burgeoning number of formal courses in labor
drama were seen as the nuclei for training working-class playwrights,
actors, directors, drama critics, and drama teachers who would gradually
fan out from these centers as an organic cultural intelligentsia. The aim was

to provide a forum in which student participants in the workers' education movement could create experimental centers of proletarian drama and workers' theater while eventually returning to their own unions and communities to organize additional theater groups. The hope, as expressed by Hazel MacKaye, was "that before so many years had passed every city and town would have its Workers' Theatre" (1926a, 37).[6]

The Ideal of Proletarian Drama

The immediate problem of dramatists involved in the proletcult movement was to organize coursework in a way that would allow worker-students to create their own drama, that is, a drama that could be described as genuinely proletarian in its production. At Bryn Mawr, Jean Carter observed that successful workshops in proletarian drama were always "based upon the hypothesis that anyone who has really lived has the elements of drama in his experience" (1935, 180). The test of that hypothesis was the ability to spontaneously generate proletarian theater from the daily lives and personal experiences of small groups of workers.

The process at Bryn Mawr usually began in one of two ways: either by attending some local performances of plays, or if those were unavailable, by reading plays aloud in the classroom. Once it was clear to an instructor that most workshop participants understood the main characters and basic storyline of a play, students were encouraged to move from descriptive comprehension to critical analysis. Analysis and criticism began with simple questions: Did students like the play? What did they not like about it? What characters did they like in it? Did they understand why a character acted in a particular way?

Two types of critical understanding were supposed to emerge from this analytic process. One type of comprehension identified by Carter may be called formal understanding. As students began to see, read, and analyze a number of different plays, they achieved a capacity to compare plays to one another. Moreover, such comparisons, in an ideal situation, would facilitate the realization among worker-students that certain formal components such as plot, character, and theme were common to all dramas. However, as Hazel MacKaye of the Brookwood program noted, a formal conception of the theater was not the primary objective of labor drama workshops. Rather, that was to provide a forum for "creating workers' plays by the workers themselves" (1926a, 38).

This goal hinged on what may be called the workers' phenomenological understanding of drama. According to Carter, phenomenological understanding would generally emerge when students began spontaneously comparing the formal elements of the play to their own lives. In other words, once students started to realize that their own lives were enmeshed with other "characters" and that life experiences could be identified as "plots," then it became evident that dramas were not necessarily about the rich and powerful, but that all lives were in some respects dramatic. Thus, a major objective of the labor drama workshop was to forge a linkage between the formal and the phenomenological, between the objective and subjective dimensions of life that are captured in the drama.

The technique for establishing this linkage started at the most concrete level of phenomenological understanding and gradually built toward a formal understanding of the structures within which workers' own lives (that is, dramas) took place. Carter suggests that phenomenological linkages were usually first established in the awareness of: "Oh, something like that happened to me" or "once I saw . . . ." These phenomenological linkages were then used as the experiential foundation for impromptu skits. At Bryn Mawr, students who successfully made connections between the dramatic form and their own lives were always asked to act out the experience. A student would select his or her actors from among the workshop participants, characters would be assigned, and the actors would quickly plan the skit. A few props would be placed in position to make the necessary backdrop, for example, an office, a boarding room, or a kitchen

Hollace Ransdell, a worker educator in the Deep South, claimed that, "Some of the most effective plays given by the labor drama groups are worked up quickly, almost—sometimes entirely—impromptu, from material which the members have seen or experienced at first hand" (1935, 122). Ransdell provides the example of a young striker at an Alabama cotton mill who in formulating a character archetype for the "boss man" stood up before the class with a woodcarved pistol and then acted out his own boss's response to picketers the previous day. Another member of the class, a stenographer, jotted down his self-dialogue and, hence, a strike skit had been produced. In this way, MacKaye notes, "out of their own lives the drama becomes an integral part of the labor movement" (1926a, 38).

According to Carter, as a workshop group became more and more experienced, the skits tended to move through three stages. The first stage focused on the external dimensions of the event. In this first stage, even though workers participated as actors, the skit's emphasis was on events that seemed to be taking place around or outside the workers, and in many respects independent of the workers' control. For example, simple events such as getting fired, asking for one's first job and being told no, a woman having to cook dinner for a family after working a ten-hour shift at a garment factory all suggest a dramatic world in which events happen to workers. Moreover, the skits tended to be slice of life, discrete, unconnected "happenings." In essence, this was the life-world of reified objects and images so elegantly analyzed by Lukács (1971).

At a certain point, it is reported, the focus of the impromptu skits tended to shift abruptly toward an internal dimension. The internal dimension surfaced when actors and skit originators became increasingly interested not so much in the event itself, but in using the event as a vehicle for exploring their own feelings about the event. To return to a previous example, rather than ending with being fired, a skit would go on to express the rage of being dismissed despite being a good worker, the subsequent anxiety of unemployment, the humiliation of reporting a job loss to one's family.

Finally, a structural dimension would surface in skits. Structures were inferred in the final stage of skit making by linking events and feelings. Objects (events) and subjects (characters) became vehicles for expressing a concept or theme, for example, sweatshop conditions, exploitation of the worker, inequalities in the household division of labor, or racism. At this point, the linkage between daily life and social structure was taking form. A class-conscious proletarian drama had been constructed. Out of several spontaneous skits, one or a few would emerge that seemed to the workshop group worth polishing into a more finished product and performance.

For example, at Bryn Mawr, Carter found that "as a group discovers its ability to recognize and portray dramatic incidents, it will go on to a linking of several incidents into a whole, or possibly to an elaboration of some incident that has captured the minds and interest of the entire group" (1935, 181). Thus, several skits would often develop into the scenes of a full-blown one-act play. At its best, a play would eventually be written down, rehearsed, and presented to an audience.

Ideally, however, the process of production did not end with a play's performance. At the Workers' Laboratory Theatre, for example, plays were followed by a discussion among authors, actors, directors, and audience members. Adjustments to plot, dialogue, and characterization would be made as a result of the discussions. The theoretical objective was to broaden the collective experience incorporated into a play so as to create an "authorless" play, or rather, a play that was collectively authored by the working class instead of by any particular individual (Reines 1931). Indeed, most of the extant plays to come out of the Workers' Laboratory Theatre have no listed author. This proletarian drama's "collective method" was reinforced through job rotation (flexible specialization) within the theater troupe and collective self-management among the theater staff.[7]

The staging of proletarian dramas was also conducted within the purview of resources available to ordinary workers. Ransdell observes that labor dramas frequently had "nothing but a cleared space in an often crowded room, or a small platform, or a grassy place under the trees, or the strip of flooring in front of the nailed-down desks in a school room, for a stage" (1935, 122). Likewise, stage setting and costuming, if there was any at all, was usually allusive instead of literal: a swastika cut out of paper would make a Hitler; a tinfoil star, a policeman; a cardboard stovepipe hat covered with black crepe paper would identify a banker or a diplomat. A table and chair sufficed for business office or the anteroom in a government relief office.

The Aims of Proletarian Drama

Adherents and practitioners of the proletarian drama articulated many different motives and objectives that can be grouped as political, existential, and social. The overtly political objectives of proletarian drama were tied to the belief that workers' theaters provided a useful cultural medium for the development and diffusion of working-class consciousness. In this respect, the proletcultists' major political aim was to create a dramatic culture that was both educational and inspirational to workers.

In terms of its political content, the goal of proletarian drama was "to make clear to a working-class audience the functioning of social forces behind the problems and struggles of workers" (Ransdell 1935, 120). Yet, for the committed proletcultist, education and class consciousness alone were not satisfactory goals. The labor drama should also motivate the working class to action. Toward this goal, Arthur Calhoun, a sociology instructor at Brookwood Labor College, suggested that proletarian drama could provide collective inspiration in two ways. First, Calhoun observed, "drama of the right sort" was supposed to encourage political activism by pointing toward exemplary actions that validated individual impulses and feelings of working-class heroism. On this point, Calhoun argued that "dramatics provide a review of experience, individual and collective, and thereby constitutes a prime educational agency, selecting outstanding types of action and feeling and revivifying and reinforcing them [as exemplary] in such a way as to make them available and functional in the individual and group life to a larger degree than would have been possible otherwise" (1926, 36).

Second, Calhoun claimed that in its anthropological symbolism proletarian drama was a "rehearsal of revolution." At this level

> drama provides a rehearsal of projected exploits. The warrior band of the savage horde gathered at night around the campfire on the edge of the enemy's country and enacted in dance and song the struggle and the triumph that was to be theirs on the morrow. This rehearsal not merely put them in tune with the next day's requirements but amounted to team practice for the impending battle. So today, while we are still this side of the revolution and the commonwealth, we may profit by symbolic rehearsal of the great days to come. (1926, 36)

A second and related set of objectives were aimed at addressing the existential needs of workers. Fannia Cohn of the ILGWU Educational Department put this aim forward succinctly: "Workers are human beings and have emotional, artistic and social needs as well" (1922, 58). Consequently, in Cohn's view, a comprehensive workers' education program should promote the development of a class culture that would also ad dress these existential needs. Yet Cohn was also convinced that once the workers' longing for beauty was awakened, they would necessarily "despise dirty tenements, oppose unsanitary conditions in their shops and bring beauty into their daily lives" (1922, 46).

Finally, proletarian theatrical performances addressed the need to be sociable in a way that would promote solidarity. In fact, Cohn thought that "the best way to develop group solidarity is to give people an opportunity to satisfy their natural desire for social intercourse." Thus, any kind of social gathering, including the theater, was seen as a way to develop "a feeling of comradeship" among workers (1922, 47). Cohn speculated that "workers who sing, play and dance together will fight together for common cause" (1929, 1451).

The Reality of Proletarian Drama

Despite its promise and its ideals, the proletarian theater was a short-lived and only minimally successful movement. Neither the personal commitment of proletcult dramatists nor the strong support of many workers' education programs was sufficient to institutionalize the workers' theater. Despite his own hopes for the proletcult movement, Arthur Calhoun was distressed as early as 1926 that "the labor movement has not even begun to draw on the power resources that might be brought in by a compelling pageantry of the epic of Labor" (1926, 36). In a similar vein, organizers of the Workers' Laboratory Theatre (WLT) in New York noted that "the Workers Theatre movement in the U.S.A., tho [sic] nearly ten years old, has been slow in developing" (*The Workers' Theatre* 1932, 3). One WLT actor observed that the short history of U.S. workers' theaters was one in which theater "groups formed and quickly died" (Roberts 1931). Consequently, as late as the mid-1930s, Jean Carter would note that "the drama is only beginning to take its place in the consciousness of the working people of America," although in Europe it had already become a "fundamental part of the worker's living" (1935, 179).

Proletcult activists offered several explanations for the failure of workers' theater in the United States. The rise of the cinema was always included as an important factor in any diagnosis of its problems. Despite the success of the Bryn Mawr drama program, Jean Carter was always fearful that the movies were slipping into the cultural niche "that should be occupied by the folk theater" in workers' lives. Moreover, the movies were not simply viewed as a competing cultural form, but as a cultural medium that was serving "primarily to make us forget the world" in which we live (1935, 180). Indeed, this anesthetic proved to be so potent that the Portland Labor Players concluded that "to compete with town entertainment is both useless and impossible" (Director 1927, 540).

However, it is also probable that features peculiar to the proletarian drama made it particularly vulnerable to such competition. Proletcult writers continually observed that as an audience, workers preferred either light comedy or *théâtre noir* with a humorous slant such as irony and satire. For example, Paul Blanshard, director of the Rochester Labor College, found that "the workers are not interested in serious singing but they like blackface comedy and they like light plays" (1921, 110). Similarly, Hollace Ransdell's experience was that "the labor plays which get the most effective response from the audiences, tend to be satiric or comic in tone, aiming for the most part to arouse laughter and thought, bringing out the ridiculous or the sardonic" (1935, 125). Nonetheless, it appears that most of the plays actually written and produced by workers were not comedies or satires, but dramas; certainly most of the theatrical criticism and theorizing in the proletcult literature focuses on the dramatic and not the comedic genre.

Thus, in many instances proletarian drama may have undercut its appeal to the working class because of its serious and uncompromising realism. For instance, Ransdell relates an incident in which women in the audience, including wives of some of the worker-actors, found the "harsh realistic treatment" of a southern cotton-mill strike too offensive. Yet, the view of the workers who had written and performed the play (and also had been in the strike) was that if anything they "had left out the worst of it" (1935, 122). The simple fact may be that workers' drama was just too bleak, too harsh, and too realistic to compete for a mass audience in a cultural entertainment market increasingly dominated by Hollywood productions.

Extant descriptions of labor dramas drive this point home. Tom Tippett described the theme of the first play produced by his miners' troupe in Illinois as "the tragedy of poverty in the southern hill country." The miners' second play, entitled *The Price of Coal*, was summarized as a one-act play "which dramatizes with telling effect the hideous truth that there is much human blood as well as sweat to reckon with in the cost of coal" (Tippett 1926, 1058). Or, as it was put by Rose Simkins, a garment worker and Brookwood student, *The Price of Coal* showed the lives of the miners; "it showed that in return for all the wealth they are producing they get killed" (Simkins 1928, 5).

One of the Brookwood Labor Players' most frequently performed plays was entitled *Peggy*. The play was written by Harold Williamson, whom Hazel MacKaye describes as a North Carolina mountain boy. She considered it a play that "brings home . . . the sheer helplessness of a large part of humanity before the devastating greed and selfishness of the present social system" (1926b, 12). A second play often performed by the Brookwood Players was called simply *Miners*, by Bonchi Friedman, a New York clothing worker whose left arm had been amputated after he was arrested during the New York garment strikes of 1926: a prison guard had literally crushed Friedman's arm with an iron bar. Helen Norton thus commented about his play that "one does not expect 'pretty' plays from such a writer, and *Miners* is distinctly not a pretty play" (1926, 19).

To be sure, where worker theaters and such dramas did achieve some degree of institutionalization, there is evidence that the theater troupes themselves preferred such "black" dramas to other "lighter" kinds of plays—whatever the audience might have wanted. Indeed, the Workers' Laboratory Theatre established an official policy to this effect. Worker-authors and others wanting to submit scripts to the WLT for consideration were reminded that "plays written for a bourgeois theatre are written with the aim of amusing, entertaining people for money. These are cock and bull concoctions, written to amuse the bourgeoisie for two and a half hours after dinner and ending in a pleasant manner so as not to upset their stomachs. . . . the worker-writer must write about the life the worker knows" (*The Workers' Theatre* 1931, 17).

The compelling feature of this proletarian realism is that there were generally no happy endings and no ironic twists. There was simply brutality, exploitation, work, alienation, and death. A brief extract from an ILGWU mass chorus recital called *Machine* perhaps best illustrates the dark themes of the proletarian drama. The initial stage setting reads as follows:

> As the curtain rises, the machines are seen at work to the monotonous beat of a gong. The lighting effect is produced by covering a single footlight unit with red gelatine. The gong is a brake drum, muffled, and struck with a wooden mallet. The "machines" are the chorus, clad in black shirts with white cog-wheels painted on the backs, and white stripes down the sleeves. Since the setting consists only of a black "cyclorama," or backdrop, the wheels and stripes appear to turn as the chorus goes through a mechanical dance. Still to the beating of the gong, the workers turn as they make their first speeches, revealing that they are workers, not yet freed from their machines.

The chorus then proceeds:

SCRIPT	MOVEMENTS
R. 3rd: (turning): We are starving.	3 strokes of the gong (hands slightly lifted)
L. 3rd: (turning): We are starving.	(hands slightly lifted)
C. 3rd: (turning): We are starving.	
(*Three strokes of the gong*)	
R. 3rd: We are crushed by Machines.	All crouch, hands uplifted to shield their heads
C. 3rd: Their weight smothers us.	
L. 3rd: The iron crushes.	
R. 3rd: The steel oppresses . . .	
(*Three strokes of the gong*)	
1st Voice: The iron hammer flattens me.	All rise and sway dully.
2nd Voice: It crushes the blood out of my veins; it fractures my bones; it makes me flat as sheet-iron.	
3rd Voice: Through the rollers my body is pressed thin as a wire. Where is my body?	

All: Where is my blood? Where is my soul? . . .

(*Three beats on gong*)

All: We are crushed by Machine
      We are parts of Machine

(*Three taps on gong*)

Front row: Oh terrible machine
Back row: Oh powerful machine
1st voice: Let us pray
All: Let us pray to Machine

(*HYMN TO MACHINE*)

All: Who is most powerful in the world?
      Most terrifying in the whole world?
      Machine!
      Who is more beautiful, richer, wiser?
      Machine!
      What is earth? Machine.
      What is sky? Machine.
      What is man? Machine.
                                        (Teper and Loomis 1941)

The image of alienation and the theme of powerlessness run through this and many other proletarian dramas. Yet this proletarian realism was a double-edged sword that, in many respects, contradicted the whole objective of inspiring workers with heroic images. Hence, it is not surprising that Arthur W. Calhoun complained to fellow worker educators that too often the proletarian drama was inclined to "take the direction of stunning, neurotic, narcotic melodrama." To this degree, he observed, proletarian drama paralyzed the audience instead of capturing "the fruitful, energizing, constructive possibilities of dramatic presentation" (1926, 35). Aaron Director also lamented that too many of the labor dramas were filled with "decadent philosophy" (1927, 540). On this point it should be emphasized, however, that even to the extent that these plays "came from below" they were always instigated "from above" and produced under the guidance of already politicized intellectuals. Consequently, it is not clear to what degree these intellectuals elicited a "proletarian realism" that was only partly the workers' own interpretation of proletarian reality.

These questions arise because of the acknowledged lack of success of workers' theaters in attracting a working-class audience. Director noted that at performances of the Portland Labor Players, "the attendance . . . while large, is drawn as much from the 'outside' as from trade union circles" (1927, 540). Indeed, the chief appeal of proletarian drama was often to what today is called a "radical chic" audience. Workers' theaters often found that their audience was a culturally radical middle class accompanied by a congeries of curiosity seekers. Sam Beder, an actor with the Rand School's Young Circle Dramatic Studio, describes a performance that conveys this point vividly. While on stage, he noticed: "Capitalism was staring directly at me in the bourgeois audience, with its women in their glaring dresses and jewels, its intellectuals, its deceivers, all waiting to see the performance that is to 'fight capitalism through drama'" (1931, 4). Even worse, from Beder's perspective, was the fact that the "bourgeois" composition of the audience inverted the play's intended social meaning. This particular play, *Squaring the Circle*, had originally been performed in the Russian agit-prop theaters and had been translated into English by the Young Circle. Its plot concerns two students admitted to Moscow University. The young men are torn between their working-class roots and political loyalties on the one hand and the temptations to adopt the comfortable petit-bourgeois life-style of the intellectuals. The moral thrust of the play was the ease with which even the most ardent radical, once receiving a university education, may lapse into "bad faith" and hypocrisy. As Beder describes the performance, the audience interpreted the play not as a tract on socialist self-criticism, but rather as a "form of burlesque to entertain the bourgeoisie, to place the Soviet workers in a ridiculous plight, to clown them whenever opportunity offers itself" (1931, 4). Audience reaction to the play transformed it from a piece about workers trying not to become bourgeois intellectuals into a satire about bourgeois intellectuals trying to imitate revolutionary workers. Such a performance of *Squaring the Circle* was a political embarrassment; taken out of its generative context the play became a chic lampoon of radical intellectuals, performed by professional actors, such as Beder, for a bourgeois audience. Yet for the workers in the audience, the play was not a "chic bourgeois lampoon" (as Beder protested), but rather a realistic portrayal of the American labor movement, particularly of its left wing during the 1920s. Still, given these disparate interpretations, it is clear that the meaning of proletarian realism often eluded the intentions of both its patrons and its performers, despite their conscious desire to use the theater to communicate a specific political message.

Conclusion

The dilemma posed by *Squaring the Circle* draws attention to an under-lying assumption that typically underpins all forms of realism. The initial assumption of United States supporters of labor drama was that such the-atrical pieces could "represent" a social reality that would appear the same to all observers, including patrons, audiences, and performers. A corol-lary of that assumption was that a realist script could permanently freeze specific images of society in the content and style (that is, the structure) of a dramatic work in such a way that the play's symbols (for example, characters and setting) would unilaterally act on different performers and audiences to consistently convey the same political message. Yet, at least three factors worked against this one-dimensional politics of patronage: the social mobility of the labor dramatists; shifting patterns of patronage during the late 1920s and 1930s; and finally the development of a more artistically sophisticated audience over time.

First, union officials and labor college directors often complained about the "social mobility" of the labor dramatists. The intent of the college-sponsored players' troupes was always to nurture amateur proletarian dramatists who would remain associated with the organized labor move-ment either through unions or political parties. However, as troupes of labor players achieved success *as actors,* many of the worker-actors became more interested in acting than in the labor movement (Director 1927).

There were two consequences of this social mobility. One result of the actors' increasing success within the art world was that it disrupted the simple "correspondence" between proletarian realism and the organiza-tional aims of the labor movement that initially gave birth to the labor players. Judith Balfe has observed that historically a linkage exists between movements of "the common man" and the generation of various forms of realism (1985). However, she has also suggested that as the artists them-selves become more artistically sophisticated and thus advance beyond the constraints of their initial generative context, they develop a predis-position for more and more abstract forms of representation (1981). The development of the American labor drama certainly lends case-study sup-port to this generalization. Thus, as labor dramatics developed over the course of the 1920s and 1930s, what the *artistically successful* prolecultists came to see as proletarian realism or as political art (for example, *Machine*) was a far cry from what union activists considered real. Thus a further consequence of the rise in actors' artistic and social aspirations was that the dramas were seen as "narcotic" and "decadent" by union and labor college officials. In turn, they often withdrew their institutional patronage from the labor players in order to redeploy scarce resources toward more "practical" fields of endeavor.

Yet the withdrawal of institutional patronage only accelerated the separation of proletarian drama from the official labor movement. In fact, the few labor players' troupes that achieved artistic success steadily shifted their patronage base from unions, political parties, and labor colleges to the marketplace. Typically, such troupes achieved institutional autonomy by establishing independent "little theaters" (for example, the Workers' Theatre) and increasingly directed their arts production toward (middle-class?) consumer markets that were already more culturally sophisticated. As one advocate of proletarian realism complained, the result was that artistically successful workers' theater troupes "degenerate to nothing more than an artistic group with a proletarian name" (Roberts 1931, 3).

Consequently, while the labor players of the 1920s and early 1930s laid much of the foundation for the WPA programs that followed in the late 1930s and the 1940s, by this later date the original proletcultists (as in Europe) were already moving toward various abstractionisms as a more radical form of cultural expression (Balfe 1985). Hence, by the late 1930s, there was a considerable gap between the artistic preferences of the original proletarian realists and real proletarians. This gap was evident along at least two somewhat contradictory axes. One consisted of a conflict between the abstract realism of dramatists and the naive realism expected by the originally generative audience. The other was between the dark proletarian drama of the performers and the working class's avowed preference for comedy and laughter. One might speculate that irony and satire could have constituted the midground between either set of these antinomies, but the extant plays do not indicate any movement toward such a synthesis. Therefore, it is no accident that workers' theaters came to rely on the market patronage of other radical intellectuals and a chic middle class who were already conversant with the increasingly abstract symbolism of socially mobile proletarian dramatists.

Finally, the development of proletarian drama during the 1920s and 1930s is illustrative of the dilemma confronted by all forms of realism in late capitalist (pluralist) social orders. On the one hand, the entry of art into the marketplace assures that it must realize its *value* as a commodity form if it is to survive at all. On the other hand, its *meaning* cannot then be reducible to the intent of its producer or owner. Rather, the marketplace tends toward a decentering and a multiplication of artistic meanings, particularly when coupled with abstract forms of expression. As Balfe has observed in another context, the commodification of artworks in the cultural marketplace means that "all artworks become subject to differing concurrent and consecutive interpretations. However, 'realistic' and 'objective' a style may be, it can still symbolize different things to different people, and participate in many forms of symbolic interaction" (1985, 6).

Similarly, the entry of proletarian drama into the cultural marketplace worked against the original patrons' desire to direct it toward ideological purposes. The multiplicity of social positions and social identities prevalent in late capitalism militates against the ability of patrons to ultimately control or dictate the meaning of art. Paradoxically, therefore, the point at which proletarian drama fails as radical politics is also the point at which it may achieve its highest artistic and market success.

Notes

This chapter was first published in *The Journal of Arts Management and Law* 20(4): 5–29.

1. Labor colleges relied on multiple sources of financial support, including tuition (usually one dollar per course), union- and party-financed scholarships, local union and party education levies, auxiliary enterprises (for example, bookstores, dances, and theaters), volunteer faculty, the free use of public buildings, private donations, and foundation grants. In general, their independence from corporate and state influence was guaranteed by a patronage system based exclusively in working-class institutions (such as unions, parties, and cooperatives) and "low end" cultural markets (*Report of the Proceedings of the First National Conference on Workers' Education in the United States* 1921, 135–36).

2. These figures are based only on enrollments at the sixty institutions affiliated with the Workers' Education Bureau in 1923 (Maurer 1924, 42).

3. The concept of an organic intellectual is best elaborated by Antonio Gramsci: "Every social group coming into existence on the original terrain of an essential function in the world of economic production, creates together with itself, organically, one or more strata of intellectuals which give it homogeneity and an awareness of its own function not only in the economic but also in the social and political fields" (1971, 3).

4. The Workers' Theatre was later absorbed as an auxiliary of the American Communist Party, whereupon its declared objective was to make theater a "weapon in the class struggle" (*The Workers' Theatre* 1931, 3).

5. In 1931, the Work People's College set up a Worker's Drama Bureau as a clearinghouse for labor and folk dramas. The bureau's purpose was "to collect dramas, ranging from short skits to five-act tragedies, and to make copies of the parts, letting them out to those wishing to use them." A description of its collection boasted that "many of the plays are descriptive of class struggle in America and have been written by those who were in the thick of them" (*American Labor Yearbook, 1931–1932*, 172).

6. In only two instances were these ambitions realized to some degree. Classes at the ILGWU's Workers' University led to the formation of dramatic groups by

many of the locals in that union (Swerdlow and Cohn n.d.). The Workers' Laboratory Theatre also opened branches in Philadelphia, Chicago, and Los Angeles (Raugh and Hartman 1931).

7. MacKaye observed that "we want to turn out students who are intelligent on this whole question of the drama with some practical knowledge of the problems involved in producing or writing plays" (1926a, 38).

References

American Labor Yearbook, 1921–1922. 1922. Report of the Committee on Curriculum: First National Conference on Workers' Education in the United States. New York: Rand School Press.

American Labor Yearbook, 1925–1926; 1926–1927; 1927–1928; 1928–1929; 1929–30; 1930–31; 1931–32. New York: Rand School Press.

Balfe, Judith Huggins. 1981. "Social Mobility and Modern Art: Abstract Expressionism and Its Generative Audience." In *Research in Social Movements, Conflict, and Change,* edited by Louis Kriesberg, 235–51. Greenwich, Conn.: JAI Press.

———. 1985. "Art Style as Political Actor: Social Realism and Its Alternatives." *Sociologia Internationalis* 23(1): 3–26.

Ball, Sidney. 1931. "Wanted: A Technique for Workers' Theatre in America." *The Workers' Theatre* (May): 4.

Barrow, Clyde W. 1989. "Pedagogy, Politics, and Social Reform: The Philosophy of the Workers' Education Movement." *Strategies: A Journal of Theory, Culture, and Politics* 2: 45–66.

———. 1990. "Counter-Movement within the Labor Movement: Workers' Education and the American Federation of Labor, 1900–1937." *Social Science Journal* 27(4): 395–417.

Beder, Sam. 1931. "Squaring the Circle." *The Workers' Theatre* (May): 4–6.

Blanshard, Paul. 1921. "Popularizing Workers' Education." In *Report of the Proceedings of the First National Conference on Workers' Education in the United States,* 109–11. New York: Workers' Education Bureau.

Budish, J. M. 1921. "The Work of the United Labor Education Committee." In *Report of the Proceedings of the First National Conference on Workers' Education in the United States,* 121–28. New York: Workers' Education Bureau.

Calhoun, Arthur W. 1926. "The Social Significance of Dramatics." In *Third Annual Conference of Teachers in Workers' Education,* 35–36. Katonah, N.Y.: Brookwood College.

Carroll, Mollie Ray. 1923. *Labor and Politics: The Attitude of the American Federation of Labor toward Legislation and Politics.* New York: Houghton Mifflin.

Carter, Jean. 1935. "Creative Expression: A Symposium." *Journal of Adult Education* (Apr.): 179–82.

Cohn, Fannia. 1922. "The Educational Work of the ILGWU." In *Report of the Second*

Annual Conference on Workers' Education in the United States, 46–58. New York: Workers' Education Bureau.

Craig, Leonard. 1918. "Workers' Education in Pennsylvania." *American Federationist* (Sept.): 1122–24.

———. 1929. "Educational and Social Activities." *American Federationist* (Dec.): 1446–52.

Director, Aaron. 1927. "A Western Experiment in Workers' Education." *American Federationist* (May): 538–40.

Dwyer, Richard E. 1977. *Labor Education in the United States*. Metuchen, N.J.: Scarecrow Press.

Fichlander, Alexander. 1921. "Workers' Education: Why and What?" *Labor Age* (Apr.–May). 49–50.

———. 1922. "How Labor Classes Operate." *Labor Age* (Apr.): 3–5.

Gleason, Arthur. 1921. *Workers' Education: American and Foreign Experiments*. New York: Bureau of Industrial Research.

Gramsci, Antonio. 1971. "The Intellectuals." In *Selections from the Prison Notebooks of Antonio Gramsci*, edited by Quintin Hoare and Geoffrey Nowell Smith. New York: International Publishers.

Hanchett, David Scott. 1922. "Labor Education in the Industrial Community." In *Proceedings of the National Conference on Social Work*, 346–51.

Hansome, Marius. 1931. *World Workers' Educational Movements: Their Social Significance*. New York: Columbia University Press.

Holwell, Raymond V. 1927. "Colorado and Wyoming Education Enterprises." *American Federationist* (Apr.): 442–44.

Kallen, Horace M. 1925. *Education, the Machine, and the Worker*. New York: New Republic.

Koven, Joseph. 1919. "The Workmen's Theatre." *Justice* (Apr. 19): 3.

Lee, Algernon. 1922. "The Rand School of Social Science." In *Workers' Education in the United States: Second Annual Conference of the Workers' Education Bureau*, 45–49. New York: Workers' Education Bureau.

Lembcke, Jerry. 1984. "Labor and Education: Portland Labor College, 1921–1929." *Oregon Historical Quarterly* 85 (Summer): 117–33.

Lukács, George. 1971. *History and Class Consciousness*. Cambridge Mass.: MIT Press.

MacKaye, Hazel. 1926a. "Our Experiment in Dramatics at Brookwood." In *The Promotion and Maintenance of Workers' Education: Third Annual Conference of Teachers in Workers' Education*, 37–39. Katonah, N.Y.: Brookwood College.

———. 1926b. "Plays for Workers." *Workers Education* (May): 11–18.

Mareg, E. W. 1931. "How the 'Workers' Theatre' Works in Germany." *The Workers' Theatre* (June): 6–7.

Maurer, James H. 1924. "Report of the Executive Committee, Proceedings of the Third National Convention on Workers' Education in the United States, 1923." In *Workers' Education Yearbook 1924*, 11–42. New York: Workers' Education Bureau.

Miller, Spencer, Jr. 1929. "Workers' Education." In *Social Work Yearbook 1929*, edited by Fred S. Hall, 480–81. New York: Sage Publications.

Morris, James O. 1958. *Conflict within the AFL: A Study of Craft vs. Industrial Union-ism*. Ithaca, N.Y.: Cornell University Press.

Norton, Helen. 1926. "Drama at Brookwood." *Labor Age* (May): 18–19.

Paul, Eden, and Cedar Paul. 1921. *Proletcult*. London: Leonard Parsons.

Ransdell, Hollace. 1935. "The Soap Box Theatre." *The Crisis* (Apr.): 122–25.

Raugh, F., and Lo Hartman. 1931. "The Rise of the Workers' Theatre." *The Workers' Theatre* (Apr.): 3–5.

Reed, Louis Schultz. 1930. *The Labor Philosophy of Samuel Gompers*. New York: Columbia University Press.

Reines, Bernard. 1931. "The Collective Method in the Workers' Theatre." *The Workers' Theatre* (June): 3–4.

Report of the Proceedings of the First National Conference on Workers' Education in the United States. 1921. New York: Workers' Education Bureau.

Roberts, S. 1931. "Consolidation of the English-Speaking Theatre Movement." *The Workers' Theatre* (May): 2–3.

Saposs, David, ed. 1926. *Readings in Trade Unionism*. New York: George H. Doran.

Simkins, Rose. 1928. "Brookwood Meets Katonah." *Justice* (Jan. 27): 5.

Sweeney, Charles Patrick. 1920. *Adult Working-Class Education in Great Britain and the United States*. Washington, D.C.: GPO, U.S. Bureau of Labor Statistics Bulletin.

Swerdlow, Irwin, and Fannia Cohn. n.d. *In Union There Is Strength*. New York: ILGWU Educational Department.

Teper, Lazare, and Sally Loomis. 1941. "Machine (a mass recitation)." In *Collection of One Act Plays*, edited by Fannia Cohn. New York: ILGWU Educational Department.

Thompson, Edward P. 1963. *The Making of the English Working Class*. London: Gollancz.

Tippett, Tom. 1926. "Workers' Education among Illinois Miners. *American Federationist* (Sept.): 1055–59.

The Workers' Theatre. 1931. "Dedication; We Must Write Plays." (Apr.): 3.

———. 1932. "A Year of *The Workers' Theatre Magazine*." (Apr.): 3.

❖ 6 ❖

"Friends of . . .": Individual Patronage through Arts Institutions

JUDITH HUGGINS BALFE AND THOMAS A. CASSILLY

Most European museums of art were founded as royal or aristocratic collections. Since then, they have been taken over for public use and supported almost entirely by national and state ministries of culture (Cummings and Katz 1989). In contrast, American art museums have been founded through the initiative of private individuals, whether actual collectors or simply civic-minded "boosters" (Burt 1977; Coleman 1939; Lee 1975; Miller 1966). The industrial expansion of the post–Civil War era brought about both new fortunes and the waves of new immigrants upon whose labor they depended; that combination contributed to the founding of art museums (and other institutions of "high culture" such as symphony orchestras) in city after city. These institutions were established and controlled by elites "in the public interest"; if any direct governmental support was provided, it remained largely at the city level where local elites were most likely to exercise political as well as cultural power, or needed to forge alliances with immigrant-supported political machines. However, such public support usually went toward operating expenses rather than to the acquisition of the artworks that were—and are—central to any museum's purpose. This was—and is—the responsibility of the trustees and their delegates, the director and curators.

The Structure of Museum Patronage

Most of the original founders were self-made business and professional men (or their widows or daughters), not all of whom had previously acquired much taste for or knowledge of the arts, but all of whom believed that public collections of art in museums would stimulate the cultural life of the community through enhancing the quality of life for individual citizens. Further, they believed that the severe urban problems caused by new immigrants could be alleviated by making European-based high culture—or even a diluted Yankee version of the same—accessible to the multitudes under their own trusteeship (DiMaggio 1986). If the museum founders thereby acquired personal prestige as public benefactors, that was to be expected; after all, they could have been spending their time and money on other pursuits, like so many less-civic-minded members of their own social class.

They could have become patrons of non-arts institutions as well; following the American practice of establishing voluntary associations to provide for social welfare, alternative philanthropic and charitable activities abounded during these years, with the development and expansion of nonprofit institutions to include civic, religious, educational, medical, and cultural organizations along with the private foundations that contributed so much to their funding (Powell 1987). Today there are over 900,000 such nonprofit organizations, of which cultural organizations like museums make up less than 5 percent, and art museums only a small portion of that (Weil 1991). Because these are proportionately few, legislation directed at the entire nonprofit sector does not always serve their particular interests.[1] Additionally, cultural organizations must compete for private and public support with others whose purposes are more clearly charitable, based on need and the alleviation of social misery, rather than philanthropic, based on merit and social betterment. As the audiences for the arts have been demonstrated to come disproportionately from the privileged sectors of society (DiMaggio and Useem, 1978; Robinson 1985; Wyszomirski and Clubb 1989), it has become harder to justify continued public subsidy in the face of pressing social needs.

In self-justification, the museums argue that they are among the most open, inclusive, and democratic cultural institutions in contemporary America, facilitating multicultural understanding in an nonpoliticized setting. Admission is either free or less than that charged by local movies; accordingly, museums claim that without being elitist, they encourage aspirations toward excellence. Indeed, long before the economic and social crises that currently affect large areas of the country, museums welcomed not just wide attendance by people of very modest means, but also the contribution of both their volunteer time and whatever donations they might make through becoming members. To be sure, the title of "patron" has been reserved for those members whose donations are substantial. Today, however, even people in the lower ranks of membership—without any collections of "museum quality" of their own to be sought after by curators, and with minimal chance of social or professional advancement through museum membership—are acknowledged by museum trustees as art patrons in the fullest sense (Grimes 1991). Their inclusion is the direct result of the founders' success in their purpose of raising public interest in the arts; now small donations from large numbers of people are solicited to replace the decline in patronage power of the heirs of the founding elites.

However, membership fees have generally been used for basic museum operations to supplement any public, foundation, or corporate funding. To raise money for acquisitions, since the mid-1920s museums have organized groups of higher-paying "Friends," whose contributions have supplemented those expected from trustees directed toward this end. Members and volunteers support the museum; Friends support the art. The latter support is more readily particularized; for example, in the frequent case that acquisition of works by any contemporary artists was hard to justify to conservative members of the board, such "Friends" were then organized with this specific purpose, often encouraged by museum education programs about modern art and with the help of a key "modernist" trustee or curator. Thus while the Cleveland Museum of Art inaugurated a general Friends of the Museum in 1925, the Detroit Institute of Art established the first museum Friends of Modern Art in 1934, to be followed by the Albright Gallery in Buffalo with a Society for Contemporary Art in 1939; Chicago's Art Institute set up its own Society for Contemporary American Art in 1941, to be followed in turn by the Cleveland Museum of Art's Gamblers in Modern Art in 1945 (Balfe 1979).

Typically, such groups of Friends were composed of young upwardly mobile professional couples, of whom the wife had first been—or was subsequently—recruited to serve on a concurrently established group of museum volunteers, its Women's Committee (at the Boston Museum of Fine Arts, this was called the "Ladies Committee"). Such groups increased rapidly after World War II to the point that a national association of the now-titled Volunteer Committees was formed in 1955. While museum trustees are also "volunteers," of course, it is the middle-class volunteers whose numbers have so expanded that today they may make up as much as 60 percent of an art museum's "staff": they work in curatorial departments behind the scenes, cover the information desk, serve as guides and docents, run picture loan and rental galleries within the museums, and organize membership campaigns, arts festivals, and costume balls. Those who donate time do not necessarily donate much money, but no American museum could function without them. The principle of noblesse oblige is now a middle-class value, for museum volunteers at least.

Volunteers and "Friends" at the Metropolitan Museum of Art

The Metropolitan Museum of Art was founded in 1870 and has long been regarded as the foremost (although it is no longer the wealthiest) American museum. It has always received municipal support for basic operating costs: New York City owns the building itself, while the private Metropolitan Corporation owns the contents and pays the staff (Howe 1946; Lerman 1969; Tompkins 1970). In recent years it has sometimes received additional funds from the New York State Council on the Arts and from the National Endowment for the Arts for specific projects (see Levine in this volume), but the vast majority of its operating and acquisition budget must be raised privately. As with other American museums, patronage continues to be elicited from wealthy individuals, corporations, foundations, and—especially in New York City—the real estate industry. At the same time, various categories of individual memberships have been designed to broaden the base of both the financial and the political support necessary to retain city funding. In addition, in order to increase the earned income under its direct control, as well as to provide welcome services for its visitors and members, like other American museums the Met has established a number of income-producing "auxiliary activities": two restaurants, elegant on-site gift shops with four satellite locations (one in Columbus, Ohio), a mail-order service, a parking garage, lectures, films, and concerts in its auditorium—in addition to its own scholarly publications available for sale.

It has also expanded its use of volunteers, even as these are limited in number to seven hundred, with a long waiting list. About half of the volunteers give one day a week on assignment to a particular department. The others undergo rigorous training before being permitted to serve as docents for both adult and student groups, for specific galleries of their choice; they may work three days a week. All sign contracts specifying their hours and responsibilities; if they are in violation, they are dropped and replaced by someone from the waiting list of those eager to give their time and knowledge to the Met. They receive neither direct monetary compensation nor even the chance to deduct the time-costs of their voluntary activity from their taxes.

There are other compensations, of course: discounts at the sales desk; entry to the museum on Monday (when it is closed to the public); free admission to the museum and to concerts and lectures that have not been sold out; a private reception in their honor and the opportunity to attend others; education and training in a specialized field of art history; hands-on experience and acquaintance with museum professionals; prestige among friends and acquaintances who have not yet been admitted from the waiting list. The Met's own prestige rubs off on its volunteers, as competition alone makes the entry requirements higher than for volunteers at the hundreds of smaller arts and cultural institutions in the same city.

Even though the Metropolitan has a full-time staff of 1,600, it depends upon its volunteers as much as do those smaller museums, especially for activities involving the general public. All volunteers are also members, of course; it is through membership that they are recruited. Still, the higher the category of membership (the more money donated), the greater the museum perquisites, regardless of volunteer activity. For the Met, love would seem to be acquired more readily than money. After all, the love of art is presumably what motivates all museum staff, paid or volunteer, and thus is more taken for granted. (Both love and money are in shorter supply for most smaller museums, but especially money.)

Some of the reasons for the apparently greater valuation of members and donors, compared to volunteers, are demonstrated by comparing the Met's budgets of 1975 and 1990 (see table 1).

Obviously, the total budget increased enormously between 1975 and 1990 (more than doubling in constant 1989 dollars), as did the amount obtained from each category of contribution. In fact, the amount and proportion contributed by New York City as it entered a period of fiscal crisis in 1989 was even greater than that contributed during the lesser fiscal crisis of 1975. As the Met frequently reminds local politicians, it is the largest tourist attraction in New York and generates from its visitors five times as much spending elsewhere in the city's economy than the city contributes to the museum. Other arts organizations granted city subsidy cannot make an equivalent claim, and in 1975 and recently they have suffered cuts that the Met has not (see Levine in this volume).

To put the Met's budget figures into a national context: in 1975, the Met's operating income in current dollars was $16.5 million, while the budget for the National Endowment for the Arts was $80 million. In 1990 the respective figures were $75 million for the Met and $172 million for the NEA. In constant 1989 dollars, the Met's budget has doubled while that of the NEA has increased less than 3 percent, totally dependent as it is upon Congress rather than receiving private as well as public patronage.

Of greater importance for our discussion here is the redistribution of proportionate shares of the Met's operating income. Over these fifteen years, the share provided by its endowment was reduced by half, while that of membership and gifts and grants more than doubled.[2] Allocation of particular items to auxiliary activities or to "other" varies in the respective

Table 1. Metropolitan Museum of Art: Operating Income, 1975 and 1990

Income Source	1974–75		1989–90	
	Percent of total	Amount in millions	Percent of total	Amount in millions
New York City	18.4	$3.0	20.7	$15.6
Membership	6.1	1.0	14.4	10.8
	(N = 30,955)		(N = 99,859)	
Admission	9.1	1.5	9.0	6.8
	(N = 3,500,000)		(N = 4,433,000)	
Gifts & grants	9.7	1.6	19.7	14.8
Spec. exhibits & purposes	13.4	2.2	6.9	5.2
Endowment	29.4	4.8	17.0	12.8
	(Net worth: $132.1)		(Net worth: $449.5)	
Auxiliary activities	7.3	1.2	2.7	1.9
	(Gross: $9.7)		(Gross: $79.6)	
	(Expenses: 8.5)		(Expenses: 77.6)	
Other	5.7	.8	9.6	7.2
TOTAL:		$16.450*		$75.190

Sources: Metropolitan Museum of Art Annual Report, 1974–1975; 1989–1990.
*Adjusted for inflation: $34.500 million in 1989 dollars.

Annual Reports (1974–75; 1989–90), which are the sources of these data; if these two categories are combined, their proportionate total is equivalent and their share is stable. In any event, the income from these categories, together with the regular admission fees (both largely derived from the general public, of whom 4,443,000 attended in 1989–90), does not equal the sums obtained from members and other private donors.

In 1991, memberships started at $30 for students and $70 for other individuals; with their perquisites of free entry, discounts, quarterly bulletins, and special receptions, they are obviously affordable to many people. Compared to the general audience (which increased by a third since 1975), the number of members has more than tripled to nearly 100,000 in 1990. However, of this total only 10,000 contributed over $100 and only 244 are in the $3500 to $5000 category, at which point they enter the official rank of "Patron," have their names listed in the *Annual Report*, are able to use the patron's lounge, and gain greater access to other museum facilities and activities. (Another 1,600 individuals are Fellows or Benefactors.

Their financial and other contributions to the institution are presumably so large that no dollar figure can rightly be assigned; in any case, none is provided in the *Reports*.)

Still, regardless of the level of membership, the sums generated along with admission fees provide revenue for the museum as a whole. In 1989–90, this totaled $10.8 million. In contrast, gifts and grants (a total of $14.8 million in 1990) are usually specified for particular projects such as acquisition, construction, or installation.

What these museum-wide data do not reveal is the fact that at the Met, as in every art museum, the various curatorial departments have their own traditional rivalries of aesthetic hierarchies and professional status (wherein Renaissance painting ranks higher than, say, decorative arts or costume, and anything European traditionally has ranked higher than anything made in America—at least until recently). Not surprisingly, the proceeds of both common membership support and private gifts to the Met have tended to be distributed accordingly, with the less-prestigious departments finding themselves comparatively less-endowed and thus more in need of raising independent funds.

Given such hierarchies, by the mid-1950s it became apparent to the curators in charge of the American Wing (especially those in charge of its decorative arts, even more than those responsible for its possibly more prestigious painting collection) that some special Friends would be useful. In emulation of comparable programs established in other American museums in earlier decades, the Friends would provide funds for acquisitions. After some lobbying, in 1960 the Met's board of trustees agreed to the following: "RESOLVED: That the organization of the group to be known as The Friends of the American Wing be . . . approved subject to the following conditions: a) each member of the group shall make an annual contribution to the Museum, which contribution shall be held in a restricted fund to be known as The Friends of the American Wing; b) expenditures from the Fund may be made only for the purchase of objects for the American Wing and for special installations and events . . ." (Rosenzweig 1990).

From thirty-two members at its inception, this organization of Friends has grown to over three hundred in 1991, even as the individual dues contribution has risen from $100 to $1,000 annually. During the past thirty years, the Friends have raised over a million dollars for notable acquisitions of decorative art that would not have been possible otherwise. Their success has engendered a more elite group that now totals sixty-four couples or individuals: the William Cullen Bryant Fellows. Automatically members of the Friends, the Fellows contribute $3,500 annually per couple; by giving at the general museum rank for "Patrons," they have their names listed in the *Annual Report* as those of more ordinary Friends are not, and their contributions are used to fund special American Wing publications rather than being allocated for acquisition.[3] Such distinctions aside, the routine administration of both Friends and Fellows activities is handled by the American Art Department itself, and they are encouraged to become more directly involved in departmental affairs as volunteers. (Alternately, volunteers trained as docents for galleries in the American Wing, under the general museum volunteer program, are encouraged to become Friends.)

American Wing Friends and Fellows have been so successful in enhancing its prestige, as well as its collections, that several other museum departments have founded comparable groups on approximately the same donor basis as the Fellows: The Friends of Asian Art (at $3,500 a year); Friends of European Sculpture and Decorative Arts (at $5,000); the Philodoroi (Friends of Greek and Roman Art, at $5,000); Affiliates of Film and Television (at $2,500). These departmental Friends have no lower-ranking "friendly" associates such as does the American Wing.

With the cost of virtually all works of art skyrocketing in recent years, even the Metropolitan, with an endowment of nearly half a billion dollars, is often unable to compete with more affluent museums in the United States (notably the Getty Museum in Malibu and the Kimbell Museum in Fort Worth), to say nothing of private collectors, especially the Japanese. In 1989–90, for example, the Met spent just over $18 million on acquisitions at a time when a single painting by Van Gogh brought $58 million at auction.[4] With seventeen departments in the museum competing for these relatively limited funds, strains and frustrations inevitably arise. In the circumstances, the advantage that Friends and Fellows give to any department is obvious.

Equally obvious, however, is the fact that the museum as a whole must compete for a limited pool of funds available both locally and nationally to museums and other arts organizations (see Galligan and Levine, in this volume). Thus contributions to the Friends of the American Wing might be seen to come at the expense of the institution as a whole. However, the museum's president, William H. Luers, concerned with raising general funds as well as with administration, insists that the advent of Friends groups has added to overall gifts, bequests, and grants (Luers 1990). The museum is too vast and its interests too broad to elicit the personal loyalty of any but a rare few. Rather, devotion to a single department, promoted by the face-to-face relations that Friends enjoy with each other and with the curatorial staff, seems to have given more people a sense of involvement, which may then be extended to the more general interests of the museum.

What do the Friends and Fellows of the American Wing receive for their contributions? Throughout the year, there is a program of lectures and receptions before American Wing openings, which is offered exclusively to them. Additionally, free visits are scheduled to the private homes of prominent collectors. On one such occasion, Richard H. Jenrette, one of this country's most renowned collectors of American decorative arts, painting, and even entire houses, played host to the Friends; on another, Ronald Lauder, former ambassador to Austria with an exceptional collection of armor and European drawings and paintings, extended the Friends' interests beyond Americana. Day trips are scheduled at a modest fee, for example to the reopening of Boscobel, a Federal mansion up the Hudson River, which was sumptuously restored by Mrs. DeWitt Wallace. On this trip, Friends were provided with luncheon in a tent on the property, where they were able to meet this celebrated patron of the arts. Another visit was to Andalusia, near Philadelphia, one of the finest Greek Revival houses in the country, built for Nicholas Biddle in 1836; there, lunch was offered beneath the portico by Biddle's direct descendent James Biddle, former director of the National Trust.

In addition to the satisfaction of feeling one has helped to preserve the best of the nation's patrimony by acquiring exceptional works of art for the museum, there is obviously a psychological satisfaction in being able to mingle with some of the most prominent collectors and connoisseurs in the country. For a relatively modest sum, Friends who could not afford the vast outlays necessary to acquire top objects of American decorative art themselves have an opportunity to meet those who have sufficient money, as well as the taste and inclination, to do so. And with the Fellows immediately above them in rank yet otherwise in the same status as "amateur" patrons, they can socialize at regular Friends events as equal devotees of the field, celebrating the arts of the United States.

Friends of the Vieilles Maisons Françaises

The patent success of such American groups of Friends has not been lost on other countries, especially in Europe where art patronage has traditionally been monopolized by the state. Accordingly, private associations have been founded to promote culture following American models in many respects.[5] Of interest here is the Vieilles Maisons Françaises (VMF), founded in 1922 by owners of French châteaux, manors, and old farmhouses as an interest group to exert pressure on the French government to help them preserve their property. It proved to be highly successful in this goal almost immediately (two years later it inspired a similar and somewhat more elitist organization, Demeures Historiques). Today the VMF has a membership of over twenty thousand, nearly all of whom are owners of buildings that qualify for "historic preservation" on a scale that most Americans can barely imagine.

Impressed by Friends groups in the United States and their recently established counterparts in France (such as the Amis du Louvre), in 1982 some American VMF members in Paris organized themselves as Friends of VMF; shortly thereafter, they decided to set up a similar organization in America with nonprofit status. Since its founding, these Friends have established twelve chapters throughout the country, as well as one in Paris, with a combined membership of fifteen hundred. Starting memberships are under $100; again, those in higher categories of "friendship" receive more perquisites.

Collectively the FVMF have raised over a million dollars to aid historic preservation in France, with projects including the restoration of Renoir's studio in Cagnes-sur-Mer and the rescue of an entire medieval village at Chatillon-sur-Saône that was in danger of being despoiled by antique dealers. Through FVMF-sponsored Richard Morris Hunt Fellowships, American architects and their counterparts in France have participated in an exchange program; American students have worked on restoration projects across the Atlantic while young French students have done the same in this country. Successive issues of the FVMF quarterly magazine are devoted to the various *departments* in France, noting their respective artistic heritage and cases of historic preservation. The FVMF newletter lists many private events and behind-the-scene tours in France and the United States open to all Friends, from the studios of Christian Dior to the Musée d'Orsay and residences not open to the public. For the past several years the FVMF has funded scholarly seminars, such as one in Fountainebleau in 1989 that assembled twenty museum staff members, academics, and others under the supervision of the curator of sculpture and decorative arts of the Boston Museum of Fine Arts. (Notably, English is the official language of these annual seminars.) This weeklong program featured lectures by prominent authorities and visits to places not open to the public (*Friends of Vieilles Maisons Françaises* 1990; Stuebe 1990). For Friends in the upper ranks of donors, members of the VMF itself are willing and, indeed, eager to open their properties for meals and even for overnight stays; it is particularly these more affluent Friends who might consider contributing to the restoration of the hosts' châteaux. (Similarly, tours to the United States by French FVMF members have led them to make contributions to historic preservation here, for example the repair of buildings in Charleston, South Carolina, damaged by a 1989 hurricane.)

As intended, the major reward for membership in the Friends of the VMF is gratification in helping to preserve an impressive range of buildings, restoring medieval frescoes, exchanging scholars and even members of the International Union of Bricklayers, and generally strengthening ties between France and the United States. Without question, of at least equal importance is the subtle snob appeal and the psychic and social satisfaction of associating with prominent Francophiles and members of the hereditary French aristocracy, in historic and elegant settings. The distinguished Honorary Committee of the Friends in Paris includes the ambassadors of both France and the United States; perhaps more important in the eyes of many Friends is the Prince de Polignac, the Grand Bailiff of the Knights of Malta and the Comte de Castries, president of the Society of Cincinnati in France. Such individuals serve in more than honorary capacities; the executive council of the FVMF board in Paris is equally distinguished, including the Princesse Georges-Henri de La Tour d'Auvergne. When she made a lecture tour to different chapters of VMF Friends in the United States in 1990, discussing the Château d'Ainay-le-Vieil—which has belonged to her family since 1467—her lectures were sold out as Friends brought their nonmember friends to hear her. Given such a response, exporters of champagne like Veuve Clicquot and Moët et Chandon have donated their wine to benefits given by the Friends, and the French ambassador in Washington and consuls elsewhere have made a point to attend Friends' functions and offer their headquarters for events sponsored by the organization.

Conclusion

As individuals, members of both sets of Friends that we have examined here obtain much satisfaction in having contributed to historic preservation in France, or to the acquisition of works of decorative art for the American Wing at the Metropolitan. Notably, these institutions themselves are "world class" in prestige, as arts organizations of more local interest are not. However, all arts organizations who have instituted Friends have recognized that their appeal must be based on something more than the desire to support the arts. They must also provide opportunities to meet compatible individuals—especially those who are wealthy and socially prominent (in these two cases, collectors and owners of historic buildings that are closed to the ordinary public). These, in turn, would seem to benefit from the intimate audience of Friends, whose admiring recognition contributes to the maintenance of their own prestige and privilege. Otherwise, there is no reason for them to offer time and space to such comparatively less-privileged people. Most Friends are in professions and positions in which they are able to advance a more sympathetic understanding of those who use their great wealth, in part, for philanthropic purposes; without their support, the wealthy would have a harder time maintaining their property and status in the face of politically exploitable resentment of inherited class privilege.

The sponsoring institutions—in this instance, the Metropolitan Museum and the Vieilles Maisons Françaises—also benefit; small groups of like-minded supporters are encouraged to extend their loyalty from their own group to the greater purposes of the institution as a whole and to the preservation of the nation's cultural patrimony. There is a paradox, however. Recruitment of Friends on the basis of their making a higher financial contribution than that of ordinary members, with the promise of access to the privileged elites of great and/or old wealth, might seem to undermine these same organizations' claims of democratic and equal access to the public at large. To be sure, the fees to join these groups of Friends are within reach of many upper-middle-class Americans, those most likely to have acquired the education in the arts and culture that would incline anyone to such membership. However, as we have seen, so many have been attracted that more exclusive groups have split off to receive even more recognition. The jump from $1,000 to $3,500 per couple, as required for Friends of the Met's American Wing to become William Cullen Bryant Fellows, is more than even most Friends can afford—yet once Friends, some feel "outclassed" if they do not go on to become Fellows and be listed in the museum's annual report accordingly.

The inevitable appeal to social distinction based primarily upon the ability to pay (there are no scholarships for "Fellowships" that are based on "worth" or knowledge alone) is, in one sense, democratic. Americans brought up to the question: "If you're so smart, why aren't you rich?," may believe that anyone—from ball players to rock stars—can rise to the top (even if they personally may have a hard time making ends meet). In effect, anyone can enter into the "Life Styles of the Rich and Famous" at any art museum, at some level: mere attendance is at ground level; joining or volunteering is more advanced; becoming a Friend or Fellow is higher still. The point is that entry is open to all, as a matter of principle. If art acquires its aura of autonomous power because it can transcend its original social location, becoming accessible to those far removed in time, place, and wealth to the enhancement of their own lives, this is demonstrated by the open recruitment of new acquaintances, some of whom become new friends and lovers.

However, while lovers want their friends to be enthusiastic about their beloved, they do not always want to share the beloved's time with mere acquaintances, pleased though they may be that the multitudes agree that the beloved is, indeed, lovable. Some kind of exclusive claim to private time alone with the object of admiration must be acknowledged by those same multitudes if the lovers are to feel worthy of the beloved. But how are these multitudes to assess the claim and that worthiness? For better or for worse, most Americans would agree that the greater the willing sacrifice of goods and resources by the lovers, the more they deserve the prize, as the greater must be their own merit. (The sacrifice of time and devotion cannot be measured for comparative purposes, not even by the IRS; voluntary activity leading to personal impoverishment, as by Ralph Nader or Mother Theresa, may be admired but is seldom recommended to one's children.) Thus the higher the financial contribution, the higher the awarded distinction. Further, because philanthropy is less necessary for the immediacies of societal survival than charity, it is seen to be more meritorious.

Through such institutions as Friends, museums have been able to keep their doors open and continue to increase their collections in an era of rampant commercialism, when "selling out"—and selling off—are ready possibilities. (Controversies over deaccessioning are all too frequent.) As they maintain the contrasting aesthetic "ethic" of beauty for its own sake and for the sake of the world's cultural heritage, museums try to satisfy their critics who would reallocate their funding toward more pressing social needs. Ironically, by building upon the status rivalry and snobbery that accompanies the qualitative distinctions they are obliged to make among the arts, museums find that the establishment of categories of Friends leaves them open to the charge that they are run by and for these elites whose claims of philanthropy are merely a mask for self-interest. And the individual Friends, motivated by the desire to sustain the old and great traditions against the cheapening assault of late-twentieth-century materialism in which price is taken as the only measure of value, find that their own worth is assessed by the same criteria.

Notes

1. This is illustrated in the 1986 revision of the tax code, which essentially penalized charitable deductions of appreciated property to the point that donations of artworks to museums dropped nearly 50 percent between 1985 and 1990 (Weil

1991). (The relevant provision was subsequently suspended for 1991 through June 1992; revision of the tax code by the Clinton administration may eliminate the provision.) Still, some dollar-equivalence can be assigned to any purchased artwork for tax purposes, as it cannot be to the time donated by the volunteers upon which museums depend, which cannot be deducted at all. On the same principle, time "volunteered" by artists in the creation of their work is not evaluated for tax purposes until the work is sold, so there is no tax incentive for artists to donate their work to museums.

2. From the *Annual Report*, one cannot distinguish gifts from grants. Presumably most of the 1990 gifts and grants category here was made up of grants, but no details are provided as to their sources or specific purposes.

3. Fellows' contributions thus support the wider dissemination of curatorial knowledge of the acquisitions and exhibitions of American decorative arts and painting. Greater prestige would seem to be accorded to this intellectual and academic purpose than to the mere collection of objects to which the fees from "ordinary" Friends are relegated.

4. Although the funds are raised privately, $18 million is 24 percent of the total budget for that year. Comparable figures for 1974–75 are $3.2 million and 19.5 percent.

5. Europe is not alone in its emulation of the United States in this respect. In June 1991, a delegation from the Hermitage Museum in newly renamed St. Petersburg toured museums in New York City. They were little concerned with curatorial concerns about preservation of their collections, but focused instead on the mechanisms of encouraging private patronage, membership support, and earned income through auxiliary activities.

References

Balfe, Judith Huggins. 1979. "The Institutionalization of the Modern Image: Modern Art in American Museums, 1913–1963." Ph.D. diss., Rutgers University.

Burt, Nathaniel. 1977. *Palaces for the People: A Social History of the American Art Museum*. Boston: Little, Brown.

Coleman, Laurance Vail. 1939. *The Museum in America*. Washington: American Association of Museums.

Cummings, Milton C., and Richard S. Katz, eds. 1987. *The Patron State: Government and the Arts in Europe, North America, and Japan*. New York: Oxford University Press.

DiMaggio, Paul. 1986. "Cultural Entrepreneurship in Nineteenth-Century Boston" (reprinted from *Media, Culture, and Society* 4 [1982]). In *Nonprofit Enterprise in the Arts: Studies in Mission and Constraint*, edited by Paul DiMaggio, 41–63. New Haven: Yale University Press.

DiMaggio, Paul, and Michael Useem. 1978. "Cultural Democracy in a Period of Cultural Expansion: The Social Composition of Arts Audiences in the United States." *Social Problems* 26(2): 179–97.

Friends of Vieilles Maisons Françaises Annual Report. 1990.

Grimes, William. 1991. "How to Win Friends and Influence Culture. *The New York Times*, Dec. 20, pp. C1, 33.

Heckscher, Morrison. 1990. Interview by Thomas A. Cassilly, September 12.

Howe, Winifred E. 1946. *A History of the Metropolitan Museum of Art*. New York: Columbia University Press.

Lee, Sherman L., ed. 1975. *On Understanding Art Museums*. Englewood Cliffs: Prentice-Hall.

Lerman, Leo. 1969. *The Museum: One Hundred Years of the Metropolitan Museum of Art*. New York: Viking.

Luers, William. 1990. Interview by Thomas A. Cassilly, September 27.

Metropolitan Museum of Art Annual Report, 1974–75; 1989–90.

Miller, Lillian B. 1966. *Patrons and Patriotism: The Encouragement of the Fine Arts in the United States, 1790–1860*. Chicago: University of Chicago Press.

Ouvert au Public: Châteaux, abbayes, et autres bâtiments. 1989. Paris: Ministry of Culture.

Powell, Walter W., ed. 1987. *The Nonprofit Sector: A Research Handbook*. New Haven: Yale University Press.

Robinson, John. 1986. *Public Participation in the Arts*. College Park: University of Maryland.

Rosenszweig, Ellin. 1990, 1991. Interview by Thomas A. Cassilly, August 1990, May 1991.

Stuebe, Isabel. 1990. Interview by Thomas A. Cassilly, September and October.

Sussek, Marie. 1991. Interview by Thomas A. Cassilly, May.

Tompkins, Calvin. 1970. *Merchants and Masterpieces: The Story of the Metropolitan Museum of Art*. New York: E. P. Dutton.

Vieilles Maisons Françaises, Patrimoine historique. 1990.

Weil, Stephen E. 1991. "Tax Policy and Private Giving." In *Public Money and the Muse*, edited by Stephen Benedict, 153–81. New York: W. W. Norton.

Wyszomirski, Margaret Jane, and Pat Clubb, eds. *The Cost of Culture: Patterns and Prospects of Private Art Patronage*. 1989. New York: American Council for the Arts.

✤ PART THREE ✤

INDIRECT PATRONAGE

BY CITY INSTITUTIONS

In contemporary societies with market economies, art patronage usually involves multiple and interrelated institutions, both private and public—particularly at the city level. There, elected officials are personally close to and held accountable by their individual constituents, whether these be artists, would-be patrons or audience members, or the larger number who have no interest in the arts at all. At the same time, they are subject to national, regional, and state policies that affect the amount and direction of the funds and power at their disposal. This situation contributes to their attitudes toward the public agencies that are openly involved in art patronage. With so little real power, city politicians tend to see these as administrative units for the convenience of their own and their constituents' non-arts agendas. Not surprisingly, such agencies have very little direct control over the outcomes of their patronage.

Meanwhile, private patron organizations such as theaters and galleries have been established to advance the arts, both on a commercial and a nonprofit basis. As they operate at the city level, they are closest to the artistic community. Yet they too are likely to have too little power and autonomy to achieve many of their artistic goals, especially when these require cooperation with politically compromised city agencies. Thus in all such "mixed" cases, institutions of arts patronage are at the mercy of wider political, economic, and social forces.

The three case studies in this section focus on artistic developments in the late 1980s in New York City, Chicago, and Philadelphia. While these large cities may be atypical in the scale of their political bureaucracies, they are also atypical in the concentration of artists available to be enlisted in the factional struggles endemic in urban settings.

Judy Levine analyzes the problems of the New York City Department of Cultural Affairs, originally set up in 1976 as an administrative unit to manage city funds apportioned to fifteen city-owned cultural units such as the Metropolitan Museum of Art. By 1990, with these units grown to thirty-one and with some five hundred other cultural organizations seeking city funding, DCA's $175 million budget had become so specifically allocated by city politicians that it had direct control over less than $900,000. With the city facing financial collapse, social service became the primary justification for any public funding: thus the much-reduced DCA funds (allocated or discretionary) were awarded for education-related projects, rather than for the arts in themselves. Yet DCA is the only city agency accountable for the health of its cultural institutions, upon which much of its shaky economy depends.

If the city bureaucracy makes art patronage byzantine and inflexible, the open market presents other problems. The independent yet related and often conflicting role played by commercial and real estate interests in New York's culture industries is explored by Anne E. Bowler and Blaine McBurney, who describe the gentrification of the East Village that occurred in the 1980s. Here the "patronage" was largely fortuitous and uncontrolled by any city bureaucracy, as investors built upon the autonomous development of the area by artists and their dealers. The area "boomed" and some artists became "stars," while community residents were displaced and art was commodified—the very things most of the first East Village artists and many of their dealers opposed.

Steven C. Dubin examines incidents that occurred during the same years in Chicago and Philadelphia. In both cases, the artist's claims to the right of free expression conflicted with the same rights claimed by other groups. Dubin's analysis shows that however diffused through different agencies, public art patronage may engender political controversy in periods of great volatility. Whether the resultant work is representational or nonrepresentational and regardless of its aesthetic quality, it can serve as catalyst for—and distillation of—previously unfocused feelings. And once focused, those feelings promote action to which politicians must respond.

Levine and Bowler and McBurney show how art and artists are at the mercy of enormously complex economic and political organizations, themselves beyond the control of both private and public officials who are presumably in charge of directing art patronage. However, Dubin reminds us that art can ignite wider social action that determines the fate of those very organizations.

New York City Department of Cultural Affairs: Art as Municipal Service

JUDY LEVINE

The arts are important because they define who we are culturally to one another, and they make it so that you can accept me and we both can accept Joey Yin, who has a totally different culture than we do, and we can figure out through the arts how we can live next door to Joey Yin and work at the desk next to his. . . . [But] it's a struggle every step of the way for this agency to promote the involvement of the artist in the community.
—Kathleen Hughes, New York City
   Department of Cultural Affairs

New York City's funding process for most of our arts organizations is an anomaly because of the politics, and it isn't that politics are not a good thing. It's just that the way the funding process works, it focuses on individual groups, rather than on policy issues. . . . Policy survives politicians; individual funding doesn't.
—Charmaine Jefferson, New York City
   Department of Cultural Affairs

The New York City Department of Cultural Affairs (DCA) was created as a separate agency in 1976. Following the momentum unleashed by the pivotal mid-sixties Rockefeller Brothers and 20th Century Fund Reports (Rockefeller Panel 1965; Baumol and Bowen 1966), New York City arts and cultural leaders began a dialogue with then-Mayor Lindsay on ways the city could become more involved in its arts activities. When Abraham Beame was elected mayor in 1973, cultural leaders saw an opportunity through which substantial change in the city's treatment of the arts could be effected. While Mayor Lindsay had been very friendly to the arts community, cultural leaders were concerned that this "not lapse with Beame, who had shown no visible interest in the subject up to that point," according to one participant (Benedict 1991). At the time, cultural oversight was spread among several city agencies, with the major activity coming under the Office of Cultural Affairs located within the Department of Parks, Recreation, and Cultural Affairs. However, cultural leaders felt that this mammoth department's priorities gave short shrift to the importance of the arts to New York City (Benedict 1991).

A group of foundation directors concerned with the arts met with Edward Weisl, commissioner for Parks, Recreation, and Cultural Affairs, to offer assistance in advising the new mayor on cultural activity. The resulting commission recommended the formation of a separate Department of Cultural Affairs to "consolidate a variety of functions relating to the city's cultural life formerly administered by several different city agencies" (New York City Department of Cultural Affairs 1981, 4).

The new department was charged with coordinating various cultural programs that had been under the Department of Parks, Recreation, and Cultural Affairs, including the administration of capital and line-item expense appropriations for what were then fifteen cultural institutions located in city-owned buildings. It was also mandated to "plan, develop, conduct, and supervise cultural activities within the city" (Glueck 1976, 40) but was not given explicit grant-making powers nor a budget commensurate with its mission. Indeed, during the first year of the new agency's existence, it was actually given *less* money than its preceding subagency the year before (Glueck 1976, 40). DCA's founding was undertaken in the hope that consolidating existing city responsibilities to the arts would lead to the formation of a greater power base with more visibility and benefit to the arts community (Benedict 1991). This expansive vision has been hampered by bureaucratic maneuvering ever since. Rather than taking its primary identity cue from the art world, the Department of Cultural Affairs is defined first by its position as municipal government. More than simply a bureaucratic accident of place, the department's link to New York City government determines its mission as well as means.

Historical Precedents

The department's history parallels New York City's 1975 near-bankruptcy, its slow climb toward solvency, and a renewal of economic difficulties in the early 1990s. The mid-seventies erosion of the city's tax base due to an economic recession and corporate flight to the suburbs, succeeded by the enormous strains that crack and AIDS have placed on the city's social service and criminal justice systems, has meant that DCA has never been able to increase its startup funding to a level consonant with the scope of the cultural activity it was mandated to serve. Indeed, most of the funds under the department's administration are reserved for city-owned cultural facilities such as the Metropolitan Museum of Art, leaving only a small percentage for other programs and the department's own administrative expenses. This pattern has been consistent over the years, as can be seen by contrasting the DCA budgets of 1980 and 1987. In 1980, of a total DCA budget of $22.8 million (adjusted for inflation, $35.5 million in 1987 dollars), 86 percent went to the group of city-owned cultural facilities (by then totaling 25 institutions), 8 percent was allocated for other programs, and 6 percent went to central administration (New York City Department of Cultural Affairs 1981, 1). In 1987, while the agency budget had doubled in constant 1987 dollars to $73.1 million, 82 percent still went to the institutions (now numbering 31), 14 percent was allotted to approximately 500 other New York City arts organizations, and 4 percent was spent on central administration (New York City Department of Cultural Affairs 1988, 33).

This funding pattern has historical roots in the 1870s founding of the Metropolitan and American Natural History museums. The city retained legal ownership of the museum buildings, while the trustees retained ownership and control over the contents of the building—the collections. At the time, this was an entirely new idea in municipal government and was propagated by the founders of the museums as an attempt to maintain private control while obtaining the massive amount of monetary support then available only in the public sector. Resultant tensions between the public and private nature of museums (and other similarly established organizations) follow these institutions to this day. And in New York City, DCA is the agency responsible for the implementation of these institutions' public mandate.

DCA and the Cultural Institutions

The wide disparity in funding levels between the major institutions and the rest of DCA's roster, and the inability of the arts community (and its supporters within the department itself) to influence that disparity in any meaningful way, has led to resentment over that distinction. The special funding categorization of the Cultural Institutions Group (CIG), overseen by a separate division within the department, has set up a distinction between "the big guys" and everyone else. The proportion of DCA funds allocated to the institutions sends a clear message regarding the importance of these institutions in relation to the rest of the art world. Indeed, the Metropolitan Museum alone receives more than does a combination of all other arts organizations supported by New York City that are not considered "cultural institutions" (see Balfe and Cassilly in this volume). The city's financial priority toward the institutions (and mostly large ones, at that) creates bitterness among many of its arts organizations, especially in a time of dwindling resources.

At DCA itself, however, this disparity is tolerated due partly to the fact that these institutions' boards of directors have substantial access to New York City governmental sources of power (and, therefore, to funds). In 1990 the department was threatened with being eliminated as a separate agency, and it was lobbying by the directors of the major institutions, along with New York City politics, that saved DCA from extinction. Early in 1991, as the department faced a 50 percent cut in funding, the heads of the major institutions testified before the city council and attracted the notice of the *New York Times*. DCA is dependent on "the majors" for political clout—for *all* departmental funding.

The long history and special nature of the cultural institutions, the need for borough- and city-wide balance, and other politically determined imperatives, together form a complex web within which both the amount and the distribution of departmental funding is determined. DCA Deputy Director Charmaine Jefferson (1991) commented on the department's attempt to address these issues:

> There are some within the cultural institutions that probably receive more money than they would otherwise, but it isn't because they're the best cultural institutions. It's because elected officials put most of their money into it . . . because in some boroughs, [such institutions] were almost the only thing happening for the longest [time] so they have a history built up. . . . [But] you still have to have a mechanism by which people can get into being a city treasure [because] when you grandfather all the preferences of the past into place then you can never correct them. What we hope to do is have a policy to formalize the concept of what a cultural institution is, and to formalize how [an arts group can] become one . . . so that it's not ad hoc.

DCA Program Funding

In recent years, DCA has begun funding smaller New York City arts groups. DCA now issues formal application guidelines and receives up to eight hundred applications per year. However, the greater proportion of funds available for these groups is also not at the department's discretion but is set into the agency's budget by New York City elected officials.

As Kathleen Hughes (1989a), DCA Assistant Commissioner for Program Services, explained:

> The agency does not set its own budget. . . . Our money comes through a political process that has a lot to do with the priorities of the borough president's office, and the city council. . . . The agency tries to affect the choices that are made in the [budget] adoption process [but] it's very much out of our control in terms of where the dollars go. . . . The agency is a bureaucracy for the priorities of others, some of whom are well informed and some of whom could be better informed. We try and do the best we can with that.

In fact, of its 1990 budget, the department had discretionary control over only $900,000, according to Hughes (1989a). She added:

> [While] that's not an insignificant amount of money—if it were somewhere else in the world, it would be a lot—when you put [it] within the frame of reference of a $13 million program budget or a $175 million [expense plus capital] agency budget, it's peanuts. And since it's the only money the agency has any discretion over, much of it gets eaten away even before the process begins. . . . [It's] such a minuscule portion of the overall budget, and it deals with every discipline, every type of arts organization, [from] tiny community-based theaters up to the Guggenheim Museum.

There is a striking discrepancy in funding amounts between the institutions, groups that receive "political" funding, and groups dependent on departmental discretionary funds. In 1989, institutions designated as part of the CIG received from $228,000 to $14.8 million (plus ongoing capital expenditures). Those organizations with enough political connections to have been designated as line-items in the city budget received from $10,475 to $420,000. But the groups that simply fell into DCA's discretionary budget or Borough Arts Development funds were granted from $1,000 to $10,000 (New York City Department of Cultural Affairs 1990, 28–32). In New York City, becoming acquainted with one's political representatives is essential to receiving any type of substantial city arts funding. Indeed, DCA staff members encourage the arts community to visit and lobby their local politicians.

However, according to Charmaine Jefferson (1991), this leads to a situation in which

> these people are trying to create art, usually with a staff of three, maybe four, maximum, sometime one at minimum. They don't have

government liaisons. They shouldn't have to become experts in lobbying. What they're producing is something of quality. . . . The way [for] people [to] get money is through individual political lobbying [but] no group should be penalized because they didn't vote for the right person . . . [or] because they only went to two offices for a visit and they didn't go to the third.

Because DCA staff has so little input into the distribution of funding, often the greatest help it can offer an arts group is to recommend that the group ask its local politician to put money into the department's budget earmarked for the group. This leaves DCA in a position of ceding control over arts resources to nonartistic judges. Regaining some of that control has been a priority of the current administration; but extra-artistic factors have complicated the process.

Charter Revision and the Allocation of DCA Funds

In 1990, the New York City Charter—the basic document under which city government is conducted—was completely revised. The change that most affects the operations of DCA is the transfer of major budgetary power from the five borough presidents to the thirty-five city council members (to be increased to fifty-one). In addition, the entire mechanism by which city contracts are approved has been overhauled.

In the past, most DCA program dollars (as opposed to CIG funds) have come from the borough presidents' discretionary money. The borough presidents, understandably, have wished to ensure that the funds they put in the department's budget go to their constituents. Indeed, arts advocates in the "outer boroughs" continue to raise questions about DCA being overly "high art" and Manhattan-focused (Segal 1976, 19; Adams 1991).

DCA has been caught in a cycle in which new money has not been added to its budget by the executive branch, and elected officials then put in their own money for specific groups. New money is not then allocated in the budget by the executive branch the next year; the assumption is that elected officials will put their dollars into the department again. Though the specific players may have changed with the new charter, the funding process for the department has remained almost the same. As Kathleen Hughes (1991) sees it:

The overall picture of where DCA funds have gone this year isn't drastically different from where they've gone in previous years [but] the process was lots more complicated [and] there remains for the future the issue of whose funds are these, anyway? [There's a process of] political gamesmanship that for the most part has been heavily affected by entities like the Office of Management and Budget. Basically, the game is: borough presidents put the money in [and the new charter now includes council members in this effort], so we'll take the money out, so they'll put the money in. The OMB views this portion of DCA's budget as rampant, uncontrolled growth . . . but they helped create the problem [by] making sure there are no, or little, new money initiatives in the executive budget, so that the department is always reacting to what happens and dealing with other people's priorities.

On the positive side, there is the presumption that a borough president or council member and a good staff have a deeper knowledge of their particular area and its resources and its needs—but this hasn't been used to inform DCA. It wasn't used in the process of setting a cultural agenda, [nor] to look at the city as a whole; it was effected piecemeal, and DCA has been viewed simply as a mechanism for carrying out their [agenda].

At the most basic level, Department of Cultural Affairs funds are taxpayer dollars, collected by the city and apportioned during a complex budget process through which elected officials attempt to allocate resources to achieve the maximum public good. Who determines the distribution that will best accomplish this result—and even what the result should be—is at the heart of DCA's struggle to fulfill its mandate to oversee the cultural health of New York.

While the department views the money in its budget as intended to support its mandate to "oversee and sustain New York City's cultural life, heritage and artistic preeminence" (Jefferson 1990, 13), those placing the money under DCA's authority—local politicians—tend to see its purpose as supporting *their* mandate to deliver municipal services to their constituents. Political officials view DCA as a resource much as they respond to their community's health care needs by allocating money to the Department of Health for a neighborhood teen pregnancy program, or place pressure on the Department of Transportation to resurface local streets.

Another issue affecting the budget adoption process is the city charter's new requirement that all contracts be "let" for competitive bidding. What this means for arts funding is unknown; how does competitive bidding work for a modern dance concert, or for a symphony orchestra series in the parks? DCA staff is hoping that an increased emphasis on competitive bidding might enable the department to wrest the decision-making process away from politicians and toward peer panels, but politicians are unlikely to give up control of "their" money for "their" community's needs.

The issue of "whose money" DCA resources actually are is more than semantic. The arts community, department staff, and various political delegations are locked in a struggle to define DCA's purview. The department must balance community needs against artistic agenda; internationally recognized creativity against crime prevention; and views of New York as a "hometown" against the aura of New York as an international center for the arts. While the tool of this conflict is the allocation of individual grants, the contention itself is about the nature of New York. The bitter struggle for control of DCA resources is one of the many mechanisms through which the future of New York City is being determined.

Funding Decisions versus Policy

The allocation of resources by the Department of Cultural Affairs is dependent on a mixture of individual political savvy and historical imperative. Charmaine Jefferson (1991) noted the consequences:

> When you have a system that allows for individual elected officials to be able to receive personal accolades for what they've done, [a politician's] entire life is dependent on: Who knows me? How many people did I get to see? and How many people did I get to like me because I did something? . . . [They] can't take [funding] away without getting into a political battle over what *they* did for this organization as a personal politician.
>
> If you end up [with] politicians arguing over individual groups . . . they're talking about pork barreling: "You give me this group, I'll give you that group."

Tying specific grants so closely to the political process (as opposed to broad priorities set by elected officials and implemented via specific programs designed and carried out by the department) means that the political mandate of being re-elected is a primary factor in designating how New York City resources are distributed to the arts. Rather than issues arising from (and related to) conditions in the arts world, political concerns such as pleasing the greatest number of people the greatest amount of time, rewarding one's friends, and otherwise attempting to ensure one's political survival are what drive New York City's allocation of arts resources (and, by extension, arts policy). Jefferson (1991) explained some of the practical outcome of this reliance on political decision making:

DCA gets bound in not being able to create [funding] flexibility . . . because then you're going to have to go and argue it with a politician. In times of budget reductions, maybe you can't take cuts across-the-board; maybe you're just going to have to eliminate funding certain organizations. In a competitive selection process, by policy you can decide, for example, that this year we're going to limit our funding to service organizations, and we're going to focus on those who are more directly involved in the art. If that is the decision I needed to make, that means I'd just simply take a group and wipe them off the line. I would [then] get called in and asked why . . . [and] asked about that group in that person's borough, that person's district. . . .

It starts to have this historical significance and no one can touch it, and it is often not . . . related to the arts; it could be a policy of you scratch my back and I'll scratch yours. . . . I think a political funding system works when you have only a few organizations, closer to the way the city was more than a hundred years ago when it created the Metropolitan Museum and the American Museum of Natural History. But now there are almost 1,600 arts organizations in the city of New York. With all the issues and concerns we have, I can't even see how politicians could possibly talk to that many organizations every year, each asking: "Won't you give me another couple of thousand dollars?" How could they possibly spend time on other issues?

Still, of all funding at a politician's disposal, it is not surprising that allocation of DCA resources is a "perk" unlikely to be relinquished. While allocating funds for extra police acknowledges a neighborhood's crime problem and substance abuse programs point to a social issue out of control, arts money is "good news" money.

Linda Adams, former special assistant for cultural affairs for the borough president of Brooklyn, explained that while the borough president, Howard Golden, put a great deal of money into the arts because he believed in the arts' capacity as an economic stabilizer and multiplier, the arts were also a highly visible form of service delivery. She gave the example of a press conference called to announce the fact that one in three people were undercounted on the census; "two and a half" reporters would show up, she remarked, while at a Brooklyn Academy of Music opening, "everyone would be there." In addition, the opening would offer the borough president the opportunity to meet and mix with his constituents, demonstrating his ability to deliver for his community (Adams 1991).

Ultimately, the distribution of resources *is* policy. What is funded is, de facto, what is encouraged and prioritized. In New York City, the competing mix of artistic, community, and political needs has meant that the Department of Cultural Affairs does not have control in setting the cultural agenda for the city. That task is carried out on fiercely protected political turf.

The Consequences of Budget Cuts

In times of economic expansion, the process by which groups get money does not seem very critical. Sufficient funding is available to satisfy basic needs, and if some segments of the artistic community receive a disproportionate share of resources, the total amount seems to be expanding and that expansion can be directed into areas needing attention. New groups to whom the circle of power and money has been previously inaccessible can be admitted to the funding cycle (as happened in the early 1970s when a number of new institutions were put on DCA's CIG roster). Throughout the 1980s, smaller organizations were also given new departmental program funding every year, through the borough arts development and commissioner's discretionary funds.

Then, in fiscal year 1989 (July 1, 1988, to June 30, 1989), cutbacks started. Kathleen Hughes (1991) described the 1990 effects on DCA:

> In FY90, we had a midyear cut. It was relatively unexpected, and disastrously imposed. It affected all the organizations that apply to us for funding that aren't fortunate enough, or politically connected enough, to get either line-item [politically designated city budget funding lines] or Borough Development Fund money. That's an extremely diverse group. It includes Paul Taylor, the Whitney Museum, and some of the more contemporary arts—some of the newer art forms [such as] media, video, television, alternative spaces, and emerging arts organizations as well [as] primarily Manhattan-based [groups]. By political fiat, we lost basically all of that money.

In fiscal year 1991, as the city's resources continued to shrink, DCA's budget received further midyear cuts, with even more occurring in 1992. New York City is currently in very poor financial shape; as of this writing, however, the Department of Cultural Affairs may not be substantially worse off than other services deemed "nonessential."

DCA, caught between competing priorities and under restrictions that make it difficult to fashion a funding policy that could deal with a reduction in resources, is at the mercy of political and financial decision making having little to do with the arts. Faced with approving drastic social service or arts service cuts, politicians are finding it increasingly hard to allocate additional discretionary monies to the arts, further reducing the department's ability to assist the arts community during a period of its own dwindling resources. DCA is facing a marginalization in both the political and artistic communities.

Pressure to Fund Public Service

Further complicating the Department of Cultural Affairs' attempt to meet the arts community's needs is the fact that the New York State constitution prohibits the city from giving outright monetary gifts to arts groups. Therefore, the department provides funding "in exchange for a specific public service, such as free or discounted performances, workshops, exhibits or cultural services that benefit the community" (New York City Department of Cultural Affairs 1988, 12). This limits the department's control over which groups it chooses to fund, since, according to Hughes (1989a),

> sometimes the people who are genuinely service providers are not necessarily the people who would win a competition based on artistic excellence. . . . The more you define public service, the more difficult it becomes to see how it's important to fund the Wooster Group [an internationally renowned avant-garde theater ensemble] as well as the Laurelton Theater [a local neighborhood-based theater company]. So we try and have it both ways. We try to find a way where the Wooster Group really is doing public service. . . . I would say we don't fund the Metropolitan Opera for what they do in Lincoln Center, we only fund the concerts that they do in the parks in the summertime. But [that answer] doesn't serve everybody . . . especially when you talk about a small organization that doesn't have the wherewithal that the Metropolitan Opera has, or when you are talking about an experimental [company] like the Wooster Group.
>
> And there is a second side to that, too: the perception of DCA. . . . Unless the agency gets involved on a certain artistic level, then it will always be thought of as [merely] . . . community stuff that is not on par with what happens [in the arts] in this city.

At its most basic level, DCA functions as a mayoral agency administering cultural funds lobbied for by politically connected constituents and designated for those constituents by elected officials. Because the department is so closely tied to city government, it takes the issue of constituent service much more literally than does the New York State Council on the Arts or the National Endowment for the Arts. This has led to an emphasis on fields in which constituent need can be easily demonstrated, such as arts in education and community arts programs, and to a stress on "numbers"—a count of New Yorkers served. This, in turn, works to the disadvantage of groups that stress art-world appeal rather than popular appeal, or those that lack the resources and administrative sophistication to collect statistics. Even before the FY1990 cutbacks (which were especially devastating to smaller, less politically connected organizations), DCA's funding roster was conspicuously lacking in experimental companies, individual artists, and other "up-and-coming" artistic communities. Even the smallest $1,000 grants have been awarded to arts organizations institutionalized enough to tap into political connections. The result of this dependence on political acumen is that New York, the world capital of artistic creativity, has a municipal arts funding agency that is irrelevant to many of the up-and-coming important artists.

The pressure to fund public service sometimes results in the artistic community and its governmental representatives speaking different languages. Jefferson (1991) reflected on this:

> A municipal government's responsibility [is] to take care of communities and neighborhoods. . . . As a municipal agency . . . we have . . . responsibility to make sure that there is service provided to the community . . . [but] the arts community as a whole has a hard time thinking of itself as a service provider. The person who wants to remain solely dedicated to creating his art, painting a painting, and never trying to share with someone else what that process is, will remain out of the funding cycle, not just in this agency, but in any agency.

Describing the arts community's historical isolation from other "quality of life" municipal services, Jefferson (1991) spoke of "that wall we created for ourselves of 'We're the arts—the higher, loftier place. You will aspire to try to reach us, and if you do, good for you, and if you don't, well, we aren't surprised.' . . . We have [to] come down from our perch and say: 'We're the same thing as a truck driver: you drive a truck, which you're dedicated to doing. It requires discipline and training. So [does] playing this cello. . . .' [If we do this, then] we will probably rise up in the ranks."

The notion of the artist as a cultural worker (so dominant in early governmental arts programs such as the 1930s WPA [Works Progress Administration] and the 1970s CETA [Comprehensive Employment and Training Act] program, yet so radically missing from the contemporary NEA and New York State Council on the Arts) is present, albeit in nascent fashion, in DCA's emphasis on contracting for services. In this way, the department is linked to early attempts to provide governmental patronage to artists, the department's limitations on assisting individual artists notwithstanding. Despite itself, the political limitations of DCA's funding have placed it squarely within the framework of America's historical attempts to connect government to the arts.

DCA-Generated Programming

The department has devised a number of programs over the years to exploit other public and private resources available in New York. The Materials for the Arts Program, begun in 1978, collects corporate and other donations of unneeded or excess furniture and other goods, and makes these available to nonprofit New York City arts groups on a first-come, first-served basis. The program has been emulated in several other cities, and is successful precisely because it takes advantage of both the high volume of business in New York and the vast size and impersonal nature of the city. While a corporation in a small city can simply donate goods to the leading theater company, the cultural cornucopia of New York makes it difficult for a business that is trying to do good to know where to start. Materials for the Arts provides a central clearinghouse certified by an official city agency, at a volume level that makes trucking and storage of donated items worth the effort. In addition, according to Susan Glass (1991), director of the program, "It costs a lot to throw things out. . . . We make it easy for [companies]. If they have a floorload of furniture or supplies, they just have to make one phone call and then it goes out to thirty groups, so it's a lot easier to distribute."

In 1989, after losing a personnel line in a DCA budget cut, Glass approached the Department of Sanitation and proposed a cosponsorship of the program (with a corresponding budgetary outlay) as a recycling/reuse program. This cooperation between city agencies is becoming common in new DCA-generated programs. However, as city agencies continue to operate under budget constraints, joint programs are often the first to be dropped. In FY92, the Department of Sanitation ended its sponsorship of Materials for the Arts.

On several occasions when city finances have become scarce the department has turned to private partners to continue public programming. In 1980, when budget cutbacks threatened the department-funded free summer concerts in the parks, DCA joined the Gulf and Western Foundation, Warner Communications, and New York Community Trust in a collaboration called the Summer Arts Fund, which raised money to help continue the concerts previously supported solely by the city. In 1989, the department began arts-in-education programming in the borough of Queens with city-funded arts organizations working in shelters with homeless children. This program has since expanded, and funding is now shared by DCA, the Board of Education, the Human Resources Administration, the New York State Department of Education, and the AT&T Foundation.

However, the department was criticized in 1989 for one such effort to obtain external funding. A DCA-sponsored poster campaign for subways, airports, and other public sites promoting New York's cultural attractions, funded by Philip Morris, garnered reproach from New York City arts groups for turning to the same donors as did the groups themselves and competing with the very organizations the campaign was intended to aid. Still, while sensitive to the issues raised, out of necessity the department seems likely to continue to seek outside resources for its programs.

Arts-in-Education

One of the major threads running through DCA programming is education, connecting the department to a municipal concern that transcends class, race, and other divisive factors: a concern for children. With New York City's strong emphasis on municipal art services benefiting a wide populace, arts education is a natural fit between arts advocates' concerns and those of municipal government, and DCA has seized on arts-in-education as a primary focus through which to carry out its service mandate.

The department's arts-in-education programming currently takes three main forms: (1) working with the major cultural institutions to facilitate their educational programs; (2) founding and supporting for the Arts-Connection Arts Exposure program; and (3) supporting of the Arts Partners Program.

Arts Education and the Cultural Institutions

Education has been considered an appropriate sphere for the city's cultural institutions as far back as the founding of the Metropolitan Museum. In 1983, DCA began to examine the ways in which the city's funding of the cultural institutions was correlated with education. The department was prodded by a report of the Mayor's Advisory Commission for Cultural Affairs entitled *Funding for Culture*, which called for assessing the funding level for cultural institutions on the basis of questions such as: "Is the institution passive in relation to its community, or does it reach out to further the education of our children and to maximize the utilization of its resources?" (1983, 100).

In 1988, the department published a booklet entitled *Reaching Out: A Review of Education and Public Programs in New York City-Funded Cultural Institutions*, which discussed the range of educational activities available in the cultural institutions, such as guided tours, exhibition programs, performances, publication of catalogues, posters, program notes and workbooks, and special children's programs or areas of exhibition. Publication of the booklet further demonstrated the department's commitment to education, and set in motion a process through which, by the very fact of the department's attention, educational programming began to receive greater prominence at the institutions. However, the political nature of the department's relationship to the delivery of city services can be seen in the report's reliance on numbers and statistics—for example, that 1,328,948 schoolchildren were served in formal programs and another 500,000 in self-guided tours in FY 1983 (Kalvert 1988, 49).

According to an arts administrator (interviewed in 1989) who did not wish to be identified, the need to prove that tax dollars are well spent on the educational programs of the cultural institutions has led to a situation in which

the institutions have to show numbers, and they all show numbers. They bring in thousands and thousands of kids. But whether that's for a real educational experience, I have my doubts. . . . If you are dealing with a couple of thousand kids a day, you can't give them a meaningful educational experience. If you are dealing with a couple [of] hundred kids a day, you can. . . . The education[al programs] of the [institutions] I think are really more about giving kids an opportunity to have lunch in another place than they are about education or introducing them to the museums.

Clearly, the fact that DCA is part of the city's system of service delivery is a determining factor in its decision to focus on the educational nature of the institutions it supports. Former DCA Deputy Director for Cultural Institutions Barbara Kalvert (1989) explained the connection of the institutions' educational missions to the department's funding:

Every year when we go for our budget hearings we always say that when you support the arts, you are supporting education, because you cannot be a well-educated citizen unless the arts are included. . . . It's important that [they are] not seen as an elitist vehicle.

It's a very important part of the budget presentation [that] it's not just scholars who go to all the museums or a particular group in society that uses concerts, but that all of these institutions make their efforts to reach out to audiences.

Just as in the founding days of the Metropolitan and American Natural History museums, when those institutions' educational functions were used to justify the institutions' receipt of public support, arts education is still the easiest mechanism by which art can make the case that it benefits the broadest swatch of New York's citizenry.

DCA Arts Education Initiatives

When facing bankruptcy in 1975, New York City slashed all programs deemed nonessential, including arts in the public school system. The newly formed Department of Cultural Affairs began designing ways in which it could help fill the gap. One of these programs is Arts Exposure, which is still collaboratively administered by DCA and an independent organization, ArtsConnection. The latter's executive director, Steve Tennen (1989), described the Arts Exposure program:

> In the fifties or sixties if you went to public school, you had music and art classes in your schools. During the fiscal crisis in 1975, all that got cut out. But what has happened is organizations like Arts-Connection have come into being to fill the gap. Our Arts Exposure program auditions [individual] artists [and looks for] artistic excellence . . . ethnic balance . . . discipline balance . . . a balance of groups that can work with early childhood and groups that can work in high schools. . . . Then we meet with someone from each school. They choose anything from five to nine groups on the roster that we then book . . . over the course of a year.

Also at work in the design of the program, explained Assistant Commissioner Hughes (1989a), was the department's wish to give work to artists: "A whole roster of artists [was] chosen to go into the public schools, and the idea was that it was a way to give them earned income. It was during the day when they were not otherwise committed, when they would have been waiting tables, when they would have been painting rooms, whatever. And it was a way of getting exposure to young people of a variety of forms of artistic disciplines." DCA's dual sense of responsibility to the arts community and the taxpaying public can be seen in this program, which attempts to meet both artists' and public schoolchildren's needs through the enactment of the artists' role as cultural worker.

A further educational initiative of the department is Arts Partners. This program was begun in 1984 and is run as a collaborative effort by the Department of Cultural Affairs, the Board of Education, and the New York City Youth Bureau, with additional support from the mayor's office and the New York Community Trust.

The Arts Partners program contracts with nonprofit arts organizations to provide arts services to public schools. According to Judith York (1989), former arts coordinator for the program:

> The school districts put together a planning team, discuss the needs of the district, set goals for the arts project, target populations, and then select arts agencies from the eligible listing. . . . A district can select as many arts agencies as they want. . . . It runs the gamut—like hotel kids in District 2, when they're looking at affective kinds of things [such as] socialization and self-esteem; to District 24 in Queens, which has over fifty different languages spoken in the homes of the kids [and enhances] cultural awareness through ethnic dance.
>
> The three city agencies have very different kinds of goals. The Youth Bureau wants affective consequences and social consequences . . . the Board of Education wants more cognitive and educational content, and the Department of Cultural Affairs is concerned about aesthetic consequences.

The lack of regular arts teachers in New York City public schools, however, has resulted in an imbalanced arts-in-education experience, according to Kalvert (1989): "You could have one hundred other [arts-in-education programs] and still not fill the needs. Certain schools get a lot, and certain schools get nothing, and within certain schools, certain classes get a lot. There's just not any kind of equity there." Mary Schmidt Campbell (1989), then DCA commissioner, noted further difficulties in the situation:

> You don't have the same growth internally in the public schools for culture [as growth within the arts community itself], so what you get is cultural groups figuring out that "Oh, I can provide something they're not providing"; . . . This rapidly growing universe [of arts groups then] begins to provide this service to the schools . . . [but they] have really remained marginal because there has been no expertise [in the schools] to absorb them in an appropriate way. The schools have no idea that we exist, for the most part.

Making the Case for Arts Education

One reason why arts-in-education is becoming a dominant concern of arts leaders is their frustration that educational leaders seem to have written off the arts as part of the educational process. According to a 1991 report, it is now "possible for a student to go from kindergarten through high school with no formal arts education. . . . arts programs are scattered among the schools with no one at the Board of Education to guide and nurture their development." Indeed, the attempt by private arts organizations and artists "to fill the void left by the decimation of school arts curriculum . . . may have unwittingly contributed to the system's abdication of responsibility for providing sustained and comprehensive education in the arts to all students" (Board of Education Task Force: Arts and Education Policy in New York City 1991, 3). In the same way that DCA's receipt of borough presidents' discretionary funding over the years may have meant that the department was granted less discretionary money of its own, the arts community's attempt to fill the gap in arts education has allowed the education sector to place less urgency on providing comprehensive school-based arts education.

DCA's struggle to maintain arts in the classroom in the face of the absence of classroom-based specialist arts teachers, and the lack of a centralized policy for arts education at the board of education, are symptomatic of the low priority given to arts education nationwide. However, while governmental resources for arts education have been scarce, corporate funding of arts in education has picked up over the past few years. For the most part, this is occurring not because of priorities within the art world, but in response to an overall corporate philanthropic shift to education.

Education, and arts-in-education alongside it, is an "easy sell" to funders not familiar with the arts—city council members as well as corporate vice presidents. DCA has managed to parlay this concern for education into a partnership with corporate sources in programs such as the Shelter Program. This further stretches the department's resources and improves the "reach" of its programs, in turn, adding to the department's case when it approaches the city council the next year.

The hybrid nature of arts-in-education as artistic yet also filling social needs serves the field by allowing it to claim priority. Diverting the mass of city arts dollars to education and other social-service-oriented arts programming, however, means that the creation of art itself gets less. By responding to New York City's social problems with arts dollars, funding sources are creating an arts hierarchy in which "pure art" takes last, if any, place. The notion of art as a tool, central to arts funding received from social-service-oriented funders, is also being reinforced in New York City by public and private *arts* funders.

Public/Private Partnerships

Much of New York City government is run on the principle of public/private partnership, the notion that government cannot completely fill the needs of its citizens and therefore must turn to the private sector. New York City does this by contracting with and overseeing private agencies in the delivery of services from cable television wiring to private bus companies. The public/private partnership notion is also applied to city services mandated by law such as housing and other social needs, at which point nonprofits often step in as the "private" partner.

DCA contracts with arts groups to provide cultural resources to the citizens of New York, in the same manner as New York City's Human Resources Administration contracts with private social service agencies to provide community-based programs such as day care or homeless drop-in centers. Thus the department does not "give grants"; it signs the same contract with arts groups that any vendor doing business with the city must sign, and its contractees go through the same approval process as any other vendor. DCA functions more like other branches of New York City government than as an "arts funder." This is a crucial point in understanding the department, which has been very difficult for the cultural community to comprehend. DCA is *not* an arts funder; it is an arm of city government. The confusion about how those two roles interrelate, given the historical and political imperatives, has shaped the struggle of DCA staff since the department's founding.

In a 1990 departmental report, *New York City and Its Cultural Resources: Strategic Policies for the 90's,* then Acting Commissioner Jefferson (1990) described the department's activities in a framework of strategic mayoral priorities such as ensuring public safety; preparing our children; promoting economic growth and opportunities; enhancing environmental quality; building and preserving neighborhoods; and maintaining fiscal stability. Jefferson also discussed the effects of New York's ten-year capital plan on cultural institutions. The document's terminology is more bureaucratic than arts-oriented in its discussion of issues such as "capital investment goals," "changing demographics," and "historical under-investment." Jefferson's report is an attempt to fit the artistic world into larger municipal priorities—economic, educational, and social. But in so doing, the needs of the arts community itself have become de-emphasized. Out of political and historical necessity, the New York City Department of Cultural Affairs has implicitly endorsed the devaluation of "art for art sake" in New York City government.

The department's programming can be understood within the context of this need to provide services designed for a nonartistic agenda. *Especially* given that DCA contractees are selected, for the most part, by nonartistic judges based on non-artistic criteria, DCA's attempt to frame the arts community within larger social concerns makes perfect sense.

Art as Municipal Service

DCA Deputy Director Jefferson (1991) commented on the department's interest in socially oriented art:

> We think the importance of the arts . . . [which] is not necessarily known by people . . . [is] its relationship to social issues, [such as] exhibitions on AIDS, which are both educational as well as serving their artistic purpose. Our groups [are] involved in drug prevention through the arts, in working with populations that may be disadvantaged or may not have had the same opportunities, [such as] our cultural programs for children living in temporary housing. We have tried to focus a great deal of attention [on] insuring and expanding the involvement of arts organizations in society as a whole, which is part of what we think is necessary for the future.

While all government arts agencies struggle with the duality of serving both the artistic community and the public whose tax dollars provide support, the arm's-length protection from legislators set up at the state and federal levels is completely absent at the city level. As Hughes (1989b) remarked: "The NEA defines itself, or [did] until very recently, as being [at] more than arm's length from government. . . . But [DCA] is right in there . . . in terms of being government. . . . There's a big [gap] between a group of arts professionals who have their own priorities and a process that is run by the elected officials . . . [and DCA's staff is] trying to figure out how to balance it all."

Education (targeted at the school-age population) and access (targeted at potential audiences of all ages) are the two main avenues the department has chosen for providing arts services to New York's broadest populace. The public service nature of the department makes it impossible to award artist fellowships or fund the creation of work. It is, however, allowed to fund that work's widest possible dissemination. In subsidizing ticket sales to the elderly, students, and other special populations, as well as sponsoring free concerts in the parks, the department is aware that it often subsidizes a company's other activities.

For groups who understand how to "package" their rehearsals as opportunities for the public, or performances as low-cost community service, DCA's emphasis on cultural service is simply another funding hoop to jump through. But for those accustomed to thinking of themselves as "artists" and to judging themselves solely on artistic grounds, DCA seems extraneous to their concerns.

City government as an instrument through which the department serves its constituency does more than govern the areas of the arts upon which it concentrates. While DCA directs its funding to arts organizations concerned with education, access, socially oriented programming, and funding determined by connections to a political constituency, the triple relationship among the arts community, the tax-paying public, and the political sector determines more than the focus of DCA's programs. The Department of Cultural Affairs' negotiation of this triple relationship *is* the shape of local arts in New York City.

DCA: A Triple Constituency

Is the Department of Cultural Affairs a medium for fulfilling local political priorities, or is it the instrument of municipal government through which the arts community's needs are met? If the answer is *both,* then the skill with which DCA's administrators navigate city government is crucial to the success of the department's mission(s).

New York City government is notoriously labyrinthine, ridden with fiercely protected fiefdoms, strewn with historical imperatives, and filled with scorn for political newcomers lacking the savvy to master its intricate and unspoken rules. DCA's concern about depoliticizing the process of arts funding is seen by some New York City political officials as naive; one official commented that all public money was political and was therefore "dirty money," and that if arts groups didn't like that they should get out of the political fray. No one, according to this official, was "above" politics if they took public money (Adams 1991). DCA's emphasis on trying to change the political process, rather than mastering the system of backhanded dealing, has not helped the department's standing in the city. DCA is seen as a lightweight agency, described as "the Motor Vehicles Bureau of city agencies [where] other people make decisions and the agency processes the paper"; its complaints about arts groups having to master the political process are seen by some as foolish. Perhaps *because* of DCA's reluctance to get "down and dirty" in city politicking, the department is not trusted as a decision maker about city monies and is therefore given even less discretion than if it "made deals."

In looking wistfully to the New York State Council on the Arts and the NEA, and spending its political capital trying to gain independence from the political process, DCA is caught between its constituencies. As a mayoral agency, the department is mandated to carry out the priorities of the mayor; it is also directed with overseeing the health of the arts in the city. The priorities of locally based politicians—the borough presidents and city council members—are of paramount importance to the funding it receives to carry out its charges.

Other mayoral agencies cope with these competing demands by the skillful exercise of city politics. But the DCA staff retains the traditional focus of the arts on talent and the quality of creative work, and it values artistic credentials over political merit. While the department is struggling to adjust to political realities, in one politician's view the arts community's adherence to "standards" and "artistic decision making" is diverting DCA from achieving any real power in city politics.

In addition, the artistic community, which *could* help the department in its quest for political power, is itself politically naive. Smaller arts groups are overwhelmed at the morass of city politics, and the major institutions are not ready for the political decentralization implied by the new city charter, according to one political aide interviewed in 1991, who requested anonymity. Though the department is holding "town meetings" to explain to arts groups how they can influence the city's budget adoption process and has published a detailed schema of the steps involved in budget approval under the new charter (New York City Department of Cultural Affairs 1991), the arts community's traditional view of itself as "nonpolitical" gives other equally hard-hit communities a head start in reaching politically connected parties. DCA's reluctance to embrace the political process may have cost it dearly.

Indeed, DCA sustained a 28 percent cut in the FY92 budget, causing many of the city's major arts institutions to substantially reduce their hours and services to the public. In addition, DCA Commissioner Mary Schmidt Campbell resigned in October 1991 to assume the position of dean of New York University's Tisch School of the Arts. Luis R. Cancel, former executive director of the Bronx Museum of the Arts, was appointed as commissioner after a three-month search during which the idea of folding DCA into the Department of Parks and Recreation was once again floated in the press. At this writing, no further reduction in DCA budget is projected by the mayor's office over the next four years: given the history documented here, that will happen only if DCA and the arts organizations it represents are able to skillfully maneuver through the shoals of NYC politics.

New York City has eight million inhabitants of widely varying ethnic backgrounds, social conditions, and cultural interests. The Department of Cultural Affairs is responsible for seeing that these inhabitants' cultural needs, and those of the business and tourist communities, are met. The extent to which the Department of Cultural Affairs can come to grips with its artistic and cultural nature, and with the political processes enmeshed within, is the extent to which it will succeed on any of these counts.

Note

The epigraphs at the beginning of this chapter were taken from interviews cited in the reference list.

References

Adams, Linda. 1991. Interview by author, Mar. 22.

Baumol, William J., and William G. Bowen. 1966. *Performing Arts: The Economic Dilemma*. New York: The Twentieth Century Fund.

Benedict, Stephen. 1991. Interview by author, Feb. 8.

Board of Education Task Force: Arts and Education Policy in New York City. 1991. *Crisis & Opportunity: A Report to the Chancellor and the Board of Education on the Role of the Arts in New York City Public Schools*. New York: Alliance for the Arts.

Campbell, Mary Schmidt. 1989. Interview by author, Aug. 16.

City Of New York. 1989. *Official Directory*.

Glass, Susan. 1991. Interview by author, Feb. 22.

Glueck, Grace. 1976. "City Forms First Cultural Agency." *New York Times*. Feb. 11: 40.

Haworth, John. 1991. Interview by author, Feb. 22.

Hughes, Kathleen. 1989a. Interview by author, May 30.

———. 1989b. Interview by author, Aug. 22.

———. 1991. Interview by author, Feb. 20.

Jefferson, Charmaine. 1990. *New York City and Its Cultural Resources: Strategic Policies for the '90s*. New York: NYCDCA.

———. 1991. Interview by author, Mar. 20.

Kalvert, Barbara. 1988. *Reaching Out: A Review of Education & Public Programs in New York City-Funded Cultural Institutions*. New York: NYCDCA.

———. 1989. Interview by author, June 1.

Mayor's Advisory Commission for Cultural Affairs. 1983. *Funding for Culture: The Cultural Policy of the City of New York*. Report to the Mayor by the Mayor's Advisory Commission for Cultural Affairs. New York: NYCDCA.

Mayor's Committee on Cultural Policy. 1974–75. Papers 1974–75. Stephen Benedict, New York.

New York City Department of Cultural Affairs. 1991. "Highlights of the City Budget Process as of May 10, 1991." New York: NYCDCA.

———. 1980–1990. *Annual Reports 1979–1989.* New York: NYCDCA.

———. 1989. "Education Report 1989." Unpublished document. New York: NYCDCA.

———. 1989. "Public Service Contract Proposal FY90." New York: NYCDCA.

———. 1988. *The New York City Budget Process and the Department of Cultural Affairs: A Guide to the City Budget Process, the Department of Cultural Affairs, and the Community Boards.* New York: NYCDCA.

Rockefeller Panel. 1965. *The Performing Arts: Rockefeller Panel Report on the Future of Theatre, Dance, Music in America.* New York: McGraw-Hill.

Segal, Ryna Appleton. 1976. *The New York City Department of Cultural Affairs, 1962 to 1973: A Record of Government's Involvement in the Arts.* New York: NYCDCA.

Tennen, Steve. 1989. Interview by author, June 14.

Tomkins, Calvin. 1970. *Merchants and Masterpieces: The Story of the Metropolitan Museum of Art.* New York: E. P. Dutton.

York, Judith A. 1989. "New York City Arts Partners: Teachers and Artists as Effective Partners for Arts in Education." Ph.D. diss., New York University.

———. 1989. Interview by author, May 13.

✤ 8 ✤

Gentrification and the Avant-Garde in New York's East Village

ANNE E. BOWLER AND BLAINE MC BURNEY

With a mixture of giddy self-promotion and unabashed hype, New York's East Village burst onto the international art scene in the summer of 1982 in a media explosion that was, even by its detractors' accounts, of astonishing proportions. Soon almost as famous for its controversial role in the gentrification of one of the nation's worst ghettos as for the aesthetic sensations aroused by its trademark neo-Expressionist and graffiti-style painting, the East Village scene was hailed by insiders and observers alike as the art world's newest avant-garde. Feature after feature on this new bohemia appeared in the pages of *Art in America, Arts, Artforum,* and even the *Wall Street Journal.* As two of its own self-styled critics proclaimed, "The art world has done it again. With no warning to speak of, a new avant-garde has been launched" (Robinson and McCormick 1984, 135).

A genuine phenomenon was officially under way. Media attention surrounding the latest bohemia peaked in 1983–84, at which point the East Village housed a network of over forty commercial galleries. Currently, as the smoke has cleared and the initial clamor has subsided, only a handful of these galleries remain, as a more routinized arts community finds itself once again at the mercy of the fickle art market. Meanwhile the gentrification process continues unabated, now forcing out many of the original artists, clubs, and galleries that were themselves responsible for initially attracting a new population of the upwardly mobile middle class. Accumulating tensions amidst skyrocketing rents and threats of displacement finally exploded in July 1988 with one of the worst instances of urban rioting in this decade. This time media attention focused not on the galleries and art scene, but rather on the clashes between club-wielding policemen and various members of the local community (*New York Times* 1988). Since then, protests over the city-sponsored demolition of a squatter's tenement and its eviction of the homeless from public parks indicate that such social eruptions are likely to continue (Ferguson 1989).

This chapter attempts to sort through the confusion of conflicting claims that have surrounded the East Village since its "renaissance" in the early 1980s. Just what is the aesthetic value and political significance of this scene? Have its artists been agents of gentrification, as some have argued, or are they merely its dupes and victims? Can the East Village rightly be described as an epicenter of the new avant-garde, or has it been merely its endgame, a simulacrum cannily exploited for marketing purposes? How much of this latest bohemia has been the creation of the institution-alized culture industry, and how much is it the expression of genuine revolt against the institutionalized "patronage system" of late capitalism? And finally, to situate this phenomenon in the center of a contemporary heated debate, are the events surrounding the East Village an example of a pernicious anything-goes postmodernism or the confused but important strivings of nascent critical cultural forms?

Material History and the Question of Cultural Continuity

The East Village has a long and lively history as an arena of aesthetic practice and political activism. As a point of embarkation for a variety of immigrant ethnic groups since the nineteenth century, the area has seen the likes of Yiddish theater, the Christodora Settlement House (now luxury co-ops), an assortment of socialist and anarchist movements, and Abstract Expressionists of the 1950s. More recently, it has been called home by a collection of 1960s countercultural representatives (Sandler 1984; R. Lawson 1986; Sanders 1979; Schoener 1967).

But an uninterrupted history or tradition should not be presupposed. Despite the romantic image suggested by the above list, the recent "renais-sance" in the East Village has involved a radically new and qualitatively different type of influx into the area, precipitated by almost twenty years of abject abandonment and decay. An impoverished working-class neigh-borhood for over one hundred years, the larger part of the East Village known as Loisaida (as well as the Lower East Side directly to its south) originally received New York's successive immigrant waves. Vastly over-crowded in the early part of the century (at one point over a half million people resided in its less than two square miles), its population steadily decreased after the 1920s, with the heaviest decline taking place through-out the 1960s. By the 1980 census, only 150,000 remained (Berman 1983,

12). As the tides of immigration slowly subsided, those who could afford to move out did so; like most major American cities, in recent years New York has seen a gradual transformation of its labor base into the growing service sector of a new and allegedly "postindustrial" society.

The term "postindustrial" has been used to describe a host of presumed theoretical and empirical changes in the structure and dynamics of late-twentieth-century Western capitalism. As such, it is a controversial term (Bell 1973; Browning and Singelman 1978; Gershuny 1977; 1978; Gustafson 1979; Kumar 1978; Mandel 1978; Offe 1985). Here, it is employed in a general sense to describe empirical shifts in occupational patterns and labor markets within the U.S. economy as a whole and the New York City economy in particular. These shifts are characterized by a decline in agricultural, manufacturing, and other manual labor-based industries along with a dramatic rise in various white-collar service industries including corporate business, health, finance, education, legal, and social services. This transformation of the labor market has had serious consequences for various urban neighborhood economies and, by extension, for the housing markets of these same urban neighborhoods (Gale 1984; Zukin 1989). A 1981 study by Stanback and Noyelle demonstrated that New York City is indeed one of the most rapidly restructuring of the "postindustrial" urban economies (see also Fleetwood 1979).

According to the U.S. Census Bureau, in 1950 almost one-third of New York's total workforce was engaged in manufacturing. By 1970, this proportion had declined to one-fifth of the total. The number of machine shops in the Lower East Side alone declined from 60 in 1950 to only 8 in 1978 (Zukin 1989, 23–33). At the same time, white-collar employment linked to New York's growing role as the international capital of business, banking, and finance expanded dramatically. During the period between March 1978 and March 1984, while over 100,000 blue-collar jobs disappeared from the city's industrial base, 215,000 new jobs were added during the same period, overwhelmingly in business and financial services-related sectors (Deutsche and Ryan 1984, 94). These transformations in the labor base of New York's economy are both the immediate causes of the decimation of the working-class neighborhoods of the Lower East Side and a precondition for their gentrification.

By the late 1960s, large-scale abandonment, brought on by the long years of impoverishment and neglect as well as a new and flourishing drug trade, began in earnest. Census records for a six-square-block-area between Avenues B and D, between Third and Sixth streets alone, show a population drop between 1970 and 1980 from 7,799 to 2,721 (Gottlieb 1982, 11). Through the haze of gang warfare, arson for profit, and a generalized culture of violence, there emerged a new "city of ruins" (to use Marshall Berman's eloquent phrase [1983, 12]). Loisaida suffered especially from this decline: large sections of blocks lay in rubble, a burgeoning heroin trade grew unchecked out of the abandoned housing shells, and a singularly destitute population, largely Puerto Rican, was left to fend for itself.

But in the early 1980s new signs of life began to emerge in a neighborhood that was the last significant low-rent district in Manhattan south of Central Park. Storefront galleries and underground performance clubs began to appear as young artists, effectively priced out of nearby (but now chic) Soho and Greenwich Village, sought cheap housing, studio space, and a new sense of community.

Yet this is not enough to explain the massive transformation of the East Village. A strong cultural component in this transformation has been an important catalyst for these economic forces. Manhattan, arguably the center of the international art market, has been the site of two previous neighborhood transformations that bear directly upon the explosion of the East Village scene: Greenwich Village and Soho (Simpson 1981; Zukin 1989). Despite vast differences, all three areas share one compelling component: the artist. So by 1980, the East Village had become, as one *New York Times* critic phrased it, "Manhattan's third art district, after uptown and Soho" (Glueck 1983, 27). The economic value of the East Village has been based as much on its unfolding art scene as its booming real estate market. More accurately, the two are inextricably bound. Long accustomed to sniffing at the heels of young artists with the successes of Greenwich Village and Soho behind them, speculators and developers lost no time in capitalizing on this hot new "art neighborhood." The image of a new bohemia in Manhattan has been an attractive one from the points of view of both the real estate and art markets. While previous cultural institutions (both formal and informal) have been a significant part of the area's history, none has provided such a strong base for both the current cultural scene and its massive ecological transformation over the last decade.

With these issues in mind, we are situating our analysis of the East Village within three interrelated axes of influence. First, we will discuss the role of urban demographics and the politics of private/public sector collusion in relation to real estate practices and processes of urban gentrification. Second, we will examine the selection processes of the commercial culture industry, organized for the maximization of profit and the commodification of modernist cultural icons. And finally, we will examine the existence of a critical, autonomous subculture that should be understood as an expression of genuine resistance. Taken in isolation, each of these three dimensions cannot offer an adequate explanation of the East Village. Understood together as a nexus of complicated and often conflicting relations, a more nuanced, critical, and nonreductive picture of events emerges. While the gentrification of the East Village cannot be understood outside of the dynamics of culture, the latter, in turn, are delimited by the realities of macro-level economic and historical processes.

Gentrification, Displacement, and the Artist

Studies of gentrification, both within and outside the academy, have tended to misunderstand many of the structural forces and consequences of this process (Sites 1987). Journal literature in the early 1980s concerning the problem of gentrification (defined as the "immigration to inner-city neighborhoods of a wealthier professional class of residents") has largely concerned itself with answering the debates of the previous decade about the existence of a true "urban renaissance" hailed by the national media of the same period (Henig 1980, 638; 1982, 344). Largely downplayed in this literature on gentrification is its major consequence: the displacement of vulnerable members of the already existing population (the poor, members of the low-to-moderate-income working class, the elderly, and ethnic or racial minorities) who are driven out as a result of the economic and social pressures that gentrification induces. Indeed, dismissing displacement as an accidental byproduct of gentrification, editors of a 1984 collection argued not only that this problem has been perhaps overrated, but even that existing evidence of its presumed reality may in fact be skewed by the general "poor renter" history and instability of the lower classes: such people would move on anyway (London and Palen 1984, 261–62). Conversely, a potentially important class analysis of displacement by Smith and LeFaivre (1984), in the end, misses the more subtle configurations of public and private-sector collusion. Here, overwhelming emphasis on the invariably determinant role of capital occludes recognition of the variety of permutations this public/private relationship can take. Unrecognized as well are both present and possible forms and structures of opposition and protest—among which are those led by the presumably gentrifying agents, the artists.

Amidst heated debate, media treatments of gentrification and displacement in the East Village have presented an equally problematic variety of assessments. Art-world commentary has largely left such critical issues unacknowledged in favor of an emphasis on artistic agendas and events. The dismissal of the human significance of gentrification is typified by local critics Robinson and McCormick's complaint about "pseudo-sociological examinations of shifts in neighborhood population" (1984, 141). More pernicious, perhaps, have been those reviews and articles capitalizing on the area's drug trade and decay as a source of decadent glamour. Again, Robinson and McCormick write of a "unique blend of poverty, punk rock, drugs, arson, Hell's Angels, winos, prostitutes and dilapidated housing that adds up to an adventurous avant-garde setting of considerable cachet" (1984, 135). The rhetoric of such articles (which have become a familiar banner of the scene) has served a dual cynical role. First, it justifies the ideology of gentrification as "neighborhood improvement involving the displacement of social undesirables," while, second, it openly markets various artists and galleries to middle-class consumers presumably in search of excitement. More recently, Neil Smith (1989) has explored the widespread use of the iconographic symbolism of the "frontier" as it has been mobilized in the media to further the "glamorous" edge of gentrification in the East Village.

Other reports have tended to ignore the structures of economic and political power behind area investment practices even while covering the vulture-like swoops of "big gun" developers following initial artist colonization (Unger 1984). In contrast, in one article that does examine the relationship between the art scene and displacement process as it applies to the East Village, Deutsche and Ryan (1984) present a carefully detailed attack on the forces behind its gentrification, pointing out the significant collusion between city officials eager to encourage private investment and a real estate market waiting to capitalize on the development of conveniently located Manhattan neighborhoods. They show that the appearance of providing direct and indirect support to artists hides the real beneficiaries of such "patronage": a burgeoning class of young Wall Street professionals.

At the same time, in this and other such analyses wherein big developers and New York "patricians" use "low-cost arts patronage as a tool of neighborhood de-stabilization" (Zukin 1989, 184), artists are viewed either as the dupes or collaborators of gentrification. Thus, the conceptually distinct social role called "artist" is conflated with the meaningful aesthetic-political choices made by various individual artists. Indeed, in these analyses, the latter is reduced to the former, and no creative or critical response is deemed possible.

This is not to argue against the view that artists did play an (often unintended) role as catalysts in the transformation of the East Village into a real-estate gold mine. Nor should the greed of certain artists' groups for securing public subsidies for low-income housing be dismissed. In 1982, public exposure of one such case, the city-sponsored debacle known as the

Artists Home Ownership Program (AHOP), provoked bitter controversy pitting artists against an already pressured, increasingly impoverished minority population (Derocher 1982; Deutsche and Ryan 1984; Goldstein 1982; MFY Legal Services 1982; *Village Voice* 1983). But one-dimensional vilifications of artists as the primary agents of gentrification shift critical attention from the larger economic and political forces at work, as well as from the city officials and political leaders who carefully ignored the condition of this devastated area for over twenty years. Indeed, through owner development and tax default, by the late 1970s the city had acquired title to nearly seven hundred buildings and lots in the neighborhood, approximately 60 percent of the area's total housing stock (Gottlieb 1982, 20; Deutsche and Ryan 1984, 97). Yet the city consistently failed to develop the low- and moderate income housing so desperately needed out of these holdings. Instead, it employed a new rhetoric of crisis, designed to provide the ideological justification for doling out economic incentives to private development. It is precisely this type of strategy that Mayor Edward Koch put forward in the spring of 1982, when he announced the privately funded AHOP as part of the fight against "abandonment and decay" on the Lower East Side (*New York Times* 1982, B6).

Yet while widespread neighborhood protests forestalled the realization of AHOP in the end, city officials employed a similar rhetoric in the promotion of its Cross Subsidy Program (or "Double-Cross Subsidy" as it became known among neighborhood residents), a deal struck in 1987 between the Department of Housing Preservation and Development and the local Community Board to sell off city owned properties to private developers for the creation of a thousand units of market-rate housing. Under the agreement, profits would then be used to develop another thousand units of vaguely specified "low-" and "moderate-income" housing. Even adjusted to this new 50/50 ratio (down from the 20/80 that city housing officials had originally proposed) the viability of any real low-income housing emerging from this plan seems nebulous at best. More controversial is the fact that Cross Subsidy, if realized, would contribute to the direct displacement of local squatters' groups who have worked to reclaim abandoned city-owned buildings for their own use (Ferguson 1989, 31).

Given the volatility of East Village housing patterns, gaining a clearer understanding of the gentrification process may be one of the central tasks for urban sociologists of the next decade. While the renewed real estate interest in older cities across America has made itself most apparent in the construction of new skyscrapers, shopping centers, hotels, and luxury condominiums in formerly blighted downtown areas, also prevalent (though far less visible) is the move toward "recycling": the trendy redevelopment of heavily deteriorated inner-city neighborhoods into chic urban enclaves. In the early stages, such areas (like the East Village) offer cheap living and spaces for small businesses, as well as a huge cache of unpopulated buildings that provide potential opportunities for upscale renovation and windfall profits. No wonder that in the early 1980s in New York, given the combination of the immediate precedent of the development of adjacent Soho (Zukin 1989), the massive redevelopment of Lower Manhattan's business district (Robinson 1976), and a city-wide vacancy rate in 1982 at the then all time low of 2.1 percent (Gottlieb 1982, 11), there was more than sufficient impetus to set dollar signs dancing in the heads of speculators and local landlords in the East Village.

Economic factors alone, however, do not fully explain the pattern of colonization and restructuring that the East Village has since undergone. Rather, as Castells has argued, changes in urban form and function, as well as processes of urban conflict, here as elsewhere have involved questions of cultural identity and meaning (1983, xviii–ix). As in Castells's own analysis of San Francisco's Castro District, initial movement into the East Village involved young artists and other individuals who expressed themselves in terms of alternative or countercultural values and norms. As the post-punk inheritors of intellectual and artistic practices and events that had existed on and off in the area during the two or three previous decades, they established crude storefront galleries, small performance clubs, and an active and vibrant street-life through which they sought to uphold the values of artistic community, creativity, and a rejection of suburban lifestyles.

In this respect, of course, "self-patron" artists in the East Village followed the path of their predecessors in Soho. But the gentrification of Soho began as the colonization of what were, for the most part, empty industrial warehouses, the concretized residue of a changing urban economy. The East Village development, by contrast, involved the displacement of an established poor minority population from the beginning. Thus, while Loisaida, especially, contained sometimes entire blocks of burned-out, abandoned, and boarded-up buildings, it was not these spaces that were first inhabited by the incoming young artists. Rather, it was only after this population had started to become visible as inhabitants of the neighborhood that its transformation into a new bohemian outpost could be successfully marketed and fully established, with the takeover of habitable space needing little renovation. That much of the area still remains garbage strewn, drug embattled, and dangerous not only seems not to have inhibited upscale colonization practices but, aestheticized in the media as part of a "decadent bohemian landscape," seems rather to have even encouraged gentrification. Thus, one *Village Voice* art critic spoke of her decision to live in luxury co-op Christodora (the building stands as something of a symbolic bellwether in the neighborhood, having been a settlement house at the turn of the century and headquarters for the Black Panthers in the late 1960s): "I like that it is very mixed and very weird. I like it in the way I like to ride subways: there's a kind of realness about it. I feel like I'm in touch with stuff here" (Alson 1989, 26).

It is the early stages of gentrification processes that bear particular scrutiny, for it is here that the promise of increased rent revenues have provided an incentive for landlords to move from the passive neglect of blighted buildings to active displacement tactics. Such tactics have typically included the installation of drug dealers into buildings, suspicious fires, inept or completely neglected repairs, verbal and physical harassment of tenants, long periods without heat and hot water, broken front-door locks encouraging activity from high-crime streets, and unpaid electrical bills leaving dark and dangerous hallways (Gottlieb 1982; Newfield 1984; Robbins 1981; Sites 1985). The success of such measures in insuring the flight of already vulnerable minority and elderly tenants likely to hold rent-controlled leases has paved the way for a higher level of renter. At the same time, "cleaning out" buildings in this way also serves to increase resale value to the generally more monied and publicly legitimate "second wave" type of owner. As a lawyer for one investment group in the area was quoted several years ago: "My investors do not rape buildings. We buy from the rapers of buildings" (Gottlieb 1982, 13). Indeed, it has not been unusual for the value of a building to increase proportionally as the number of its empty units has gone up.

Crucial to this war of upheaval in neighborhoods like the East Village are the city- and state-sponsored agencies that, however unwittingly, have given tacit or even explicit support to such methods. What needs to be understood here is the web of conflicting interests and values embedded within the public agencies organized for the protection of tenant rights but which provide ambiguous services at best. This dimension of gentrification is usually ignored by the existing literature—whether written by sympathetic urbanologists who tend to decry the role artists have often played in the process, or the art critics who have applauded the artists instead. Both groups of analysts may deplore the upscale developers but they differently identify their "victims."

Unstabilized commercial rents help insure that long-time, inexpensive neighborhood fixtures like the family-run Orchida Restaurant are, despite a widespread and highly publicized battle, eventually displaced by a well-known ice cream chain. For residential tenants, ostensibly protected by rent stabilization laws, the results are proving much the same. Poorly enforced housing code regulations, safety guidelines, a labyrinthine bureaucracy of public agencies, and an overburdened housing court have allowed dynamic slumlords like Paul Stallings and Maurice Roth (who from 1980 to 1985 owned up to one hundred buildings in the area) to amass hundreds of safety violations without censure (Newfield 1984, 42). Pressured by legal action from a well-organized tenants association, such landlords may then "flip" ownership back and forth, in the process artificially inflating the value of a decimated building as it is gradually vacated. As one frustrated community housing worker said in an interview with the author: "We inform people of their legal rights which the city and government says they want tenants to know . . . but they don't like it when these people are aware of their rights and fight for them. People complain and the city responds very slowly—how do these people who are sick from no heat, the cold, deal with this?" (Bowler 1985, 19).

The success of displacement at this early stage provides the groundwork for large-scale speculation and development to begin in earnest. Once buildings have been emptied, lax warehousing laws have encouraged new owners to keep vacant apartments unrented for long stretches of time, allowing one vote per empty unit in the typical co-op conversion plan (Pileggi 1985, 34–37). Even more significant, however, have been the consequences of displacement for the economic and ecological restructuring of the neighborhood as a whole. As a *Village Voice* journalist, Martin Gottlieb, noted as early as 1982: "The Lower East Side is no longer a neighborhood where rents are pegged to the maximum welfare rental allowance or to what poor working families can afford. It is a neighborhood where the open market and the poorly enforced rent stabilization limits have taken over" (11).

Apartment by apartment and building by building, gradually the neighborhood has been transformed. Small slumlords like Stallings and Roth gave way to a new wave of owners like Harry Skydell or "Baby" Jane Holzer, Manhattan socialite and self-styled real estate entrepreneur, whose company name, Lower East Side Redevelopment, foreshadowed a radically altered rent clientele. As the city has continued to auction off its holdings to private investors and as rental rates have soared to as much as $1,000 per month for a railroad flat in a tenement building on the still drug-embattled and garbage-strewn Avenue B, not only minority populations but finally even the artists themselves have been forced out.

The Cultural Politics of the East Village:
The Good, the Bad, and the Ugly

It bears repeating that the dimension of housing and gentrification alone cannot begin to explain the extraordinary phenomenon of the East Village. Indeed, a more robust understanding, one that would account for the unprecedented amount of international attention the neighborhood has received, must include an understanding of its specifically cultural nature.

With this task in mind, we now turn to the remaining axis of influence. On the one hand, we may speak of the substantive revolt of a younger generation of artists against the complacency and expanding vacuity of the patronage system typified by the Soho scene in particular and the art world in general. This rebellion calls into question many long-held modernist assumptions regarding the values of the avant-garde, the effects of the commodification of art, and the relationship of the art world to a public. At the same time this "revolt" has been itself patronized by the established New York art media in particular, which has mobilized the cultural icon of the avant-garde in order to both solidify New York's tottering position in the international art world and stimulate a sagging art market at home.

The degree to which the East Village may be described as a "bohemia" illustrates the conflicting social roles and historical ambiguity of bohemia itself. With respect to this ambiguity, bohemia may be understood in the broader symbolic sense of a cultural icon or in the more specific sense of the recurring phenomenon of urban arts communities existing in opposition to established social, political, and, in particular, aesthetic norms. The two senses of the term are, of course, related; bohemia may exemplify a genuine revolt against bourgeois capitalist life (Clark 1982; Graña 1964), or an institutionalized enclave where middle-class youth may harmlessly experiment with the problematic boundaries of modern individualism before returning to the fold of more conventional lifestyles (Siegel 1986). Victor Turner's (1974) structuralist approach argues that bohemia, understood as "institutionalized anti-structure," serves as a pressure-release valve vis-à-vis the tensions and divisions within social systems. Thus, bohemia ultimately serves the interests of social integration and the established order. Other analysts simply present a highly depoliticized account of bohemia, opting rather for an "artworld" interpretation that locates the activities of bohemia well within the boundaries of noncritical, nonrevolutionary reform (Easton 1964; Richardson 1969).

One would expect that a specific bohemia may go through several transitions from one aspect to another over a period of time. Critical moments where genuinely radical challenges are articulated may be buried under ameliorating histories that emphasize only the end results. Thus, in the case of the East Village, aspects of bohemia as a radical and critical subculture have existed along with aspects of bohemia as a harmless, chic party-playground for middle-class consumption (Dowd 1985). These latter dimensions of the East Village are directly related to the unprecedented rapidity with which, in concert with private and public developers, the leading organs of the established art world descended upon, publicized, and labeled the East Village art community. Within months of the appearance of the area's first new galleries in July of 1981, both the art press and mainstream media sprang into action. The reasons behind this rabid enthusiasm are not hard to discern. By the end of the 1970s, critics, dealers, and museum curators alike agreed that the New York art world was moribund and provincial or, as one commentator put it, "it's kind of boring, nothing's really happening" (Taylor 1987, 101). Others warned that such a state of affairs could undermine "America's dominance of Europe," possibly leading to a disastrous "shift in the balance of aesthetic power" (Taylor 1987, 101; Brenson 1983). Thus, the spectacle of the East Village came as a breath of fresh air to a New York art industry desperately in need of something new to recapture its international hegemony.

Once again dipping into the seemingly bottomless well of the "cult of the new" and avant-gardist renewal, the industry sought to portray the East Village as the epicenter of dramatic aesthetic events (Pincus-Witten 1985). However, the established art media have used their institutionalized power as the gatekeepers of aesthetic value to effectively censor much of the more radical, interesting, and critical art, thereby trivializing the East Village as a whole while supporting a more palatable group of artists to its conservative, upper-middle-class-based market.

Striking examples of this culture-industry phenomenon may be seen in the cases of painter Kenny Scharf and writer Tama Janowitz. In both instances national and sometimes international publicity was directed at these artists in a manner that illustrates the distorted values of the culture industry. In the case of Scharf (who paints wild and colorful images as well as "customizing" mass-produced objects in the same style), a feature-length cover story in the September 1985 issues of *ARTnews* is representative of the culture industry "plugging" and labeling processes that produce the art world "star system" (Marzoratti 1985). The *ARTnews* piece actually spends a great deal of time discussing everything but Scharf's artworks. Instead we are treated to a journalistic tableau of downtown parties, clubs, and "personalities." The opening words of the piece are indicative of its entire tone and style: "Andy Warhol said, 'You have to go to it.'" We are then told that at a party attended by Scharf, Jean Michel Basquiat was seen, that "Matt Dillon was leaning in a corner," that Steve Rubell and Tatum O'Neal were spotted, and that Scharf once met Sean Lennon and Yoko. We are also told what Scharf wore to the event ("pink hip-hugger pants by Stephen Sprouse") and that as a child of seven Scharf liked to spend his time sitting extremely close to the television set until (in his own words) he "would see these intense colors, like dots." We also learn that Scharf likes to fingerpaint.

When remarks are actually directed at Scharf's art they are generally occasional, disconnected, and highly problematic. Thus we are told that Scharf's painting "owes something to Surrealism," and the names of Miró and Tanguy are duly dropped. But as Gerald Marzoratti, author of the piece, observes: "Scharf's paintings for all their oneiric strangeness, don't work on you the way Surrealist paintings do. There is none of the still spooky dread. There is no sex or sexual terror. There is no suffering, no anxiety of any kind. . . . Scharf's are not dreams you wake sweating from or brood about. It is surrealism without the dark edge of night, surrealism for the fun of it" (1985, 77).

Indeed, the core of Scharf's aesthetic does seem to be "fun." As Scharf himself remarks: "The whole thing about fun—I think about that alot. I think everyone wants to have fun. I think that having fun is being happy. I know it's not all fun, but maybe fun helps with the bad. I mean, you definitely cannot have too much fun. . . . It's like I want to have fun when I'm painting. And I want people to have fun looking at the paintings. When I think, what should I do next?, I think: more, newer, better, nower, funner" (Marzoratti 1985, 77–78).

Scharf's strategy of nostalgic reference and quotation from 1960s cartoons is ultimately arbitrary. There seems to be literally no point to it other than having "fun." Much the same could be said for Scharf's aesthetic of customization. Television sets and radios are painted in bright day-glow colors and covered with tiny plastic tubes, figurines, or tufts of mohair. Says Scharf, "Customization is saying it's plastic anyway, so go all the way."

In the case of Tama Janowitz, the process by which her 1986 novel *Slaves of New York* became the most recognized literary work to emerge from the East Village and Janowitz herself an oft-photographed celebrity and society-page figure illustrates similar problematic culture-industry processes. Indeed, according to many local observers of the literary community, it is not at all clear which came first, Janowitz's "success" in the society pages and club circuit or the "success" of her collection of short stories. Janowitz had already published two other books that had received scant attention, when she began to appear regularly in photographs with Andy Warhol and other socialites in the pages of magazines like *Interview*. Shortly thereafter, her third book, *Slaves of New York*, began to "take off" with the help of active plugging by Warhol. Subsequently, in combination with the (widely panned) film version of *Slaves of New York*, Janowitz appeared at the opening celebration for a Bloomingdale's boutique of the same name. Yet, while several of Janowitz's short stories are interesting, even the casual observer of the East Village's literary scene could not fail to have noticed that far more interesting and aesthetically provocative works have appeared regularly in the pages of local journals like *The Portable Lower East Side* or *Between C and D*. However, these works have typically been ignored by the "tastemakers" of *Interview*, *Vanity Fair*, and their ilk.

For the East Village arts community, the cumulative and negative effects of culture-industry hype and labeling (as evidenced in the cases of Scharf and Janowitz) should not be underestimated. Such practices have distorted the real picture of events in the East Village, making it easier for observers who are not directly familiar with events to ignore the possibility that serious artists are at work there and otherwise to dismiss their significance. At the same time, this publicity has contributed directly to the perpetuation of a one-sided view by both attracting and rewarding a certain element or type of art and artist. Indeed, observers pro and con have noted an overwhelming propensity among East Village artists and dealers for unabashed self-promotion. Thus, the critic Carlo McCormick (1984) has characterized these young artists as the generation who grew up believing in art history's myths and set out to mythologize themselves.

Other fallout from the culture-industry publicity of the East Village was subtle at first glance, yet ultimately devastating in its real effects. For instance, widespread publicity of the East Village as a "scene" has attracted tourists and shoppers to the neighborhood. The influx of these groups has created a market that has fueled the process of storefront conversions. What at one time were second-hand stores, family-run restaurants, low-budget galleries, and other esoterica have now been transformed into luxury boutiques, corporate-based retail stores, and the particularly omnipresent upscale pasta/wine bars.

The same groups who make up the market for these storefront transformations have also invaded the local clubs and cabarets. These venues have played a central role in the community life of artists in the East Village. Yet there is evidence that this invasion has disrupted the delicate social fabric and networks nurtured in the clubs. Film maker Jim Jarmusch

(*Stranger Than Paradise, Down By Law,* and most recently, *Mystery Train*) summarized the situation:

> There was a lot of excitement because you'd go to CBGB's or Max's, which still existed then, later the Mudd Club, and there was really a good spirit of exchanging ideas which now is completely gone. But at that time it was a really strong kind of, I don't know, energy that was going on. . . . Everyone seems to have pulled their ideas back and there's no real scene anymore, there's no real exchange of energy, there are no places to go where people are really enthusiastic about new ideas . . . the scene became more a spectator scene than one of participants, whereas initially it seemed like everyone at CBGB's was doing something, everyone wanted to make films or paintings or had a band or something. . . . [But then there were] more people that were spectators rather than people who were interested in creating something. . . . it's just a little disturbing that the energy exchange doesn't really exist anymore. (Belsito 1985, 60)

Of course, the most obvious effect of culture-industry publicity's attracting tourists and consumers was the advancement of gentrification. It becomes fashionable, chic, and thus desirable to live in the neighborhood, literally to rub shoulders with the free-spirited artists. However, the process of gentrification has also produced effects more subtle than the obvious one of class displacement. In particular, it has led indirectly to a radical decline in the amount of public and noncommodified art displayed in free public visual space. In the pre-gentrified East Village, boarded-up, abandoned brick buildings and long stretches of street-level brick walls became the site of public exhibition spaces and bulletin boards. Large-scale paintings on paper, masks in clay, murals, chalk drawings and stencil works of various kinds coexisted with announcements of events and performances. Today this "public art" and communicative culture has all but disappeared as abandoned buildings have been converted into luxury condos or boutiques. The long brick walls that functioned as community bulletin boards have been replaced by plate-glass windows advertising the wares of a large-chain retail clothing store. Community gardens are increasingly threatened by city-sponsored development schemes. Abandoned and/or unclaimed urban space has been "recolonized" and organized into a seamless web of controlled visual presentation. Art itself has retreated into the commodified indoor environment of the galleries.

There, artwork becomes subject to the machinations of the art market dominated by the art media. The very tone and rhetoric of the media attention directed at the East Village, characterized by an emphasis on the qualities of the "chic" and glamorous, is also highly problematic. Indeed, it is indicative of certain aspects of the changing form of the commodity structure within late capitalism in general. Commodities are increasingly supercharged as symbols of desire, of a dream world replete with images of glamour, wealth, satiation, and reconciliation. Store windows resemble religious shrines presenting fantasies of enchanted, sparkling commodities that take on an aura formerly reserved for cultic objects. The allure of fashion, glamour, big money, and bright lights becomes the measure of value, and helps to define art as commodity. The underside of the aestheticization of commodities is a degraded aesthetic. As several critics have noted, the line between art, fashion, and the club circuit is effaced, and the "art stars" take their place alongside "the demistars of music and television" (T. Lawson 1986, 97).

It is in this sense that we may speak of a degraded simulacrum of the avant-garde, cynically manipulated for its presumed legitimacy in the eyes of the market. The avant-garde and its so-called "spirit of revolt" itself have become a commodity for consumption in the constant search for the ever-new and latest thing; it has become an ensemble of gaily starving young artists amidst the rubble of a neighborhood long since in ruins. Within this context, the explicitly ironic poses toward the market adopted by some artists appear all the more cynical and pernicious when one observes how quickly such strategies meet with attention and success. Mark Kostabi, a painter who once told a critic that paintings are the doors to collectors' homes and that his middle name should be changed to "et" (for Mark-et), is perhaps the most notorious example of this unabashed strategy (Robinson and McCormick 1984, 157).

Still, the market has proven as fickle as ever. It is now no longer important or even noteworthy to present oneself as an East Village artist. In the words of the critic Thomas Lawson, "At lightning speed, flirting with what became the neo-Expressionist fashion as well as with what became its bedfellow—appropriation—the young Turks of the East hyped a hyped market" (1986, 102). Indeed, the area has recently declined as an art center as the more successful galleries have moved to Soho and many of those left behind have faltered in the recession, with fewer buyers and skyrocketing commercial rents. And yet the penchant for denigrating the aesthetic worth of the East Village as a scene has become almost too easy, itself too much the fashion. Indeed, from within the art media itself, a certain irony arises when a number of those artists originally most denigrated (like Scharf) now sit comfortably in the hands of the more successful Soho galleries, themselves the "derrière-garde" of the art-world establishment, as McCormick aptly phrased it (1984). More important, other critical and significant works have been less noticed. The attack on an elitist and insular Soho that was so integral to the birth of the first East Village exhibitions can be understood, in part, as an important critique of the often insular and sectarian vanguardism of late 1970s minimalism. The reinvigorating of painting by East Village artists has inaugurated a new pluralism in the realm of style, from the trademark neo-Expressionists to graffiti art and playful "takes" on cartoon and pop imagery that, in the case of several young artists, provide ironic critiques of both mass culture and canonic aesthetic codes.

Part of this new pluralism can be seen in the wide variety of aesthetic styles, genres, and practices that have been largely unnoticed within the media's streamlined presentation of the East Village. Although larger alternative venues like P.S. 122 have garnered a certain amount of media attention with the popularization of performance artists like Laurie Anderson or Eric Bogosian, small performance spaces and clubs like Dixon Place, ABC No Rio, or the now defunct Darinka and 8BC have remained, for the most part, firmly in the background.

ABC No Rio originated in January 1980 with the organization of "The Real Estate Show" by a group of approximately thirty-five young artists who unofficially occupied and held an exhibit in an abandoned city-owned building on Delancey Street, in the area of the Lower East Side south of Loisaida. The exhibition offered a multiplicity of mediums, genres, and styles that included photo-text appropriation and collage, sculpture, found objects and graffiti, cartoon images, and expressionist figures painted on paper and directly on walls. Organizers' statements spoke of three goals behind the exhibition: to critique the role of capital and profit over residence and the organization of everyday life; to protest the noncooperation of city housing officials with whom they had been negotiating for the building as an exhibition space for over a year; and (as organizer and sculptor Rebecca Howland stressed) to put forth the idea of a "post-gallery" movement with a commitment to the creation of a neighborhood "citizen's space" as much as an art center (Weichselbaum 1985, 53). Far from the explicitly decontextualized aesthetic mannerisms of the self-styled graffitist Scharf, the "Manifesto or Statement of Intent" that accompanied The Real Estate Show demonstrated an explicit concern with the artist's role in site-specific issues and events: "The intention of this action is to show that artists are willing and able to place themselves and their work squarely in a context that shows solidarity with oppressed people, a recognition that mercantile and institutional structures oppress and distort artists' lives and works, and a recognition that artists, living and working in depressed communities, are compradors in the revaluation of property and the 'whitening' of neighborhoods" (Moore and Miller 1985, 56).

Critically, ABC No Rio, along with Collaborative Projects (Colab), Political Art Documentation and Distribution (PADD), and Group Material have represented groups of East Village artists whose expressed values and practices run divergent from, if not directly counter to, those generally valorized by the art and mass media (Moore and Miller 1985). Similarly, alternative exhibition and performance spaces like ABC No Rio that continue to survive in the area have represented a radically different construction of cultural terrain, where patterns of cultural production and consumption are less likely to be organized according to the dictates of the art commodity and principles of acquisition or profit.

Other practices and institutions generally omitted from the usual compendium of breathless "profiles" dedicated to the advertisement of the East Village "downtown scene" have included a thriving dance community, the long-standing St. Mark's Poetry Project, the Hispanic arts center and language school Taller Latino Americano, the Knitting Factory, and theaters like Cuando and Theater for the New City. Especially interesting are "no-profile" storefront enterprises such as the nonprofit, bilingual bookstore Embargo, run by artist Richard Armijo, which has been a highly eclectic bilingual source of small-press material ranging from both local and international journals for art, politics, fiction and prose to Mexican dime-store romance novels. Indeed, characteristic of the East Village has been an interesting and varied collection of small-press publications like the fiction-oriented *Redtape* or the previously mentioned *Portable Lower East Side*, anarcho-punk fanzines, underground comics, tenant/housing-issue newspapers, and assorted hand-stapled tracts.

In the visual arts, the critical variety of works found in the East Village is barely suggested by established media coverage. But more to the point is the existence of similar styles and genres employed with very different results. The work of David Wojnarowicz, one of the most interesting and visually imaginative artists to have come out of the East Village, has been simultaneously labeled graffitist, neo-Expressionist, and postmodern. Wojnarowicz's canvases present emotionally and politically charged bursts of rage mediated through a highly personal and idiosyncratic aesthetic. But the expressive content of his work has done little to promote the romanticist portrait of a unified individual subject awash in a modern sea of means-end social exploitation and cultural debasement. Early works of Wojnarowicz, which used crude expressionist figures and pictographic images painted on supermarket posters, undercut any of the usual ahistorical romanticism characteristic of much neo-Expressionist fare through the blatant artifice of collage and the use of stencils. Later work combining photography and image/text appropriation with intimate painted vignettes resembling dream landscapes increasingly moved into a complex investigation of the historical constitution of individual desire within the disciplinary structures of church, society, and the state, and, in his last works, the policing of the sexual body politic through official responses to AIDS. As the case with other contemporary artists whose work confronts issues of sexuality and politics, Wojnarowicz became a target in the debates over NEA funding. While this chapter has focused primarily on the impact of the *market* on artists, these debates raise serious questions about the influence of the *state* on future artistic practices, for example, the extent to which artists may engage in forms of self-censorship.

Evidence of a sustained new aesthetic pluralism itself can be read in a critical light. Many East Village artists are struggling to represent a positive version of the critical "postmodern" spirit. Several small commercial galleries, nonprofit exhibition spaces, and alternative performance clubs have attempted to preserve a critical niche in the East Village scene and have continued to mount shows of consistent integrity and imagination.

Thus, in conclusion, we wish to emphasize that despite the current fashionable tendency (present among even left cultural critics) to engage in one form or another of "East Village bashing," a number of critical and progressive cultural practices are even today surviving in the neighborhood. For this reason we have chosen to highlight the coexistence of disparate, often conflicting elements and forces that make up the cultural politics of the East Village. Thus the persistence of critical counterpractices against the hegemony of industry forces, both real estate and cultural, can be more fully understood. Its cutting edge at this time seems to be the blend of activists, artists, musicians, and youth who constitute the beleaguered forces of opposition in the neighborhood. As many have realized, without their efforts, the truly ugly specter of gentrification threatens to make all questions of political struggle in the East Village a foregone conclusion.

Note

A version of this paper appeared in *Theory, Culture and Society* 8(4), 1991.

References

Alson, Peter. 1989. "The Building that Ate Tompkins Square Park." *Village Voice,* July 18, p. 26.

Bell, Daniel. 1973. *The Coming of Post-Industrial Society.* New York: Basic Books.

Belsito, Peter, ed. 1985. *Notes from the Pop Underground.* Berkeley: The Last Gasp of San Francisco.

Berman, Marshall. 1983. "A Struggle to the Death in Which Both Sides Are Right." *Village Voice,* July 12, pp. 10–24.

Bowler, Anne E. 1985. "Gentrification and Displacement: The Case of Loisaida." Unpublished manuscript. New York: New School for Social Research.

Brenson, Michael. 1983. "City's Position Secure as Focus of Art World." *New York Times,* Feb. 28, pp. B1, 6.

Browning, Harley L., and Joachim Singelmann. 1978. "The Transformation of the U.S. Labor Force: The Intervention of Industry and Occupations." *Politics and Society* 8(3–4): 481–509.

Castells, Manuel. 1983. *The City and the Grassroots: A Cross-Cultural Theory of Urban Social Movements.* Berkeley: University of California Press.

Clark, T. J. 1982. *Image of the People: Gustave Courbet and the 1848 Revolution.* Princeton, N.J.: Princeton University Press.

Cohen, Ed. 1989. "The 'Hyperreal vs. the Really Real': If European Intellectuals Stop Making Sense of American Culture Can We Still Dance?" *Cultural Studies* 3(1): 25–37.

Derocher, Rob. 1982. "Artists Housing Meets Resistance from Local Residents Who Fear Displacement." *Villager,* May 13, pp. 5, 24.

Deutsche, Rosalyn, and Cara Gendel Ryan. 1984. "The Fine Art of Gentrification." *October* 31 (Winter): 91–111.

Dowd, Maureen. 1985. "A Different Bohemia: Youth, Art, Hype." *New York Sunday Times Magazine,* Nov. 17, pp. 26–33, 36–37, 100.

Easton, Malcolm. 1964. *Artists and Writers in Paris: The Bohemian Idea 1803–1867.* New York: St. Martin's Press.

Ferguson, Sarah. 1989. "Occupied Territories: Inside the Squatter Movement." *Village Voice,* July 18, pp. 22–32.

Fleetwood, Blake. 1979. "The New Elite and an Urban Renaissance." *New York Sunday Times Magazine,* Jan. 14, pp. 16–34.

Gale, Dennis E. 1984. *Neighborhood Revitalization and the Postindustrial City: A Multinational Perspective.* Toronto: Lexington Books.

Gershuny, John. 1977. "Post-Industrial Society? The Myth of the Service Economy." *Futures* 9: 103–14.

———. 1978. *After Industrial Society? The Emerging Self-Service Economy.* London: Macmillan.

Glueck, Grace. 1983. "A Gallery Scene that Pioneers New Territories." *New York Times,* June 26, p. 27.

Goldstein, Richard. 1982. "Portrait of the Artist as a Good Use." *Village Voice,* Dec. 14, pp. 20–22.

Gottlieb, Martin. 1982. "Space Invaders: Land Grab on the Lower East Side." *Village Voice*, Dec. 14, pp. 10–50.

Graña, Cesar. 1964. *Bohemian vs Bourgeois: French Society and the French Man of Letters in the Nineteenth Century.* New York: Basic Books.

Gustafson, Bo, ed. 1979. *Post-Industrial Society.* New York: St. Martin's Press.

Hall, Stuart, and Tony Jefferson, eds. 1976. *Resistance Through Rituals.* London: Hutchinson.

Henig, Jeffrey. 1980. "Gentrification and Displacement within Cities: A Comparative Analysis." *Social Science Quarterly* 61(3–4): 638–52.

———. 1982. "Neighborhood Responses to Gentrification." *Urban Affairs Quarterly* 17(3): 343–49.

Kumar, Krishan. 1978. *Prophecy and Progress: The Sociology of Industrial and Post-Industrial Society.* New York: Penguin Books.

Lawson, Ronald, ed. 1986. *The Tenant Movement in New York City, 1904–1984.* New Brunswick, N.J.: Rutgers University Press.

Lawson, Thomas. 1986. "Toward Another Laocoön or, the Snake Pit." *Artforum* (March): 97–106.

London, Bruce, and J. John Palen, eds. 1984. *Gentrification, Displacement and Neighborhood Revitalization.* Albany: State University of New York Press.

McCormick, Carlo. 1984. "The Periphery of Pluralism." *The East Village Scene* (exhibition catalog). Philadelphia: Institute of Contemporary Art, University of Pennsylvania Press.

Mandel, Ernest. 1978. *Late Capitalism.* Translated by Joris De Bres. London: Verso.

Marzoratti, Gerald. 1985. "Kenny Scharf's Fun-House Big Bang." *ARTnews* 84(7): 72–81.

MFY Legal Services, Inc. 1982. "The New York City Artist Homeownership Program." Unpublished legal brief. Oct.

Moore, Alan, and Marc Miller, eds. 1985. *ABC No Rio Dinero: The Story of a Lower East Side Art Gallery.* New York: ABC No Rio with Collaborative Projects.

Newfield, Jack. 1984. "The Worst Landlords: A New York Bestiary." *Village Voice*, Feb. 21, pp. 16–42.

New York Times. 1982. May 4.

———. 1988. Aug. 8–11.

Offe, Claus. 1985. "The Growth of the Service Sector." In *Disorganized Capitalism.* Cambridge, Mass.: MIT Press.

Owens, Craig. 1984. "Commentary: The Problem with Puerilism." *Art in America* 72(6): 162–63.

Pileggi, Nicholas. 1985. "Here Are 25,000 Great Vacant Apartments You Can't Rent." *New York Magazine*, Dec. 16, pp. 34–37.

Pincus-Witten, Robert. 1985. "The New Irascibles." *Arts* (Sept.): 102–10.

Richardson, Joanna. 1969. *The Bohemian: La Vie de Bohème in Paris, 1830–1914.* London: Macmillan.

Robbins, Tom. 1981. "The Changing Face of Norfolk Street." *City Limits* (June/July): 8–10.

Robinson, Walter, and Carlo McCormick. 1984. "Slouching toward Avenue D." *Art in America* 72 (6): 135–61.

Robison, Maynard Trimble. 1976. "Rebuilding Lower Manhattan: 1955–1974." Ph.D. diss., City University of New York.

Sanders, Richard. 1979. *The Lower East Side: A Guide to Its Jewish Past*. New York: Dover.

Sandler, Irving. 1984. "Tenth Street Then and Now." In *The East Village Scene* (exhibition catalog). Philadelphia: Institute of Contemporary Art, University of Pennsylvania Press.

Schoener, Allan. 1967. *Portal to America: The Lower East Side 1870–1925*. New York: Holt, Rinehart, and Winston.

Siegel, Jerrold. 1986. *Bohemian Paris: Culture, Politics, and the Boundaries of Bourgeois Life 1830–1930*. New York: Viking Penguin.

Simpson, Charles. 1981. *Soho: The Artist in the City*. Chicago: University of Chicago Press.

Sites, William. 1985. "Landlord Stallings Forced from Lower East Side." *Tenant* (Feb.): 5.

———. 1987. "Gentrification: A Critical Review of the Literature." Unpublished manuscript, City University of New York.

Smith, Neil. 1989. "Tompkins Square Park: Riots, Rents and Redskins." *The Portable Lower East Side* 6(1): 1–36.

Smith, Neil, and Michele LeFaivre. 1984. "A Class Analysis of Gentrification." In *Gentrification, Displacement and Neighborhood Revitalization*, edited by Bruce London and J. John Palen. Albany, N.Y.: State University of New York Press.

Spencer, Lloyd. 1985. "Allegory in the World of the Commodity." *New German Critique* 34 (Winter): 59–77.

Stanback, Thomas M., Peter J. Bearse, and Thierry J. Noyelle. 1981. *Services: The New Economy*. Totowa, N.J.: Allanheld, Osman Publishers.

Taylor, Paul. 1987. "How Europe Sold the Idea of Postmodern Art." *Village Voice*, Sept. 22, pp. 99–102.

Turner, Victor. 1974. *Dramas, Fields and Metaphors*. Ithaca, N.Y.: Cornell University Press.

Unger, Craig. 1984. "The Lower East Side: There Goes the Neighborhood." *New York Magazine*, May 28, pp. 32–41.

Village Voice. 1983. "Why Artists' Housing Went Down." Feb. 22, p. 41.

Weichselbaum, Lehmann. 1985. "The Real Estate Show." In *ABC No Rio Dinero*, edited by Alan Moore and Marc Miller. New York: ABC No Rio and Collaborative Projects.

Zukin, Sharon. 1989. *Loft Living: Culture and Capital in Urban Change*. New Brunswick, N.J.: Rutgers University Press.

❖ 9 ❖

Impolitic Art and Uncivil Actions:
Controversies in the Public Sphere

STEVEN C. DUBIN

I resent the insinuendos.
—Mayor Richard J. Daley, May 15, 1965

Gentlemen, get the thing straight, once and for all—the policeman isn't
there to create disorder, the policeman is there to preserve disorder.
—Mayor Richard J. Daley, September 23, 1968

Political issues beget social dramas. Some events concisely express widespread anxieties, whether they be agrarian, antimili-
taristic protests over the building of an airport in Japan (Apter and Sawa
1984), the symbolic airing of artisans' complaints through their ritual massacre of cats in eighteenth-century France (Darnton 1985), or the kidnap-
ping of a prominent Italian politician and factional feuding over his fate
(Wagner-Pacifici 1986). In such instances social actors extend the pro-
scenium to include the largest of audiences. Many become players and
spectators, guaranteeing that the episode becomes part of a group's subsequent cultural history.

Airport insurrections, animal carnage, and celebrity abductions are unusual situations, but they have commanded in-depth analyses. On the
other hand, dramatic scenarios that develop when art is politicized have
generally escaped systematic scrutiny by social scientists. Artistic work
commonly incorporates political concerns both extrinsic and intrinsic to
the art world itself. But when outsiders attempt to combine art and politics
for their own purposes it can seem especially intrusive; then these pursuits often repel one another, much like the similar poles of two magnets.
In other words, artists resist politicization of their work in ways *they* did
not intend. Such problems have become more evident in the recent past,

183

coincident with the increased promotion of public art. There is, therefore, both an affinity *and* antipathy between these realms.

Controversies over public art have erupted in a number of locales, largely because art can crystallize otherwise unexpressed sentiments and display them prominently. These disputatious events signal how various groups uphold incompatible definitions of the situation and jockey for power. A morality play is generally enacted as each party promotes its own values and attacks its opponent's assumptions and integrity. These are narratives that can be read, much like any script.

In some cases it is easy to anticipate the action: conflict seems inevitable. The well-known episode of Diego Rivera's inclusion of Lenin in a mural painted at Rockefeller Center in 1933 is one such example (deLarrea 1986). Other incidents are less predictable, however, highlighting opposed concepts of "good taste" instead of politically partisan disputes. Richard Serra's now infamous *Tilted Arc* in New York City is a case in point (Balfe and Wyszomirski 1986), as are sculptures at a Colorado penitentiary considered by some to be "depressing" and "grotesque," a mosaic mural picturing slavery at the city hall of Edwardsville, Illinois, assailed as racially insensitive (Hochfield 1988), or bus placards and el-platform billboards proposed to the Chicago Transit Authority whose subjects were deemed "disquieting" (Tesser 1985) or "inappropriate" due to their representation of same-sex and interracial couples (Lazare 1990; Olson 1990).[1]

It would be simple to dismiss these as instances of unsophisticated constituencies and their uninformed leaders recoiling from the unfamiliar. But such negative reactions have occurred even in such supposedly enlightened communities as Greenwich Village, New York (Lubell 1984). The common denominator in many of these incidents is the failure of artists to confer with local residents and to involve them actively in the process of creation and placement, nor has the sponsoring public agency considered neighborhood (as opposed to "universal artworld") reaction. Interestingly, it has been suggested that women have become more successful in the public art arena because they are more sensitive to community needs and "more conciliatory" in their approach—regardless of agency strategy to ignore or involve the public (Rosen 1987).

Repeatedly, however, art has been exploited for distinctly political purposes by both community and "universal artworld" groups. For example, the proposed removal of a 1922 sculpture in Queens, New York, presenting "civic virtue" as a man tempted by the female characters of vice and corruption demonstrates how the shifting of the relative social positions of different groups can recast the appropriateness and continued desirability of once-approved works (Fried 1987). And even though the ascendancy of nonrepresentational art since World War II supposedly "depoliticized" it (Guilbaut 1983), controversy has surrounded both representational and nonrepresentational works (such as *Tilted Arc* and the Vietnam Memorial in Washington, D.C.).

The present task is to examine how and when such problems arise. I will focus most specifically on one case in Chicago in 1988 concerning a painting of the late Mayor Harold Washington, a negative caricature that exploded into public awareness about six months after this leader's death. I will explore how rival sides framed the controversy, selected their allies and opponents, and scripted and acted out their respective parts.

The Preconditions of Controversy

I argue that particular circumstances contribute to the likelihood of controversy over public art, especially when the dispute—let alone patronage of the work itself—is initiated by public officials. First, when the legitimacy or effectiveness of local government leaders is in question, the probability of conflict over art is heightened. This condition generally derives from the recent empowerment of political constituencies, or from the death of a political leader and the transfer of power. The first situation has prevailed in a number of American cities in the past two decades: old coalitions have broken down, as have barriers to participation based on race, ethnicity, and gender. Groups that were formally served to a greater or lesser degree by paternalistic power brokers have succeeded in wresting more control from the hands of those in power. So a black alderman in Chicago recently typified this development when he reacted to the furor over the exhibited portrait of the late mayor, and to the assertion by a white former public official that action to censor it should not have taken place: "That's a white fellow talking for black people again. We will not allow whites to tell us what to do" (*Newsweek* 1988, 25). Significantly, this statement was made during a time of civic mourning, dismay, and confusion. When there has been a recent ascendance to power or recent transfer of power within a community, the right to rule is so new and the record of accomplishments may be so slight that public officials are apt to feel defensive and define many forms of artistic expression as threatening.

Second, public officials are likely to react negatively when art critically assesses them or social conditions for which they can be held responsible. Such art often identifies the "soft underbelly," the most vulnerable part of an individual or the group he or she represents. It can challenge the most mundane abilities: for example, in Chicago in 1979 a sculptural piece satirized the failure of the snow removal efforts by the new mayor, Michael

Bilandic. This piece hit a strategic target, implicitly contrasting the ineptness of the current regime with the efficiency of the old. In effect it tapped the widespread sentiment that such a problem with municipal services would not have occurred "if Mayor Daley were alive" (Dubin 1987, 171–74). In Philadelphia, artists took similar aim, focusing on trash-removal problems or creating work seen as commenting metaphorically on the catastrophic MOVE incident (*Philadelphia Inquirer*, 1987; *New York Times*, January 10, 1988).

Art can also lampoon the most sacred, as did the 1988 painting that represented the late mayor of Chicago dressed in women's underwear. This work was a direct assault on Washington's character, although it broached the subject of his administrative ability as well: someone as ridiculous or perverted as this could hardly be capable of making governmental decisions. In either case, most at issue are the capacity to rule and "fitness" for power.

Finally, controversy generally erupts when art is displayed in spaces that are public or publicly supported. It is here that the question of accountability is most pointedly raised and the disregard of such responsibility is deemed most critical. It is also in these locales that threats to withhold funds can most easily be made and enforced, directly affecting the fate of artists and their work.

Thus I propose that public art controversies are most likely to occur at times when there is a high degree of communal fragmentation and polarization, along with widespread civic malaise and low communal morale. Works that become controversial are generally those which address volatile, unsettled issues—especially when these works are exhibited at strategic public locations. While any of these circumstances is likely to spark trouble, their combination virtually assures conflagration.

The Emperor's New Clothes: A Case Study

Such a coalescence of circumstances occurred in Chicago in May 1988, when a posthumous portrait of Mayor Harold Washington was catapulted into public controversy. In the painting, Washington is displayed full-length, frontally, staring directly at the viewer. He is clothed only in a woman's brassiere, panties, garter belt, and hosiery. A slight foreshortening of the arms makes them somewhat flipper-like and draws attention to the swelling of his entire midsection. In fact, the center portion of his body appears as an immense balloon over the top of which the brassiere is stretched while the other garments cling onto the bottom. An important iconographic element is a pencil he is clutching in his right hand, a reference to the fact that he dropped a pencil when he had his fatal heart attack and aides thought he was reaching to pick it up when he slumped over in death.

The painting is primitively rendered and falls somewhere between a cartoon and a photograph. On close examination the head appears to be grafted onto a neckless body, and there is only one breast encased in a brassiere whose straps hang unnaturally. Some features are only crudely modeled: for example, the figure's legs look more like Christmas stockings or snow boots than human appendages. Standing stiffly at attention, Washington seems like someone in a mug shot. His face registers bewilderment; he is presented as a grotesque gender-incorrect paper doll waiting to be dressed.

Although this is one contested view of the man, some facts about Washington's public life and character are undisputed. In 1983 Washington became the first black elected mayor in Chicago, and he was reelected in April 1987. His entire first term was stymied by a city council deadlocked by white aldermen who represented the working-class ethnic wards that had routinely supported the Democratic machine of Richard J. Daley, who died in 1976. As Washington's second term started, he was much more successful in effecting his will, largely due to a reapportionment plan that gave more representation to minority groups. He was just beginning to consolidate his power when he died suddenly in November 1987.

His death elevated his reputation and also created a power vacuum. The desire to capitalize on Washington's accomplishments and share his charisma resulted in a struggle by different political factions, generating the epithet "legacy police" to denote those claiming to be his legitimate heirs (Stamets 1988, 31).[2] It was they who were most offended when this portrait of Washington was displayed in an exhibit of student work at the School of the Art Institute of Chicago (SAIC). As a group, several aldermen marched from the city council chambers to the school to have the painting removed. (At this point, it was displayed in a nonpublic part of the building.) After meeting with the school's director, the aldermen had the police "arrest" the painting by confiscating it; in their minds this seizure was necessary in order to avoid a riot.

The school subsequently issued a public apology in the major Chicago newspapers,[3] the city council dropped a threat to withhold public funds from the institution, the painting was returned to the artist with a gash across it, and the ACLU took up the case as a violation of the artist's rights under the First, Fourth, and Fourteenth Amendments.[4] The incident also generated multiple interpretations of the artwork and the reaction to it.

Here we have the *Rashomon* effect: for nearly every witness there was a different view of what had happened. Paired and opposed explanations emerged. For example, the entire incident could be seen either as artist-generated or the result of extra-institutional factors. Supporting the first position were those who saw this as an iconoclastic or satiric gesture that got out of hand (Brenson 1988; Schlesinger 1988), as well as those who believed the painting was part of a larger "performance art" piece that succeeded admirably in highlighting cultural currents and exposing socio-political hypocrisies (Miner 1988).[5] Others recognized that what ultimately transpired was far beyond the artist's control: timing (for example, a tele-vision ratings "sweep" period transformed an insignificant incident into a media event [Greene 1988]) and financial vulnerability (the Art Institute was about to launch a fund-raising drive to expand school facilities and was understandably cautious [Strahler 1988]) molded how this event was framed and received.

A number of other such opposed views emerged. According to one argument, this reaction was a sign of the political naiveté and political infancy of the black community. But this could also be seen as a pro-active stand: the black community experienced the painting as an affront and was standing up for its rights and demanding respect. In this sense there is a parallel to the concern over pornography that directly links it to the negative treatment of women. Here we have the argument of "ad-verse climate," a compelling one for those who can construct a history of past assaults and a slippery, nonpersuasive concept to other groups. Similarly, based on vested interest and past history, there were either clear expressions of racism here (Strausberg 1988c) or signs of homophobia (see coverage in the *Windy City Times* 1988; or *Outlines* 1988).

Certainly the reaction to this painting was overdetermined. It obvi-ously touched both individual and collective nerves, and the cultural, biographical, contextual, and historical synapses that were triggered can be disentangled analytically only after the fact. I will analyze this case according to what I would call the "*dayenu* principle." *Dayenu* is a phrase re-peated during the retelling of the Passover story, where Jews recount each positive deed God committed on their behalf. For each favor extended, the response is "*Dayenu*, it would have been enough," until the entire litany is recited. In this present use the *dayenu* principle demonstrates that any of several factors could have been sufficient to elicit the *negative* re-sponse to this painting. For each, we might say: *dayenu*, it would have been enough. Instead, a dizzying additive process was set into motion, where a number of factors interacted, synergistically creating an explosion of great intensity.

One such factor deals with image, which we can call the *cultural or reputational* component. A connection can be drawn between the typically masculine image of Chicago and the contradictory theme of the painting. Perhaps more than any other American city, Chicago has a long-standing and widely accepted "macho" reputation. Whether it be Sandburg's image of the city of "the big shoulders" or the association with 1920s gangsters, Chicago is typically portrayed as brash, violent, and most of all, masculine. This is an image that has been alternately resisted and cultivated. At the same time that Mayor Washington insisted that something be done about Chicago's "rat-tat-tat" image, the chairman of the International Visitors Center there saw it as something to capitalize on in a proposal for a museum of crime and corruption (Schmidt 1987).

Since the death of Mayor Daley—who was commonly seen as a father figure—those occupying his office have had to wrestle with this impression. Washington's predecessor, Jane Byrne, had the most difficulty. European observers were puzzled when they tried to understand her election in a city characterized as a "world symbol of masculinity" (Dubin 1987, 6). As it turned out, a black man would also have manifold problems leading a city stubbornly resistant to change and heir to a legacy of racial divisiveness.

As mayor, Washington made real efforts to cope with these problems, in part by self-conscious identification with his revered late predecessor. (Washington jokingly referred to himself as the "sepia Daley," even retrieving Daley's desk from storage for his own use [*New York Times* 1987, November 26, D19].) But what was more problematic to contend with was another *biographical* factor. Washington's bachelor status generated many rumors regarding his sexual orientation and his sexual conduct. Throughout his tenure in office, these rumors were a whispered subtext and emerged as tales of homosexuality, child molestation, and transvestism. In fact, the artist of the painting under scrutiny here cites such a rumor as one of his sources of "inspiration": Washington was said to be wearing women's underwear beneath his business suit when he was taken to the hospital after his fatal heart attack (Stamets 1988, 30).[6] *Dayenu*, it would have been enough.

This theme was amplified by the controversy. One way it emerged was through sensationalistic headlines: "Ex-Chi mayor art is dragged away" (*New York Daily News* 1988, 23) or "Late Chi mayor dragged through art flap" (*New York Post* 1988, May 13, 5). Even the staid *New York Times* acknowledged this when they described the painting by noting that "everything about him is ambiguous" (1988, May 29), while an early-morning radio commentator suggested the work might be dubbed *The African Queen* ("America in the Morning," 1988). To savvy observers the link was clear,

with the painting's title *Mirth and Girth* evoking another interesting association: it was unmistakably similar to the name of a local organization for
overweight gay men, Girth and Mirth.

While Mayor Washington was in office, such rumors remained largely
submerged. They were a widely suspected and unsubstantiated—but generally unspoken—facet of Washington's incumbency. Even after his death,
only a few commentators brought them up, among whom were a well-
respected black journalist (Jarrett 1988), an ACLU representative, and
writers in the Chicago gay press. Yet the association between life and art,
and the desire by some to deny this possible connection, undoubtedly
contributed to the negative reaction to this painting.

We can also cite *contextual* elements that helped guarantee the response.
A number of events had already contributed to a racially charged mood in
the city. For example, an "equity law" had been proposed to protect home
values by establishing a state-financed fund to pay the difference between
a home's sale price and its appraised value. The intention of the legislation was to decrease the probability of rapid racial transition of neighborhoods through panic selling. The message it broadcast to many was one
of racism, however, with its tacit acceptance of the notion that property
values inevitably decrease when blacks move into a neighborhood.

But the most racially divisive matter centered on mayoral aide Steve
Cokely. Shortly before the incident over the painting, this city official
made anti-Semitic remarks (such as accusing Jewish doctors of injecting
black babies with the HIV virus, and charging that Jews were in a con-
spiracy to rule the world). At first, Washington's successor, acting mayor
Eugene Sawyer, resisted pressure to fire Cokely. This earned Sawyer
greater respect from those fellow members of the black community who
felt that he had previously worked too closely with anti-Washington forces
to be the late mayor's legitimate successor. But when Sawyer finally ac-
ceded to the pressure, many blacks felt outraged that Cokely's right to
free speech had been abridged. The wound thus opened was enlarged by
the painting's display and then even further irritated by the outcry that
the artist's rights had been curbed by the painting's "arrest."

What followed was a dredging up of past insults along with a reluctance to admit fault on either side. As the leader of the black organization
PUSH asserted when she defended black leaders under fire: " 'You didn't
ask the Art Institute to apologize,' she bellowed. . . . 'We ain't apologizing
no more. . . . We are grown . . . we can count too' " (Strausberg 1988b [in a
black newspaper]). These remarks highlight the sense of impropriety and
outrage the painting evoked because of its appearance relatively soon after
Washington's death, and also underscore the newness of black political

power in Chicago. Blacks saw the painting as part of a pattern of assaults, not as an isolated incident.[7]

This racial climate was augmented by sexual politics in the city. Just before the painting was seized, George Dunne, president of the Cook County Board and head of the county Democratic party, was accused of trading patronage jobs for sexual favors from several young women— who were also alleged to be lesbians. Rather than garnering a negative public reaction, his presumed potency at age seventy-five was publicly celebrated. As a female county commissioner admitted, "I'm glad to see we have a heterosexual at the head of government" (quoted in editorial, *Windy City Times* 1988, May 12, 11). To this we can add the fact that a proposed local human rights ordinance extending protection to homosexuals had been stalled in the city council, largely because of resistance from churches in black communities. *Dayenu;* this sexual climate would have been enough to provoke the reaction against the painting.

Finally, there were *historical precedents* for the official suppression of art in the public realm in Chicago. The attempt in 1979 to censor the previously mentioned sculptural piece picturing Mayor Bilandic as a complacent observer of a snow emergency is a case in point, where the effectiveness and reputation of a public servant were on the line. Several years later the same artist created a similar tableau that showed Washington and his electoral rival Edward Vrdolyak stalemated in debate, a work that Washington himself told aides to leave alone (Stamets 1988, 31). This reflects a pattern of tolerance of free expression that Washington established: he resisted attempts to censor a black poet on a city-sponsored Dial-a-Poem program (Hentoff 1988), defended an artist whose frescoes in a neighborhood library provoked an outcry for being "fertility symbols" (*New York Times* 1988, August 31, L9), and refused to support the assertion of two black aldermen that the city seal was racist and should be redesigned (Newman 1988, 36). But Washington's strong civil liberties stance kept the forces of censorship only temporarily at bay. Once he was gone, a pattern of many prior attempts to limit artistic expression provided ritual stances and precedents for conduct that commanded a great deal of popular support.

It is no wonder that this painting, presented at this historical juncture in Chicago, was destined to provoke controversy. The next task is to examine exactly how that controversy was shaped and in what terms.

Of Nooses and Nostrums

Although this may seem like a frivolous event, it resulted in cuts in public funding to SAIC, as well as in threats of violence directed against the artist, the art school, and the school's director. While these threats were not acted out, violent language was used by both sides. What transpired was in essence a symbolic lynching: group characteristics were blurred and information was distorted, representative victims were targeted, and mob action was both threatened and committed. What is most unusual is that in some respects the traditional roles of perpetrator and victim in such a scenario were here reversed.

It is impossible to overlook the symbolism associated with the "arrest" of the painting by the Chicago aldermen. Two images predominated in press accounts: the vigilante or posse of the American West, and the Gestapo storm trooper of Nazi Germany. Such motifs surfaced in many news articles, modified occasionally by a note of triviality, as when one story also characterized the scene as a "panty raid" (Newman 1988, 3). Further, key facts in the scenario were difficult to ascertain: the number of aldermen who confiscated the painting, the number of threats directed at individuals and institutions, and even the age of the artist were all subject to variable reports. Most important, however, was the confusion regarding the artist's background. Some of the detractors immediately assumed he was Jewish, which in their minds would have explained everything about his work (for the record, he was not Jewish).

In this instance both sides felt they had been violated and both acted to enforce their views. The painting's supporters maintained that an illegal action had been committed and that a legal remedy was necessary. They argued that the "hecklers' veto" had triumphed, that is, that there was denial of rights of free expression on the basis of real or imagined threats to those wishing to express themselves (Hentoff 1988).[8] By seizing the painting to the supposed end of *preventing* a riot, the aldermen ironically used the same rationale that had been used historically against blacks to deter them from publicly demonstrating for and exercising their civil rights (Donahue transcript 1988, 5; *Washington Post* 1988, May 14, A26).[9]

But for those who were offended by the painting, their call to action was supported by another set of assumptions: "There's a higher moral law than the Constitution and that's what I'm concerned about. Nothing else counts" (Alderman Allan Streeter in Donahue transcript, 1988, 3). Such individuals felt that the first punch in this skirmish had been thrown by the artist, and they justified their response as retribution for a provocative action. To their minds a lynching or symbolic emasculation had already occurred, and the black community was the victim, not the perpetrator.

Nothing highlights the racial polarization in Chicago at this time more than the conjunction of the Cokely firing and the display and seizure of the painting of Mayor Washington. For many in the black community, the "muzzling" of a public official was an assault against that community; it signaled the need to close ranks and protect one's fellows, albeit in a manner some might term a tyranny of the masses (see Lester 1988 for a similar view of some related matters). As a community organizer passionately argued at a rally for Cokely: "We're here to tell the Jewish community and sell-out Negroes that we'll not allow them to snatch the manhood of black men in this community. . . . It's Steve Cokely tonight, but it'll be us tomorrow" (Muwakkil 1988, 6). This sentiment was also found in Allan Streeter, one of the aldermen who "arrested" the painting. As reported by one journalist, "In his ward publication, Streeter said that he would not be a part of any move to 'silence or castrate another black person' [beyond Cokely] and added that [Mayor] Sawyer should not bend to pressure from outside groups in dealing with blacks" (Strong 1988).

Blacks were thus found enacting the roles of both victim and aggressor, in the latter respect inverting the standard drama. And once again, we can locate an uncanny precedent for this rhetoric that undoubtedly contributed to the outlook of blacks in Chicago. In 1987 a judge had declared that any resident of the South Side (a predominately black portion of the city) who did not vote for Harold Washington in his campaign for a second term "ought to be hung." In March 1988—shortly before the incident over the painting—the state Judicial Inquiry Board filed a complaint with the Illinois Courts Commission charging this judge with violating the state code of conduct (New York Times 1988, July 24, 29). Not only did the image of lynching have currency, but the judge's protestations that his remark should not be taken literally were officially overruled. For some this was another example of a supposed aggressor actually being the victim.

Inflammatory remarks were not restricted to blacks, however. In an editorial that only thinly veiled his racism, the well-known Chicago columnist Mike Royko confirmed the worst that many blacks must have feared. After mocking black street jive, speculating that the black aldermen had never been to the Art Institute before they removed the Washington painting, and using the moniker "alderboobs," Royko cut loose: "If anything, I find a painting far less offensive than an alderman. A painting is nothing more than an inanimate object. You just hang it on a wall and it stays there. Some aldermen are inanimate, too, but you can't hang an alderman that way, although it would be fun" (1988, 3).

To bring together these different accounts and summarize these events: An irreverent young white artist felt that a recently deceased black mayor should be humbled because his image had become sacrosanct. His painting offered an alternative and unflattering point of view, reflecting larger racial and gender ambiguities. It symbolically castrated the man, paralleling a traditional reaction to "uppity niggers" who exceeded their pre-scribed social position. Both the painting itself and its fate in the hands of its detractors were additionally marked by dimensions of rape, a tra-ditional method of "controlling" women. This feminine identification was heightened because of a conflation of aspects of Washington's biography with his assumption of leadership of a city that was weakened first by its loss of a powerful paternal leader, and then by the impact of critical structural problems that have contributed to the decline of many major U.S. cities in the 1980s. Chicago was becoming flaccid, and its late mayor was portrayed similarly. In a city with an over-masculinized identity, this was a particularly potent image.

The reception to this painting was orchestrated by actors from two "worlds" that in this case had little overlap: the elite Art Institute and the city government. Within their respective domains, the social positions of the "challengers" was similar, however: on the one side a student against the elite establishment, and on the other, minority members newly em-powered in municipal politics. While each was joined by various partisans, neither side brought with it much practical experience in accommodating or negotiating conflict as they confronted one another in this new—and newly "democratized"—territory. Armed with perspectives formulated in such different contexts, these parties and their allies constructed the operative rules *de novo*. However, the outcome called up a familiar sce-nario, as "frontier justice" triumphed. The staging of an ersatz lynching occurred because legitimate authority did not appear to exist, and gov-ernment officials became outlaws when they used force in an extralegal manner.

Thus this pictorial image was the tinder that ignited what was already an incendiary racial situation. In the classic sense, it was a disaster wait-ing to occur. But for some it was also an opportunity to flex political muscle, consolidate local alliances, and generate political capital. As men-tioned earlier, many of the participants in the seizure of the painting were those who most zealously joined the "Washington legacy police." In some cases they needed to confirm publicly their allegiance to the late mayor, and in some instances they wished to counter being cast as racial traitors because of their association with the firing of Cokely. In both instances they upstaged the acting mayor by taking matters into their own hands. Was this essentially a case of political opportunism? Most likely; but this action also stands as a marker for the changing state of politics and of the complexities of art patronage or support by public agencies. As such, it warrants a reconsideration of the criteria I earlier proposed for predicting such events.

The Last Shall Be First

To extract the fullest degree of meaning from this conflict, we can consider additional incidents (and non-incidents) to determine how well the explanatory model I am suggesting for public art controversies fits other circumstances. Let us review three different Chicago examples of artworks and the reactions they provoked: they provide a time-lapse exposure of Chicago's political terrain. Mayor Daley died in December 1976. Fifteen months later, he was "feted" by a large exhibit at an artist-run "alternative space" just north of Chicago's Loop. This show, called "Daley's Tomb," consisted of the work of forty-five artists, including a Renaissance-style painting presenting Daley as an angel hovering over city hall as deals are enacted below; an architect's proposal to add crosses to major downtown buildings, thereby transforming the city into a giant memorial park; a musical sarcophagus; and pinball machines, file cabinets, and other miscellanea. Many of the artists incorporated Daley's words and deeds into their presentations (in most cases radically reformulated). Even though Daley was then still very much a hero to a large part of Chicago's population, it is hard to imagine a more satirical or overtly political art exhibit. Yet there was no public outcry or negative critical response to this exhibition.

Approximately one year later, Michael Bilandic, Daley's immediate successor, was lampooned as the head of what was perceived to be an inept and insensitive bureaucracy after months of winter storms had immobilized and frustrated city residents. During this period, there were specific complaints that predominantly black areas had been routinely underserved by the public transportation system and by the city snow-clearance efforts. February 1979 was also the time for the primary elections, when Bilandic's record was directly on the line. Politically appointed employees of the city's art council covered up the piece of sculpture satirizing Bilandic and attempted to have it removed—an action that was then overturned in court (Dubin 1987, 171–74). These loyal workers led the public outcry on behalf of their leader, who nonetheless lost his bid for his party's nomination that same month.

Finally, in 1988 we have the incident regarding Mayor Washington that has just been detailed. What sense can be made of the similarities and differences between these incidents? Recall the criteria determining public art controversies I delineated earlier: low communal morale combined with high communal fragmentation and polarization; artwork that addresses sensitive issues; and public locations. In the case of the "Daley's Tomb" exhibition, we have a period marked by low community morale and a sense of loss, but more time had passed after the former mayor's death than was the case in the Washington incident. In addition, there was no marked sense of polarization. Daley commanded a high degree of allegiance from a wide variety of people, although his support was eroding by the time of his death, particularly in the black community (Green and Holli 1987). In some ways he was "everyone's mayor" and even those who disliked him could acknowledge that his personal identity and the city's were practically coextensive. While disaffection was clearly present, opposition had not yet coalesced to a significant degree; the volatile issues of black enfranchisement and empowerment had not fully erupted. And last (and perhaps most important), as irreverent as the work in this show was, it was relatively hidden from public view. Although reviewed in the media, it was exhibited in a place known primarily to the avant-garde. The exhibition gallery was also a cooperative venture, neither beholden to public funds for its operation nor subject to governmental oversight. While the potential to offend was certainly there, the public issue did not emerge.

In the Bilandic incident, however, all the criteria were met. Sufficient time had passed after Daley's death for groups to have waged battles for power; civic morale was low and polarization increasing; and an image was presented in a public setting that went for the political jugular vein. Controversy erupted. Such was also the case with the Washington painting, with the same conditions present, although more exaggerated. The difference in reception is best summarized by the following comment by an art critic for the *New York Times:* "Perhaps in no American city has this iconoclasm [in art] been more prevalent than Chicago . . . It thrived in response to the ascendancy of the white middle class, which was generally secure and powerful enough to tolerate being attacked. . . . [But] at the same time that the middle class is now generally harder to provoke, those who feel relatively powerless as a result of race, gender, nationality or religion are more unwilling to tolerate being depicted in an unflattering light" (Brenson 1988, 37).

A Philadelphia Story

Evidence from Philadelphia provides further confirmation that the conjunction of these particular factors maximizes the potential for controversies over art. In recent years the political landscape has been roughly comparable to that of Chicago: a white "boss" ruled from 1972 to 1980; a liberal white man became mayor for one term; and then Philadelphia's first black mayor, Wilson Goode, was elected in 1983. Mayor Goode's administration has been dogged by problems, both mundane and persistent (sanitation strikes and trash removal difficulties), and spectacular and unique (in 1985, police bombing of the house of a black militant group known as MOVE resulted in several deaths). It has also had difficulties dealing with art.

The city established an "Art in City Hall" project in 1985 to bring juried shows to the halls outside the mayor's office and the city council chambers. Since then there have been several instances of controversy, related either to issues of race or to the efficacy of the city administration. For example, in two shows in 1985 artworks were mistakenly interpreted as making references to the MOVE incident: one painting featured huts and stick figures, and the other pictured a burning house. Both pieces were threatened with removal but subsequently allowed to stay, but only after the artists successfully explained the symbolism and intent of their work in different terms than those assumed by their detractors.

In 1987, however, an artist's work was ejected from a show after it directly addressed a municipal problem. *Doorway with Pilasters* featured a doorway framed by columns made of trashcans, littered by actual trash from Philadelphia streets (Price 1988; Fleeson and Sozanski 1987). It was presented just after Mayor Goode had failed to win support for a trash-to-steam plant proposal that might have alleviated the city's chronic trash disposal difficulties. Later that year Goode ordered the removal of photographs displayed in city hall that depicted the annual Mummers parade because he judged them to be racist. In point of fact, the black-and-white photos depicted the blue-and-green makeup used by the participants (a rather recent change from the traditional blackface that had been deemed insensitive to the black community [Price 1988]). However, these photographs were being interpreted through a race-conscious lens.

These incidents were all played out against a set of conditions meeting the criteria for public art controversies. Increased black political participation in Philadelphia has been accompanied by increased racial polarization. This is evidenced by a white backlash, such as a well-publicized burning of the home of an interracial couple who had moved into a white, working-class neighborhood in 1985 (Stevens 1985). And the fact that a black mayor and other key city officials were held responsible for the murder of other blacks in the MOVE incident (also in 1985) produced a very complicated and sensitive political scene.

There is an additional and important similarity between these efforts to remove artworks in Chicago and Philadelphia. In both cases explicit censorship was deemed necessary because other controls were insufficient. In the case of the Washington portrait, the works that students exhibited at the Art Institute's school had not been screened. In fact, the artist reported that he created the painting one night at his home, shortly before the show. As a faculty member averred: "I heard the painting was not done in any class. If it had been, any teacher would have talked to the student about the appropriateness of this sort of thing" (Schlesinger 1988). What could not be intercepted in process was instead removed after the fact. And a similar circumstance occurred in the case of the "trash" sculpture in Philadelphia. The artist submitted a proposal that was evaluated and accepted, but he later altered his concept during the actual process of creation. A major part of the rationale for banning the piece was that it didn't conform to the original design, but instead had slipped through a screening apparatus that should have caught potential problems before they surfaced (Sozanski 1987). In each case emergency measures were taken when more subtle devices did not successfully check problems (Dubin 1987, 155–79).

The Continuing Drama

Less than a year after the Washington uproar another controversy erupted in the same venue. In February 1989, a mixed-media installation by a black SAIC student named "Dread" Scott Tyler entitled *What is the proper way to display a U.S. flag?* called out large-scale protests and legal wrangling. This piece included a collage of visual images such as the U.S. flag being burned overseas and flag-draped U.S. coffins. In addition, Tyler placed a real U.S. flag on the floor and positioned a shelf above it with a book in which viewers were invited to write their responses to the work. The easiest way to do this, however, involved stepping on the flag. And once again, radically opposing views regarding art and aesthetics, patriotism, loyalty, freedom, responsibility, and propriety were aired, with local and national politicians and veterans largely constituting one side of the debate and artists and civil libertarians the other.

The framework offered here for analyzing such situations fits this set of events remarkably well. There are striking similarities with the other incidents I've discussed, including all the preconditions for controversy: time, place, and circumstance. There is even a parallel with the aforementioned Mayor Daley example from 1978: Tyler's piece had been exhibited previously without incident in an alternative gallery space prior to its SAIC showing. This other context had been a show devoted to political art, the audience was more specialized, and there was a much greater convergence of intentions and understandings. Ironically, Tyler's inclusion in the SAIC show reflected an organizational commitment to highlight the work of minority students with the intent of partially redressing the accusations of institutional racism that had emerged earlier as a result of the Washington brouhaha.

Problems inherent in the public patronage of the arts also have emerged repeatedly on the national level since the Mayor Washington incident, as the arts, public funding, and alleged obscenity have become a routine theme of contemporary political life. Aesthetic judgments have emerged from the small, somewhat closed world of art; they are now just as frequently issued from the halls of Congress and daily newspapers as from art experts writing in specialized journals. Mapplethorpe, Serrano, Finley, and others have become the bogeymen and -women in the contest between groups and their respective sets of values (for example, fundamentalism versus "secular humanism") for control over the nation's standards and behavior. While a significant number of contemporary artists have chosen to reflect the concerns of recently enfranchised groups in their work, others have felt threatened by the representation of the experiences of gays and lesbians, women generally, and people of color, and have argued for a withdrawal of public funds from these nontraditional expressions. These conflicts not only concern the artworld but reflect larger structural, demographic, and attitudinal shifts within our society.

Conclusion

The regulatory outbursts I've discussed are just one consequence of the social conditions I enumerated as their setting and cause. They represent—but do not exhaust—the possible forms that civic controversy can assume. I have laid particular stress on those periods when the sense of community is tenuous and many people may be looking for representations of who they are and who they are *not*. This partially explains the magnitude of the response against public art, feeding on old frustrations, disappointments, and previously unfocused yet pervasive anxieties. Public art puts form on inchoate concerns and in turn provides a convenient target. Like a magnet, it then attracts scraps of civic discontent. In these cases we can also understand the direction of the negative response, which typically is aimed against both understandably critical forms as well as incomprehensible ones. Either way, public art can insult large numbers of people and be seen as an offensive intruder in the community, not as a good neighbor.

This analysis has focused primarily on one type of art and art controversy, although I believe it provides the basis for drawing conclusions regarding public art controversies more generally. Different types of art can elicit remarkably similar responses, whether from "the community" or from its designated representatives. Work that breaks convention often draws resistance, especially from those relatively uninvolved in the worlds of art (Becker 1982, 50). Specifically, with non-representational art there is a problem in relation to the range of what many people will recognize and accept as legitimate. If the community were consulted in regard to a proposed non-representational work, there might be attempts to push it toward something more traditional, more understandable, as was the case with the Vietnam Memorial in Washington (Balfe 1989).

In the case of representational art, on the other hand, people *can* accurately read meanings, and they often find them offensive. In these cases the push is to strip work of its overt social or political commentary, thus seeking to generalize, not particularize the message.[10] When a well-developed review process is in place either type of art is likely to elicit attempts to standardize and neutralize it toward more routine, "clean" representations. Both types of negative reaction therefore converge toward a similar (and safe) outcome.

It is also important to recognize that the instances where the artist is a passive and unknowing victim are probably rare. Some artworks are provocative—as are some artists—by almost any standard. What happens to them is rather predictable, and without imputing blame we need to examine what any artist contributes to a problematic scene. This should not detract from the significance of the regulatory acts directed against them, and it might even dilute somewhat their sense of outrage. Those artists who do not take into account the probable response of their patron and the potential audience are likely to experience difficulty, as are those who are able to anticipate these reactions but deliberately disregard them and inflame controversy. In either case we see how works of art are generally the product of an interaction, dependent upon the input of creators as well as others (Becker 1982, chapter 7; Griswold 1986, chapter 1). Those others include the various institutions and agencies that support—directly or indirectly—the public exhibition of works almost guaranteed to offend some audience, even as other constituents may applaud. What emerges is often the result of imagined and anticipated audience responses, but when that response has been unanticipated intervention, new rules for future play are established for all concerned.

Although I have cited a variety of problematic situations and a range of outcomes, seemingly disparate phenomena can be analyzed along two important dimensions. First, the *production* of the work and the artist's relation to the larger world must be considered. An artist can either draw directly from the immediate social and political milieu (as in the case of the Washington painting), or act as if the outside world does not exist (as with Richard Serra's *Tilted Arc*). Concurrently, *reception* and the nature of the community in which it occurs must be examined. A community's aesthetic may be in formation, with diffuse definitions of good/bad and proper/improper (for example, during and just after Mayor Washington's tenure), or its aesthetic may be highly articulated (for instance, during and just after Daley's tenure).

Controversy is not aberrant; it should be expected when there is vulnerability along any of these dimensions. "Daley's Tomb" did not provoke controversy because there was an established aesthetic at the time and the challenges mounted by the show could not disrupt it. Although the exhibit championed an alternative aesthetic, it played to a select and sympathetic audience—a strategy that effectively managed and safely "contained" its reception. In the Washington incident, on the other hand, it was impossible to contain the controversy. The School of the Art Institute, the official "patron" of the exhibition of student work that included the offensive painting, was inherently committed to a "value-free," "hands-off" posture out of its emphasis upon artistic freedom. This allowed an open field for action by individuals on both the immediate production and reception sides—respectively the artist and the aldermen—who surely were somewhat conscious of the impact of their actions. As additional diverse constituencies were drawn in, each felt threatened in different ways, and the situation quickly spun out of control. The painting was like a fumbled football in a game without referees: everyone was grabbing for it, each side deemed possession critical for its own ends, but there was no one recognized to have the authority to call "Time out!" or "Out of bounds!"

Such controversies have increased; there is both more support for the idea of public art, and more public and private agencies involved in sponsoring it, as well as more competing definitions about what is desirable in many spheres of contemporary life. This echoes conditions in the 1930s, another time when there was low-value consensus and a large number of art controversies, the latter in part due to the steady supply of artworks produced under direct government sponsorship. In the 1930s the "devils" often took the shape of persons associated with foreign ideas like Communism and its accompanying specter of revolt. Today, however, we are more commonly plagued by inner devils, with portrayals of our own leaders and their capabilities providing one of the troublesome themes.

These contentious events demonstrate once again that problematic public art—like other material that some judge to go beyond community standards—highlights the very values it has transgressed. It unites both those who respond negatively to it as well as those who rise up in its defense, reminding each side of what they hold dear. Therefore, even art that seems to be oppositional can have unintentional, supportive consequences. What might appear to be the most assaultive cultural products may clarify troublesome social situations. In the short run the controversies these works generate cause hurt and dismay. But in the longer view such struggles can also stimulate dialogue and provide catharsis, and may eventually activate a healing process.

Notes

I thank George Chancey, Jr., and Randy Martin for comments and suggestions on an earlier version of this essay. One such version was presented at the 84th Annual Meeting of the American Sociological Association, August 1989, in San Francisco. In addition, it appears in somewhat different form in Dubin (1992).

1. The oddest incident I have seen reported regards a painting that was banned from a small college in Virginia. The painting presented an American family scene with a child represented by the remains of an aborted human fetus. School administrators feared the work violated a state law restricting the transport and display of dead human bodies; they also claimed it violated propriety because it was a "disgusting morsel of human tissue." On the one hand, the definition of what is human was involved; on the other, the limits of free speech (Hentoff 1984a, b).

2. As outspoken as some players became in this drama, they could also maintain silence. In June 1988 I surveyed all fifty Chicago aldermen by mail, soliciting any public statements they had made in relation to the incident, relevant ward publications, etc. I carefully worded my cover letter so it would not offend any side to the dispute, highlighted my past residency in Chicago and my ongoing professional interest in public art and "the social role and responsibility of the artist," and also included self-addressed, postpaid envelopes. Significantly, I received not one response to my request.

3. The SAIC is particularly sensitive to public opinion. It is a private professional college of art, separate from but associated with the Art Institute of Chicago. Together they make up the Museum-School Corporation. The main buildings stand on public land, and both establishments receive public funds. In this instance, SAIC further agreed to intensify efforts to recruit more minority administrators, faculty members, and students (Huntley 1988).

4. The ACLU highlighted its defense of this artist in a June 1988 mail membership drive and solicitation for donations. The organization also emphasized that by accepting this case it did not wish to appear to be taking a position against the interests of blacks.

5. The artist's motives were much debated. In the black press he was castigated for being opportunistic (Strausberg 1988a) and for trying to build publicity for himself (Strausberg 1988c). Such calculation was intimated by others as well (Artner 1988), but one of the most damning charges was made by a columnist who reported that before the controversy had erupted, he'd gotten a call from someone claiming to be the artist and urging him to write about it (Greene 1988). And even though

the artist was placed in a tradition of prankster art dating back to the nineteenth century (Miner 1988), he claimed he did not intentionally provoke this controversy. He has acknowledged producing other iconoclastic paintings, however, and affirmed, "I don't want to make art that everybody loves" (Schlesinger 1988).

6. The artist was frequently quoted as saying his idea for the painting was derived mainly from a poster he saw that showed Washington and Jesus looking down on Chicago; the public transformation of the late mayor into an icon was what he was satirizing (Hornung 1988).

7. The sense of siege in the black community is vividly conveyed by this additional quote from the director of Operation PUSH: "We are still suffering from that great loss [Mayor Washington's death]. When a community is divided, it makes it more vulnerable to attack by its enemies . . . like flies to an open sore. . . . A united Black community should not continue to have to defend itself against questionable charges of anti-Semitism and racism. . . . [T]he gross depiction of Washington . . . is but the latest in a series of escalating attacks and assaults against the Black community" (Strausberg 1988b).

8. The actual justification for the seizure was under a local statute regarding incitement to riot. The constitutional basis for bringing legal action against the seizure rests on the rights of free expression, freedom from unreasonable seizure, and freedom from deprivation of property without due process. Also potentially relevant is the 1988 Supreme Court decision in favor of *Hustler* magazine, which upheld its right to publish a scathing parody of Jerry Falwell. This reaffirmed the broad protection of editorial criticism of public figures. And according to the local ACLU director, there is nothing obscene or inherently defamatory about the painting (Donahue transcript 1988, 5).

9. There is a further irony: one of the aldermen who seized the painting was formerly a Black Panther Party member who had been defended in 1969 by the ACLU, which had argued for the protection of his right to distribute his group's literature (Donahue transcript 1988, 14).

10. Dichotomizing the art world into representational and nonrepresentational spheres does not accurately reflect contemporary realities. With postmodernism, concrete imagery can be used in unexpected ways, blurring traditional distinctions. However, I would argue that the public often responds negatively to such innovative "realistic" expressions because they challenge established rules of comprehensibility. And while this reaction parallels the negative response to nonrepresentational forms, it may be even more pronounced: the familiarity of much postmodernist imagery sparks recognition and allows partial readings, but ultimately causes frustration and resentment among those uninitiated into the aesthetics of this world.

References

"America in the Morning." 1988. Mutual Broadcasting System. May 13.

Apter, David, and Nagayo Sawa. 1984. *Against the State: Politics and Social Protest in Japan.* Cambridge, Mass.: Harvard University Press.

Artner, Alan G. 1988. "Two Sides Hit a Wall in Art Institute Furor." *Chicago Tribune,* May 22, p. 13.

Balfe, Judith H. 1989. "(Re)presenting Social Reality, (De)constructing Public Sculpture: Two Vietnam Memorials." Conference on Writing the Social Text. College Park, Md.: University of Maryland. April 11.

Balfe, Judith H., and Margaret J. Wyszomirski. 1986. "Public Art and Public Policy." *Journal of Arts Management and Law* 15(4): 5–31.

Becker, Howard S. 1982. *Art Worlds.* Berkeley: University of California Press.

Brenson, Michael. 1988. "A Savage Painting Raises Troubling Questions." *New York Times,* May 29, pp. 29, 37.

Darnton, Robert. 1985. "Workers Revolt: The Great Cat Massacre of the Rue Saint-Severin." In *The Great Cat Massacre and Other Episodes in French Cultural History,* 75–104. New York: Vintage.

deLarrea, Irene Herner. 1987. *Diego Rivera: Paradise Lost at Rockefeller Center.* Mexico City: EPICUPES, S.A. de C.V.

Donahue, Phil. 1988. Transcript of broadcast on censorship. #061488, June 14. Cincinnati: Multimedia Entertainment, Inc.

Dubin, Steven C. 1987. *Bureaucratizing the Muse: Public Funds and the Cultural Worker.* Chicago: University of Chicago Press.

——. 1992. *Arresting Images: Impolitic Art and Uncivil Actions.* New York: Routledge.

Fleeson, Lucinda, and Edward J. Sozanski. 1987. "Artist's View of the City Gets Trashed." *Philadelphia Inquirer,* July 13, p. A10.

Fried, Joseph P. 1987. "Statue Showing Women as 'Evil' May Be Moved." *New York Times,* Oct. 13, p. B3.

Green, Paul M., and Melvin G. Holli, eds. 1987. *The Mayors: The Chicago Political Tradition.* Carbondale: Southern Illinois University Press.

Greene, Bob. 1988. "Editors Choose to Say 'No.'" *Chicago Tribune,* May 18, 5:1.

Griswold, Wendy. 1986. *Renaissance Revivals: City Comedy and Revenge Tragedy in the London Theatre, 1576–1980.* Chicago: University of Chicago Press.

Guilbaut, Serge. 1983. *How New York Stole the Idea of Modern Art: Abstract Expressionism, Freedom and the Cold War.* Translated by Arthur Goldhammer. Chicago: University of Chicago Press.

Hentoff, Nat. 1984a. "Has This Painting Committed a Crime?" *Village Voice,* Feb. 28, p. 6.

——. 1984b. "If It's Not a Human Being, What's the Crime?" *Village Voice,* Mar. 6, p. 6.

——. 1988. "The Day They Came to Arrest the Painting." *Village Voice,* June 21, p. 37.

Hochfield, Sylvia. 1988. "The Moral Rights (and Wrongs) of Public Art." *ARTnews* 87(5): 143–46.

Hornung, Rick. 1988. "Big City, Dim Bulbs: Painting Incites Chicago Riot." *Village Voice,* May 31, p. 17.

Huntley, Steve. 1988. "Racial Parity Urged at Art Institute School." *Chicago Sun-Times,* May 26.

Jarrett, Vernon. 1988. "Art Deserves a Lot Better Judgment." *Chicago Sun-Times,* May 15, p. 13.

Johnson, Dirk. 1988. "In Chicago, Outsiders of 1968 Are Insiders Now." *New York Times,* July 24, p. E4.

Lazare, Lewis. 1990. "The Culture Club: CTA to Ban Busses?" *Chicago Reader,* May 25, p. 1.

Lester, Julius. 1988. "When Black Unity Works against Critical Inquiry." *New York Times,* July 12, p. A25.

Lubell, Ellen. 1984. "Eye of the Beholder." *Village Voice,* Oct. 30, p. 51.

Miner, Michael. 1988. "Outlaw Art." *Chicago Reader,* May 27, p. 4.

Muwakkil, Salim. 1988. "Harold Washington's Fractured Legacy." *In These Times* (May 25-June 7): 12.

Newman, M. W. 1988. " 'Posse' Grab of Student Art Stirs Protests." *Chicago Sun-Times,* May 15, p. 3.

Newsweek. 1988. May 23, p. 25.

New York Daily News. 1988. May 13, p. 23.

New York Post. 1988. May 13, p. 5.

New York Times. 1987. July 26, p. 30; Nov. 26, p. D19.

———. 1988. Jan 10; May 29; July 24; Aug. 31.

Olson, David. 1990. "Read Their Lips: Illinois Moves to Ban AIDS Poster." *Village Voice,* July 24, p. 14.

Outlines. 1988. June.

Philadelphia Inquirer. 1987. July 13, 14, 15, 19.

Price, Debbie M. 1988. "Philadelphia Asks: Is It Art or Politics?" *New York Times,* Jan. 10, p. 35.

Rosen, Steven. 1987. "Women Are Reshaping the Field of Public Art." *New York Times,* Nov. 8, p. 78.

Royko, Mike. 1988. "Alderman's Brain Is a Museum Piece." *Chicago Tribune,* May 17, p. 3.

Schlesinger, Toni. 1988. "The Mayoral Painter's 15 Minutes of Fame." *Chicago Tribune,* May 22, pp. 4–5.

Schmidt, William E. 1987. "Chicago Still Haunted by the Ghost of Capone." *New York Times,* Sept. 20, p. 26.

Sozanski, Edward J. 1987. "Politics versus Art." *Philadelphia Inquirer,* July 19, pp. K1, 14.

Stamets, Bill. 1988. "Theater of Power, Theater of the Absurd." *New Art Examiner* (Summer): 29–31.

Stevens, William K. 1985. "Philadelphia Neighborhood Torn by Racial Tension Starts to Simmer Down." *New York Times,* Dec. 1.

Strahler, Steven R. 1988. "Uproar Trips Resurgent Art Institute." *Crane's Chicago Business* (May 23–29): 1, 53.

Strausberg, Chinta. 1988a. "Aldermen and Artists Clash Over Student's Portrait of Washington." *Chicago Defender,* May 12, p. 3.

———. 1988b. "Barrow: No More Apologies for Remarks." *Chicago Defender,* May 16, p. 3.

————. 1988c. "Racism Cited at Art School." *Chicago Defender*, May 16, p. 1.

Strong, James. 1988. "Sawyer Puts Salve on Racial Wounds." *Chicago Tribune*, May 19, p. 2.

Tesser, Neil. 1985. "Art Police: CTA Takes Gallery for a Ride." *Chicago Reader*, July 5, p. 4.

Wagner-Pacifici, Robin. 1986. *The Moro Morality Play: Terrorism as Social Drama*. Chicago: University of Chicago Press.

Washington Post. 1988. May 14, p. A26.

Windy City Times. 1988. May 12; May 19; May 26; June 2.

PART FOUR

DIRECT PATRONAGE
BY STATE INSTITUTIONS

National governments in the modern world—whether in the postindustrial West or elsewhere—have been obliged to develop arts policies to control competition among the diverse groups seeking support and claiming freedom of expression and individualized creativity. Since one group's definition of artistic genius is another group's definition of artistic license, the state becomes the national arbiter of taste, eagerly or reluctantly as the case may be. As we have seen in the last section, city bureaucracies are at best ineffective, and potentially counterproductive, as structures for art patronage. Yet from the perspective of a national government, the absence of structured (hence bureaucratically administered) arts policy— or simply too permissive an arts policy—is recognized to lead to the kind of social divisiveness that has also been detailed in the last section.

Understandably, national art policies accord with the prevailing political and economic perspectives and institutions. Thus national policies designed to facilitate freedom of expression usually focus primarily on regulating the processes of public art patronage (and by regulating commerce and through taxation, affect private art patronage as well). However, when a state government wants to define and advance social goals whose attainment depends upon a strengthened national identity, it is likely to follow the elitist patronage model of Louis XIV—even when its overarching ideological commitment is populist. Thus officials in newly formed states have usually tried to exercise considerable control over the arts, in order to forge a new "public culture" across the various constituent groups. Such new "patron states" have particular problems in their efforts to coopt the allegiance of the artists so that their art will support the public ideology, rather than oppose it.

Here, Marilyn Rueschemeyer describes the art policies followed by the German Democratic Republic (East Germany) during the forty years of its existence between the end of World War II and German unification in 1990. As a socialist regime committed to Marxist views of art "for the people," it controlled the production of all aspects of art through the Artists' Union. But given a heritage of artistic freedom from the prewar period and the prominence accorded to the arts by the regime (to say nothing of the increasing freedoms and support for the arts in nonsocialist countries), GDR artists were able to pressure the state to permit greater freedom of artistic expression. Indeed, the singularity of their source of patronage contributed to their focused resistance to it. They thus became instrumental in bringing down the regime that had provided them with full material support.

The complexity of such state policies is even greater in former colonies, which need to establish a cultural identity that transcends both the immediate and the precolonial pasts. Vera Zolberg considers the current situation in India, focusing on the role played by the state museums in fostering the new "public culture." In contrast to the monopolistic model of (royal) state patronage developed by French kings, contemporary state patronage enters an arena already crowded by vigorous forms of commercial culture, tempered in India by tribal and religious subcultures. In the museums promising equal valuation of the cultural products of various groups, the very categories of thought used to order the collections and displays that celebrate tribal traditions—and through such celebration overcome the related traditional conflicts—often exacerbate them instead. Again, the single visible patron, the state, becomes the focus of any resultant resentment.

✦ 10 ✦

State Patronage in the German Democratic Republic: Artistic and Political Change in a State Socialist Society

MARILYN RUESCHEMEYER

Modern art has a complex and deeply problematic relation to society and politics. This is generally recognized in the capitalist West. It is equally true of the state socialist countries of Eastern Europe. An exploration of the role art has played in these countries is often blocked by a simple stereotype, that Stalinist policies overwhelmed and deformed an art that otherwise—if granted its own integrity—would take on the forms and social functions of the arts in the West. While this simplistic view arises out of moral outrage, one can share the outrage and still reject the stereotype. Implicit in this stereotype is a conception of art that sees its historical development as ultimately determined from within, provided that art is given the social and political autonomy that it ought to have. This is naive reductionism, whether it is applied in the West or in the East.

Stalinism did indeed impose its will on art as on other spheres of social life in Eastern Europe. But this proposition does not describe fully the life and development of art in postwar Eastern Europe. The demands and dilemmas facing the artist in these state socialist societies were enormously varied and complex both before and after the decline of Stalinism. Stalinist impositions and total state control of art patronage must be seen as one extreme in a wide variety of patterns relating art to society and politics. At the opposite extreme is the model of the alienated artist without any formal patron or audience, producing for a market that neither directly sponsors nor values the creations. Exploring the interrelations of artist and patron in a state socialist country can help to broaden our view of the different relations possible between art and society. This, in turn, can tell us much about the variable social nature of art.

Here I am concerned primarily with visual artists in the German Democratic Republic, but their political situation was similar to that of creative artists in other media. Regardless of the art form selected, then, studying art and politics in the GDR is particularly informative because the historical background of the Weimar Republic and contemporary developments in the art of West Germany after World War II remained important reference points for artistic creation in East Germany after the war. At the same time, the establishment of the GDR represented a radical break with the past, a social and political transformation very different from the trajectory of change in West Germany.

So too, from its very beginnings, was modern art. In all media, it intended to make a radical break with the past by rejecting traditional forms of patronage, just as it rejected traditional styles (though at the same time reacting to them). On both counts, it deliberately distanced itself from the established expectations of the audience. Early Impressionist exhibits in Paris were jeered at by visitors, as the autonomous development of art increasingly conflicted with any expectation that it serve society. Artistic autonomy came to be symbolized by a bohemian lifestyle that (while not in fact typical of most artists) was viewed as spiritually akin to and even necessary for artistic creativity. By the 1920s, rapid stylistic change became the accepted norm for art in the West. Such norms became dominant in critical discourse as well as in the marketplace, and artists had to conform to a standard of constant change in their own styles if they expected critical acclaim and access to the elite market—or to any market in which art was taken seriously.

Artists and art traditions rooted in this historical background confronted a radically different situation after World War II in the newly created state of the GDR. There, rather than facing the choice of creating for an avant-garde or intellectual elite (often *nouveaux* in wealth) or else starving totally unappreciated, artists were supposed to meet the needs of the working classes and serve the development of a new social order—the creation of a socialist society. In this new situation they faced contradictions for which they were unprepared by past experience. After the Nazi period, even artists politically committed to the new political order retained many attitudes and ideological positions associated with the earlier development of modern art, as they began to work under the new regime.

The first dilemma faced by GDR artists involved conceptions about the function of art. Modern art had not only reflected the individual experience of artists in often marginal positions in society. It also tended to look critically at the surrounding society, focusing on suffering, fragmentation, and disorientation, and it rarely either praised the status quo or provided visions of the future. For artists to support—and be supported by—the now dominant socialist political elite meant a radical about face vis-à-vis society and the state. A second contradiction was closely related, concerning the audience for art. Art in the new GDR society was to be accessible to the working people. Yet the more esoteric standards of earlier modern art could not be easily dismissed; in fact, for most artists, these continued to define artistic integrity and existential commitment. A third dilemma corresponded to the first two and concerned the increasing political control of artistic production and the need to conform to official expectations in order to carry on an artistic career at all. The dilemma was a serious one, because along with control came opportunity. For many, there was real pleasure in being economically secure as an artist, rather than continuing to live under very marginal economic conditions. Thus the temptation was strong to conform to the wishes of the new political order.

Of course, such security required overt support for the new vision— and increasingly the defective reality—of a socialist society that insisted on art's popular accessibility. Both security and accessibility were formalized through political control that was a central feature of the obligatory style of "socialist realism." Still, as we will see, the meaning of this official doctrine as well as the artistic responses to changing political demands varied over the forty-five years of GDR history.

While visual art in the GDR was obviously affected by complex relationships with both the Soviet Union and the Federal Republic of Germany, it also evolved internally. Recognition of the influences of societal change on the art world and, in turn, the impact of internal developments in art on GDR society increase our understanding of the multifaceted relationship of art to political developments in a socialist society. On this basis, we may conclude that the difficulties encountered by state patronage structures in the context examined here are similar to those experienced by institutional patrons of the arts in the contemporary world, regardless of type of political economy.

The Beginning: GDR Art after World War II

The heritage of GDR art was rooted not just in the immediate past of the Nazi period but more importantly in the more distant Weimar Republic and in the traditions of even more remote periods such as the realism of nineteenth-century painting. For twelve years during the Nazi regime, Germans had been allowed to view only art that may be described as heroic and sentimental. Thousands of modern paintings were removed from museums and other collections. Goebbels said that the people wanted to see "the beautiful and sublime . . . a world of wonder shall open here before their eyes."[1] Those artists who would not conform to these Nazi criteria of acceptable art either emigrated or stopped working altogether, in order to escape severe punishment or even death.

Immediately after the war, in 1946, the new socialist authorities celebrated particularly those artists who had been persecuted during the Nazi period. Their works were featured in the first major postwar art exhibits in Dresden and Berlin, which included approximately 600 works by 250 artists from both West and East Germany. Represented were Expressionists, former members of the Association of Revolutionary Artists of Germany (ASSO, 1928–33), as well as artists identified with a number of other artistic movements existing before World War II. The openness to a variety of artistic styles at this time was reinforced at the First Central Cultural Congress of the Communist Party (KPD), meeting in 1946. On this occasion, Wilhelm Pieck (who was to become first president of the GDR) emphasized the inviolability of an artist's freedom to choose the form he or she considered the best (Thomas 1980, 17).

In apparently full agreement, Major Alexander Dymschitz, representing the Soviet Military Administration (SMAD), pronounced that "during the Nazi period, art was the victim of a barbaric regimentation. . . . When families were represented, the artist had to make certain that the German family was portrayed with at least four children. This nonsense is over forever" (Feist and Gillen 1988, 10). This comment was consistent with the general policy of the SMAD, which aimed for a broad united front of antifascist forces, but this policy lasted only until mid-1948.

Indeed, already evident in the GDR were different attitudes toward the social role of art that flowed from the Soviet Union and became intensified by the Cold War. Put into practice, these soon restricted the diversity of views permitted expression within the artistic and political community. Even in 1946, a report appeared in *Neues Deutschland* (the leading East German newspaper) on a meeting of the Saxonian Artists' Congress. There Colonel Tulpanow (then head of the information section of the SMAD) talked about the importance of a democratic development in art and the duty of the artist to express the feelings and goals of the people. He advised artists to pay attention to what was happening in the Soviet Union (Feist and Gillen 1988, 11). Since the early 1930s, art in the Soviet Union had been dominated by socialist realism (a conception of art that actually might better be described as socialist idealism). The diversity of visions in the GDR that had survived the Nazi period to find expression in the 1946 Dresden exhibition had long since disappeared from the Soviet art world (Rueschemeyer et al. 1985).

To be sure, the reaction of most GDR viewers to the art shown at the Dresden exhibition was largely negative. After all, they had been looking at Nazi "social realist" art for many years. Such negative responses provided grounds for new accusations condemning formalism (the opposite extreme from socialist realism) by GDR political authorities; while anti-Nazi, these authorities also needed to establish an independent GDR identity separate from Western "bourgeois" developments. Yet it was also on these grounds that, after the end of the Stalinist period, artistic development in East Germany was able to diverge from the Soviet model—a matter to which I shall return.

In any event, from 1946 on, those who conformed to the new political demands quickly took over positions of power in GDR artistic organizations and academies. The interest of many artists in gaining access to important positions and commissions, or merely in finding simple exposure, encouraged conformity and a turning away from styles that could be criticized as decadent, Western, formalistic. Other artists left the country altogether. The disillusionment and emigration of some of the most prominent artists left a deep gap in the GDR art scene, as previously sympathetic authorities turned against modernism. Indeed, only two years after his 1946 talk noted above, Major Dymschitz wrote in the *Taegliche Rundschau* (the SMAD newspaper) that "although Fascism had shaped the artistic experience of a considerable percentage of the German people, that does not save decadent-formalist art from the criticism of the people. The Germans have basically healthy ideas about art but the art of the formalists is sick" (Feist and Gillen 1988, 15).

Still, in the early years of the new regime, the diversity among GDR artists was considerable. A variety of groups built on traditions of the Weimar period, especially those that had been associated with leftist causes. The association of socialist artists of the Weimar period, ASSO, had included artists of expressionist, surrealist, and abstract constructivist styles, and these traditions were renewed in (and immediately after) the 1946 Dresden exhibition, even if the more realistic artists were given more representation.

But in 1949, the Second German Art Exhibition was utterly dominated by socialist realism (although there was still a small representation of Expressionists). The direction was clear: in 1951, the new GDR chairman, Walter Ulbricht, characterized modernist painting, sculpture, and graphics as backward and said no such work could be taken as a model for the future development of the arts. A year later, *Neues Deutschland* attacked the pessimistic character of much contemporary art (Thomas 1980, 25). Accordingly, at the Third German Art Exhibit in Dresden in 1953, virtually all work permitted exhibition was natural illustration, socialist realism similar to work in the Soviet Union, or involved the use of stereotyped symbols such as flags, peace doves, and clasped hands. Correspondingly, in 1951 and again in 1959 at its second and fourth congresses, the Artists' Union (Verbandes Bildender Kuenstler Deutschlands [VBKD]) took rigid stands in favor of realism and against formalism (Werner and Thomas 1985, 229).

The modernist styles were not forgotten, but since they could not be practiced, they could not be developed. Indeed, a current analyst of the period, Karin Thomas, suggests that there is probably no reputable German art historian who does not regret that the movements spawned by ASSO in the late 1920s were repressed by both the Nazi and socialist regimes and that so many years had to pass before young artists recovered these traditions as possible models for their own work (Thomas 1980, 30). In fact, it was not until 1988 that an exhibit was held in Berlin of former ASSO artists, commemorating the sixtieth anniversary of the founding of that association.

With the death of Stalin in 1953, the political pressures in the arts eased somewhat; as in the Soviet Union, the Khruschev period promised greater artistic freedom from total state control. Artists such as Willi Sitte, Bernhard Heisig, and Werner Tuebke turned to more individualist forms of realism. They were the typical representatives of GDR art seen abroad in the 1970s and 1980s, although there were also other styles that could be described as impressionist, decorative, and expressionist. The 1969 Leipzig district exhibit of the Artists' Union included artists oriented to the *Neue Sachlichkeit* of the 1920s.

Nonetheless, access to artistic developments in the West was still difficult. Though less isolated than their Soviet counterparts had been for long periods of time, East German artists had little information about contemporary Western trends. Subscription to Western journals was forbidden, and special permission was needed for access to libraries and other collections of material. (Some of the new developments in Western art became known later through West German television, increasingly available to nearly all GDR citizens.)

Thus one cannot speak of a continuous liberating development in the arts after the difficulties of the Stalinist period. In 1959 we see renewed efforts to bring artists into line with party expectations at a series of conferences. For example, at a meeting that year in Bitterfeld, artists and writers were urged to increase their contact with workers both in the art that they produced and through programs set up to involve them in direct exchange with workers. Amateur groups in the arts received greater attention and funding, inhibiting any sense of art's autonomy that might be associated with professionalism. Not surprisingly, in the same period (and intensifying after the fall of Khrushchev), artists in the Soviet Union experienced a tightening of the reins. Thus the cultural scene was bleak throughout the Ulbricht era, even if there were some intense controversies about art. It was only in 1971 when Erich Honecker became first secretary of the Socialist Unity Party (SED) that artists could begin to hope for a greater acceptance of diversity in style and content.

In a talk to the Central Committee in 1971, Honecker declared that provided one started from the standpoint of socialism, there could be no taboos in art and literature, neither in content nor in style. Honecker was responding to increasing pressures in the society for social and economic improvements as well as to the ongoing demands of artists and writers. From that point on, artistic developments in the GDR reflected the continuing tensions between these demands and the self-defined needs of the state bureaucracies and ideologies. After a brief description of the way GDR art was organized, I will return to these issues.

The Organization of GDR Art

As in the Soviet Union, the Ministry of Culture (responsible for policy on the arts, museums, and exhibitions as well as for the allocation of important funding) and the Artists' Union shaped the official institutional world of GDR art and monopolized patronage. Both were linked to the leading party, the SED. Hans Joachim Hoffmann, minister for culture, and Willi Sitte (until 1988 head of the union) were members of the Central Committee of the SED. Under state control, exhibitions and sales of art took place in thirty-five national galleries. The Kulturbund was another relevant association—an umbrella organization sponsoring activities related to a broader audience (such as lectures, exhibits in small galleries, amateur circles of a variety of sorts, and hobby groups). These activities often took place in the Kulturhaeuser, or clubhouses, which existed all over the region but which differed considerably in the scope and quality of their offerings to the public.

It was very difficult to work as an artist in the GDR without being a member of the Artists' Union. Eighty percent of the artists in the GDR joined the union as candidates for three years after graduating from the five-year program of art school. During this candidacy period, they were paid three hundred marks a month. (The money was available only if they returned to their hometowns to work; if they insisted on remaining in the larger cities, they forfeited this stipend.) The union enforced official policy on the arts, but it also played a mediating role between official policy and the demands of the artists. It had the seldom-realized potential of becoming an institution that could provide great protection and support for its members.

Until the end of the GDR regime, the union negotiated collective or individual contracts for socially important art such as sculpture and murals commissioned by the various social organizations, enterprises, and the state. The cultural arm of the Freierdeutscher Gewerkschaftsbund (FDGB, the national umbrella union of the workers' collectives) organized such contracts with state-owned industry. The offices of fine arts in the fifteen district governments were also important sponsors. Typically, the people who staffed these offices had studied cultural politics and art history. The six thousand members of the Artists' Union itself (which also included designers, commercial artists, and craftspeople as well as art critics, scholars, and administrators) were organized into specialty sections. Artists generally worked through the district branches of their union section to receive commissions, contracts, interest-free loans, and a number of other benefits.

To be sure, it was not impossible to work as an artist outside of the union, but it was much more difficult to gain access to jobs and studios, participate in major exhibits, pay for materials, travel abroad, or earn as much when selling work (because there was a higher tax for income from self-employed nonunion work). Furthermore, a number of welfare benefits, including access to vacation houses, were tied to union membership. As in the other Eastern Bloc countries, conformity to prevailing norms was a criterion for general exposure of one's art and for receipt of all the other benefits that come with being a member of the official artistic community.

One might ask why anybody remained outside of the union, and who did so. The answers are complex: aside from personal tensions and rivalries, they involve the issue of nonconformity, to either artistic or political norms. Throughout the four decades of the GDR's existence, some artists (including those with international reputations) were not acceptable to the regime because of the work that they produced or because of the views that they expressed about art or other sensitive issues. Ultimately, their presence and survival pressured the state patrons to grant some of these artists a degree of recognition. Even before the collapse of the regime, the union was able to incorporate a wider variety of artists, usually because of the recognition that they found outside the GDR but also for a variety of other reasons, which will be discussed later.

On occasion, artists were rejected for union membership because they had not graduated from the official art institutions. This requirement became more stringent over the years, supposedly because of the increase in the number of would-be artists. Admission to the art schools was competitive, favoring those who moved toward professionalization (with its appealing as well as its limiting aspects) and giving an advantage to those who accepted the established positions, both artistic and political. Some critics have claimed that candidates were rejected because they had worked with noninstitutional artists before applying, and not merely because they were unwilling to comply with prevailing artistic norms. The mechanisms of professionalization and professional education (well known in many different contexts in the West) merged here with an ideological and political selectivity specific to the GDR.

Although the art schools varied in artistic disciplines and emphasis (as well as in their adherence to socialist realism), all GDR art students went through a traditional training where the emphasis was on the figure; abstraction was discouraged. Not surprisingly, it was primarily the artistically conservative students who were chosen to participate in prestigious and specially supported programs after graduation and to work with a Master at the Academy of Arts.

While the Artists' Union maintained policies of both exclusion and conformity, it made efforts to integrate young and innovative artists. The union was at once pulled in the direction of what it saw as its traditional responsibilities and toward new developments in the international art world. Political ideology alone was not at the heart of the ensuing conflicts; regardless of artistic predilection, those wishing to maintain positions of dominance and power, with all the attendant privileges, equally encouraged arrangements that reinforced traditional notions of art. Indeed, when advocates of new forms did become accepted and established, they too developed similar patterns of defense. Thus Willi Sitte, whose work was seen as innovative and new in 1971 at the end of the Ulbricht regime, ultimately became such a symbol of stagnation and limitation in artistic style and philosophy that in 1988 he was unable to maintain his position as head of the union.

Art Galleries and Exhibitions

Galleries in the GDR were run by a variety of institutions, including both the national and city governments, the Artists' Union, the Kulturbund, and subordinate parties such as the National Democratic Party (NDP) or the Christian Democratic Party (CDU). None were privately owned. They showed work that appealed to a variety of tastes and gave exposure to artists with diverse styles and aspirations—if not a universal range. However, such gallery exhibits were neither the only nor the major way in which artists earned money. Even with the union's support, it was difficult for artists to gain commissions for large projects and to sell their work for what they considered an adequate amount. They still had to cultivate their own connections to institutions sponsoring artwork, even if there was some mediation by the union. To sell one's work abroad was attractive because it could bring valued foreign recognition as well as foreign currency earnings. Still, the state took 85 percent of all earnings paid in Western currency, and to achieve such exposure and sales was a very complicated affair that few had the resources to arrange.

Within the GDR itself, even gaining a commission of some importance did not always mean public acknowledgment or even exposure. Sometimes a museum, a factory, or a city government commissioned and bought but then simply stored the art; eventually the artist was perhaps asked to suggest where it should be placed. If the style was unacceptable either to the politicians or to the lay audience, it would be stored for a long time. This happened because of popular resistance as often as for political reasons.

In interviews I conducted in 1987–88, several gallery managers complained that for years the galleries were empty and that few people came to look at the art. Some galleries offered lectures on art and concerts to attract visitors; some of these were well attended and others were not, according to the managers. Even the official, state-supported galleries still depended upon sales to individuals (in one, doctors were prime customers) and in recent years, a variety of styles became acceptable, however they might have been interpreted. For example, abstract works by two young artists were described as part of the realistic tradition. For those state galleries (such as those in the Alte Museum and the Unter den Linden) that were to appeal to foreign visitors, the range of artistic styles was more extensive.

The national exhibition held every five years in Dresden continued to attract both domestic and foreign attention. While it gave art greater visibility, it also continued to evoke anger and frustration among many artists both inside and outside the union. From its founding in 1946, this exhibit had developed into an affair of state, an occasion at which the highest representatives of party and state acknowledged the great and changing importance of the role of art in the GDR. Given the exhibit's prominence, controversy over the exhibition in 1972–73, the first under Honecker's regime, led to major changes in GDR arts policy.

For each of these enormous exhibitions, the works selected had to survive a competition that started at the local and district levels, following which they were reviewed by the national union section representatives. Some people sat on both district and national boards and thus had enormous decision-making power. Cultural functionaries were involved in the selection process at all levels, even though the board was mainly composed of artists. One curator told me that even after the jury decided, nonvoting representatives of the party and ministry added their views on particular works, and that these views were usually decisive, especially if there was conflict, for example, between the district and the national sections of the union.

Not surprisingly, a number of important artists were still not shown, even in the last Dresden exhibit (1987–88). At the same time, the exhibit included many mediocre works, most notoriously a portrait of a member of the Central Committee that was an embarrassment to many of the people involved. However complex the process of selection, increasing fury about the resulting show contributed to the important changes taking place in the Artists' Union even before the demise of the regime.

GDR Arts Policy and the Audience

Over the forty years of GDR existence, the goals of policy on the arts changed considerably. Throughout, they reflected specifically political considerations as well as the changing overall cultural climate. Influenced to some extent by the internal dynamics of the GDR art world, they were also affected by relations with the Soviet Union and with the West; after the events of 1989, they became transformed again, both in reaction to past difficulties and, more important, in reaction to the prospects of unification. As noted above, at the outset GDR officials wanted the public to be exposed to art that would re-educate them out of their old, reactionary views and increase their general aesthetic understanding. Accordingly, emphasis was put upon German traditions of art, especially on those artworks that would presumably encourage a positive view of socialism to counteract any cosmopolitan "decadent" influences. Art was to be embedded in popular culture and understood by the people. People's own lives were to be reflected in what they saw. A common culture was to be created through the participation of many people in amateur art groups of all sorts, through visits and exhibits by artists in the enterprises, and through work-collective excursions to art exhibits. Judged by this goal of a common culture, there were real and positive changes in the GDR. There is little question that the general educational level was enormously increased; it is also true that masses of people who never before set foot in a museum or theater have been exposed to the arts—even if it is apparent that for a number, these initial visits were strange events, experienced mostly as a compulsory union work-collective activity.

An American artist visiting the last Dresden exhibit in the winter of 1987–88 might at first have envied the scene. Altogether, attendance totaled approximately one million in a country of barely seventeen million. People lined up to enter every day, filling the exhibition halls. Art students served as guides for groups and other interested people, explaining the goals of artists and how one might understand the works themselves. At the same time, the American artist could not help but notice that most of the audience remained totally confused about the very few works exhibited that were outside of the realist tradition as broadly interpreted— even as some people were attracted by the gradually increasing diversity of the art that was on exhibit from 1972 onward.

Their confusion is not surprising; in the schools, students had virtually no exposure to contemporary art and were taught only about the established and approved traditions. The myriad amateur art circles produced realistic painting and sculpture. Of course, all this is not fundamentally different from the situation in the West, except that in the GDR (as in the other state socialist countries of Eastern Europe), the state took an official position and actively sought to promote its own conceptions of the arts, one based totally on this "lowest common denominator" factor. Yet it is probably fair to say that despite the efforts of the GDR to reach the masses and to create a single common culture, there was always more than one culture in the GDR. Intellectuals created and supported more complex forms of the arts, even though they could not attract many workers to the more contemporary expressions of music, theater, and art that they preferred.

In an effort to gauge the success of the tenth national Dresden exhibit of 1987–88 in reaching a broad audience, researchers interviewed viewers systematically, querying visitors to a Dresden district exhibit that was considered particularly innovative.[2] According to Bernd Lindner, a sociologist involved in this study, approximately a quarter of the visitors attended under the auspices of their work collectives. Fully half of all the visitors were graduates of universities and technical schools; 20 percent were skilled workers and masters, and 30 percent were students and apprentices.[3] According to another informal estimate, 70 percent of the visitors were university students or graduates. (These latter proportions are similar to those of visitors to contemporary art exhibitions in the West as well.)

The high education level of most visitors to the 1987–88 exhibition accords with that of people who were surveyed at the previous exhibition in 1984, over 90 percent of whom gave their full approval to the exhibits of applied arts, whereas for paintings, graphics and sculpture approval was given by only 56 percent (Kober 1984, 141). Even with the vast majority of exhibited works being in realistic style, it was difficult for many to understand or appreciate what they were seeing.

From these surveys and his other research, Lindner thought that about 650,000 people in the GDR were seriously interested in visual art, of whom two-thirds had traditional tastes. Thus only about 200,000 (only a small percentage of the adult population) were more developed in their understanding of complicated works.[4] Despite (or perhaps because of) its small size, this latter group had very intense artistic interests, visiting on average about ten exhibits a year and traveling all over the GDR to see international and local GDR exhibits. Among the most important of these were retrospectives on the work of Paul Klee, German Expressionists of the 1920s, and Joseph Beuys. In each case, the Ministry of Culture approved exhibition of German art of international acclaim; to fail to do so, the GDR state would have continued to alienate its most educated citizens and to create additional difficulties in presenting itself as a viable alternative German state in the international community.

Accordingly, from the mid-1970s, there was an increase in the variety of styles shown; these included works in the tradition of late Impressionism, a small number of Constructivist and Surrealist works, as well as pictures based on montage and collage. Changes in artistic form and also in subject matter were considered important, even if controversial. There was a growing interest in depicting problematic aspects of everyday life, including expressions of isolation, alienation, and difficulties in interpersonal relationships, as well as in such broader issues as pollution, aggression, and war. Even historical paintings were designed to be more directly relevant to contemporary issues, some done in stereotyped forms but others in much more subtle and sophisticated styles. Concurrently, GDR literature became known for its revealing and beautifully expressed understandings of personal life in a socialist society and the complex interweavings between ideal and reality. Thus it is not surprising that some GDR visual artists were interested in making a similar contribution with their work by bringing into the public discussion issues that were rarely if ever dealt with in newspapers or on television. That they could do so at all depended upon certain cultural functionaries, personally sympathetic and supportive of new artistic movements, who showed great courage in exhibiting these usually "unofficial" artists.

Emigration to the West

Part of the pressure to permit such exhibitions came from outside the country. After the end of the Nazi period, many intellectuals and artists returned to what later became the GDR. However, disappointed with the increasingly negative official reception to their work and frightened by the criticism of the Stalinist period, a number of artists again emigrated and contributed to external criticism of the GDR's civil liberties record. As we have noted, after 1972, in part to address such criticism, Honecker accepted new art forms under the premise of socialism. Yet insecurities continued among emigrés and their domestic followers—and with reason. Thus even during the first exhibition to follow Honecker's official pronouncements, certain critical paintings were put in a side room during his visit along with a number of cultural functionaries, while other abstract works that were difficult to move were hidden behind photo equipment. No wonder artists did not completely trust the recent developments, even as they hoped for the future (Pohl and Pohl 1979, 21).

Despite the gradual lifting of taboos after 1972, art in the GDR still had definite official and quasi-official tasks. Although it became possible for artists to criticize such conditions as the pollution of the environment and general issues of war, still forbidden were themes that linked material shortages in the GDR to its political system, criticism of atomic energy, the Berlin wall, the military structure, and even references to the "other" Germany expressed in nostalgia for certain landscapes. It remained the case that those artists who conformed to the articulated norms were advanced and honored over those who were critical. The irritation of those artists who were excluded, or whose opportunities were limited, again led some to emigrate from the GDR even as greater freedoms were permitted.

Visual artists were not alone in suffering these restrictions. Dramatists, composers, and poets joined the painters in a continuing stream of talent to the West, particularly to West Germany, greatly enriching its cultural life at the expense of that of the GDR. Feeling these losses, cultural and political functionaries proclaimed again and again the importance of open discussion about all issues. There were increasing attempts at integrating artists into the official artistic institutions. However, many artists who were belatedly accepted felt tolerated at best rather than feeling really cherished; when given the opportunity, even more left for the West. According to one estimate, about a third of the fifty best artists in Dresden left between 1982 and 1987; these are figures comparable to the proportion of artists that emigrated during the worst period of Stalinist influence in the 1950s.[5]

In my interviews with some of these emigré artists, it became apparent that they held quite dissimilar attitudes toward the GDR and dissimilar ideas about art. Several had felt guilty about emigration and saddened by their inability to bring about change in the existing system. Others believed that the GDR would never change its basic political structure or its policy on the arts, so that there was no sense in attempting to be creative in such a restrictive atmosphere. For both groups, however, emigration to West Germany in the 1980s had many advantages: the language was the same, citizenship and several important health and other benefits were automatically granted to GDR emigrés, there was immediate attention and public support for artists of any prominence, there were enticing financial rewards for those who were successful, and, most important, the whole world of Western art was now open and easily accessible.

During this same period, many Soviet and East European artists also emigrated to Western Europe and the United States (Rueschemeyer et al. 1985). Most had additional difficulties of dealing with an entirely strange culture and a new language. But both Soviet and GDR emigré artists experienced problems in their lives specifically as artists, including an acceptance and enthusiasm at the initial point of their arrival as "political refugees," followed by a benign neglect of their work and their fate. Some artists in both groups remained nostalgic for the intensity of the artistic atmosphere that they had known at home. As one of them put it: "I'm not someone who hates the GDR. Actually, I found more people there interested in art and books and not just money. There was also a greater respect for the artist. I miss going into the countryside and painting with a group of people. I don't have much work here; my life is harder."

However, many artists who have had limited success since emigration have not regretted their decision to leave the GDR at this time. It is my impression that this is especially true of the younger artists, those who came of age after Honecker started to loosen the controls in 1972 and who thus were most exposed to avant-garde art. Even if they have not yet established themselves as artists, they have had an easier time integrating themselves into the cultural life of the West than have the older artists who are more comfortable with socialist realism. However, the emigré artists from both the Soviet Union and the GDR have benefited from the increasing diversity of styles that had become acceptable in Western contemporary art.

Diversity in the Subsequent GDR Art Scene

The complex political maneuvering and the debates on the role of art in a socialist society that took place in the 1980s, along with the growing diversity of independent artistic expressions, made the GDR a fascinating place to observe these transitions even before the autumn of 1989. During the decade, those who advocated the artist's responsibility to the public typically retained a loyalty to some variety of realism and did not view themselves as alienated artists in the Western sense. Bernhard Heisig, one of the most established artists in the GDR (and in 1988 first vice-president of the Artists' Union under then-president Willi Sitte), made the following comment: "You want me to make myself into something I don't want to be. . . . I always have to make something new, a strange idea of artistic freedom. If I am, here and there, an outsider, that is not my intention. I want to be a part of the aggravations as well as the joys of the society" (*Der Spiegel* 1988, 151).

Among those I interviewed in 1988 who had not emigrated, however, at least one was more upset with the financial difficulties of being an artist in the GDR than with the existing restrictions: "It's better to have something to work against rather than having it all open." Another (who had waited fifteen years for his first exhibit) commented: "It is good to be fighting for something and working outside the system for what you want. It's not such a tragic thing. Artistic production is individual production." These attitudes are potentially very important because in some sense modern art is an enclave enterprise in relation to society as a whole, oppositional to the dominant culture whatever form this may take. Thus there is some legitimacy and even structural base for resisting pressures from the authorities, who are defined as illegitimate because they speak for the state. This is true even after the structuring of a reunified Germany, when the result for artists is now the absence of political pressure: the state that grants freedom is to be critiqued as has been the state that denies it—even if for opposite reasons.

From the mid-1980s on, the exhibits, concerts, readings, and happenings in Prenzlauer Berg (a neighborhood in Berlin) showed the kinds of activities that were already taking place outside the official GDR culture system. The participants varied from members of the Artists' Union to young people who worked at a variety of odd jobs and remained outside of any formal artistic institutional structure. Their attitudes toward the regime also could not be easily classified; at the very least, however, there was a notion about the importance of art's independence and a rejection of restrictions prohibiting any real critique of their own society. Visual artists crossed beyond the boundaries of their own media and cooperated with poets, dancers, and musicians. Tapes were made of such groups as Musik aus dem Land, Demokratischer Konsum, and the Bolshovistisches Chor Orchester. The members of these groups played openly, earned little money, and paid high taxes on their income (and were usually in debt because of what they owed for their technical equipment). Christoph Tannert, an art scholar and critic who worked with young artists in the union as well as lending his support to unofficial artists, walked a fine line in his efforts to legitimize the latter. He played a role in providing increased exposure for the music groups as well. (In fact, the tapes of these groups were played on the state radio even though they were not sold in state stores. Many of the artists did not want the state directly involved in the production of their work, in order to remain uncompromised before their audience.)

During this same period, however, some of these independent efforts were stopped by the authorities. For example, at a festival held in a culture house in Dresden, which included contemporary art with jazz and rock, an artist reading from *Neues Deutschland* threw the headlines to the audience. Two artists were arrested and the director of the culture house was fired.

Although the artists involved in these developments emphasized individuality of expression, they also remained closely in touch with each other, meeting regularly in cafes and informing each other of unofficial exhibits and concerts. Exhibits were and still are held in ateliers or apartments, with as many as a hundred people showing up for openings. As mentioned above, people interested in contemporary art and music traveled across the GDR for many of the events, although it is understandable that a young artist having an exhibit would be more likely to attract an audience from the same city. The balance between individuality and communal commitment has provided an interesting example of these transitions in a socialist society.

Artists also worked with poets in the creation of beautiful hand-produced books; such printings were typically in ninety-nine copies that were sold openly, and collectors have bought them for very moderate prices. Still, joint poetry and art books (as well as journals) were somewhat easier to collaborate on and to market than joint productions involving sophisticated technology. The lack of technical equipment for all sorts of artistic productions was a problem in the GDR, and artists still remained behind the West in this respect even if they had more exposure than before to what was being done abroad.

Throughout this period, in addition to individual private initiatives in artistic production outside the state apparatus, the Protestant church was a haven for various independent art exhibits. As an institutional umbrella for a number of independent groups of all kinds (including environmental and peace groups), it allowed its facilities to be used for exhibits and performances as well. Some of these rooms were very simple; some included an informal cafe. In 1988, in one such room in the Zionskirche in Berlin, the minister, an energetic young man not so different in style from some of his contemporaries in the Communist party, spoke of creating a church "from below" where people such as social workers or nurses who studied some theology could be given space to establish alternative groups. Along these lines, the Evangelischer Kunstdienst, a Protestant artists' service, also maintained a gallery space. It sponsored seminars on the arts with people from Western Europe, collected art journals, and offered some church contracts for artists. One of its publications, *Dialog mit der Bibel*, included a contribution by Herbert Sandberg, who was both Jewish and an SED party member (Rennert 1984). This group kept a delicate balance in asserting a degree of autonomy in GDR society. The involvement of artists in other church activities resulted in difficulties on more than one occasion. Within the SED itself, there seem to have been opposing views on how these various church activities should be handled, and, even as the pattern of an antagonistic cooperation between church and state became increasingly established, at times the authorities came down hard on young activists.

Still, all along the West was an important and consistent orientation point in the development of autonomous art. The GDR had claimed that it would not be tied to any changes taking place in the Soviet Union, and that the significant opening for new art forms in 1972 was consistent with the changes in cultural policy under Honecker. At the same time, the enormous changes in the Soviet Union in the late 1980s could not go unobserved. GDR citizens traveled there; the House of Soviet Science and Culture in East Berlin sponsored talks and exhibits; certain newspapers and journals were sold (though they were on occasion banned)[6] and West German television closely followed Soviet developments while also informing viewers about the changes in Poland and Hungary.

As these liberating events occurred, however, the artists of the GDR still did not have the financial resources of some of the independent Soviet groups, and they were careful about the challenges in which they engaged. In part, this was because in the GDR, as noted above, there had been serious changes within the official union, which was opening the door to a degree of democratization and thus to an increasing pluralism among the artists. Since 1972, despite or perhaps because of the improvement of conditions, the complaints of union members had increased along with a growing demand for autonomy. In response, the union officially identified itself with a degree of pluralism and acceptance of a wider variety of art; "art in socialism" rather than "socialist realism." Referring to the 1988 Dresden exhibit, Willi Sitte, then union president, asked for courage to engage in an open discussion of differences with a tolerance for variety and mutual respect (*Information* 1988, 4–5). He also called for a greater participation of artists in determining contracts and payments, as well as for a greater role in deciding aesthetic concerns. The union had given permission for more artists than ever before to travel abroad; a few were allowed to work in the West for long periods of time and yet retain their GDR passports. However, it is clear that those in control attempted to maintain their power even in the face of pressures for change within the union, and the implications of decisions by the Congress of Artists in November 1988 were uncertain for nearly a year.

The district elections for section leaders that preceded the 1988 Union National Congress indicated that changes would take place in its formal structure and that the Congress elections might be affected. (To be sure, those elected in the districts did not necessarily openly pursue alternative policies; a number were primarily concerned with exhibits, travel, and similar activities, and remained careful of what they said.) Still, with the vote of 54 percent of the artists eligible to participate, nearly half of those elected to the 635 leadership positions were new, and many of those had no party affiliation. Nearly a third of the new people elected were women, mainly designers, craft workers, and art scholars. The small proportion of painters and graphic artists (those who had been favored in the past if they were stylistically safe) was in striking contrast to their greater representation in the concurrent Dresden exhibit (*Bildende Kunst* 1985, 434). Among the newly elected was Christoph Tannert, the art scholar-activist noted above.

The results of the congress elections were debated for many months. As a result of the consensus building in informal meetings beforehand, Willi Sitte did not run for reelection to president of the union; he was to remain honorary president for life and a member of the Central Committee. The new head, Claus Dietel, was elected by acclaim, along with calls for greater democracy. While many of the old establishment people were reelected, others holding important positions in the art establishment were not. In sum, the leadership of the union was threatened and pressured by the criticism of a number of its members, even as many of the people elected to the Congress were members of the state-affiliated artistic establishment. These tensions were still playing themselves out as reunification proceeded.

The Fall of 1989, the Spring of 1990

Some GDR artists participated in drafting resolutions advocating political reform and transformation both before and after the resignation of Honecker in 1989 and the collapse of the GDR state apparatus. Many took part in the protests and actions that brought an end to the regime and were prominent members of the newly formed political groups and parties.

Since then, like every other former GDR social institution, the art world has become radically transformed. Artists experienced dramatic changes in their union, in their relations to buyers and sponsors, in their connection to the art world of the rest of Germany, and frequently in their very self-understanding of what it meant to be an artist in contemporary Europe.

By May 1990, although the union was still receiving funding from the state, it had a severely diminished role. A specially convened Congress resulted in a thorough restructuring of the organization. With a changed name (which dropped any reference to the GDR), it proclaimed its political independence and increased decentralization. Autonomous state organizations that concerned themselves with welfare issues were combined with specialized sections (for photography and graphics, for example) that were represented in the overall organization at both the state and the central level and which focused more on artistic interests than on social benefits (*Vorlaeufig Satzung* 1990). Despite these changes made in anticipation of German reunification, the future of the union itself was in jeopardy because West Germany had no union counterpart. In the period of transition, the new GDR parliament formed a special committee to examine and evaluate all existing groups and organizations in the GDR and their subsidies; the union, too, had to submit and justify its programs. The outlook for continued state subsidies is bleak. In the meantime, a few of the upper-level union functionaries opened a new gallery near the union headquarters, where they will exhibit work by GDR and other artists, in addition to continuing their union work as long as they are able to do so.

Thus while some artists have reaped immediate benefits from the transformation of the GDR (such as the opportunity to exhibit without political restraints), others have felt the negative aspects of those same changes. There is a great deal of apprehension about the future material condition of artists. Many fear that art will not fare well in competition with the full spectrum of consumer goods that the population was denied for so long. As of this writing in late 1990, however, art sales do not seem to have declined; foreigners, especially West Germans, have bought up a great deal of the art at what were for them moderate prices. (Indeed, some GDR artists have complained that their prices had been too low.) A number of other artists fear that they will not be able to sell their work at all because their former state organizational patrons no longer commission works of art. Commercially unsuccessful artists who previously still enjoyed state support and all the fringe benefits that were provided through the union will have to find other work. In the meantime, however, the union pressured the state to continue its support and to maintain the existing Culture Fund (now secure until the end of 1994), which is financed by a tax on all cultural events and contributes to the welfare of artists.

Although most previously state-sponsored galleries remain open, some (for example, the Kleine Gallery in Pankow) had to close because the municipality dropped its support. Christoph Tannert opened one of the first "public" private galleries. While several hundred people showed up for the opening, he and his partners (one of them a West German) feared that after the end of the year, they might not be able to continue using their present space; it is owned by the municipality, and because it is in an advantageous location, the city is trying to rent the space to a more profitable business. By the end of 1990, their rent had indeed soared.

One further conclusion is unquestioned: the artists who were or will be successful in the international art scene will no longer be able to capitalize on their political opposition. Instead of a focus on the content of their work, formal aesthetic considerations will play a more prominent role; and these, according to Christoph Tannert, were precisely those qualities that were comparatively neglected in the past. On the other hand, since GDR art was more "national" and "realistic" in its character than West German art, Tannert believes that these features will become more prevalent in German art overall.

Thus, the very role that art has played in culture and society is being challenged by the dramatic social and political changes that have taken place. Painters and sculptors, who through their work and actions were noticeable critics of existing political conditions, soon will be merely one voice in a multitude of voices in the public arena. Like their West German colleagues, they will create works of art for a more diffuse and less attentive audience, without official patronage and scant protection from the market.

Today, the artists of the former GDR find themselves exposed to a multiplicity of influences and there is a corresponding multiplicity of reactions. At the same time that many feel uncomfortable about the pressures in the Western art world that force the artist to respond to ever-changing demands and chase after galleries and patrons, they want to be innovative and take their place in the contemporary art world. Most do not view these new tendencies as irresponsible and completely individualistic. Indeed, they see their own development as well as the transitions in the dominant institutions of GDR art as part of the overall change that is taking place in Eastern Europe as well as in their own society.

Conclusion

In the GDR, art was considered a powerful tool used to influence society in ways that were supportive of the system. It was expected to express the dominant goals and values, to be broadly accessible and to contribute to a common, nonfragmented culture. Because of this role of art and artists, art received substantial state patronage through the Union of Artists, through museums and exhibitions, through public recognition and efforts at art education, and through sponsorship of commissions by institutions not previously involved in art.

Yet a growing number of artists came to view these expectations with reserve and made insistent claims for more artistic autonomy. They believed it was crucial to develop new styles, techniques, and aspirations that included critique and negation of what was the dominant artistic culture. For some, this also meant a critique and negation of the dominant political system.

Nonconformist artists found support for their efforts in the very concepts of modern art and in the self-understanding of the international community of contemporary artists, most of whom do not see themselves as integrated in a similar way into their own societies. Indeed, the history of modern art fundamentally contradicts the vision of one common culture shared across divisions of work and education. To be sure, this vision is appealing to many, and yet it is at odds with the ideals of expressive individualism and artistic creativity; in this case it also was at odds with the fact that GDR society had become increasingly differentiated and heterogeneous, making even more difficult the maintenance of any common culture. Modern art also contradicts one classic role that art has traditionally played: celebrating the status quo. On the contrary, it has tended to favor critique and negation. The developments of the 1980s deepened these tensions that had been alive throughout the four decades of GDR artistic history.

Ironically, over the years, nonconformist artists acquired a strong voice precisely because art had been established as an important component of official culture. If the expected praise was valued, then critique from the same source was even more audible. Yet allowing greater variety did not turn arts policy on its head. In fact, after 1972, artistic innovations and the tensions engendered with the official cultural views advanced by the party not only enlivened the art scene itself; they also stimulated a much broader and more intense interest in art, an art that yet did not fully reject its role in society and challenge hegemonic views.

The dissatisfactions continued to increase with each effort by the state to meet them. The deteriorating economic system in the late 1980s meant that a number of artists could not count on easy commissions. They were then granted coveted foreign exhibitions and commissions, which constituted a new patronage system and provided opportunities for responding to different incentives and for increasing their artistic autonomy. However, most of the foreign earnings were paid in GDR currency, and in any event, only a few GDR artists benefited from these exchanges. For the rest, dependence on the union bureaucracy for permission to exhibit necessarily resulted in frustrations, and restrictions in the styles that were officially promoted left most GDR artists still excluded from the international art market. Again, as with other spheres of GDR life, partial reform did not succeed in meeting the demands of those with complaints.

Thus the success of the artists' efforts presented increasing challenges to the existing patronage system and to rapidly increasing demands for deeper changes in cultural policy overall. From the point of view of the artists, these successes were critical not only for their individual interest (though that was important) but for the common good. And that gave a special meaning to their art and to their politics.

Though enormous change was expected with the fall of the GDR, there were major unintended consequences of the dramatic events that plunged GDR artists into the different political economy of West Germany. The advantages of integration were clear. West Germany not only had a complex system of art markets and public and private patronage that give a high premium to individual choice and autonomy; at the outset at least, it also showed an intense interest in learning about and buying East German art. But this interest of many individuals and institutions and the generous West German subsidies for public art have not eliminated the uncertainty of working in a private market system in the arts and the difficulties of even understanding how that system can work to the artists' advantage. Artists now have enormous freedom, but they have lost the backing of a familiar—if often detested—patronage system. Many are having to find a different way of earning their living, and many of those who persist are not yet able to deal with a system that is both less imposing and less secure.

Notes

This chapter was first published in *The Journal of Arts Management and Law* 20(4): 31–55. The bulk of the research for this paper took place during 1987–88 when I was supported by a grant from the American Council of Learned Societies for a study of mass organizations in the new towns of the GDR. After the completion of that project, I began intensive interviewing with managers of several art galleries in Berlin, Dresden, and Rostock, as well as with art students, art professors, and artists in these three cities. I also interviewed museum directors and union representatives on a variety of levels. These talks were complemented by a visit to the Bauhaus in Dessau and talks there with students, professors, and the director, Rolf Kuhn. During the spring of 1990, a small set of follow-up interviews was done with a few artists, gallery managers, and union representatives I had spoken with before. I am very grateful to Hartmut Zimmermann and other colleagues at the Free University for the use of the GDR research institute's library; to Dietrich Muehlberg, Christiane Zieseke, and Dietrich Rueschemeyer for their insightful comments and enduring patience with this project; and to Simone Rueschemeyer for her help gathering the material on the Berlin artists.

1. Comments at the Degenerate Art Exhibit in Munich in 1937 and the First Great German Art Exhibition, housed opposite in the House of German Culture.

2. Nearly four thousand questionnaires were given out, to one out of every seven visitors in the two exhibit places, covering one exhibit place in one day and the second exhibit place the second day. About half of these were returned. In addition there were personal interviews with viewers who came to both the district and national exhibits, as well as with the tour guides.

3. The exhibit and survey results received considerable coverage: see reports in *Bildende Kunst* 1988; *Bildernisches Volksschaffen* 1988; and *Sonntag* 1988.

4. Talk with Bernd Lindner, *"wir"* 41 (14 Oct. 1988): 3.

5. A number of artists had been given permission to visit and even have extended stays in the West in the hope that they would remain in the GDR.

6. *Sputnik*, for example, was taken off the stands, and thereupon caused an uproar among intellectuals.

References

Bildende Kunst. 1985. "Zu den Sektionswahlversammlungen der Bezirks-organisationen des Verbandes Bildender Kuenstler der DDR." Heft 10: 434.
———. 1988. Heft 1: 41–43; Heft 2: 89–91.
Bildernisches Volksschaffen. 1988. 2:30–33.
Feist, Guenter, with Eckhart Gillen. 1988. *Stationen eines Weges*. Berlin: Museumspaedagogischer Dienst Berlin, Verlag Dirk Nishen.
Information. 1988. 1 (Jan.): 4–5.

Kober, Karl Max. 1984. "Art Exhibits and Art Galleries: Their Role in Art Appreciation." *Journal of Popular Culture* 18(3): 125–43.

Pohl, Edda, and Sieghard Pohl. 1979. *Die ungehorsamen Maler der DDR*. Berlin: Verlag europaeische Ideen.

Rennert, Juergen. 1984. *Dialog mit der Bibel*. Berlin: Evangelische Haupt-Bibelgesellschaft zu Berlin und Altenburg.

Rueschemeyer, Marilyn, Igor Golomshtok, and Janet Kennedy. 1985. *Soviet Emigré Artists: Life and Work in the USSR and the United States*. New York: M. E. Sharpe.

Sonntag. 1988. 13:3.

Der Spiegel. 1988. "Rembrandt hatte auch nicht immer recht" (an interview with Bernhard Heisig). July 2, pp. 147–54.

Thomas, Karin. 1980. *Die Malerei in der DDR 1949–1979*. Koeln: Dumont Buchverlag.

Vorlaeufig Satzung des Verbandes Bildender Kuenstler. 1990. April 10/11.

Werner, Wilfriede, and Karin Thomas. 1985. "Bildende Kunst." In *DDR Handbuch*, edited by Hartmut Zimmermann, Horst Ulrich, and Michael Fehlaluer, 229. Koeln: Verlag Wissenschaft und Politik.

❖ 11 ❖

Remaking Nations: Public Culture and Postcolonial Discourse

VERA ZOLBERG

I was born in the city of Bombay . . . once upon a time. No, that won't do, there's no getting away from the date: I was born . . . on August 15th, 1947. And the time? The time matters, too. Well then: at night. No, it's important to be more . . . On the stroke of midnight, as a matter of fact . . . at the precise instant of India's arrival at independence, I tumbled forth into the world. There were gasps. And outside the window, fireworks and crowds.
—Salman Rushdie, *Midnight's Children*, 1980

For a former colony, becoming independent is akin to being born. As with the biological process to which the analogy refers, this is not a simple matter. With independence comes the necessity of constructing the elusive and integrated systems of meaning that anthropologists have come to treat as culture. In postcolonial nations a firm sense of one's culture may be very elusive. The immediate colonial past, with its distasteful memories of scorn and discrimination, is to be rejected. Instead, makers of the new postcolonial culture must turn to the precolonial past, or what is considered worth resurrecting from it according to criteria that are themselves uncertain. They must combine it with "progressive" steps—innovations deemed appropriate and necessary to modern times. A synthesis of these elements is expected to result in a new cultural identity that transcends both that associated with imperial domination and those particular aspects of the several component traditions that may appear incongruous in a modern nation state. Beyond the personal level, this new identity is expressed in what has come to be called the "public culture" (Appadurai and Breckenridge 1988).

Broadly speaking, a nation's public culture encompasses representations of history, geography, and the arts consistent with the self-definition and goals of its people (or at least those of its elites in charge of public institutions). But whether this new public culture has a broad base of support or not, it is important because of its role in legitimating the nation to its own citizenry and (perhaps more important) to outsiders.

Here I consider certain aspects of postcolonial Indian public culture, more than four decades after its independence. Because of India's vast size, heterogeneity, and dynamic qualities, I make no pretense of dealing with its totality, let alone with the more private cultures of its diverse peoples. I focus primarily on the foundations of the issues of national identity that continue to plague the India of today (as well as other nations), contested as they are in different ways by subcultural tribal and/or religious affiliations. As a manageable "indicator" of these issues, I will examine the way in which subnational groups are represented in official discourse, especially (though not exclusively) in relation to museums.

As distinct as each may be, neither India nor any other postcolonial nation exists in a vacuum. It is necessary, therefore, to consider the creation of its specific public culture within the context of the international social order (in certain respects inherently based on Western traditions); these new international standards and media of cultural expression have come to determine the various cultural policies of most nations, postcolonial or not.

For the sake of comparison, I will first review the cultural policies of France, whose tradition of valorizing certain art forms through state sponsorship has long been the exemplar of the process by which the official culture of the centralized state becomes seen as hierarchically superior to other types of culture, whether commercial or regional. The French case reveals how cultural policies may result in advantages for artists, art forms, and languages given official recognition, with corresponding disadvantages for those excluded. Following this discussion, I will consider how the Indian experience may provide guidance for those nations with an enormous diversity of cultures, in contrast to the more homogeneous culture of France. India's counterparts are not only the many former colonies that succeeded in breaking apart the empires of Western European power; its experience may have lessons to offer to the now-demolished Soviet imperium as well.

Exemplar for Public Culture: The French Academy

In France, as an administrative structure encompassing educational institutions as well as structures of competition and rewards for talent, from the seventeenth century on, the academy became the major institution for commissioning art for public purposes. Initiated by Louis XIV, the academies were extended by his successors, at the urging of certain key artists, to train their own successors. From the outset the French academies were selective in admissions, in order to establish and maintain standards of quality. They legitimated certain art forms, subject matter, and styles, following rationales derived from the prestigious bases of humanistic classical scholarship. From the standpoint of the monarch, institutionalizing certain art forms by elevating them hierarchically over others both established an official "great culture" and enhanced the symbolic glory of the state (Corvisier 1978; Heinich 1987).

Whatever benefit they promised artists as professionals and for developing high quality for art itself, the successive French academies were first of all instruments of national aggrandizement. Their prestige depended reciprocally upon the standing of the nation state. In contrast to the parochialism of local or regional cultural traditions on the one hand, and to the sacred universalism of the Catholic Church on the other, the artistic culture sponsored by the academy embraced (and helped to create) a newly defined national culture under the protection of whichever ruler followed Louis XIV and who equally identified the state with himself: *L'état, c'est moi*.

Artists gaining official recognition under the historical academic system benefited from the combination of esteem, material comfort, and predictability of income that became envied by others. Artists and art forms excluded from official recognition were relegated to the comparative oblivion of separate development in "little cultures," to a weakened, marginalized position as a client of the Church (Corvisier 1978), or to the "mercies" of market forces. Painters whose works were not admitted to official academic salons (where they could be viewed by private collectors or officials with funds to purchase art for public buildings) instead had little recourse but to display their paintings at public (usually outdoor) markets and fairs, to an indiscriminate clientele of lesser standing. At best they came to depend on the emergent dealer-gallery system that much later outshone the academic salons. Meanwhile their financial rewards were considerably lower and their careers more precarious. During the nineteenth century, such "independent" artists might be forced to eke out a living as writers or illustrators for the growing publishing market or commercial advertising world. Although some such nonacademic artists (Dumas, Eugene Sue, Zola, many of the Impressionist painters) became rich and famous, in most cases these fields of the arts entailed the exploitation and unreliable rewards of Grub Street. Not surprisingly, while deploring official policy, most independent artists and writers devoted considerable energy in trying to gain the rewards provided by state agencies.

Official cultural policy entailed much more than the arts alone. Equally important, the academic system monopolized control over the language of the nation. Grammar, syntax, vocabulary, and usage were a matter of official policy. The autochthonous languages of provinces such as Brittany and Provence were suppressed in favor of the French of the Ile-de-France. As a result, those who were fluent only in these provincial languages became marginalized from the important networks of influence emanating from Paris.

Many of the ideas embodied in this official public culture turned out to be extremely durable. For even after its dissolution (along with many *ancien régime* institutions) during the Great Revolution and its recreation in an altered form thereafter, the academic system continued to play an important role in defining culture for France, with or without a monarch, throughout most of the nineteenth century and even much of the twentieth. To be sure, in recent decades French cultural policy has not been confined to the institutions cited above, although much of the central purpose has been maintained. Thus aspects of official culture have been assigned to ministries with primary functions in other domains than that of culture per se. For example, the Ministry of Labor deals with working conditions, including those of artists; Social Affairs concerns itself in part with culture as leisure activity of employees both in the public and private sectors; Foreign Affairs continues to publicize and reward achievements and quality of French arts and culture more generally to maintain national prestige (Andraul and Dressayre 1987; Mesnard 1974).

The example of France suggests that the creation of a national culture has often been achieved at the expense of weaker groups. The centralized absolutist state crushed or absorbed (after distorting) those cultural components that were politically threatening or seemed unsuitable. The lesson here is that even if the central authority does not deliberately seek such dominance—indeed, even if it is committed to preserving a diversity of cultures—it may still endanger them because of irreconcilable conflicts of value and custom among contenders.

There are long-standing tensions in France between the functional groups that compose civil society, and the individualized rights of the citizens vis-à-vis the state. These have erupted over such issues as cultural categorization, expressed in demands for the use and general recognition not just of provincial languages, but also the literature and history of the groups excluded from official standing under the centralized state.

Increasingly, their proponents are learning to make effective use of the procedures and universalistic principles embodied in the centralized state itself to demand and sometimes gain concessions. But demands for the inclusion of religious subject matter in school curricula, acceptance of religious customs or holidays, and greater freedom for private religious schools from centralized oversight have tended to be viewed as marks of disloyalty, as separatist ventures. (To be sure, many of these demands have been designed to engender this response.) In turn, supporters of the state's right to maintain its dominance over education argue that giving in to these group demands would result in deprivation of civil rights for many individuals. They argue that the state has the obligation to impose universalistic standards that protect individuals from the injustices associated with particularism. For example, they have tried to free Muslim girls from "excessive" patriarchal authority by requiring their attendance in school, participation in physical education, and the discarding of traditional head coverings.

Some such "provincial" protesters have gained limited success through central government concessions and compromise: chairs of Breton and Occitens language and literature have been created in regionally situated universities; news broadcasts are now televised locally in some regional languages; Breton parents may give their children Breton names (rather than be obliged to use the names of the Catholic saints calendar in French only, as had been the practice); and a minister of education who had attempted to exert greater secularizing control over Catholic private schools was forced to resign.

Recognition at the ministerial level is essential if new art forms are to gain standing in contemporary France, and it is here that the transformation of attitudes toward culture has recently been most striking. Whereas in the nineteenth century the French government (both through its ministries and academic structures) tended to oppose innovations in art styles and forms, now the opposite is more likely. State support given for movies, comic strips, dissonant music and jazz (all three of which have been recognized as being of national importance by the French Ministry of Culture) would have been unimaginable just a few decades ago.

Moreover, unlike the United States where, as a rule, government support is confined to not-for-profit art forms, in France culture worthy of state support is construed more broadly. Certain commercial art forms are assumed to contribute to national honor and cultural prestige, as demonstrated by the various culture industries and tourism, all of which benefit the nation more generally and therefore receive state support (Brebisson 1986).

Establishing Public Culture in Less-Centralized Societies

Though seldom as centralized, academies modeled on those of France proliferated throughout Europe and elsewhere (Corvisier 1978; van der Tas in this volume). Although France's reputation as patron of the arts was admired by artists who found themselves dependent upon a market or on unappreciative patrons for their livelihood (Morgan 1978), in the United States the idea of an official culture in the French manner was deemed incompatible with the distrust of state control that was written into the Constitution. The arts were conceived as a private pleasure, in whose support the state had neither obligation nor right to disburse public monies (Meyer 1979; Mulcahy 1987).

Until the Great Depression of the 1930s, any national public art support in America was limited primarily to what became relatively routine projects: monuments to late statesmen and the more anonymous dead, the design of money, official seals, postage stamps, government buildings, uniforms, military music. However, during the Depression, New Deal arts programs were launched like other WPA programs to provide work for the unemployed—in this case, artists and writers. With the United States entry into World War II, these always controversial programs were allowed to lapse. For some time after the war, support for the arts was confined to practical and/or propaganda concerns. Only since the 1960s was political pressure by cultural supporters sufficient to overcome the three-decade hiatus (see Galligan in this volume).[1]

It is important to note that relatively little support for the arts in the United States comes from the federal government. Compared to many European nations, most arts patronage stems from a combination of private sources: corporations, foundation, individual donors, and users who pay admission fees (Balfe and Cassilly in this volume; Montias 1986). The amount of direct government funding is relatively low (combining federal, state, and local arts funding, government provides only a third of the total institutional—as opposed to individual—arts support [Wyszomirski 1987]). However, as it has increased proportionately in recent decades (while declining at both federal and state levels in the late 1980s and early 1990s), it has come to serve as symbolic recognition for the arts and their creators because of its association with the sacredness of the nation. As important, despite occasional accusations of favoritism and questionable choices, government agencies that select artists and artworks provide an imprimatur for other potential patronage sources that are tapped to meet the state-funded matching grants. Without such a combination of funding sources, certain art forms (such as grand opera) would probably not be able to exist at all (Netzer 1978). While other musical forms (such as jazz) still depend largely upon commercial success for their survival, like painting and sculpture they are often nonprofit in organization, and thus compete for state patronage.

For the visual arts in particular, the highest form of recognition for artists is attained through having their works acquired by or displayed in museums. Once this occurs, they have entered a realm of highly desirable symbolic value, whereby the artists improve their chances of receiving other types of recognition, such as funding from government agencies, private or corporate commissions, not to speak of sales at higher prices.

Entry into museum collection benefits not only art but other categories of "collectible" culture as well. Museums specializing in history, science, or the cultures of groups of ethnically or regionally distinct people confer a different yet equally important kind of recognition. However, as previously excluded or marginalized groups have gained political voice, they have questioned both their exclusion and the terms of their inclusion in such "collections." Such protests have been occurring with increasing frequency in American settings, especially in exhibition sites commemorating the nineteenth-century wars against Native Americans. Until recently these "Indian Wars" have been represented as glorifications of white conquest over "the savages," or of tragic defeats when whites were beaten by Indians (for example, the defeat of General Custer at the Battle of Little Big Horn). Today Native Americans contest these interpretations and demand an active voice in reinterpreting the past. Moreover, they are succeeding in bringing about change. In the face of their pressure, museums are increasingly ending their practice of treating Indian remains as specimens for study by physical anthropologists and are returning them to their descendants for religious burial. Instead of being objectivized as biological categories, Native Americans are being treated as total human beings. (Whether this is in terms of Westernized notions of individuality or in their own terms is a matter of some dispute [see Karp and Lavine 1991; and Karp, Kreamer, and Lavine 1992].)

Beyond the realm of officially created or supported culture, in recent times the conception of "public culture" has been broadened well beyond the creation and dissemination of those cultural products in the arts and sciences that receive official governmental support and patronage. In the modern world in which culture industries have become prevalent, public culture is now recognized to embrace other substantive domains, all of which make any direct government support even more problematic. As Arjun Appadurai and Carol Breckenridge (1988) suggest, commercial, regional, and ethnic cultural products and processes constitute an enlarged arena of public culture that provides a "zone of public debate." This may include discussion directed not only at content, but at the nature of categories of thinking that underlie public culture (6). For example, the 1990 film *Mississippi Burning*, whose makers had promoted it as a paean to the civil rights movement, aroused opposition among many black Americans who saw it as an insult to their leadership and a whitewash of the FBI's passivity in the face of antiblack violence. Increasingly, whether officially supported or dependent on the market, the realm of public culture is becoming the zone of debate that Appadurai and Breckenridge perceive it to be. As public and commercial sectors interact, the content of the official culture sphere is not necessarily totally separate from that of unofficial culture. All sectors are likely to be targets of attempts to control their content, by both official and private patrons (Dubin 1992).

Implications for Postcolonial Nations

When the kings of France began to see the benefit of sponsoring the creation and production of culture to foster the aggrandizement of the state and their power, they did so in an environment lacking an important commercial sector of culture. In effect, they created what was virtually the only game in town. Today, India and other postcolonial nations must deal with a far more complex world than that of early modern Europe. Not only does the government reward certain forms of art by its support, but a lively commercial sector has grown up beside extremely varied folk and religion-based cultural expressions. European historical and sociological processes are not replicated in new nations, although postcolonial nations sometimes face questions that run parallel to them.

As Razak Ajala of Nigeria has pointed out in his analysis of third-world policy making in the arts (1989), once the colonizers left, "groups, long separated by history, language and culture, whether in Asia, Latin America or Africa, found themselves bound up in new nationalities." Beyond that, as he shows, having suffered an epoch of denigration and rejection of every aspect of their culture—religion, language, art, values—many seek to reacquire the culture of the past. These trends leave cultural policy makers face to face with conflicting demands: whether to support art forms that transcend their own societies' cultures (symphony orchestras, productions of Shakespeare as "national flagships") or to emphasize indigenous artists and art forms. As these often express ancient tribal rivalries, to promote a few is to insult the others. But as Ajala also notes, many of these cultural elements have come to be hybridized with Western forms, and many artists have chosen to direct their efforts to the world outside of their own locality.

It is never simple for anthropologists, as Clifford Geertz puts it, to read the "ensemble of texts, themselves ensembles . . . over the shoulders of those to whom they properly belong" (Geertz 1973, 452). Not only do historical trends make problematic any definition of the spatial and temporal boundaries of cultures, but even when these boundaries are relatively clear, cultural construction is difficult due to impediments stemming from sources both internal and external to the nation in which the culture is supposed to inhere. This is equally true for forms of "public" culture, especially when this confers value to groups associated with it. One of the distasteful features of the colonial past was a sense of exclusion from autonomous standing in this symbolic domain. Where the traditional cultural forms were the object of admiration, collection, and patronage by the colonial regimes, they became disconnected from their own makers. Once themselves "colonized," art and artifact, philosophy and history became severed from their living heirs in India as elsewhere.

Independence did not automatically result in a return to a status quo, in which civilizational matters could proceed unproblematically. Indeed, determining what the "legitimate" tradition should be itself required hard choices. Which elements of the precolonial traditions should be adopted and which discarded or transcended? The problem is compounded where a substantial part of the tradition itself is based on previous imperial histories. In India the British Raj had succeeded earlier conquests and empires, with the result that the modern Indian nation encompasses past victors as well as losers. Under these conditions it is hardly surprising that the subcontinent finally came to independence only after being partitioned, and that the boundaries of the resultant new nations have been recurrently contested ever since.[2] Transcending tradition, therefore, entails reshaping older categories in order to create viable new ones.

Despite the end of its authoritarian domination, the overthrown imperium remains an important element of a nation's public culture. According to Immanuel Wallerstein (1974), its persistence is due to the fact that in most cases, the former colonial power continues to exercise authority among the advanced industrial societies in the world economic system. Former colonies constitute a periphery still linked to the preeminent centrality of former colonial powers. Beyond coercive or monetary power, however, the colonial experience exercises a more subtle effect.

Considered positively, despite their habitual authoritarianism, England and certain other imperial powers embodied Enlightenment ideals of universalism and democracy. In fact, these ideals and the legal institutions on which they were founded have been tellingly used against the colonial powers' domination by leaders of the nationalist movements, and more recently by "internal" ethnic groups against the new national governments. However, considered negatively, colonial regimes encapsulated pejorative classification of the peoples under their control. This is part of the process that Edward Said convincingly analyzes, which produced the discourse of "Orientalism" (1978).

With its more or less subtle denigration of the peoples and cultures under colonial empires, Orientalism became translated into relationships of hierarchical distinctions. It attributed to the peoples and cultures of the Orient, including the Middle East and Far East, attributes of irrationality, sensuality, barbarity, passivity, and generalized inferiority as compared to their European conquerors. The discourse gained influence not simply through the exertion of sheer power, but through eliciting the consent of the oppressed in a hegemonic form (Said 1978, 7). It would be mistaken to believe that these ideas are confined to the West alone. Similar idea structures and categories are found in the "Orient" itself, and may even be embraced (though not necessarily consciously) by national leaders vis-à-vis certain groups in their own new nations.

In contrast to traditional categories of thought (whether pre- or post-colonial), the new secular forms of public culture may also provide the bases for the processes of social reproduction (although their own consequences for creating and maintaining social inequality are well known [Bourdieu 1984]). Even if political leaders have no intention of institutionalizing the bases of cultural inequality, they need to be aware of how they may do so inadvertently. As Pierre Bourdieu and others urge, only by adopting a reflexive stance is it possible to transcend the ingrained structures of thinking that make intellectuals, no less than other members of society, bondsmen and handmaidens in the relegation of the already weak to cultural marginality.

In light of these pitfalls, I focus on two aspects of cultural policy as they pertain to India: how categories of thinking and concepts that pervade museum discourses may represent orientalizing categories; and how ethnic and regional differentiation themselves may have the same effect of reinforcing marginality.

Museums: Discourse and Contents

A glance at the approximately four hundred and more museums of all kinds in India reveals in their form, facilities, and purposes much that should seem familiar to Western observers. As in Europe and America, museums are intended to preserve the national patrimony in their collections, educate the public, entertain the ordinary visitor. That these purposes are familiar is not accidental, since museum functioning nearly everywhere has come to be modeled on the example of museums in the West.[3]

Museums are not altogether a new phenomenon in India, dating at least as far back the 1870s in Goa, as well as other states. As in many countries, however, the bulk of them have been created in the four decades since independence.[4] Their importance to the nation state is attested to by the fact that the large majority are financed and run under government auspices, whether national, state, or municipal. A number of museums are a part of universities, and only a very few are private.[5] Not surprising for a land with ancient civilizations, by far the bulk of Indian museums specialize in art or archaeology. In keeping with the nation's modernizing goals, however, science museums (especially the university-connected ones) are becoming increasingly prominent. The association of science with modernity is strikingly revealed in the well-illustrated *Annual Report* of the National Council of Science Museums (1987–88), a document that compares favorably in style and format with similar publications in Western countries. In the many photographs of visitors that illustrate the document, girls are as prevalent as boys—a choice that may be a deliberate statement of commitment to "modern" ideas promoting gender equality.

Art and science museums seem to present few problems of public culture. When it comes to the third most prevalent type of museum, those specializing in anthropology, the term "tribal museum" used for this category should arouse concern. It suggests the persistent and recurrent debates in India concerning discrimination, revealed in the terms used to characterize various ethnic, religious, or cultural groups. As suggested in the following example (taken from an essay by Zail Singh, president of the Republic of India, which appeared in the bulletin of the major state anthropological museum), certain words bear much of the same pejorative loading as when employed in orientalizing modes by Westerners:

Our late beloved Prime Minister Shrimati Indira Gandhi always took pride in our rich cultural heritage and strived for the revival and propagation of our creative arts—music, dance, theatre, sculpture, architecture, painting and so on, as well as film and photography at national and international levels. The conceptual plan of this Centre is indeed very broad and seeks to concretise through its programmes the vision of India which Shrimati Gandhi lived and strived for. In particular I am happy to note that a systematic and scientific study will be carried out at this Centre into the tribal and folk arts which are a special gift largely of scheduled castes and scheduled tribes of India. (Indira Gandhi National Centre for the Arts, 1985)

The endorsement by the president of the republic of the "systematic study" of tribal and folk arts, of the "scheduled castes and scheduled tribes of India" is surely meant benignly at a conscious level. But the creation of a separate sphere of museology for these groups recalls the historical development of Western anthropological museums and their underlying intellectual structures. In the nineteenth century, natural history or ethnographic museums served to encapsulate American slaves, freed blacks, Native Americans, and colonial "native peoples" as separate species who were qualitatively distinct from the "civilized" races.[6] Although this is not the conscious intention of enlightened officials in India, it is necessary to take seriously the warning of scholars such as Edward Said to be wary of conflating crafts and artifacts with particular human identities. Not only is this kind of formulation an oversimplification, but it lends itself to the stereotyping associated with national character analysis. Among the problems faced by new nations, therefore, is the risk of falling into the trap (much as anthropologists, especially under the aegis of colonial authority had habitually done [Clifford, 1983]), of reifying existing cultural groupings in terms of a fuzzy essentialism. This assumes that certain groups are qualitatively different from dominant or mainstream groups, and therefore were not capable of enjoying the rights of citizenship.

Ethnicity as Reification and Marginalization

With the best of intentions, this tendency is revealed in the "habit of speech" where an entire people are treated as "the." For example, in a statement by Jawaharlal Nehru referring to the unity in the midst of the heterogeneity of Indianness, the following appears (my emphases):

> The Pathan and the Tamil are two extreme examples; the others lie somewhere in between. All of them have their distinctive features, all of them have still more the distinguishing mark of India. These have been expressed, among other things, in the persistence of unequal treatment of women; caste discrimination; regional separatism; and infringements on artistic and press freedom. It is fascinating to find how the Bangalees, the Marathas, the Gujaratis, the Tamils, the Andhras, the Oriyas, the Assamese, the Canarese, the Malayalis, the Sindhis, the Punjabis, the Pathans, the Kashmiris, the Raj-

puts and *the* great central block comprising *the* Hindustani speaking people, *have retained their peculiar characteristics for hundreds of years, have still more or less the same virtues and failings of which old tradition or record tells us, and yet have been throughout these ages distinctively Indian, with the same national heritage and the same set of moral and mental qualities.* (Indira Gandhi National Centre for the Arts, 1985)

To be sure, these usages do not precisely parallel the kind of thinking that Edward Said, following Foucault's "archaeology of knowledge" (1969), attributes to the "enormously systematic discipline by which European culture was able to manage (and even produce) the Orient politically, sociologically, militarily, ideologically, scientifically, and imaginatively during the post-Enlightenment period." However, one cannot discount their potential for creating or maintaining the kind of hierarchical distinctions among cultures and the people associated with them that eventuate in the consolidation of dominion over them. No nation or individual is immune to the creation of discriminatory institutions and structures of thought even if at some level they are abhorrent to its most cherished beliefs. In light of the strongly hierarchizing cultural structure of Hindu culture, this is a persistent hazard.

Conclusion

In this essay I have insisted upon the fundamentally political nature of the tensions surrounding public culture in India today. The dimension of political conflict by which interested parties contend for the right to be associated with the state has tended to be submerged or ignored by many anthropologists. Bernard Cohn has characterized Indian history as being pervaded by cultural renovation with strongly syncretizing and Sanskritizing tendencies. Despite often violent lapses, he has contended, in time tolerance of diversity has overcome local conflicts (1971). Clifford Geertz refers to the complexity and superimposition of primordialisms in India in which "Indian civil politics amounts to a disconnected series of attempts to make the temporary endure." He is only hinting at the tensions and the outbreaks of violence that have typified Indian since its independence when he describes the Congress party ("its slightly North Indian complexion aside") as "ethnically neutral, resolutely modernist," as "a cosmopolitan central party with provincial machines fighting a multifront war against every sort of parochialism known to man (and a few known only to Hindus) in India" (1973, 290; 306). Since cleavages among the heterogeneous peoples of India persist, the future warrants little equanimity, and the task of establishing a common national culture remains as difficult as ever.[7]

Statesmen who would sincerely avoid the hegemonistic sins of their former oppressors need to remember that the gap between official policy and its practice is most likely to be felt first by those most aggrieved. As implied in Edward Said's analysis, intellectual and political leaders need to consider that unreflexive thinking may turn into a dogmatism that becomes a tool, obtrusive or unobtrusive, in the conflicts themselves (1978, 327). Their responsibilities give them no choice but to recognize these tensions and deal with them as democratically as possible.

Nations that try to make themselves anew face multiple tasks, from establishing new economic and political institutions to creating a legitimating public culture. A nation like India, immense, heterogeneous, endowed with a long succession of widely revered civilizations and deeply rooted autocthonous populations, rather than benefiting from its cultural riches, confronts problems that seem ever more intransigent. With the end of previous arrangements and the loosening of constraints, tensions among groups—ethnic, religious, linguistic—have been freed to surface openly. The movements to which this has given rise are often dismissed as the "irrational" reactions of backward peoples. But the yearnings expressed need to be understood, especially when the nation in question is profoundly committed to democracy.

This is not to urge acceptance of particularistic ideas that may deprive individual citizens of political and human rights just to maintain peace. But it is important to bear in mind that those who reject the demands as incompatible with universalistic principles of fairness may be unaware that their own preconceived ideas and categories of meaning may be similarly biased. The retention of essentializing categorical structures that I have highlighted above helps to anchor thinking which reinforces and may even create parochialism.[8] The blindness of politicians, administrators, and intellectuals to their own habits of thinking may affect their policy decisions with consequences that they and their successors will have to contend with for a considerable time. The propensity of the formerly oppressed to oppress in their turn needs to be guarded against. If independence merely substitutes one set of cultural inequalities for another, it would be a sham.

Notes

1. This was a profound change coinciding with America's new importance as a leading world power (Zolberg 1990). By now, although budgetary allocations

fluctuate, it has come to be taken for granted that the national government has an obligation to support the arts. This seems to be the case despite recent disputes over the continued existence of the National Endowment for the Arts.

2. In 1947 British India was first divided into India and Pakistan (West and East); in 1971, East Pakistan broke away to become Bangladesh; currently a number of separatist movements, some ethnically based and others religious, have wracked the subcontinent.

3. Aside from learning from the British model, a large proportion of Indian museum directors, especially of the national museums, were trained by a retired member of New York's Museum of Modern Art, Grace Morley, who worked in India until her death.

4. Over a dozen were in existence by 1900, but since independence, new museums have outnumbered earlier ones by more than two to one (Agrawal 1971). The enormous growth in museums in every Western country since World War II has produced similar proportions.

5. All central and most state museums are open free of charge; some municipal and many private museums have an entry fee. Central government museums tend to be open every day; state government museums are generally closed one day a week, and on holidays; university museums are open during the term (Agrawal, 1971).

6. Among the photographs Louis Agassiz collected for the American Museum of Natural History was a set taken of Southern slaves, along with plaster casts of heads and other body parts. Similar collections were formed of other native subjects, such as Inuit and Native Americans, in American natural history museums and in colonial museums of Europe. Objectifying as these practices were, these are relatively mild examples of these ideas. The extreme of horror must surely have been reached in Nazi plans to place the material remains of exterminated Jews in a specially designed museum for an "extinct" race.

7. The question of what constitutes official Indian public culture is far from simple—whether seen from Indian or from Western perspectives. In 1985, on the occasion of the major "Festival of India" exhibition at the Metropolitan Museum of Art (whose original state patron was Indira Gandhi herself), Arthur C. Danto, an American, took the museum and the organizers to task for misleading the public. Aside from seeing the exhibit as an aesthetic failure and an undignified carnival, he contended that the sponsors were promoting it as a "comprehensive exhibition of 14th to 19th century Indian art," while in fact it reflected primarily the tastes of Hindu India's Islamic conquerors (Danto 1985). Danto's opinion may be overstated, especially if Bernard Cohn is correct to emphasize the syncretic and Sanskritic character of India. He considers Mughal courtly culture and style "a model in content and form of a cosmopolitan culture for most of urban India and even for the countryside" (Cohn 1971, 99). Danto also ignored the various contemporary political agendas behind this exhibit, both in Great Britain and the United States (Balfe 1987).

8. Even when the central government under the Congress party has tried to compensate for inequality by opening special opportunities for devalued castes, they and other central government leaders have been attacked by many of their

supporters who consider this "affirmative action" to be carried out at their own expense.

References

Agrawal, Usha, ed. 1971. *Brief Directory of Museums in India*. New Delhi: Museum Association of India.

Ajala, Razak. 1989. "The Politics of Third World Policy Making in the Arts." Annual Conference on Social Theory, Politics, and the Arts, October 7. Toronto, Ont.: York University.

Andraul, Marianne, and Philippe Dressayre. 1987. "Government and the Arts in France." In *The Patron State: Government and the Arts in Europe, North America, and Japan*, edited by Milton C. Cummings and Richard S. Katz, 17–44. New York: Oxford University Press.

Appadurai, Arjun, and Carol A. Breckenridge. 1988. "Why Public Culture?" *Public Culture* 1(1): 5–10.

Balfe, Judith Huggins. 1987. "Affinities of Art and Politics: Gilt by Association." *Controversies in Art and Culture* 1(1): 1–19.

Becker, Howard S. 1982. *Art Worlds*. Berkeley: University of California Press.

Bourdieu, Pierre. 1984. *Distinction: A Social Critique of the Judgement of Taste*. Cambridge, Mass.: Harvard University Press.

Brebisson, Guy de. 1986. *Le Ménècat*. Paris: Presses Universitaires de France.

Clifford, James. 1983. "On Ethnographic Authority." *Representations* (2): 118–46.

Cohn, Bernard S. 1971. *India: The Social Anthropology of a Civilization*. Englewood Cliffs, N.J.: Prentice-Hall.

Corvisier, André. 1978. *Arts et Sociétés dans l'Europe du XVIIIe Siècle*. Paris: Presses Universitaires de France.

Danto, Arthur C. 1985. "The Neai Pavilions!" *The Nation*, Oct. 26, 412–14.

Dubin, Steven C. 1992. *Arresting Images: Impolitic Art and Uncivil Actions*. New York: Routledge.

Elias, Norbert. 1978. *The Civilizing Process: The Development of Manners*. New York: Urizen Books.

Foucault, Michel. 1969. *L'Archéologie du Savoir*. Paris: Gallimard.

Geertz, Clifford. 1973. *The Interpretation of Cultures: Selected Essays*. New York: Basic Books.

Heinich, Nathalie. 1987. "Arts et sciences a l'âge classique: Professions et institutions culturelles." *Actes de la Recherche en Sciences Sociales* 67–68 (Mar.): 47–78.

Indira Gandhi National Centre for Arts. 1985. Brochure. New Delhi.

Karp, Ivan, and Steven D. Lavine, eds. 1991. *Exhibiting Cultures: The Poetics and Politics of Museum Display*. Washington, D.C.: Smithsonian Institution.

Karp, Ivan, Christine Mullen Kreamer, and Steven D. Lavine, eds. 1992. *Museums and Communities: The Politics of Public Culture*. Washington, D.C.: Smithsonian Institution.

Mesnard, André-Hubert. 1974. *La Politique Culturelle de L'Etat*. Paris: Presses Universitaires de France.

Meyer, Karl. 1979. *The Art Museum: Power, Money, Ethics.* New York: William Morrow.

Montias, J. Michael. 1986. "Public Support for the Performing Arts in Europe and the United States." In *NonProfit Enterprise in the Arts: Studies in Mission and Constraint,* edited by Paul J. DiMaggio, 287–319. New York: Oxford University Press.

Morgan, H. Wayne. 1978. *New Museums: Art in American Culture.* Norman, Okla.: University of Oklahoma Press.

Mulcahy, Kevin V. 1987. "Government and the Arts in the United States." In *The Patron State: Government and the Arts in Europe, North America, and Japan,* edited by Milton C. Cummings and Richard S. Katz, 311–32. New York: Oxford University Press.

National Council of Science Museums (India). 1988. *Annual Report 1987–1988.*

Netzer, Dick. 1978. *The Subsidized Muse: Public Support for the Arts in the United States.* New York: Cambridge University Press.

Rushdie, Salman. 1980. *Midnight's Children.* New York: Viking.

Said, Edward W. 1978. *Orientalism.* New York: Pantheon.

Wallerstein, Immanuel. 1974. *The Modern World System.* New York: Academic Press.

Wyszomirski, Margaret J. 1987. "Art, Philanthropy, and Public Policy." *Journal of Arts Management and Law* 16(4): 5–30.

Zolberg, Vera. 1990. *Constructing a Sociology of the Arts.* New York: Cambridge University Press.

PART FIVE

INDIRECT PATRONAGE

BY STATE INSTITUTIONS

Given the recognized difficulties of direct state patronage, many governments have established independent agencies to which are delegated decisions over the forms and recipients of art support, "at arm's length" from their own sponsors. By stretching out the chain of patronage, the state is freed from direct responsibility and the problems of controlling the rewards to the many groups competing for support. However, with the democratic diffusion of patronage power to various independent agencies (which then serve as catalysts for the raising of private funds), the state still remains the primary identifiable source of funding. It is thus held responsible for any "mistakes" made by its delegates, as these are variously defined by the wider audience (including the nonarts audience) whose competing values may not be represented.

In the United States, the National Endowment for the Arts was established in 1965 as an independent federal agency to administer national programs of arts support, both directly and indirectly through the states. As Ann M. Galligan describes the NEA's evolution, a system of peer review panels was designed to delegate funding decisions to professionals in the field. In time, ideals of panel autonomy and professional judgment have conflicted with those of democratic accountability and public stewardship to the point that the very existence of the NEA in particular and of state arts support in general have been threatened. Yet through their politicization, the panels have served unintentionally—if providentially—as the lightning rod that has so far protected the NEA from total destruction.

Richard A. Peterson discusses another institution to which the government has delegated art patronage: the National Public Radio network of 350 stations, dependent upon both federal funds and local listener support. NPR founders saw their mission as bringing classical music to listeners whose local commercial stations did not program it; thereby they would stimulate understanding of—and attendance at—live concerts. Newscasts were programmed as well, which then attracted listeners with no apparent interest in classical music. To hold this new audience, NPR has changed its programming, to some degree denying the tastes of its original supporters. In further irony, its success in broadcasting polished musical entertainment, or "lite classical" music, has diluted audience understanding of more serious works. Patronage intended to foster classical music has unintentionally weakened its structure.

If such policies of delegated patronage cause difficulties in a single country, policies of international cultural patronage are even harder to establish. Esther Gelabert discusses the European Community as it was planned to come into formal existence in 1992. Since this chapter was written, it has become apparent that cultural—let alone economic—cooperation among intended EC members is not easy to bring about. Still, with economic cooperation as the core of the EC's intended mandate among the member states, it is not surprising that its major planning initiatives in the arts and culture have concerned their most commercial forms, in the media and the so-called "culture industries." Regarding private and individual art forms and groups, EC objectives have involved distribution more than production (as, of course, with the New York City Department of Cultural Affairs, the NEA, and NPR). Artworks and artists are to be able to move freely across borders; so too may capital investment in arts industries. The intention is that a common culture is to be shared, to reinforce the concept of European identity distinct from national or regional identities on the one hand, and from a fully "Americanized" culture on the other. At the same time, regional cultures are to be promoted as part of the "non-homogenized" European "mosaic," and some existing structures of national arts patronage and protectionism are to remain in place. Otherwise, the open EC market is likely to destroy the European "soul" it is intended to assert. Indeed, at this moment, it is precisely from such "nonhomogenized souls" that resistance to the EC has erupted, even as it was to be brought into formal existence. The final outcome, with whatever compromises, remains problematic.

Thus even when state patronage is intentionally indirect, controversy is inevitable and outcomes uncertain. This seems true whether the patronage is delegated procedurally through policies and agencies that are staffed and supported by those geographically and professionally close to the field, or through agencies that are intended to supersede ingrown and parochial rivalries in the common interest. Yet relegation of all financial and institutional support for the arts and culture to the commercial market has obvious consequences that are not always welcome, as we have seen.

Public patrons are between the rock and the hard place: their efforts are not likely to produce immediate and providential results, yet the absence of those efforts will guarantee a commercialized culture of the lowest common denominator on the one hand, and of highly fractionalized markets on the other—neither of which is particularly desirable if a rich and unified national culture is to be developed.

❖ 12 ❖

The Politicization of Peer-Review Panels
at the NEA

ANN M. GALLIGAN

Since the establishment of the National Endowment for the Arts (NEA) and the National Endowment for the Humanities (NEH) in 1965, peer-panel review has developed into one of the most vital and central components of both agencies' grant-making operations. Both endowments have come to rely on panels of experts to advise them on funding decisions and operating policy. The NEA has primarily employed discipline-based panels while the NEH has opted for project-based or more subject-oriented panels. The panel system has been effective for both endowments, aiding them in choosing among a vast number of groups and individuals requesting federal assistance within the confines of budgetary constraints.

Several basic questions are central to any discussion of peer-panel review at the NEA. First, why did the endowment opt to use panels over other forms of grant review and award selection? Second, has peer-panel review been an effective mechanism in making funding choices? Third, is it still the most effective and viable system the NEA could employ? Finally, there is the issue that this essay does not discuss: the overall appropriateness of the NEA as a vehicle for federal patronage of the arts. While this is to some the most important question of all, it is for a different time and place. Here, the major concern is the question of ongoing panel effectiveness in light of the changes wrought in its overall shape, size, and composition: as this issue is explored, it may shed light on the larger question of arts policy in general and the role of the NEA within those policies in particular.

In order to understand the role of NEA peer panels, it is necessary to examine the reasons why panels were first created and the reasons

254

behind the changes during the course of their twenty-five-year history. This review will concentrate on their role as a mechanism that allows the endowment to separate its own administration, as a federal agency most directly involved in government arts patronage, from the actual tasks of grant review and policy formation. Special attention will be paid to the history of peer panels at the NEA, including the tensions engendered by the conflicting ideals of panel autonomy and professionalism versus those of democratic accountability and public stewardship.

Underlying this conflict are two central and opposing principles. Peer-review panel members are expected to maintain a commitment to the ideals of autonomous, almost "scientific" neutrality and specialized expertise that distinguish them as representatives of their profession; at the same time they are entrusted with the power to make funding recommendations as public servants, responsible to the electorate. As will be discussed later and in greater detail, the tensions between professional and independent artistic judgment and that of public accountability for the funding outcome has been a major point of contention in every one of the debates over the endowment since its inception (Mulcahy 1985).

Under the National Foundation on the Arts and Humanities Act of 1965, the chairperson of each agency was authorized, with the advice of their respective and presidentially appointed National Councils, "to establish and carry out" programs to assist groups or individuals of exceptional talent engaged in or concerned with the arts and humanities. The chairs were further authorized to "prescribe such regulations" as they might deem necessary, "governing the manner in which the chairman's function shall be carried out"; further, they were "to utilize from time to time, as appropriate, experts and consultants, including panels of experts" (*National Foundation on the Arts and Humanities Act of 1965*).

Roger Stevens, the NEA's first chairperson, appointed by President Lyndon Johnson in 1966, turned to panels only as a procedural necessity once the National Council on the Arts could no longer cope with the vast amounts of material to review. Stevens was at first a strong opponent of panels, preferring to place the responsibility for decision making on staff and with the National Council. This was feasible when the NEA was small (its original budget was a meager $2.6 million), but it soon became impossible as applications and budgets grew. Despite Stevens's apprehensions, the use of peer-panel review began to evolve.

In composition, members of the National Council on the Arts represented all disciplines then considered appropriate, but they could not keep pace or do justice to all the various subdisciplines as applications grew. Thus after its first year, panels were composed of non-council members.

Each panel emerged differently. The first NEA panel to be appointed, for the field of dance, initially met in January 1966. This special advisory panel was comprised of twelve members of the national dance community, representing "the broadest aspects of dance expression nationwide," and was set up to review requests for assistance from both dancers and dance organizations. The panel was also charged with developing plans and programs to meet some of what was perceived at that time as "the urgent current and future needs of a chronically poverty-stricken art field" (Taylor and Barresi 1984, 83).

Panels for literature, visual arts, and music were then formed. Roger Stevens, himself, set up the eighteen-member music panel, naming Aaron Copland as its chair. This panel soon found it could not adequately review each application as a whole and, as a result, its numbers were increased and the panel subdivided into a number of smaller panels to better cover all the tributaries. There had been some criticism of the previous music award, especially regarding the scale of funding for the "Young Artists" and chamber music awards. The creation of the panel as a broader advisory body helped allay those fears (Taylor and Barresi 1984).

Before long, Roger Stevens, the National Council, and the program directors themselves all recognized that an ad hoc, project-by-project response could no longer be sustained. Still, for all the experimentation of the Stevens years (1965–69), there was no systematic structure to the peer-review panels and the process of grant application: this would be one of the first changes made by the in-coming chairperson, Nancy Hanks.

When Nancy Hanks was appointed by President Richard Nixon to be the head of the NEA in late 1969, she expanded the role of panels both administratively and in terms of policy. She brought with her many of the ideas and concepts of panels from her previous experience as program officer at the Rockefeller Fund. For Hanks, panels were seen as key factors in a number of ways. Not only did she give them increased responsibility and decision-making power, but in effect, she gave them a life of their own. Hanks's method was to bring the best and the most qualified individuals together on a number of discipline-based panels and then, with the advice of an informed program director and staff, let them arrive in their own way at a consensus for grant awards. It was for this reason that NEA panels did not follow a unified system of ranking all applications as did NEH panels. It was rare that Hanks ever interfered with the dynamics of the various panels. Although she was completely involved in panel selection and day-to-day endowment affairs, she had complete trust in the panel review process once it began. Only once did she overrule a decision after a panel had voted;[1] as a rule, she expressed any opinion to the panels only before they began their deliberations.

Meanwhile, at the Endowment for the Humanities, its first chairperson, Barnaby Keeney (1966–70), also employed panels to assist with its increased volume of applicant review. At the NEH, the first panel structure was based on the system of collegial review popular within academia. The NEH also borrowed aspects from the National Science Foundation model for the design of its administration and review. This system has remained fairly constant over the course of NEH history, with the addition of minor adaptations similar to those at the NEA during the 1970s to broaden representation on the panels. For both endowments, the workload has increased dramatically since their inception; peer-review panels have been a necessary resource in filling the need for increased assistance in applicant review. Instead of hiring additional staff to meet this need, as did the National Science Foundation, the endowments have opted to bring an increased number of panels into the process.

Still, until 1977, the NEA peer-review system was able to rely heavily on staff direction and guidance. Each panel worked differently and the structure and operation of each reflected both the needs and character of the program area. For instance, widely different and multifaceted programs like those for architecture, planning, and design relied more on ad hoc panels to meet their needs than did the more institutional-oriented theater program. Policy formation differed among the various programs as well. Theater developed its program policy over time and within the continuity of standing panels; from the outset the architecture program had tighter and more centralized policy control.

As an illustration of NEA's tremendous expansion from 1969 to 1977, the number of applications coming into the NEA multiplied over nine times, from about 2,000 in 1969 to nearly 20,000 in 1977; the grants it awarded grew nearly six times, from 584 in 1969 to over 4,000 in 1977 (Wyszomirski 1987, 208). By 1990, 85,000 grants had been awarded from a pool of 500,000 applications during the NEA's twenty-five year history. Without peer-review panels (which today total over 100) the NEA could never have handled the sheer volume of review. To have dealt with this expansion through an increase in staff would have gone against the "hands-off, once-removed" policy of federal-funding involvement that Nancy Hanks had developed. Her political "instincts" were sound: there was widespread belief that patronage for the arts was "primarily a matter for private and local initiative." This belief, both within and outside the arts community, supported Hanks's view that the solution would be found in an increase in panel members over staff. With panels, the NEA could decentralize decision making and put the emphasis on the recommendations made by representatives or "peers" of the profession rather than by paid governmental employees. This would sidestep the highly charged political question of the creation of a formal ministry of culture.

On the whole, as appointed by the early chairpersons, the NEA peer-review panels did represent the various professions; their members have tended to be closer to the field than the respective National Council members, and their focus has brought to the review process a discipline-based point of view. The NEA chair and the National Council have generally accepted panel judgments within each program area and have concentrated instead on overall, long-range issues relating to the arts for society as a whole. Instead, the panels have tended to focus more on specific funding decisions concerning individual awards. In addition, panels have drafted recommendations for council consideration concerning the established categories and standards for such review. As this system developed, it provided the NEA with a fairly effective method of distributing workload and keeping policy formation as broadly conceived and empirically field-based as possible.

The panels were based on the premise that they would bring both integrity and aesthetic judgment to the review of grant proposals. Panels had to operate with a well-defined set of professional standards. Michael Straight, NEA deputy director under Nancy Hanks, listed three criteria for panelists: they must always be appointed on merit; they must serve as individuals and not as representatives of particular interests, institutions, or viewpoints; they must be insulated from external pressures. This last point was not difficult to enforce when the endowment's budget was small, but as appropriations increased so too have the political pressures upon the endowment mounted, many of which were quite legitimate (Straight 1979).

Nonetheless, despite the pressures and the increasing importance of professional credentialism, the panels were appointed on a rather random basis between 1966 and 1970. By the latter date it was clear that if they were going to meet the demands of a growing agency, their structure would have to be institutionalized. Heretofore, the panelists had been appointed by the chairperson for terms up to four years. In the NEA reauthorization hearing of 1973, Congress reaffirmed this right but warned that the panels must be both "qualified" and have "broad geographical representation." Going further in specification in the NEA's 1976 reauthorization, Congress added that the panels should reflect "the broadest possible representation of view point . . . so that all styles and forms of expression which involve quality in the arts . . . may be equitably treated" (*National Foundation of the Arts and Humanities Act Amendments* 1976).

The need for balance in terms of representation in the funding process became increasingly evident as the 1970s wore on. As the NEA developed in size and budget, groups both within and outside the arts community began to demand a say in the decision-making process. Over the course of the NEA's first twenty years, its budget grew from $2.5 million to $163.7 million; given the stimulus of the mandated distribution of 20 percent of the NEA budget to the states, the state arts agencies' budgets themselves expanded from $2.7 million to $164 million, collectively. The similarly charged local public arts agencies received over $300 million dollars. With the obvious success of their stimulus to state and local funding, the NEA panels developed in both stature and scope: they came to be recognized as potentially powerful vehicles for a host of growing constituencies within the country as a whole. In turn, among the groups demanding representation in the panels were women's organizations, ethnic groups, minorities, and the states. Nancy Hanks herself had nurtured many of these groups. In particular, the state arts agencies came to challenge NEA autonomy in cultural funding, by the middle part of the 1970s demanding "partnership with the federal government rather than simple patronage from it" (Wyszomirski 1987, 234).

By the time Livingston Biddle (1977–81) came to head the NEA in 1977, the panel system had been firmly established, with the basic administrative duty to assist the National Council and the chairperson in the review of grant applications. Given this mandate and Biddle's own populist thrust, during his tenure the panels were broadened to better reflect the growing diversity of the endowment constituencies. As Eva Jacob (an early reviewer of the NEA panel system) remarked in a 1979 in-house document, "The need for diversity has always been acknowledged at the Endowment; the problems and priorities in each field are different and continually evolving" (1979, 2). This diversity expanded to include the needs of a wider representation of the American public. As a result, panels began to serve a new function for the endowment itself: advocacy.

While Biddle focused on new areas of artistic talent (initiating the program in jazz, for example), he also made policy changes in personnel areas to create greater movement within the staff and the program area. All of these implicitly (if not explicitly) involved new efforts at advocacy. Thus the endowment instituted a number of structural changes in the panels and introduced the Office of Minority Concerns in order to broaden the scope of minority review. Finally, panelists were rotated on a regular basis of three-year terms, to ensure infusion of new ideas and points of view.

(By rotating the panels and thereby increasing the sheer number of former and present panelists linked into the system, the NEA increased as well its "alumni" advocates and recruitable lobbyists.)

By this time, obviously, the panels had become central to the NEA's legitimation, especially at review and reauthorization by Congress. In 1978 the National Council on the Arts affirmed its reliance on the "tested principle" of review by peer panels. Shortly thereafter, the NEA issued an in-house Panel Study Report affirming both the vitality of the panel system to the working of the agency, and the belief that peer review is the fairest way of making difficult decisions on artistic quality within the framework of a government agency (Jacob 1979).

The results of the in-house study were incorporated into a formal document (*Report: a Study of the Panel System at the National Endowment for the Arts* 1979) and were approved for implementation by the chairperson. The study recommended that in order for the panel system to keep pace with the changing needs of the endowment, in each program area the panels should be divided: into a policy panel of twelve to fifteen members; and a grant panel, as needed, whose duties would be limited to application review. The specific recommendations arising out of application review were then to be addressed through "specific and structured linkage" between the panel subdivisions. (Although many of the programs today have abandoned the split-panel concept, it was an important move at the time in finding new ways to make the panels more flexible in meeting the agency's mandate to respond to its conflicting mission of fostering innovation in the arts and, at the same time, of responding to often more conservative taxpayer taste.)

Clearly, a primary goal of the restructuring and the split between program and policy was to provide the panels with greater specialization and to provide for more expertise and broader representation from the field. Not only did this move bring many new panelists into the endowment decision-making process, it brought with them many new artistic and cultural points of view. Biddle agreed that it was important to recognize the emergence of new art forms and arts constituencies, and to have those attitudes reflected on the panels.

Under the old system, approximately 385 panelists advised the NEA per year. Under the new system instituted by Biddle in 1979, the number rose to 475 panelists. The overt benefits of the changes were to bring "the range of professional experience, and the diversity of aesthetic, cultural, regional, and minority viewpoints" into the decision-making process. An implicit intent was that the representation on the panels would buffer congressional and other criticism that the panels operated as closed systems with little regard for the aesthetic needs and positions of outsiders (Mulcahy and Kendrick 1988, 51).

There were substantive grounds for such criticism: while the original "closed" system had worked quite effectively with the smaller, more traditional and institutionally oriented programs and panels when dollars were fewer and projects more narrowly defined, it was less effective when the allocated funds blossomed and the applicant pool diversified and grew. To recognize the merits of minority and nontraditional perspectives and cultures is one thing; to have those viewpoints represented on a federally funded panel is quite another. In short, it was realized that because the NEA is a national agency and is responsible for the expenditure of federal tax dollars, at the same time, efficiency is not its only mandate, and it must make sure all points of view are reflected.

Yet Congress did not think the NEA's measures sufficient and far-reaching enough. In 1979, the House Appropriations Committee's investigative staff released a report highly critical of both endowments and their operations. Regarding the NEA, the staff charged the agency with "cronyism" and called its funding structure a "closed system." It further charged that the NEA was "deficient in its management policy and practices" to the extent that the NEA failed "to meet its legislative mandate" (*Report to the Committee on Appropriations* 1979, 9).

The 1979 House report saw the NEA as failing to establish a coherent policy position and to develop uniform systems of evaluation within its programs and panels. To be sure, there were many flaws in both the methodology and in the conclusions drawn by the House report (including the fact that the report failed to make clear the distinctions between panels at the NEA and its sister agency, the NEH), but the charge that the NEA operated with a "closed circle of advisors" is relevant to this particular discussion in that it points to the growing reaction to the autonomous power of panels.

Indeed, the House report recognized that panels "are the heart of the Endowment operation," and that the selection of panelists is "the keystone." The system had operated up to this point with a sincere desire to bring the "best" and "most qualified" reviewers into the NEA process. Although the individuals who were selected previously were from a limited pool, they were generally regarded as the "finest" in the country. For the most part, the endowment critics were not challenging the credentials of those panelists; instead, they were calling for representation on panels to include a broader range of experts with a wider lens concerning artistic viewpoints and traditions.

For many at this time, the problem with the method of panel selection was that it was conservative in nature and tended to reinforce certain kinds of art and artistic viewpoints over others. As such it drew upon a fairly small range of both reviewers and applicants: in effect, it narrowed both the definition and the range of NEA supported art, leaving the system open to charges of operating as a "closed circle."

Included in the House report were charges that the endowments failed to meet their legislative mandate; were poorly organized and run; and did not live up to their mission to clearly define public policy in either the arts or the humanities. The report also charged that the endowment staff in fact determined the outcomes of panel decisions, by hiring consultants to develop project proposals for submission by applicants. Indeed, it charged the NEA in particular with having lost control of its programs and having major flaws in both its contracting system and in its relationship with a variety of service organizations. The focus of the criticism of the report was directed toward two areas: first, it focused on what it perceived were the structural problems of peer-panel review; and second, it expressed deep concern over what it saw as the "politicization" of the review process, and as noted, the creation of a "closed system" with the resulting byproducts of "cronyism" and "conflict of interest."

Both the NEA and the NEH responded that those who compiled the report misread the legislative mandate, especially in terms of the endowments' policy role, and failed to comprehend much of their internal organization and procedures. At the time the report was issued, the endowments were nearing the peak of a major period of expansion and growth, both in terms of programs and funding. As a result of this trend, both agencies were grappling with the side effects, including the need for increased institutionalization and bureaucratization. Panels had been an important component in this expansion process and, as has been outlined, both the NEA and NEH were quick in trying to adapt their systems to meet the needs and demands now placed on them.

While the House report expressed a concern that panels at both the NEA and NEH did not rotate as much as they might (thus creating a somewhat "closed" environment for applicant review), the report feared as well the opposite: that the panel system was plagued by structural "looseness" as an aggregation of "ad hoc" assemblies rather than organized panels. The NEA denied this charge and replied that the very strength of the panel system lay in its nonprescriptive nature and that panel reactiveness and independence should not be misconstrued as disorganization or lack of direction.

Although the report did not criticize the sheer number of panels and other mechanisms of review, it did express concern over how information was shared among the groups, asserting that outside consultants and individual reviewers often made comments on applications that were not shared with either panels or the National Council. It charged that in the case of NEA programs, the staff deliberately misled the National Council and contended that there were cases where applications that had been turned down by panels were nonetheless forwarded on by the staff to the council for approval without the panels' comments. (Information is provided to the National Council based on staff-prepared summaries of reviewer and panel findings.) In the overwhelming majority of cases, the National Council concurred with the decisions made by the review panels, but in a tiny percentage the decision was reversed or the applicant received a chairman's grant from a special discretionary fund. In its reply to the report, the NEA commented on the infrequency of this occurrence.

The report also found that the NEH was stronger than the NEA in its processing of grant applications. NEH panelists submit individually written preliminary reviews; then they meet together as a panel to further consider the applications. Usually two votes are taken on a single application before a final panel recommendation is made to the council. Unlike the NEA, NEH panels use a standard ranking system across all panels that will then be used for an overall funding grade. The transcript of the panel proceeding (minus names) is available to an applicant upon request. The report suggested that the NEA adopt a similar procedure of providing feedback to rejected applicants (presumably those who would care most to learn criticism of the project proposal).

The influence of endowment staff on peer panels was also at issue. One of the major contentions was that staff actually "ran" the panels by assisting in the writing of the grant proposals. Further, the report charged that the National Councils spent too little time in reviewing panel recommendations for grants, (an average of four and a half minutes per grant for the NEA), placing too much control of applicant review in the hands of both the panels and the staff, thus adding to the overall weakness of both systems. Yet sheer volume alone would preclude more than a brief review by the National Council, whose role was becoming more and more an overall policy overseer and less of an arm of actual review.

It is important to note the differing levels of staff involvement between the two endowments. The NEH staff plays a much more active role before an application goes to the panels than does its NEA counterpart. Before NEH proposals reach the panels, they are studied and evaluated both by in-house staff and by outside experts. Applications are weighted both on their own merits and in relation to other applications under consideration. The division's senior staff ensure that the criteria for the program are adhered to and that endowment policy is understood. The NEH staff also has more direct contact with both the applicant and external reviewers, similar to the project-oriented National Science Foundation Model of review. In contrast, the NEA staff plays a more indirect role, with no reliance on staff-recruited external reviewers and with its panels chaired internally rather than by staff. Still, both endowments are similar in that the staff does have an effect, more or less subtle, on an application's outcome.

Yet it was not the control of the staff over the review process or how the various agents of review communicated that was the House report's greatest concern. It was most worried that the endowments had "lost control" of the overall process by granting panels so much autonomy that, as noted above, they had become "closed" and rife with "cronyism" as previous grant recipients came to serve as panelists and vice versa.

Such charges are not limited to the endowments, to be sure: procurement decisions in the Defense Department suffer from similar accusations. Yet the central question of the House report still lingers: How valid *is* peer review itself? In 1985, in a major survey of the general issue, the American Council of Learned Societies Survey of Scholars found that three-quarters of its nearly 5,400 respondents (polled from the various affiliate organizations) considered the peer review system used by the major journals in their respective disciplines to be biased, especially in favor of established scholars. Nearly half of those polled said reform was needed (Morton and Price 1986).

In a highly critical attack on peer review that appeared in 1980, Michael Mooney, a critic of the endowments, paints the NEH review system as a secretive, conspiratorial operation, totally misusing its power, with the NEA not much better. He questions the impartiality of those chosen to review endowment projects. More than a question of "cronyism" or "conflict of interest," Mooney charges that "peer" panels reflect a certain bias toward the status quo that often stifles creativity and originality. Echoing the age-old adage that genius has no peer, he adds that it is doubtful that genius could ever survive a review by peers (1980, 347).

Mooney's second major objection to peer review is that its base is constructed on the premise that even "fundamental new knowledge" is expected to be both "rational" and, "insofar as possible, put forward from previously accepted scholarly work" (1980, 178). The primary question then comes down to the difficulty of balancing the needs for rigorous "objectivity" based on established criteria with that of inspired creativity and individualism.

Obviously, neither the practice nor the problems of peer panels as a part of a "scientific" process of evaluation is unique to the NEA. The system of peer review itself originally came from academic traditions and in recent times has also been employed within the fields of medicine, law, and the behavioral and social sciences. As one analyst has described it, peer review in these fields is build on consensus and the scientific method. The scientific process answers to three fundamental constraints: logical consistency; testability; and that science must be a public, self-correcting process. The last point does not refer to public acceptance in terms of popular opinion, but "public in the sense of one's peers, one's fellow scientists" (Hanrad 1982, 1). Science operates on a consensual basis in light of published criteria. Its strengths are its general acceptability and its repeatability. Given these standards, many feel that peer consensus is the basic objective of peer review (the absence of consensus indicates "chance" or bias, and hence should be minimized or eliminated), while others acknowledge that peer disagreement can be "rational" and even creative (Hanrad 1982). But however characteristic of science, ready acceptability and repeatability are not characteristic of innovative art. Thus the critics of NEA peer review in the late 1970s and early 1980s tended to challenge the process more in terms of the openness and representativeness of the awards selection process, than for its lack of rationality.

In 1981, President Ronald Reagan convened a Special Presidential Task Force on the Arts and Humanities to examine the overall operation of the endowment process and its commitment to the public as an instrument for awarding federal funds for culture. The task force report concluded that the endowments and their programs were basically sound and in need of only minor revisions. It found that federal funding for the arts and humanities was appropriate, even as private-sector support could and should be increased through the inducement of matching federal funds (Special Task Force on the Arts and Humanities 1981). While the task force thus reaffirmed the role of the private sector, both as independent donors and as cooperators in matching grants, at the same time it reaffirmed the primary role of the NEA and NEH as patrons of the arts and humanities.

The task force report concluded that the panel review process of the two agencies was an effective and fair method of recommending endowment grants, and should be continued. Although critical of other aspects of the endowments' operation, the task force held that the benefits of the peer-review panels outweighed any advantages of the alternatives: either centralizing the decision-making process within the purview of federal employees, or basing grants solely on predetermined formulas (Special Task Force on the Arts and Humanities 1981, 17).

By the late 1980s, however, critics of NEA panels began to argue for alternatives, toward decentralization and toward greater reliance on pre-scribed funding. While the panels had grown in power and stature during the administrations of Stevens, Hanks, and Biddle, criticism from both liberals and conservatives increased to the point that two recent NEA chairpersons—Frank Hodsoll (1981–89) and John Frohnmayer (1989–92) had to fight to maintain their structure and role within the agency.

Pressure to decentralize federal arts funding by channeling it through state and local arts agencies increased not only on the endowment as a whole, but also within the panels themselves. Accordingly, in the NEA's reauthorization concluded in fall 1990, 35 percent of its funds are to be allocated to state art agencies, compared with the previous 20 percent formula. (However, these new federal funds put at the states' disposal do not make up for the simultaneous cuts in arts funding made by the state legislatures trying to cope with severe deficits; decentralization combined with the 1990 recession thus meant a reduction in both federal and state arts support.) Administratively, the NEA responded to the pressures urging decentralization by trying to include representatives from state art agencies on many of its panels.

However, while making concessions to the movement to decentralize, the NEA fought pressures to rely on formulas for decision making. For example, one extreme formula solution would have the NEA simply match the sums raised by communities or institutions in accepted categories of art activities, with no NEA input as to what art or institution to support. A less extreme approach would be to have the panels recommend applicants for funding on the basis of perceived merit. A funding formula could then be applied. In effect, this is what former NEA chairperson Frank Hodsoll proposed in his budgetary revisions of 1989. While he did not recommend the standardizing of the panel process, a more standardized ceiling in funding was in fact implemented.

All these recent developments have reduced the central role of the panels in endowment decision-making. The congressional reauthorization hearings of 1990 raised the question of direct congressional involvement, placing preconditions on the content of art even to be eligible for panel review. If implemented, any such threatened sanctions against "obscene" art would further erode panel professional autonomy by questioning the authority of panelists in their areas of expertise.

Ironically, the devaluation of the authority of experts—either through a change in panel composition to include "non-peer" members or through congressional efforts to restrict the content of art eligible for NEA funding—can be seen as an unintentional consequence of the panel system's prior success. Over the twenty-five years of its existence, the NEA has made art more widely accessible and more readily available. It has encouraged previously marginalized groups to see themselves as equally worthy of federal support, as artists with creative expertise and professional skills to match those of the "established great." As the NEA and others have come to recognize the validity of those claims and to expand both programs and panel participation to be more inclusive, still more marginalized sectors have demanded their *own* right to autonomy and "expertise." As "members of the audience" and as taxpayers, they have declared their unwillingness to delegate to others the authority to determine the nation's public art.

Thus by demystifying art and bringing it into the public arena, the NEA with its process of peer-review panels has undermined the traditional distinction between patron and audience. As the process of patronage has become more open, the intended audience both to the art and to the act of patronage has become broadened to include those who are unsympathetic to the original aims of federal patronage. The new audiences insist that their own standards (philistine or not) be given equal respect.

Responding to these tensions within the patronage process, in the summer of 1990 Congress created an Independent Commission to review the NEA's grant-making procedures and to examine the endowment's direction with respect to the original aims of federal patronage. This action was prompted by two 1989 controversies surrounding exhibitions deemed "offensive" by some members of Congress and by a vocal group of endowment critics. In the first instance, the controversy arose over a $15,000 subgrant given by the Southeastern Center for Contemporary Art in Winston-Salem, North Carolina, to Andres Serrano for an exhibition that included photographs of a plastic crucifix submerged in the artist's urine. The second involved a $30,000 grant to the Institute of Contemporary Art in Philadelphia to organize a traveling exhibition of photographs by the late Robert Mapplethorpe, which included pictures showing sadomasochism, homoeroticism, and nude children.

After a series of public hearings, the Independent Commission issued a report that affirmed that freedom of expression was essential for the arts. While the commission recognized obscenity as speech not protected by the Constitution, it asserted that determinations of obscenity should be made by the courts, not by endowment staff nor its advisory panels in the grant-review process (Independent Commission 1990). The commission was critical of certain aspects of the endowment's operations, however, and called for a strengthening of the role of the chairperson (as the sole authority to make grants) and increasing the role of the National Council in the review process. Finally, the report recommended "basic structural and procedural reforms at every level." Among the recommendations concerning panels were steps to eliminate the "real or apparent conflicts of interest" by delineating the scope of the panels' operation and by broadening their membership to include "knowledgeable laypersons" to guard against charges of special interest and cronyism. Such structural reforms would presumably help to prevent the recurrence of the 1989 controversies over "obscene" content by introducing more "outsider" control over panel decisions.

The Independent Commission was given a second charge by Congress: to study the question of whether there are, or should be, different standards for publicly funded and privately funded art. The commission found that standards for the former did exceed those for the latter—not in terms of the level of artistic quality, but in terms of increased sensitivity by applicants for funding as to the nature of the source of the patronage. In general, when public funding was sought, the projects appeared to have fit within the limits of public acceptability—that is, projects that were inherently less "risky" than those for which only private support was expected. To the degree this was true (criticism based on the Serrano and Mapplethorpe cases to the contrary, notwithstanding), it suggested that panel approval would then serve to legitimate as "public culture" art that was safe, rather than promoting the cutting edge of individual creativity. Recognizing the difficulty, the report states that the NEA should continue to "seek to offer a spacious sense of freedom to the artists and the arts institutions it assists"—even though "at the same time, the NEA must, if it is to maintain public confidence in its stewardship of public funds, be accountable to all of the American people" (Independent Commission 1990).

As discussed, much of the disagreement over the NEA as the primary vehicle for federal arts patronage has centered on its use of peer-panel review and its near-total reliance on the authority of its panels of experts to make funding decisions. The negative byproduct of panel autonomy has been the perception that the panels operated by peers and for peers, without consideration for the public that is both the ultimate source of the funds and the intended audience—and without ongoing administrative control by the president's appointees responsible to the electorate.

In recommending that the NEA be maintained in its primary mission to foster artistic excellence and to live up to the public trust in making the arts available to all the American people, the Independent Commission reaffirmed as well both the authority and the responsibility of the chairperson for the NEA's operation. Indeed, rather than referring to the panels as "peer panels," it used the term "grant advisory panels" to stress their function rather than their composition, and to suggest that their use in funding decisions was only one of many avenues available to the chairperson in award selection.

All along, the problem has been one of democratic accountability for the NEA and for the system of federal patronage of culture as a whole: how to remain sensitive to the interests of *all* the American publics yet at the same time remain true to the mandate for artistic excellence. The panels have been at the center of this dynamic, reflecting each shift in the composition of the arts patronage equation. As outlined, changes in the panels have occurred in response to calls, in turn, for greater specialization and professionalism, for broader geographical and artistic diversity, and for increased minority, state, and local representation. Now the call is for the inclusion of individuals from outside the artistic community altogether, as representatives of the "lay public."

The endowment has allowed the panel system to absorb these changes, preferring politicization of the panels to that of the endowment as a whole and thereby the entire structure of public arts patronage. As a result, the panels have provided a necessary safety valve for the NEA, giving the system a flexibility that permits change without compromising artistic standards or the public trust. But how far can the panel system be stretched before it no longer provides such protection? Recent events have suggested that the system may be near its limits. Yet once the panels have reached a point of saturation in terms of representativeness, they may return to an emphasis upon professionalism. If history does in fact repeat itself, the panels will remain the most likely target of pressures to change the system of public patronage, and they should be able to adapt to these new conditions, securing the endowment's continued survival and success.

Note

1. In 1970, Nancy Hanks directed the removal of an erotic story from an NEA-backed anthology. Other awards during her tenure were challenged by some members of Congress and the public, but she allowed the awards to stand.

References

Hanrad, Steven. 1982. *Peer Commentary on Peer Review*. New York: Cambridge University Press.

Independent Commission. 1990. *A Report to Congress on the National Endowment for the Arts*. Washington, D.C.: GPO.

Jacob, Eva. 1979. "A Study of the Panel System at the NEA." Unpublished report. Washington, D.C.

Mooney, Michael. 1980. *Ministry of Culture*. New York: Wyndham Books.

Morton, Herbert C., and Anne J. Price. 1986. "The American Council of Learned Societies Survey of Scholars: Views on Publications, Computers, Libraries." *Scholarly Communication* 5 (Summer).

Mulcahy, Kevin V. 1985. "The NEA as Public Patron of the Arts." In *Art, Ideology, and Politics*, edited by Judith H. Balfe and Margaret Jane Wyszomirski, 316–29. New York: Praeger.

Mulcahy, Kevin V., and Harold F. Kendrick. 1988. "Congress and Culture: Legislative Reauthorization and the Arts Endowment." *Journal of Arts Management and Law* 17(4): 39–55.

National Foundation on the Arts and Humanities Act Amendments. 1976. Washington, D.C.: GPO.

National Foundation on the Arts and Humanities Act of 1965. Washington, D.C.: GPO.

Report: A Study of the Panel System at the National Endowment for the Arts. 1979. Washington, D.C.: NEA.

Report to the Committee on Appropriations. 1979. Washington, D.C.: United States Congress; House. March 22.

Special Task Force on the Arts and Humanities. 1981. *Report to the President*. Washington, D.C.: GPO.

Straight, Michael. 1979. *Twigs for an Eagle's Nest*. New York: Devon Press.

Taylor, Fannie, and Anthony Barresi. 1984. *The Arts at a New Frontier: NEA*. Madison: University of Wisconsin Press.

Wyszomirski, Margaret J. 1987. "The Politics of Art: Nancy Hanks and the National Endowment for the Arts." In *Leadership and Innovation*, edited by Jameson W. Doig and Ernest C. Hargrove, 207–45. Baltimore: Johns Hopkins University Press.

✦ 13 ✦

The Battle for Classical Music on the Air

RICHARD A. PETERSON

From the early days of broadcasting there has been a continuous effort to ensure that classical music is presented regularly over the air, the prevailing rationale of those encouraging such performances being that on-air availability of this music whets the appetite of the listeners for live performances. Although the various interest groups advocating classical music broadcasts have been in substantial agreement on the goals of their program, there has been disagreement over the means, and this conflict in approach has been regularly rekindled as new issues have surfaced over the years. One of the enduring issues has been whether commercial or public radio can better inculcate a taste for classical music.

This chapter begins by reviewing the phases of the commercial/public struggle. The chapter concludes by outlining the constraints faced by public and commercial stations that have lead to the creation of a programming format here termed "classical lite," programming that does not seem to whet the appetite for any more serious classical music.

Art Music on Commercial Air

On January 13, 1910, two years before the first regularly scheduled radio broadcast, Lee de Forest broadcast Enrico Caruso live from the Metropolitan Opera House to show that radio was not a plaything, but could become an "elevating cultural force," bringing art music to the masses who could not afford to attend performances (Barnouw 1966, 27). In the decade preceding World War II, classical music programming became a staple of commercial network radio. However, this was due less to its commercial value than to its prestige and the desire of radio industry owners to curry favor with Congress and government regulatory agencies (Barnouw 1968; Horowitz 1987).

Thus, initially, the disagreement between the advocates of commercial radio networks and the proponents of a British BBC-like public radio was resolved in favor of the commercial radio interests. In order to protect themselves from further federal regulation, the networks agreed to subsidize a great deal of classical music programming. During a typical week in the late 1930s, as Major (1979) notes, one could hear the New York Philharmonic on CBS, the NBC Symphony under Arturo Toscanini, the Philadelphia Orchestra on Mutual, the Metropolitan Opera's "Auditions of the Air" and its Saturday matinees shepherded by Milton Cross, "Ford Sunday Evening Hour" with the Detroit Symphony, and many more.

Public Radio to the Rescue

Following World War II, the issue of commercial versus public broadcasting was joined again when high-fidelity FM radio was introduced simultaneously with commercial television. As commercial television took the network programming, prestige, and national advertisers from commercial radio, in order to survive at all commercial radio stations became, in effect, jukeboxes, each playing phonograph records in a single format. These formats varied from top-40, soul, country-western, easy listening, and Latin, to news/talk and classical (Barnouw 1970; Peterson 1990a). Live classical music was virtually eliminated from radio broadcasts by the 1960s, and even taped live music performances were greatly reduced in number.

There was a small but highly visible public outcry about these events, and the newly available FM radio provided an apparent resolution. A narrow band at the lower end of the FM spectrum was set aside for noncommercial stations and mandated for "educational" purposes, with many municipalities, school systems, and universities thereupon acquiring licenses (Barnouw 1970). Since the rationale for these stations was education, classical music was inserted into the programming mix in order to increase music appreciation.

Because of the low cost of records, very little of this classical music programming consisted of live performances. In 1970, to pool their financial resources and facilitate the underwriting of live performance, ninety of these "public" radio stations founded National Public Radio with a mandate to produce, purchase, and distribute programs among members, aided by a subsidy from the federal government. Initially, NPR distributed classical music programming and some jazz. Increasingly after 1980, however, it became involved in news and public affairs, most notably "All

Things Considered," "Morning Edition," and "Weekend Edition" (Jensen 1987; ARA 1988a; NPR 1988).

NPR has continued to distribute classical music concerts, jazz, radio drama, ethnic, and folk music. But another public radio programming service, American Public Radio (APR), has become by far the biggest distributor of classical music to public radio stations (ARA 1988a). Here it was a pseudo–public affairs variety program, "A Prairie Home Companion," and its successor, "The American Radio Company," which have taken primacy of place; they have been APR's most popular programs, featuring an eclectic array of dated pop and folk music, ads for fictitious products, and public service announcements for nonexistent causes, and Garrison Keillor's weekly news stories from a fictitious Minnesota town.

Public radio stations can (and many do) belong to both NPR and APR. Accordingly, especially when supplemented with locally programmed music, it is possible for a station to play a wide range of musical styles or to go "all classical," "all jazz," or "all news and public affairs." Specialization has been most common in the largest cities where there are several classical music stations and several NPR affiliates. Still, today most NPR affiliates offer the news programs and play a mix of classical, semiclassical, and jazz music as well.

However, recent shifts in funding resources for public radio have caused new pressures for change in this mix of programming. Beginning with the Reagan administration, federal subsidies to public radio have been cut year by year. In response, to demonstrate that public radio was worthy of continued government support, to attract larger grants from program underwriters, and to build membership donations, in 1985 the director of NPR, Douglas J. Bennett, vowed to double NPR's audience in five years (Variety 1987). This seemed like an attainable goal at the time, since the public radio audience had grown steadily through the 1970s and the first half of the 1980s.

Public Radio: News and the New Audience

As the number of public radio listeners increased, it became evident that the programming preferences of the new audience were somewhat different from those of traditional NPR members. As noted above, from the outset public radio stations had not been devoted entirely to classical music. They broadcast other forms of music not often available on commercial radio stations, and increasingly they broadcast news and information. In fact, the rapid growth of public radio listenership in the 1980s was due largely to growth in the public radio audience for news and public affairs (Jensen 1987). The weekly audience for NPR's news magazine programs ("All Things Considered," "Morning Edition," and "Weekend Edition") grew from two million in 1980 to six million in 1987. Indeed, over half of all those who tuned to public radio during the week (a total audience of over ten million) listened to these three programs. The only public radio program that rivaled their drawing power was "A Prairie Home Companion" (ARA 1988a; NPR 1988).

NPR officials inferred from the accumulating evidence that while the majority of NPR station listeners are attracted by news and public affairs, many—perhaps most—of the new recruits to the ranks of NPR listenership are not classical music fans.[1] More troubling were survey findings that the musical tastes of nonmember NPR listeners differed from those of dues-paying members: the latter, upon whom the stations depend for direct financial support, are far more likely than nonmembers to choose classical music and to avoid adult contemporary rock music (NPR 1988). Generally, NPR station donor-members are much like the national audience for live classical music in terms of education, occupational status, and general values, while the more numerous nonmember listeners, whose support the stations want to attract, are more like the average American adult (Peterson 1990b).

Supporting evidence comes from a 1983 survey of adult purchases of recorded music, which demonstrates that a much higher proportion of public radio listeners (aggregating here both NPR station members and nonmembers) buys classical music records than does the general public (NPR 1984). While public radio listeners are also more likely to buy records of the other types of music played on NPR stations (Broadway musicals, jazz, folk, and new wave), they are also likely to buy contemporary black and rock music, which NPR stations do not typically program. What is more, a significant number of NPR listeners buy pop, country, and disco records. Clearly then, contrary to the assumption made by professional radio people up through the 1970s (Routt 1978; Major 1979), by the late 1980s the typical public radio listener was not necessarily a classical music afficionado. A wide range of other sorts of music finds its devotees among public radio listeners and, what is more important for the present discussion, most nonmember public radio listeners do not choose classical music at all. The most dramatic evidence of the growing number of public radio listeners who are actively repelled by classical music is provided by looking at the program-by-program listenership over the course of the day. While most commercial radio stations experience a gradual ebb and flow during their broadcast hours, the listenership to NPR stations spikes up during "Morning Edition," drops through the day and spikes up even higher for "All Things Considered" in the late afternoon, plummeting again as soon as the evening music programming begins to air.

Still, in the mid-1980s it was possible to say that NPR stations were holding their classical music audience and also serving the increasingly large news-oriented audience, many of whom did not like classical music, as we have just seen. But then, precisely at the point when the NPR leadership committed itself to doubling the audience for public radio, the growth of this audience slowed and has since become virtually flat. Understandably, policy makers and station programmers looked for the cause of these difficulties. While it would have been possible to argue that the potential audience for news programming had been nearly saturated, they reasoned differently. Since news had been responsible for the great audience growth, and since the new generation of public radio leadership itself had risen to prominence by championing news and public affairs, members of that leadership found it difficult to blame the news format for their problems. However, art music audiences had been flat for years: audiences were said to be deserting the performance arts generally (*New York Times* 1987; Harris 1988; Balfe 1989). Since a number of commercial classical music stations were going off the air (Major 1979; *Variety* 1987), it was easy to blame NPR's classical music programming, or to point to the apparent disjunction between it and the news programming, for the disappointing growth in public radio listenership (ARA 1988a).

Two major strategies were thereupon proposed for putting NPR audience growth back on its desired track and for increasing its dues-paying membership. One involved tailoring the programming along the lines of commercial radio stations so that listeners would always know what to expect no matter when tuning in the station. The second strategy involved shaping the mix of types of music aired and changing the way they were presented, to appeal to the new and younger listeners who had come of age since 1955 and who are known to use radio very differently from the older audience (Peterson 1990b). Each of these strategies will be discussed in turn.

Making Public Radio More Like Commercial Radio

What does it mean to "double the audience," as NPR officials intended? One possible meaning is to have twice as many people listen during a week or year. Another meaning is to have no increase in the number of people listening, but to have each person listen twice as much. The former corresponds to what in broadcasting is called the "cume," that is, the cumulative number of persons who have listened during a specific period of time. The second is conventionally measured as "AQH": the average number of persons listening during a specific quarter hour of programming. Other measures of size are possible as well, but the question of which is chosen as the criterion for "doubling the audience" has important consequences for the strategies of programmers, the mix of programs presented, and ultimately, the nature of art music in America.

The strategy advocated by Audience Research Analysis, the radio industry consulting firm hired by the Corporation for Public Broadcasting (NPR's link to the federal government), was to build audience by trying to greatly increase the AQH (the time each listener stayed tuned) even at the expense of considerably reducing the cume (the total number of people who listened) (Giovannoni 1988; ARA 1988a). This is exactly the strategy that had been adopted by commercial radio since the mid-1950s (Peterson 1990a). Under this system, a station concentrates on a narrow range of programming (called a "format"), such as "top-40 music," "news/talk," "soul," "sacred," "album-oriented rock," "country music," or "adult alternative." It expects to alienate most radio listeners as the cost of gaining the devoted loyalty of some 5 to 15 percent (Peterson and Davis 1974; Routt 1978).

However, the programming on most *public* radio stations does not follow this pattern of targeting one narrow segment of the market. As noted above, although a few stations in the largest markets are able to specialize as "all classical," "all news and public affairs," or virtually "all jazz," most NPR stations around the country mix these sorts of programming and others as well. In effect, they approach what is called a "block format" (Routt 1978), where one kind of program is followed by another that might be quite different. In 1980, for example, on Saturday afternoons a Washington, D.C., station programmed in succession a block of light classical, followed by 1960s Chicago-style blues, followed by reggae, followed by bluegrass. The potential advantage of this smorgasbord sort of programming is that each of the different programs attracts a different audience. Skillfully crafted, this makes for a greatly expanded cume because many more people listen to the station during the course of a week. However, this is at the expense of some AQH, as loyal fans tune in their favorite program and then tune out as the next block starts. This high-cume/low-AQH pattern of serving diverse communities is seen as pathological by most commercial radio consultants, who disparage its high turnover ratio (NPR 1988). In their view, to be discussed below, public radio should become more like commercial radio.

Public Radio Is Radio

It is helpful at this point to review the way such consultants categorize and evaluate radio audiences, which in turn largely determines the advice they give (ARA 1988a, 1988b, 1988c; Giovannoni 1988, PRC 1988, 1992). NPR's primary consultant, Audience Research Analysis (ARA), identified three components of the public radio audience: "core" listeners who listen more to NPR stations than any other, "fringe" listeners who listen to NPR stations some of the time each week, and "samplers" who listen from time to time over a year. Respectively, these comprise 2, 4, and 13 million persons over the age of eleven. Approximately 35 million people live beyond the reach of any NPR station-signal, but some 140 million could listen and evidently choose not to. According to the consultants, these nonlisteners should be ignored. As Giovannoni says, "You couldn't pay these people to listen to public radio" (1988, 10). As in the case of nonlisteners, "samplers" too are ignored in the further analysis of the consultants, who focused entirely on those defined as the core and the fringe.

Although the two million in the core are relatively few in number, they account for 70.6 percent of the AQH, the total time spent listening to public radio. Nonetheless, most members of the core also listen to stations other than public radio stations. Indeed, on average 20 percent of their listening time is devoted to commercial radio. The consultants recommended trying to capture more of this 20 percent.

However, fringe listeners received most of the consultants' attention, because "they have the most radio listening time to convert to public radio listening time" (ARA 1988a, 39). Most fringe listeners are drawn to public radio news and public affairs, and then tune to a commercial station for music (ARA 1988a). The consultants recommended programming that would induce these listeners to stay tuned longer. Summing up their advice to target only the core and fringe who already listen with some regularity, the consultants concluded: "If programming is to create listeners for public radio, public radio must create programming for listeners" (ARA 1988a, 6).

It is not that the consultants simply dismiss block formatting and the goal of increasing the cume. Their experience in commercial radio suggests that small blocks don't add up to a large cumulative audience. They believe that radio listeners do not tune to particular programs. Rather, people dial stations until they hear what they want. Thus, they argue, if a public radio station has a number of different sorts of programming, most people will be disappointed and tune out the station most of the time, as they will rarely find the programming they like. Being disappointed with the station most of the time, they also will not respond at the time of fund-raising drives (ARA 1988a; 1988b).

Such analyses are drawn from the consultants' experience with tightly formatted commercial radio stations. Not taken into account is the fact that NPR member-listeners receive a monthly program guide, that announcers often mention upcoming programs of interest, and that since stations maintain a consistent schedule of programs day-to-day and week-to-week, whether NPR members or not, people come to know well when their favorite programs air (LL&A 1986).

Program Diversity with Consistent Appeal

To be sure, the consultants recognized that "public radio is not a format" (ARA 1988a, 23), meaning that it cannot be expected to be "all classical" or some such. A public radio station should have consistency of appeal, but they argued that this "does not require consistency of genre; nor need it result in bland homogeneity. When carefully crafted, a diversity of programming styles, genres, and sources can serve a sizable and appreciative audience segment, but only when all elements maintain a highly consistent appeal" (ARA 1988a, 24).

These are lofty goals—and vague. What do they mean in practice? The nearly identical makeup of the listeners to the news magazine program "All Things Considered" and the variety musical program "A Prairie Home Companion" is cited as an example of the fact that consistent appeal does not necessarily mean programs of the same genre (ARA 1988a, 41). However, the consultants were troubled by what they saw as a serious "inconsistency" between several traditional NPR genres. For example, they found only a small co-listenership between "All Things Considered" and NPR opera programs. Both types of program draw highly educated persons, but they tend not to be the same individuals. While over half of the news program's listeners are twenty-five to forty-four years of age, half the opera audience is over fifty-five (ARA 1988a, 27). Live-opera audiences and those for children's programming and dramatic programs show little overlap with those for the other public radio formats.

The consultants diplomatically suggest that such nonoverlapping formats be dropped from the "programming mix" altogether, or be repackaged to increase their affinity with the "mix." As an example of repackaging, they suggest, "programmers desiring to increase the affinity of NPR news and classical music may take steps to 'youthen' [sic] the appeal of their station's classical music programming" (ARA 1988a, 25). Just what this means or how it is to be accomplished, they do not say. Still, the net effect they seek is quite clear: "audience service is maximized when a program schedule appeals to one type of listener all the time" (ARA 1988a, 41).

Efforts by NPR stations to follow this advice have often been costly, and not always successful. For example, in 1992 the city-owned public radio station in Nashville, Tennessee, thought it could best accommodate both its classical music fans and its news and public affairs listeners by buying a second station and dividing the formats between them. As it turned out, that purchase proved impossible, much to the relief of many classical music supporters who reasoned that without the contributions of news and public affairs listeners, the very existence of the music station would soon be in jeopardy (Goldsmith 1992; Parsons 1992).

The New-Age Music Idea

Rather than dividing and then specializing among separate types of listeners, a number of NPR stations devised tactics intended to draw listeners closer together. One of these involved the programming of "new-age" music. A new-age music format had been introduced by commercial radio stations in a number of the larger cities at the time ARA was preparing its report. The initial audience surveys, run periodically by the Arbitron Corporation, showed that these commercial stations had increased their audience considerably by making this move, and that their new listeners were primarily affluent, well-educated, young adults, that is, from the huge affluent "yuppie" component of the baby-boomers. Consequently NPR was under considerable pressure from some member stations to produce (or purchase for distribution) a program devoted to new-age music, even as other member stations treated this suggestion with dismay or contempt.

Certainly many NPR stations in the affected markets became concerned that these new-age commercial stations were drawing listeners from them, in particular the many NPR news listeners who were known to be disaffected with NPR music. They further reasoned that new-age music fans were people whose lifestyles included participation in "good causes," who presumably would then feel good about donating to a public radio station that played their sort of music. (This contrasts with jazz fans who are clearly devoted to their chosen music but who typically do not donate to support stations that play jazz.) For other reasons, new-age music was considered desirable by the promotion and development departments of member stations. They reasoned that the lifestyle of the yuppie listener oriented to new-age music would be attractive to a wide range of local program underwriters who had been unwilling to underwrite the programming of traditional art music. In their own parlance, "New-age would be an attractive new product to promote."

What is this new-age music? As with any creative activity, particularly one that has emerged so recently, it is difficult to identify new-age precisely. It is generally associated with the New-Age movement—a mix of mysticism, Asian philosophy, environmentalism, and 1970s self-absorption (Friedrich 1987; Blow 1988). In the words of Jerry Wood, a *Billboard* editor, the commercial music industry has characterized new-age music to include "many genres within the genre—space music, instrumental rock, contemporary acoustic, electronic/progressive, crossover pop, soft jazz, ambient/experimental, crossover classical, meditative, and of course, hard-core transcendental music" (Wood 1988, N4).

At the same time, defenders of the classical music aesthetic hold new-age music in utter contempt. Writing in *The New Republic*, Richard Blow characterized new-age as: "a sort of high-brow version of Muzak that its purveyors describe as 'soothing,' 'spiritual,' and 'peaceful.' That's if you like it. If you don't, the words 'boring' and 'insipid' come to mind" (Blow 1988, 26). A *New York Times* music critic, Jon Pareles, agreed: "New age music is spreading like kudzu, and for good reason. It eliminates the most complex, time-consuming, mentally draining part of the musical experience: paying attention. . . . Listening attentively is like watching Mr. Rogers on television gently repeating every word for his audience of pre-schoolers" (Pareles 1987, 28). Writers for the rock-music press have been just as disparaging (Fricke 1986).

Nevertheless, on Valentine's Day in 1987, new-age became a recognized radio format, when long-time Los Angeles commercial rock station KMET changed its call letters to KTWV—"The Wave"—and went full-time new-age. Initially, it enjoyed considerable success in attracting listeners. It focused great attention on sustaining the mood of the music. Station personnel were instructed not to refer to KTWV as a "radio station," but rather as a "mood service." Advertising was low key. DJs did not announce the names of records played: this information was available "as a personal service," along with a promotion for the station, by calling a 1-800 number. And news programs were replaced by "wave breaks" in which "information was shared" (*Newsweek* 1987).

Following KTWV's initial success, other commercial stations in major cities switched to a new-age format and were able to attract a relatively small but loyal following. However, none of these stations was able to build an audience large enough to rival the top half-dozen stations in the market. Thus, while clearly not a panacea for commercial radio, the new-age format stations garnered about as many listeners as classical music stations already held. Accordingly, many public radio programmers became concerned that commercial new-age stations could be cutting deeply into their current and potential listenership, especially those under forty years of age.

At their insistence, in 1988 NPR launched its own hour-long new-age program, "Hearts of Space," which was soon picked up by 230 affiliates. Stephen Hill, its producer, characterizes it as "a new auditory consciousness that creates mind-worlds for listeners" (Hill 1988, 1). Typically, this and other locally produced new-age music programs are broadcast late in the evening when, programmers suppose, most of NPR's aging classical music fans are asleep and unaware of this alien presence on "their" station.

By the early 1990s, however, it became clear that new-age music had not continued to grow in popularity on either public or commercial radio. In fact, *Billboard* has changed the designation from "new age" to "adult alternative," in order to include an even wider range of programming variations. Indeed, since the early euphoria a number of commercial stations have switched away from the new-age format, and the story is much the same for public radio as well. Thus new-age music has neither displaced classical music nor does it appear to be melding with it to become the "world music"—the art music of the future—as some had predicted (Peterson 1990b). Rather than become a great boon to NPR station memberships and revenues, as its advocates had hoped, new-age music has simply joined the roster of minor specialty programs available on many public radio stations.

Commercial Radio and "Classical Lite" Programming

As we have seen, with the advent of NPR those interested in promoting classical music broadcasting had good reason to focus on public radio. From 1960 through the early 1980s the number of for-profit commercial classical music stations steadily dwindled as their corporate owners switched to more popular and presumably more profitable formats, despite frequent and vociferous listener protest. At the lowest point, fewer than fifty commercial stations programmed *any* classical music (Kahn 1982). However, in recent years the number of commercial stations has slowly increased, and with the establishment of several classical music programming networks, the number may soon total over two hundred (Oestreich 1991).

In part the reason for the new interest in classical music is purely financial. Some station owners have (re)discovered that it is not difficult to turn a profit with a classical music format. Since selections are long and there is no concern about keeping abreast of a weekly changing list of "hits," it is easy to create automated programs that run for a month at a time. Further, unlike. the "star" DJs at competitive rock stations, classical announcers can be paid comparatively low salaries. Finally, although classical listeners may be similarly low in total numbers, since they are disproportionately affluent, advertising rates can be set high relative to the ad rates of other radio formats.

Still, these factors have not changed significantly in the past decade, so they can't easily account for the recent growth in commercial classical music programming. What has changed dramatically, however (and does help to explain much of that growth), is the nature of the classical music that is being programmed and the way it is presented to the audience.

As James Oestreich notes (1991), both the Philadelphia and the New York Philharmonic orchestras have recently lost national broadcast syndication of their concerts. In the place of their concerts and other full symphonic works, many classical stations now program pieces that are shorter, lighter, and aesthetically undemanding. Chamber works of Baroque composers (such as Vivaldi, Albinoni, Boccherini) are played frequently, as are classical-era concertos bereft of their slow movements. Howard Tanger of Philadelphia's WFLN has commented that the station plays "shorter works, by and large, not entire movements." In reference to contemporary classical work, he added: "we will not use our airwaves to experiment." Mario Mazza of WNCN has described the programming policies in force at the New York City station to include: "eliminating organ music, avant-garde, atonal music, waltzes, virtually all vocal music [except during the Christmas season], monaural and historical recordings" (Oestreich 1991, 30).

On such stations, announcers now introduce musical selections in a light conversational tone rather than in the starchy, slightly condescending tone of their predecessors. Moreover, they seldom discuss the pieces as *music*. Rather, in introducing the selection announcers provide tidbits of information about the personal life of the composer, or amusing anecdotes about the work's initial performance (Ames 1990).

Such moves to what may be called "classical lite" programming are not restricted to commercial stations. As Annette Griswold, program director of Denver's public radio station KCFR, told James Oestreich: "part of our mission is to educate, and part is to entertain. . . . We play excerpts, but we also play entire pieces. We don't talk very much musicologically. We talk about composers and performers in human terms, like 'Nadja Salerno-Sonnenberg smokes Camels and plays baseball.' Or the fact that women swooned over Saint-Saëns's music" (1991, 30).

"Classical Lite" for Audience Share

If one is counting numbers, the recent changes in classical music programming have been quite successful on both public and commercial stations. Since 1982 the daily classical music radio audience has risen from approximately 2.1 million to 5.3 million (Ames 1990). This increase has been gained at a high cost, however. As has just been suggested, this newly popular "classical" music might more accurately be termed "classical lite." While this light programming and presentation might be seen as a means to attract and educate larger numbers of listeners to the full range of classical music, this argument is not supported, for two reasons. First, all available evidence suggests that the pressure on radio stations to increase their listenership consistently outweighs their response to demands for more genuine classical music (PRC 1992). Second, experience shows that exposing adults to *The 1812 Overture* does not lead many to seek out works by Mahler.[2] In practice, classical lite music radio programming is increasingly used as an upscale form of Muzak, a background sound that adds a relaxed, classy tone to the homes, offices, and shops where it is played (Peterson 1990b).

The current classical lite programming does not seem to be whetting the appetite for the broad range of classical music played, whether it is played on the radio or performed live in the concert hall. If anything, it stimulates an interest for more of the same (Balfe 1989). Classical music orchestras around the country are still having great difficulty filling their concert halls when playing the standard range of classical works (*New York Times* 1987). To survive financially, many orchestras now offer a "classical music" series devoid of aesthetically challenging works and a parallel "popular music" series featuring Broadway songs and movie music, with featured soloists drawn from the popular music field (Peterson 1990b; Zeigler 1991). Thus the noble experiment pronounced in the fledgling days of radio, that classical music on the air would help the masses acquire a taste for such music and draw many of their number into the concert hall to enjoy its live performance, now seems to be a great failure. By developing audience taste for polished musical entertainment, that "experiment" has surely contributed to the ill health of the very musical institutions it was to serve.

Notes

I greatly appreciate the information and critiques of each of the following along the way in the creation of this work: Judith Balfe, Cal Bean, Joseph Bensman, Dean Boal, Jeffrey Feldmesser, Eric Friesen, David Giovannoni, Steven Greil, Howard Gutin, John Hatcher, Stephen Hill, Milt Hinton, Jennifer Jasper, Barrett Lee, Brenda Loftis, Krister Malm, Rolf Meyersohn, Claire Peterson, Ruth Peterson, Steve Rathe, John Schaefer, and Vera Zolberg.

1. When not otherwise referenced, evidence cited is drawn from the 1979–80 year I spent as a Senior Research Analyst for the Research Division of the National Endowment for the Arts, from the time spent consulting for National Public Radio in 1987–88, and from subsequent conversations with public radio personnel. A summary report of the NPR consultation was presented at the 1988 Public Radio Conference and a fuller report is given in Peterson (1990b).

2. The dangers of this strategy of programming classical lite to gain audience share are amply demonstrated by the recent experience of parallel trends in public television. In 1990 Jennifer Lawson was appointed executive vice-president for national programming of the Public Broadcasting Service (PBS) with a mandate to centralize programming decisions (Galloway 1990). Her announced goal is to increase ratings by cutting the PBS programs that are "plagued by [what she calls] the nerd factor" (Motavalli 1990). "In a push to broaden its appeal, especially among corporate sponsors, PBS is making a major new effort to retool its image into a new, streamlined network that appeals to younger, more 'action-oriented' audience" (Motavalli 1990, 10). Yet the more PBS tries to compete directly with commercial TV, the less distinctive it is, the more expensive it is to produce, and the less attractive it becomes to corporate underwriters (Motavalli 1990).

References

Ames, Katherine. 1990. "A Little Radio Music." *Newsweek*, Mar. 12, p. 88.

ARA (Audience Research Analysis). 1988a. *Audience '88: A Comprehensive Analysis of Public Radio Listeners: Programming*. Silver Spring, Md.: Audience Research Analysis, Inc.

———. 1988b. *Audience '88: A Comprehensive Analysis of Public Radio Listeners: Underwriting*. Silver Spring, Md.: Audience Research Analysis, Inc.

———. 1988c. *Audience '88: A Comprehensive Analysis of Public Radio Listeners: Advertising and Promotion*. Silver Spring, Md.: Audience Research Analysis, Inc.

Balfe, Judith Huggins. 1989. "The Baby-Boom Generation: Lost Patrons, Lost Audience?" In *The Cost of Culture*, edited by Margaret Wyszomirski and Pat Clubb, 9–25. New York: ACA Books.

Barnouw, Erik. 1966. *A Tower of Babel*. New York: Oxford University Press.

———. 1968. *The Golden Web*. New York: Oxford University Press.

———. 1970. *The Image Empire*. New York: Oxford University Press.

Barol, Bill. 1987. "Tuning In, Tuning Up: Over-the-Air Car Repair." *Newsweek*, June 1.

Billboard. 1988. "Spotlight: New Age." Oct. 29, pp. Nl-N13.

Blow, Richard. 1988. "Moronic Convergence: The Moral and Spiritual Emptiness of New Age." *The New Republic*, Jan. 25, pp. 26–28.

Bogue, Donald J. 1973. *The Radio Audience for Classical Music*. Chicago: Community and Family Study Center, University of Chicago.

DiMaggio, Paul, and Michael Useem. 1978. "Social Class and Arts Consumption." *Theory and Society* 5:141–61.

Fricke, David. 1986. "New Age, Old Hat." *Rolling Stone*, Dec. 18, pp. 95–100.

Friedrich, Otto. 1988. "New Age Harmonies, a Strange Mix of Spirituality and Superstition Is Sweeping Across the Country." *Time*, Dec. 7.

Galloway, Stephen. 1991. "Some Hand Wringing at PBC as Power Base Shifts." *TV Guide*, Sept. 29, pp. 42–43.

Giovannoni, David. 1988. "Framing Audience '88." *Current: The Public Radio Weekly*, May 11, p. 10.

Goldsmith, Thomas. 1992. "WPLN Must Tune in to Listeners." *Nashville Tennessean*, Mar. 19, p. 32.

Harris, Louis. 1988. *Americans and the Arts V*. New York: National Research Center of the Arts.

Hill, Stephan. 1988. *New Age Music Made Simple*. San Francisco: Hearts of Space.

Honan, William H. 1989. "Pleas for the Arts Take On a Nervous Edge." *New York Times*, Mar. 26.

Horowitz, Joseph. 1987. *Understanding Toscanini: How He Became an American Culture-God and Helped Create a New Audience for Old Music*. Minneapolis: University of Minnesota Press.

Jensen, Elizabeth. 1987. "National Public Radio Today Is All Things Considerable with News Its Driving Force." *Variety*, Sept. 16.

Kahn, Frank J. 1982. "Radio: Regulating Format Diversity." *Journal of Communication* 32:81–191.

LL&A (Lauer, Lalley and Associates). 1986. "Summary Report on Focus Groups of Public Radio Listeners." Washington, D.C.: Lauer, Lalley and Associates.

Major, John K. 1979. "Whither Good Radio?" *High Fidelity*, May, pp. 39–43, 129–33.

Motavalli, John. 1990. "PBS Shucks Its Tutus for Sweats." *Inside Media*, Feb. 15, 10, 14.

Newsweek. 1987. "The Wave Hits Los Angeles." Apr. 3, p. 32.

New York Times. 1987. "Many Orchestras in Financial Straits." Jan. 19, p. C11.

NPR (National Public Radio). 1984. *The NPR Audience 1982/83*. Washington D.C.: Office of Audience Research and Program Evaluation, National Public Radio.

———. 1986. *The NPR Audience 1984/5*. Washington, D.C.: Office of Audience Research and Program Evaluation, National Public Radio.

———. 1988. "State of the Audience: A Mid-Term Assessment of NPR System Performance." Washington, D.C.: Office of Audience Research and Program Evaluation, National Public Radio.

Oestreich, James R. 1991. "Is It Mahler? Or Is It Happy Talk?" *New York Times*, Jan. 6, sec. 2, pp. 1, 30.

Pareles, Jon. 1987. "New Age Music Booms, Softly." *New York Times*, Nov. 29, sec. 2, pp. 1, 28.

Parsons, Clark. 1992. "Dialing for Dollars." *Nashville Scene*, Mar. 19, p. 9.

Peterson, Richard A. 1972. "A Process Model of the Folk, Pop, and Fine Art Phases of Jazz." In *American Music: From Storyville to Woodstock*, edited by Charles Nanry, 135–51. New Brunswick, N.J.: Trans-Action Books and E. P. Dutton.

———. 1990a. "Why '55? Explaining the Advent of Rock and Roll." *Popular Music* 9:97–116.

———. 1990b. "Audience and Industry Origins of the Crisis in Classical Music Programming." In *The Future of the Arts,* edited by David B. Pankratz and Valerie B. Morris, 207–27. New York: Praeger.

Peterson, Richard A., and Russell B. Davis, Jr. 1974. "The Contemporary American Radio Audience." *Journal of Popular Music and Society* 3:299–313.

PRC (Public Radio Conference) 1988. "Public Radio Conference: In Tune with the Future." St. Louis, Mo. May 18–22.

———. 1992. "Public Radio Conference: Challenges and Opportunities." Seattle, Wash. May 2–6.

Routt, Edd. 1978. *The Radio Format Conundrum*. New York: Hastings House.

Schaefer, John. 1987. *New Sounds: A Listener's Guide to New Music*. New York: Harper and Row.

Variety. 1987. "NPR Back in the Pink after Brush with Death." Sept. 12.

Wood, Terry. 1988. "Carving Out a New World of Sound for Tomorrow." *Billboard,* Oct. 29, pp. N4, N9.

Zeigler, Joseph Wesley. 1991. "Collapse: A Seminar on Crisis in the Arts." *Journal of Arts Management and Law* 21(3): 232–52.

❖ 14 ❖

The Arts and Culture
under the European Community

ESTHER GELABERT

This chapter will analyze the cultural policies of the European Community (EC) and focus on the artistic implications of the Single European Market as originally planned to be instituted in 1992. Culture remains one of the most intractable issues in the emergence of a united Europe. The reasons include the economic nature of the EC (the current institutionalized form of a united Europe), as well as the inherent complexity of the very concept of "culture," let alone its role in preserving the political autonomy of Europe and the identity of its individual component states (Morin 1987).

The Cultural Panorama of Western Europe in the Nineties

Europe is a mosaic of nation states and cultures, with complex cultural links among its institutions, minority groups, and individuals, both ancient and newly forged. At the cultural level, opposing centripetal and centrifugal forces are simultaneously reorganizing and revitalizing its diverse cultural scene. As to the former, a Europe-wide regionalization movement in the 1970s brought about a revival of regional cultures and languages such as Flemish, Gaelic, Breton, and Catalan. The recovery of indigenous cultures has been widely embraced as progressive, and it is linked to a general movement toward political and cultural decentralization, with a transfer of powers from central to regional and local administrations. As cultural and political collaboration and exchange increase at this new level, a new map of a Europe of distinct regions, sometimes crossing national boundaries, is slowly emerging.

At the same time, a Europe of unified culture is also slowly emerging, despite the difficulty of defining its core principles and its geographical boundaries. Several supranational institutions (foremost among them—but not limited to—the Council of Europe and the European Community) are fostering this unification process through the rediscovery and enhancement of values rooted in collective history. Despite its problems, the advent of the single European market in 1992 is contributing to a "European momentum." A very dynamic combination of cultural and educational exchanges is taking place. Optimistically, over the long term these practices will reduce national chauvinism and foster a new European identity, however hard it may be to define that identity at present and however intense is some nationalist resistance. Among the artistic manifestations of the new "identity" are Europe-wide contemporary visual art fairs (ARCO in Madrid, FIAC in Paris) and theater festivals (such as those in Avignon and Edinburgh).

The advent of a "global village," facilitated by advanced communication technologies and competitive international economic and cultural pressures coming especially from the United States and Japan, has compelled European countries to redefine themselves at the regional, national, and supranational levels. The global process of homogenization and Americanization, spread through the mass media into popular culture everywhere, has posed a severe threat of dilution and even eradication of the traditional European cultures. Within the last several years the upheavals in Eastern Europe and the former Soviet Union have added a new and radical dimension to regional nationalisms and to any definition of European culture. At this writing, the real impact of these political changes upon the EC is still unpredictable. It is clear that the economic focus of society is changing from industry to services, and the cultural challenge in Europe remains to integrate the new and the old, to preserve diversity within a progressive technological orientation and thus avoid the stagnation of its various cultures.

The European Community's Role in Culture

The European Community, a confederation of twelve sovereign nation-states, has unique supranational powers in administering policies, particularly economic ones. EC membership currently includes the 1951 founding members: Belgium, France, the Federal Republic of Germany, Italy, Luxembourg, and the Netherlands. In 1973 they were joined by Denmark, Ireland, and the United Kingdom; in 1981, by Greece; and in 1986, by Spain and Portugal. The EC is administered by four principal bodies: the European Commission, the Council of Ministers, the European Parliament, and the Court of Justice. The European Commission, with seventeen members appointed by the various states on the basis of respective population and with a staff of nearly 17,000, is the primary administrative unit. It is charged with implementation and enforcement of EC policies and management of the budget through twenty-three different departments. It can propose and initiate legislation. The Council of Ministers varies in membership, its meetings attended by different national ministers according to the agenda and the issue under consideration. With a staff of 2,200, the council acts on commission proposals and is the core decision-making body of the EC, on the basis of majority vote. The European Parliament has 518 popularly elected members and a staff of 3,500: it serves as a forum for public debate and has final control over the budget. Its approval of legislation is required after the Council of Ministers reaches consensus, prior to enactment. The thirteen-member Court of Justice rules on interpretation and application of EC law.

Based upon the 1987 European Economic Community Treaty (EEC), which founded the EC, a single European market without internal frontiers and with free circulation of goods, labor, services and capital was to be established by 1992. The twelve states have also cooperated closely in areas such as research and technological development, monetary policies, the environment, and targeted regional development. However, while the EC has already achieved some degree of political policy coordination among its member-states, its goal of economic integration by 1992 has not yet coincided with a highly defined cultural ideology and related policy directives. The cultural realm of the EC remains at an elementary level of development. It is largely focused on areas such as the mass media, where economic stakes are high and which clearly come under EEC mandates for close cooperation among the states in research, regional development, and employment. Although there was extensive discussion about the possibility of including a "culture clause" in the EEC, this failed to materialize during the final negotiations.

There are two paradoxes in the failure of the EEC to establish a legal framework for initiating and implementing EC arts and cultural policies. First, sizable economic issues are at stake: since the development of the contemporary "leisure society," culture industries account for 5 percent of the Gross National Product (GNP) of the major EC countries, and employ 3 to 4 percent of the working population. Thus the EEC treaty does address many of the physical and fiscal problems affecting the production and distribution of the arts and cultural services, as well as professional training. Second, the various national heads of state have made many declarations of intent to support Europe-wide cultural initiatives in an

attempt to promote political integration. However, this discussion has remained largely at the ideological level. At a 1973 summit, the heads of
state defined a common heritage of a multicultural nature as one of the
three elements of European identity (parliamentary democracy and social
justice were the other two [*Seventh General Report* 1973]). This "common
culture" was to be a primary basis in the political proposals for developing
European political unity, on the assumption that when united by common
aesthetic, historic, and social values, Europeans would be more likely to
support economic and political integration. However, as will be detailed
below, only a few of the initiatives described in these cultural proposals
have been implemented. (Among these have been the creation of a Culture Council, the policy-making body to address cultural affairs within the
EC, which was finally instituted as one arm of the Council of Ministers in
1984. It will be discussed below.)

Despite many declarations of intent, the national leaders have not entrusted the EC with the legal power to put cultural policies into practice.
Those cultural programs that have been instituted for 1992 are largely the
byproduct of EC economic policies and not political proposals (to be analyzed below). It is important to understand the reasons for the omission
to any real legal jurisdiction, since it handicaps the formulation—let alone
the implementation—of cultural policies at the European level.

Some national governments (Denmark and Great Britain among them)
believe that the EC is not competent in cultural matters. They perceive
EC objectives to be narrowly economic. Notions of political autonomy are
very much involved in this view and underlie the negative vote on EC
membership by citizens of several states. It is true that by joining the EC,
member-states lose some of their national sovereignty by transferring it
to supranational organs. What remains under state (and regional) control
and patronage—the arts and culture—then becomes the most important
component in the definition of a distinct national identity. No wonder
that the various states are protective of the maintenance of their cultural
autonomy and have been reluctant to entrust the EC with any direct legal
power in cultural affairs.

In any case, if defined by geopolitical criteria the European Community
is not culturally united. For one thing, its cultural life has long been nurtured by artists and trends coming from other European countries than
those belonging to the EC. This would be enough to deny any specific and
restrictive cultural identity to the EC. Many ask whether linguistic zones
might be more appropriate for fostering cultural cooperation.

To be sure, cultural coordination among the different nations and cultural institutions has a long tradition in Europe, facilitated mainly through

the Council of Europe with a membership of twenty-three European countries. Thus there is an assumption that EC cultural policies can overlap with policies of the larger Council of Europe, while impacting a smaller geographical area. But this disregards the fact that these supranational organizations differ in structure and power and thus in their ability to cooperate with each other: the council has only the power to make recommendations for its member states, while the EC has the power to enforce its legislation.

One major problem is that the amount and the structure of public patronage of the arts and culture varies widely among the member-states. This inhibits the creation of a single European model to support common policies and activities. While some countries (for example, Great Britain) have philosophical objections to the role of the state in this regard, others, like France, provide considerable direct public support (Cummings and Katz 1987). Indeed, many in the political and artistic communities believe that support coming from any new European-level economic institution through the EC is likely to accelerate this market trend and favor the homogenization of popular culture (the so-called "Euroculture"). In addition, it would inevitably lead to complex bureaucratic structures, which are widely seen as antithetical to the arts. Accordingly, they believe that cultural diversity and artistic creation are better protected by national, regional, and local policies, and that patronage should be as individualized, direct, and as close to the art as possible.

The European Community Cultural Program

The European Commission

At present, regarding both inclusions and exclusions the 1992 cultural program of the EC is the result of actions and recommendations of its different institutions: the European Commission, the Council of Ministers, and the European Parliament. (As the parliament can approve only programs initiated and passed by the other two institutions, its role will not be considered here [see Pacco 1983].) Even today, national interests through the Council of Ministers tend to prevail over the supranational policies of the European Commission; not surprisingly the EC cultural program reflects those tensions. Indeed, due to a scanty pre-existing legal framework it was not until the late 1970s that a small structure within the commission was created to handle supranational cultural issues at all: the Division of Cultural Problems.[1] Limited as it was, the support of the parliament was critical for its creation. Even here, however, its role was not to formulate a cultural policy of European dimensions, but rather to study and propose potential applications of the EEC treaty to the arts and culture. Thus, as the commission states in a 1982 communication to the parliament, any cultural effects of EC action are by definition unintentional, as no specific policy direction has been established: "Community action does not expound a philosophy of culture, for it would imply coming in favor of specific ideological and aesthetic options, which is something the Community has no right to do" (Commission of the European Community 1982, 5).

Nonetheless, the European Commission has submitted three cultural proposals to parliament (Commission of the European Community 1977; 1982; 1987). The 1977 and 1982 proposals maintained a rather rigid economic and social approach. They were centered on the application of the EEC's "four freedoms" in the cultural sector: freedom of movement of goods, of labor, of services, and of capital. The proposals consisted of legal and fiscal measures regarding cultural aspects of EC economic and social policies. Examples of these practical measures included the simplification of administrative formalities and costs involved in moving cultural property across borders; the protection of author- and performer-rights though pan-European legislation on royalties and copyrights (to settle the question of "transfrontier" services); and social security assistance for artists. In addition, a small program was instituted to fund cultural activities of EC-wide impact. These have included traveling exhibitions, such as "150 Young Painters in the Community," and scholarships for restoration specialists.

The 1987 proposal, titled "A Fresh Boost for Culture," was the first to be approved under the mandate of the Culture Council, as noted above, the decision-making body for cultural affairs that was established under the Council of Ministers in 1984. It is the basis for the EC cultural program being instituted with the advent of the single European market in 1992 and indicates a shift in thinking on the part of members of the commission. Generally, as the economic structure of society has changed from industry to services, the commission has become increasingly sensitive to the growing economic importance of cultural activities and the role that they play in economic development. It has also become more aware of the cultural and economic implications of the rapid growth of new technologies. (All of this lay behind the establishment of the Culture Council in the first place.) Thus in contrast to the earlier declarations of neutrality regarding "aesthetic options" and culture, the 1987 proposal recognizes the need to strengthen a common sense of a shared European identity through high levels of culture exchange among the various European peoples. In a span of ten years, the commission has broadened its ideological commitment beyond the initial restrictive treaty description; its new philosophic focus is reflected in the plans for cultural activities in and after 1992.

Initially, the Culture Council defined four priority areas: culture industries; media and publishing; training of culture-related professionals; and measures to encourage business sponsorship. Once these areas were defined, they were sent back to the commission for specific proposals. Some of the ensuing measures were recommended by commission departments other than those responsible for cultural affairs; these have not always taken into consideration the needs of the artistic community, and thus have caused some controversy.

For example, the commission's approach to the national film industries is a classic case of ongoing conflict between the cultural ambitions and the economic goals of the EC. It demonstrates that cultural values are not always better protected by the free market economy that the EC promotes. According to the EEC treaty, the EC objective of freedom of services requires revision of the various national systems of funding the cinema industry. Current practices are thus seen as discriminatory and against open competition. However, there have been strong reactions against the implementation of such revisions, both from the national governments that see cinema as an expression of their national culture, and from special (nationally based) interest groups, such as film producers.

Another example along this line is a controversy over fixed pricing, which is permitted in the EC countries for books but not for other commercial products. In the 1979 and 1982 proposals (even before the advent of the Culture Council), the commission questioned the policies that permitted fixed pricing of books on the grounds of competition, and envisaged possible direct European Community intervention.

The following response in the European Parliament shows that all were not convinced by the commission's arguments: "The possibilities available to the Commission with respect to influencing book prices on the basis of the relevant articles of the Treaty are limited. So, the Community's role in respect to books should be an integral part of cultural policy as appropriately formulated by the Community" (Wiesand 1981, 56). And since the apparent cultural policy was to have no direct policy, the existing practices of fixed pricing of books were to remain intact. Indeed, while many other proposals were developed after this date, EC intervention in the field of publishing was provisionally disregarded until very recently (as considered below).

Obviously, the commission's role in the cultural sector continues to be viewed with some mistrust by many of the groups who are directly concerned. As they see it, cultural interests are not always reconcilable with those of the marketplace, whether one argues from the position of the nationally restricted market or the common market. Given this response from those who are expected to produce the art and culture that is somehow to work wonders (in ways that are not altogether clear), the commission has become increasingly receptive to arguments about the importance of maintaining national or regional cultural policies, even if they go against the deregulatory principles of the EC.

The Culture Council

The Culture Council first met in 1984, and is intended to be the EC's principal decision-making body regarding proposals made by the commission itself in the area of the arts and culture. As initiated by the commission, it is an institutional structure intended to contribute to European political integration. Since 1987, majority voting—rather than the unanimity that was originally required—has facilitated its decision-making propensities.

Theoretically, like other EC Councils of Ministers the Culture Council is made up of the various national heads of cultural affairs. This presupposes a uniform centralized support system across the states. However, in practice there are significant variations among them, from centralized to mixed to decentralized structures of state support (Cummings and Katz 1987). Thus areas that are under national control in France are under the control of the *lander* (individual states) in Germany, and under the linguistic communities in Belgium. Inevitably, the national representatives to the Culture Council speak from different structural positions and with different sets of priorities, adding even more complexity to council meetings.

Overall, the Culture Council has had a positive impact on institutional cultural cooperation. Under its imprimatur, several agreements have been passed in the fields of media, publishing, professional training, business sponsorship, and the organization of cultural events. These agreements vary in the degree of discretion permitted. Binding agreements in the media field include: film distribution; an increase in the proportion of European-made programming on television; and coordination of the national regulations concerning broadcasting. Nonbinding are agreements concerning the collaboration among libraries in the field of data processing.

Understandably, there have been a number of difficulties in reaching agreement, as different national positions have been asserted to protect national cultural values and the economic interests of national cultural markets. The 1989 agreement to increase the proportion of European-made programs shown on EC television channels is an example. As described by one reviewer: "Italy with a high level of imported programming wanted to apply a strict quota of 40% for programs made outside Europe. In contrast, Great Britain and the Netherlands, with 85% of their programs made in Europe, simply proposed an agreement that more television programs should be of European origin" (*Economist* 1989, 48). The limits of EC cultural cooperation are well captured by Stanley Hoffman, well-known theorist of the common market, whose 1982 comment still holds true: "Policies [of cooperation] in the framework of the EC are more likely to be established in areas where, and in a moment when, sovereign national actions are likely to be insufficient or unproductive, when joint actions produce better results for each member-state than 'uncoordinated individual calculations of self-interest' " (33–34).

EC Cultural Priorities

The Media Sector

Building on the 1989 agreements, the EC program has the following goals for the advent of the single "audiovisual" market in 1992:

To harmonize legal and technological standards that still impede transnational flow of broadcasting;

To promote European media production capabilities;

To ease other obstacles, such as language differences and different structures of film distribution;

To harmonize different technical standards of broadcasting and to promote communication technologies, such as High Definition Television (HDT).

Traditionally, the information and entertainment industries in Europe developed nationally and were viewed as "national monopolies." Until the 1980s most of the European countries regulated these industries through state institutions (such as the BBC [British Broadcasting Corporation] in the United Kingdom). In addition, each country had its own regulations that applied to broadcasting received from outside its territory. Nationalistic interests and the structure of media industries contributed to the partitioning of media programming in Europe. However, since the 1980s, the emergence of private television channels and the development of new communication technologies and TV distribution systems have changed the way media industries are organized. As programs can be broadcast more effectively and cheaply across frontiers, the media are increasingly international and more profitable.

The Culture Council has responded to these particular issues with little hesitation (especially when compared to its reluctance to intervene in book sales). Thus in relation to the free flow of broadcasting, the 1989 agreement, "Television without Frontiers," was the first step in the harmonization of regulations concerning advertising (its production, distribution, and broadcast scheduling) in order to protect children. In addition, steps are being taken to eliminate the different technical standards of broadcasting by satellite.

Obviously, the development of an internationally competitive media industry is an important cultural and economic EC goal for 1992. There is wide concern about the weakness of European production, especially in a context of both the increased demand for, and reaction against, American penetration in the television and cinema markets. There is a general consensus that both of these have contributed to a weakening of European identity, and have generated a process of American homogenization of popular culture. At the time of the 1989 Culture Council agreement, imported television programming accounted for more than 70 percent of TV fiction programs (of which nearly two-thirds originated in the United States, a proportion that had increased by half during the preceding ten years). The agreement recommended a limit of 50 percent for imported programming—"whenever practicable."

Here again, however, the policy recommendation has been very controversial. On the one hand, those in the European media community have complained strongly about the weakness of this measure, which does not protect them with a system of mandatory quotas. They perceive the commission as abandoning them to the laws of the marketplace. On the other hand, the American media community sees this as a protectionist measure and a threat to its TV and cinema markets.[2]

In line with its free-trade mandate within EC borders, the Commission has increased the resources available for the development of media programming, rather than centering the development of a competitive television industry through truly protective measures. The EC has encouraged this through its program with the acronym MEDIA (measures to encourage the development of the audio-visual industry), budgeted at $260 million spread over a period of five years. It has established different structures throughout the community to promote distribution, production, training, and financing. Examples of funded programs include: cross-frontier distribution of European middle-size budget films in cinemas; promotion of independent producers; research and development of new production technologies and graphics; production of series-length TV programs; support for dubbing and subtitling; development of multilingual television programs or broadcasts; encouragement of structures to stimulate media investors. Throughout, these initiatives are sensitive to countries with limited media production capability and limited linguistic range.

The Book-Publishing Sector

This is another priority area for 1992. The commission's 1989 report, "Books and Reading: A Cultural Challenge for Europe" (Commission of the European Community 1989), analyzes the policy ramifications of the EEC treaty on the different cultural, economic, and social aspects of the production and reading of a book: the creative work, translation, publication, dissemination, promotion and, finally, reading. Its priority recommendations for the intended advent of the single European market include: harmonizing of copyright legislation; collective agreements guaranteeing writers and translators a minimum level of protection and fair remuneration; launching a pilot scheme to provide financial aid for translators of contemporary literary works; extension of the European network for training colleges for translators; adoption of an action plan for interlibrary cooperation in data processing; a community campaign to promote the use of "permanent paper"; facilitation of open import/export of books through a proposal for new postal policies and the harmonization of VAT rates (value added tax) on books. At this writing in spring 1992, these recommendations await approval by the Culture Council. Still largely unreconciled are issues defined as economics (pricing) and as culture (the books themselves).

Professional Training

Professional training is another priority area. The commission's aim is to identify existing problems in the field at the EC level, and to help enhance the quality of that education and training by improving the flow of information and promoting exchanges of expert personnel. Priority areas for training are the media, preservation, and translation. The commission appropriated $2.5 million for professional training projects in 1991.

Currently, there are several such EC programs that deal with education and training, known by their acronyms: MEDIA (already noted above); ERASMUS (European Community action scheme for the mobility of university students); COMMETT (European Community action scheme for the education and training for technology); PETRA (European Community action program for vocational training of young people); and FORCE (European Community action program for the continuing of vocational training). These programs include some projects in the field of historic preservation, the media, visual arts, and music.

Additionally, EC structural funds support national employment policies, particularly through training programs such as the European School of Heritage in Barcelona.

Specific EC Cultural Programs

From its Directoriate-General X (successor to the Division of Cultural Problems), the commission runs a program to promote cultural activities of Europe-wide interest. However, this has a derisory budget of $12 million, less than one-tenth of 1 percent of the total EC budget and less than a quarter of that allocated annually for the media alone. While its value is important as a catalyst for a culture of European dimensions, its impact is severely constrained by its budgetary limitations.

There are several categories under this program. The "Europe Cultural Scene Project Laureate" is aimed at funding and promoting transnational artistic and cultural manifestations about any aspect of European culture; guidelines require a participation of at least three EC countries. The commission also funds artistic organizations such as the European Community Youth Orchestra and the European Baroque Orchestra. (Appropriations for these subprograms totaled $1 million for 1991.)

The commission also funds cultural cooperation with other countries outside the EC. With a current budget of approximately $1.5 million, this subprogram is concentrated on cultural exchanges with Eastern Europe.

A further commission-funded program is an annual festival held on a rotating basis at a designated capital "European City of Culture." Its aim is to help the European publics become aware of the particular aspects of a particular city, region, or country, with a concentration on cultural overlapping and commonalities among the EC countries. Madrid was the capital city in 1992. While this scheme was initiated by the EC, it receives the bulk of its funding from national governments. From 1993 on, this event will be opened to European cities outside the EC.

An additional EC cultural program, on historic preservation, is based on the manifold importance attached to the conservation of the architectural heritage, in cultural, regional, social, and economic terms. For example, it has provided important funding for restoration of the center of Lisbon and for the Parthenon on the Athenian Acropolis. This program is particularly successful, but here too the available funds (of $12 million) are quite inadequate: in 1990, money could be allocated to only 26 out of a total of 1,138 applications submitted.

Several attempts have been made to enlarge and consolidate the EC cultural program, as the commission and the national heads of state acknowledge the role that cultural relations play in the integration of the states and peoples. Some national governments (such as the Greek and the French) have put forward requests to see this recognition translated into budgetary terms. Indeed, in the late 1970s, there was an effort to create an autonomous cultural foundation, the "European Foundation," isolated from the structure, politics, and interests of the EC. At that time, differences in views toward the desirable extent and direction of role of the EC in cultural affairs were a decisive handicap, with a resultant temporary failure to establish such an autonomous foundation.

Toward a "European Cultural Area"

The historical nationalistic partitioning of Europe involved many cultural, physical, and fiscal barriers. These made the flow of cultural goods more complex and inefficient. Now, with the application of the principles of the EEC treaty, many of these barriers are being removed. However, the measures proposed for the cultural sector (as is shown below) only partially address the intended EC practice of unlimited freedom of movement and settlement for cultural goods, let alone of artists. Obviously, cultural barriers remain: languages, cultural tastes and demands vary widely among the EC. These are handicaps for a European cultural market. At the same time, they demonstrate the most important cultural asset of the European Community: its cultural diversity.

Freedom of Cultural Goods

With the advent of the single European market in other sectors, efforts toward the free movement of cultural goods have increased. Presently, the EC has agreed in principle to the following measures, however difficult may be their implementation:

Simplification of administrative formalities for the import/export of artwork across internal EC borders, particularly those involved when artists themselves move artwork and equipment;

Harmonization of existing tax provisions applicable to various categories of the art market;

Promotion of actions to fight against illicit trade;

Definitions of the criteria used to identify "national treasures" of historic, archaeologic, or artistic nature, which are exempt from the freedom of movement by the EEC treaty.

These measures should have a positive impact in cultural exchanges and the dynamics of the art market. However, the latter of these present particular difficulties of definition, and thus of legislation.

Reflecting the high value of national treasures to their countries of origin, Article 36 of the EEC treaty gives national governments the right to "prohibit or restrict imports, exports, or transit which are justified by the protection of national treasures having artistic, historic or archaeologic value." However, this article also specifies that "this provision must not constitute either a means of arbitrary discrimination or disguised restriction among member-states." Among EC members, systems of implementing art export regulations vary widely and countries differ as to what constitutes the "heritage" of the nation. Thus, the commission initially proposed the formulation of a standardized definition of the term "national treasures," based on criteria such as antiquity, rarity, and cultural significance. However, it has recently been agreed that no further attempt will be made to harmonize these concepts; rather, each nation-state's definitions of its own national treasures will be respected.

It is simpler to harmonize laws affecting art trade and therefore art theft, although given the varying definitions of national treasures, trade that is illicit in one country may be perfectly legal in another (Branagan 1992). Still, new EC regulations will contribute to the expansion of the records describing artworks; the establishment of a European information center on stolen work; and the drafting of a code of ethics applicable to intracommunity art trade.

Otherwise, by creating a united customs, the European Community has already abolished all taxes on import-export within its borders, including those on artworks. These taxes were formerly a significant source of income in art-exporting countries, such as Italy; their removal raised some controversy. Still, these taxes remain in effect for art trade outside the EC.

Freedom of Labor

Theoretically, this EC goal means that all member-state citizens in culturally related professions (such as performing artists) would be free to work or tour in all EC countries, without any restriction. Compared to other fields, in many respects the art-labor market has already been liberalized to a significant extent (particularly in the fields of dance and music, less so in theater). However, many barriers still exist, such as nonrecognition of the equivalence of diplomas and other formal credentials.

In this regard, the EC goal of freedom of labor implies a common vocational training policy and the recognition of diplomas and certificates of competence; across the board such resolution will take a long time, and in the cultural sector it is still in a preliminary stage. Not even begun is the initial task: close interaction and exchange between arts professionals, educators, and the commission itself in the analysis of the needs and the problems of vocational training and definitions of the criteria of competence. With less than $1 million of the current budget allocated to this issue, the commission can act only as a catalyst in this process.

Another (and perhaps greater) barrier to freedom of labor in the cultural sphere is the general preference of national trade unions for the hiring of native rather than foreign artists. Here the commission is finding that even the role of catalyst is hard to attain. Given the varying and complex national policies and social security structures, it is unlikely that they can soon be harmonized.

Freedom of Services and Capital

As part of the freedom of services described in the EEC treaty, the EC called for free flow of broadcasting, an issue that has been dealt with above. The effects of the new policies are already evident: this is an intense period of pan-European mergers of professional and service organizations, and the cultural industries are among them. Film, book-publishing, recording, and advertising industries are not just advancing toward an internationalization of their contents, but also toward a transnational integration of production and distribution structures. Through mergers and acquisitions (such as those by the French company Hachette and the German company Maxwell), companies are seeking to diversify their holdings and provide national industries with business opportunities in other member-states. This business concentration is making the European cultural industries more competitive at the international level. However, the resultant increase in market pressure threatens the production of quality products and cultural diversity. To counterbalance the homogenizing and reductive tendencies of the marketplace, at least so far as the film industry is concerned, the above-noted EC MEDIA program aims to help independent producers and middle-size production and distribution structures. Similar proposals have been launched for the book-publishing sector.

Conclusion

This study has focused on the aims and limitations of the European cultural policy in the context of the EC. Several intractable questions remain, and they will have to be addressed with the advent of a new level of European economic integration after 1992:

Is it possible to strengthen regional and national cultural identities, while at the same time developing a European cultural identity?

How should the EC organs reconcile the need to protect regional and national cultural individuality with EC economic and political goals?

Should culture be a tool to further economic and political integration or should its cultivation be a goal in itself?

What kinds of legal and budgetary provisions should be developed to allow for legal and budgetary provisions that could further cultural action?

What steps should the EC take to give more tangible expression to Europe as a whole, by expanding EC provisions to states outside its boundaries—especially those whose needy economies require massive support?

Clearly, one of the problems for a solid and expanded EC cultural program is the lack of an explicit legal basis in the EEC treaty to support its actions. A major priority should be the amendment of the treaty to include provisions affirming and promoting European cultural identity. Further, the EC cultural budget must be raised dramatically, well above the present scanty funding for cultural programs with no direct economic component (as noted above, at one-tenth of 1 percent of the total EC budget). No wonder that its impact so far has been very limited, even as it has been entrusted with an enormous task.

It may be that the issues of cultural cooperation, both within and outside the EC, could be better promoted from an autonomous structure, like the never-achieved "European Foundation" mentioned before or following the Arts Council model of Great Britain. With some independence from political and bureaucratic concerns, by standing slightly outside the EC structure such an autonomous institution might help EC policy-making bodies to recognize the special nature of the arts, the media, and their role in maintaining the cultural diversity—as well as the cultural unity—of their member-states and regions.

This analysis of the development of cultural policy in the European Community has shown that the community has taken the lead in those fields, such as professional training and cultural industries, which will be particularly affected by the advent of the single European market in 1992. Only recently has it given attention to the broader cultural issues, considering specific and intentional policies of patronage structure that will affect them rather than letting them be affected unintentionally and by default, in the exercise of other policies. Accordingly, European Community cultural action should gain increasing importance and credibility as the EC expands its ideological commitment beyond its initial restrictive economic or political goals.

All along, two categories of cultural activities have been of concern to the EC: commercial culture, that is, the culture industries; and noncommercial culture, that is, artists and nonprofit cultural organizations. To date, while the EC has developed proposals and projects in both categories, obviously its major policy focus has been the commercial sector, particularly the mass media. It will be most unfortunate if the noncommercial sector is not addressed more thoroughly. With the abolition of all the market barriers in 1992, the European Community is contributing directly to the emergence of a culturally united Europe with a common and progressive technological outlook. But technology and the market should not be seen as the only grounds for integration. "Today the European Community is still perceived by the great majority of its citizens as a vast economic machine and a large capitalist market. At a time when homogenization is threatening Europe's cultural identity, culture is more than ever a *sine qua non* for the kind of economic and social evolution with which the citizens of Europe can identify" (Fatouros 1989, 81). Through EC efforts, European citizens are becoming increasingly aware of their common destiny, but the challenge remains to consolidate this new European cultural identity at a higher level of coherence. There is an increasing consensus that if this does not occur, Europe risks the dilution of its historic identity to the single dimension of economics; it will then have lost both the diverse particularities and the common culture of the European "soul" that it was trying to save from international homogenization.

Notes

1. The formal successor to the Division of Cultural Problems as the principal commission department dealing with cultural affairs is the Directoriate-General X, concerned with films and television, culture, and EC public relations.

2. The proliferation of private channels and new ways of television distribution (such as cable TV) are demanding an endless stream of new entertainment, which the current European industry cannot presently supply. In any event, several studies indicate that increased broadcast exchanges of European origin are still not likely to meet these needs for reasons of taste, cultural identity, and

national values. Although the market for American-produced entertainment might decrease, the profile of the market is unlikely to change considerably.

References

Anderson, M., and Dominguez, L. 1984. *Cultural Policy in Europe*. Report for the Center of European Governmental Studies. Edinburgh: University of Edinburgh.

Borchardt, Klaus-Dieter. 1986. *European Unification: The Origins and Growth of the European Community*. Luxembourg: Office of the Official Publications of the European Community.

Bouaert, Ingace Claeys. 1988. *Le Régime Fiscal des Foundations Culturelles et du Mécènat dans la C.E.* Brussels: Report to the European Commission.

Branagan, Susan. 1992. "The Effects of Completion of the European Community on International Illegal Art Trade." Unpublished paper. New York: Graduate Center, City University of New York.

Carbery, John. 1985. "La fondation Européenne." *Revue du Marche Commun* 283 (Jan.): 45–48.

Commission of the European Community. 1975–91. *Bulletin of the European Communities*. Luxembourg: Office of the Official Publications of the European Communities.

————. 1990. *Completing the Internal Market: Current Status December 31, 1989. Elimination of Frontier Controls*.

Council of Europe. 1984. *A Future for Our Past: Heritage and Tourism* 24. Brussels.

Cultural Council Report. 1984–91. "Report for the European Commission." Brussels.

Cummings, Milton, and Richard Katz, eds. 1987. *The Patron State: Government and the Arts in Europe, North America, and Japan*. New York: Oxford University Press.

Delacourt, Jacques, and Roberto Papini, eds. 1987. *Pour une Politique Culturelle de la Culture*. Paris: Economica.

Domenach, J. 1990. *Europe: Le Defi culturel*. Paris: Editions la Decouverte.

The Economist. 1988. "A Survey on Europe's Internal Market." July 9, pp. 5–44.

————. 1989. "Rubbish It May Be, But Euro-Rubbish." March 18, p. 48.

Europe in Transformation: The Cultural Challenge: Culture, Technology and Economy. 1987. Brussels: Directoriate-General X.

Fatouros, D. 1989. *Culture and the European Citizen in the Year 2000*. Brussels: Commission of the European Communities.

Forrest, A. 1987. "La dimension culturelle de la Communauté Européenne: Les Ministres de la Culture explorent le terrain." *Revue du Marche Commun* 307: 326–332.

Gelabert, Esther. 1989. "The European Community and Culture." M.A. thesis, American University.

Hoffmann, Stanley. 1982. "Reflections on the Nation-State in Western Europe." *Journal of the Common Market* 21(1–2): 21–39.

Hunne, Christopher. 1988. "The 1992 Earthquake: Do You Hear a Rumble?" *The International Economy* (July-Aug.): 93–96.

Lang, Jack. 1988. "The Future of European Television and Cinema." *European Affairs.*

Lemaire, R. M. 1984. *Evaluation Economique du Patrimoine Monumental.* Brussels: Report for the European Commission.

Lerner, Ralph E. 1990. *The Law and Business of Art.* New York: Practicing Law Institute.

Lewis, Sulwyn. 1967. "Principles of Cultural Cooperation." *Reports and Papers on Mass Communication.* UNESCO 5(61): 7–22.

Lohr, Steve. 1989. "European TV's Vast Growth: Cultural Effect Stirs Concern." *New York Times,* Mar. 16, p. A1.

Lutz, Colleen, and Diana McCaffrey, eds. 1988. *The European Community's Program for a Single Market in 1992.* Washington, D.C.: United States Department of State.

McCartney, J. R. 1989. "The Fight for Jobs in a United Europe." *Washington Post,* Jan. 15, p. H8.

Massart-Pierard, Françoise. 1986. "Limites et enjeux d'une politique culturelle pour la Communauté Européenne." *Revue du Marche Commun* 293:34–39.

Montgomery, Paul. 1989. "Europe Sets Standards for TV Programs." *New York Times,* Mar. 15, p. D1.

Morin, E. 1987. *Penser l'Europe.* Paris: Editions Gallimard.

Official Journal of the European Communities. 1977–91. Luxembourg: Office of Official Publications.

Pacco, Veronique. 1983. *L'Action du Parliament Européen dans le Secteur Culturel.* Brussels: Report of the European Commission.

Perry, Susanne, ed. 1987. *The European Community.* Washington, D.C.: European Community Office for Public Affairs.

Purdom, Lillian. 1983. "Help for the Arts: How Far Should the E.C. Go?" *Europe* 241 (Jan.–Feb.): 27–28.

Rawlinson, William, and Malachy Cornwell-Kelly. 1990. *European Community Law.* London: Waterlow.

Rowen, Hobart. 1989. "Europe's New Crusade." *Washington Post,* June 18, p. H8.

Schlesinger, Phillip. 1986. "Any Chance for Fabricating Euro-fiction?" *Media, Culture, and Society* 8.

Seventh General Report on Activities of the European Communities. 1973. Brussels: Office of the Official Publications of the European Communities.

United States Department of State. 1989. "The Community Program for the Single European Market in 1992." Washington, D.C.: Western European File.

Vessillier, Michele. 1988. *La Situation Sociale des Travailleurs Culturels dans les Pays de la C.E.E.* Brussels: Report for the European Commission.

Wallace, William. 1982. "Europe as a Confederation: The Community and the Nation-State." *Journal of the Common Market* 21 (Sept.–Dec.).

Wiesand, Andreas Johannes. 1981. *Cultural Policy in Europe and European Cultural Policy.* Brussels: Report for the European Commission.

Zentrum fur Kulturforschung. 1985. *Handbook of Cultural Affairs in Europe.* Baden-Baden: Nostresen.

✛ CONCLUSION ✛

Art Patronage: Perennial Problems,
Current Complications

JUDITH HUGGINS BALFE

This volume opened with a question: Why should anyone take on the expense and risk of art patronage? One possible answer— if the arts matter to you and you can afford it, why not?—is as playful and exuberant as are many of the arts themselves. At the same time, that answer opens the way to cost-benefit analysis and bureaucratized structures ensuring accountability: it is easy to find many reasons "why not." Among these is the uncertainty of the outcome. In all of the cases presented in this collection, patronage had consequences for both artists and patrons that were not always anticipated by either, as artists and the newly attracted audiences took advantage of the opportunities that the patrons had provided (intentionally or not). Beethoven established new rules for listening—as well as more difficult music to listen to—and his aristocratic patrons had to adjust to protect their higher status over his *haut bourgeois* supporters who eagerly embraced his new style. So important has audience predisposition become two hundred years later that officials at National Public Radio have attempted to change their music programming to follow (rather than to form) the tastes of their news audience.

Almost always, patrons discover that the reward structure toward which their original patronage had been directed becomes changed through their own activities. Given support and applause, artists (whether in Dutch academies, in Santa Fe pueblos, in Workers' Theater groups, in the East Village, in the German Democratic Republic, or elsewhere) have aspired first to improve—and then to expect greater recognition of—the formal aesthetic qualities in their work. As they become self-identified as *artists* and thus professionalized, they have encouraged the development of an art market structure that has allowed them to disassociate themselves from their original sponsors. Either they have "sold out" to popular stardom, or they have insisted on a new and superior "ethic"— a hierarchy of "pure" art under their own control—with which to subvert or even directly attack the aesthetic, social, and political ideologies of their patrons. In both cases, as the artists have "advanced," among those whom they leave behind are often their original patrons, whether in turn-of-the-century London literary circles or in late-1980s city and federal bureaucracies.

How might social science help us to understand these issues? In the words of Auguste Comte, "founder" of sociology in the early nineteenth century, the purposes of social science are "to know, in order to predict, in order to control." From the evidence presented here, while patrons have usually had considerable knowledge of the art and the artists they have supported (if, perhaps, not so much understanding of the wider audience who was to be impressed), they have been less certain in predicting the consequences. And they have had little chance at all to control.

The Sources of Artistic Charisma

It is clear that the interests of artists have frequently been in distinct opposition to those of their patrons. Putting this in a classical sociological framework, at issue is the legitimation of authority through charisma and its frequent association with an "aesthetic ethic" (Weber 1973 [1920]). If art has a charismatic aura—an autonomous and "magnetic" power located in the artwork itself—it matters to political and economic elites whether the source of this charisma is the artist, who alone has the power to produce the work, or the patron, who has the power to direct its production and ownership.

Since the time of the Renaissance and Lorenzo de' Medici, artists have become so successful in justifying their claims to being the source of artistic charisma that today it seems ludicrous even to question them. Yet artists of consummate genius like Michelangelo and J. S. Bach accepted full patronage control until they became sufficiently independent—usually through the help of those same patrons—to set a few of their own terms. Several generations later, Beethoven's aristocratic patrons still thought that they were "in charge"; several centuries later, so did the variously situated (but hardly aristocratic) founders and supporters of the Indian Art Fund, the Metropolitan Museum of Art, National Public Radio, and the cultural ministry of the German Democratic Republic. Even in the contemporary gallery scene in New York's East Village, dealers vie with each other to establish and then exploit the "charisma" of the artists they have "collected."

To be sure, despite their divergent purposes, both artists and patrons need to impress and convince the immediate audience and the wider public as well; supply and demand must come together. Both immediate applause and long-term public acclaim is necessary to validate the meaning and power of the charisma that patrons and artists respectively sponsor and create in the art. If they do not work together in mutual (if rivalrous) support, there is no applause. If there is no applause, how can they be sure that there is any charisma?

But whose recognition and applause for the artwork's charisma is both necessary and sufficient? Artists and patrons tend to look for approval from different sectors of the audience. On these grounds alone, their interests vary. Artists tend to judge their success almost entirely by the reaction of their peers, the discerning few; patrons are more likely to seek approval of the sponsored art not just among their peers, but also among the wider audience, the less-discriminating many.

For artists, mutual approval is vital whether or not further support is necessary or attained: witness Cézanne and Degas, both with inherited money, involving themselves in cafe discussions with other "Impressionists"; in relative poverty, Picasso and Braque worked together to "invent" Cubism. But without external recognition and patronage—without dealers such as Ambroise Vollard or Durand-Ruel in the first case, Daniel-Henri Kahnweiler as dealer and Gertrude Stein providing a salon in the second—how long could they have kept this up? Solitary artists whose creativity can support itself without recognition are exceedingly rare and "maverick" (Becker 1982): even Van Gogh had his brother Theo—not incidentally an art dealer rather than, say, a plumber.

For artists the issue then becomes how the select few kindred souls are to be identified and recruited, free of the "compromising" pressures by a patron to "adjust" the work so that it will appeal to a larger public. We have seen here the difficulties of this search, in case studies of Dutch painters among the dilettantes in the eighteenth century, of writers shifting from publishers to literary agents in London in the nineteenth, and artists becoming part of the "stable" of commercial galleries in the East Village in the twentieth. In such instances, until the potentially exploitive but also collegial patron becomes established in that role, artists are left to promote themselves competitively, inevitably undermining their support of each other. Typically, they welcome a structure of patronage that can encourage and direct beneficial and comprehending attention, discourage the destructiveness that often accompanies artistic rivalry, and deflect crass commercialism at the same time. Such mediator-patrons exact a cost, of course. As they succeed in promoting the arts, more artists—and more patrons—enter the competition. For artists, the difficulties of establishing peer support become even more complex once competing institutions of private and public patronage become established, leading to bureaucratic inflexibility, as in New York, or controversies over the political implications of public support in censorship controversies, whether in Chicago, Philadelphia, or elsewhere.

As for those who seek reflected glory as patrons, the question is how to impress the many in the wider audience with their acts of artistic philanthropy, when that audience is unable or unwilling to acknowledge the authentic power of the charismatic artwork being supported. Hence the quandary of program officials at New York City's Department of Cultural Affairs, the National Endowment for the Arts, National Public Radio, or in national ministries of culture in Europe or India: if they dilute the "purity" of their program to appeal to a wider, less-informed audience, its short-term meaning may soon be "used up" (Hall 1976, 92), and its charisma will cease to exist over the long term. In any event, some "disenchantment" of artwork, artist, and patron is likely once critical attention is attracted, given the propensies of many contemporary critics to unconvincing hyperbole, on the one hand, or to "deconstruction" on the other. All the more is any inherent artistic charisma removed from the patron's control.

Elitist and Populist Traditions of Patronage

The degree to which artists and patrons have different perspectives on the sources and comparative distribution of charisma depends largely upon whether they follow elitist or populist traditions. While these are "ideal types" rooted deeply in European civilization, comparable antithetical ideologies and practices can be found in virtually every society with a ruling elite. To be sure, they are not found in pure form in any specific empirical case. However, the distinctions are useful for analytical purposes, as they help us to understand the reasons why art patronage is such an uncertain pursuit. Considering them here allows us to reformulate the structural variables of patronage—whether private or public, direct or indirect—which have served to organize the discussion so far. This helps to reveal the inherent tensions between structure and ideology.

In the elitist tradition, art patronage flows from ancient theocracies and aristocracies, building from these hierarchical principles of distinctiveness and perpetuating them along with the aesthetic claims of "high" culture (Bourdieu 1984). Such patronage is often for private enjoyment, of course; when it is not, it is understood as noblesse oblige—in contemporary parlance, as philanthropy. On these terms, the arts are supported as an investment in the future through the activities of unique and superior individuals, whose creative and interpretive expressions are needed both to sustain the quality of today's civilization and to advance it. Within the European tradition, this perspective emerges from the usually conservative aristocracies and flows through the Enlightenment into the structures of the liberal democracies, with their general emphasis upon individualism to be protected and fostered by the secularized administration of the state. Whether such efforts concentrate on preserving the glories of the past or, on the contrary, on supporting the untested avant-garde, it is assumed that the arts are to be developed for their own sake by unencumbered and individualized artists. In time society will recognize or catch up to—and profit from—their visions. If the state becomes involved at all, as direct (or even indirect) patron, it should advance such "recognition" by helping people gain access to the meritorious art of the past or the future that—in the eyes of elitists—they ought to have.

The populist tradition of patronage is, in principle, more egalitarian and communitarian. In its European forms it flows through provincial subcultures and Reformation sectarians oriented toward charity as a response to the human needs of the present. Here the arts are supported as "social glue," as the means of social inclusion of everyone in the collective here-and-now.[1] The assumption is that art's purpose is to secure and enhance the health and safety of society as it is, idealizing neither the distant past nor the distant future at the expense of the present. From this perspective, both private and public patronage should help people to have more of the art that they already want (Gans 1985).

If there is less to be said about this line of patronage, it is partly because the patrons themselves are usually less distinguishable among the group for whom the art is produced. They are certainly known individually (and doubtless honored) by their fellow members of the tribe, the citizenry, or the bureaucracy. However, to outsiders they are as mutually replaceable as are the artisans and folk or popular artists they support, as in the eighteenth-century Dutch academies, the pueblos before the organization of the Indian Art Fund, labor colleges in the 1930s, or in the Artists' Union in the GDR. Not surprisingly, the products of populist traditions have usually been valued less highly by outsiders to those collectivities—especially the scholars, critics, and producers trained in the first tradition, which confirms their own claims to individualized freedom of interpretation and expression.[2]

With modernization, the broad social structures favoring both hierarchy and equality have been legitimated by specific political ideologies. But as the ideologies have become enshrined in governmental institutions, inconsistencies have developed with the artistic ideologies and practices that previously accompanied them (Balfe and Wyszomirski 1985). Let us examine the respective affinities of the two "ideal type" traditions with forms of artistic patronage, in order to understand why they so frequently break down in contemporary practice.

On hierarchical principles, elitist patronage assumes that artistic charisma is unique and cannot be routinized. Once the patrons accept the view that *artists* are the source of such charisma, they expect to bask in the reflected glory of recognition and promotion of the artists and the artworks that embody such uniqueness. In contemporary versions of elitism, then, elites are thought to be composed of a "natural aristocracy" based on ability and discernment (whether that of self-selected artists, aesthetes, or patrons) rather than being exclusively hereditary. All the more must any inherited status be affirmed through public demonstrations of superior taste. To be sure, such patronage often supports arts institutions like museums, symphony orchestras, and opera or classical ballet companies that preserve the masterpieces of the past. Those works are usually associated with earlier elites, yet in the immediacy of contemporary "framing" or performance, they also retain enough idiosyncratic aesthetic qualities to affirm today's elitist principles of superiority based upon highly skilled yet individualized artistic practice. Thus the self-made as well as those with inherited position have discovered the usefulness of affiliation with the artistic "virtuosi" who have produced the distinctive works that have commanded attention over time.

While elitist patronage supports the masterpieces of the past, it also supports individual creative artists working on the cutting edge of innovation and cultural critique.[3] In either case, as noted briefly above, elitist patronage has the overt philanthropic purpose of helping the many to enhance their lives and to become ennobled through the great art produced by the few. Attention is focused on public access to, and education in, those arts and cultural artifacts that presumably will provide the greatest degree of social enrichment through their ability to transcend (and perhaps submerge) subcultural parochialisms. As such art is almost inevitably the product of urban cosmopolitan experience in creation and/or in interpretation, its institutions find the necessary critical mass of both patrons and audiences in large cities. But as these cities also include large numbers who oppose their social and artistic interests, this circumstance does not necessarily make for easy and uncontested artistic outcomes, whether in London, New York, Chicago, New Delhi, or Berlin.

In contrast are the affinities associated with the populist position, based on principles of commonality and equality rather than on distinctiveness. Here, patronage has traditionally moved toward the crafts and folk arts, toward amateur creation and performance, toward community-based, subcultural, volunteer and collective activities—that is, toward support of arts by which the community expresses its current experience, which it already understands and wants.[4] As modernization has progressed world-wide, such groups tend to be relegated to the peripheries of any society, in ethnic enclaves and religious ghettos in large cities or in isolated rural provinces, whether in India or New Mexico. Alternately, once members of such peripheral groups are cast adrift from those traditional moorings and migrate into the core cities, they tend to become part of an anonymous mass whose unschooled tastes present commercial opportunities for the media, on a vast scale.

Whether for folk or mass audiences, populist artistic charisma is inherently "routinizable," intended to be experienced as the lowest common denominator uniting the collective heart rather than being appreciated through the individual mind. Accordingly, from this perspective art is to respond to people's needs for social solidarity and consolation, providing group stability for subgroups or for larger collectivities, rather than advancing individualized and idiosyncratic changes.[5]

Paradoxically, while contemporary patrons who stand on populist principles are often politically radical, the art they support is likely to be conservative in both style and content, if it is to speak to the anonymous masses or the subcultural groups with whom they identify. (The genres of popular culture may appear to change rapidly in terms of style, as mere fads, but they change far more slowly in terms of substance. Boy continues to meet, lose, and regain girl; good men triumph over evil oppressors; "bad" women come to tragic ends. The genres and styles of many subcultural groups change even less.) Such art cannot move far from the traditional tastes and practices of its intended audience, if it is to help maintain their collective solidarity. The ostensible populism of politically radical postmodernists is based on the fact that they take seriously the genres and artifacts of popular culture, as the subject of their analyses of mind-numbing linguistic complexity; therefore they cannot, themselves, be guilty of elitism (Balfe 1990).

For politically conservative elitists, however, the reverse problem is likely to occur. If they are to support hierarchy as a matter of principle and therefore address and stabilize the interests of the superior few against those of the subordinate or inferior many, they must support art that is either innovative or ancient, respectively arcane or obscure (at least until it is identified as fueling a disruptive critique of the political status quo). This is especially true in contexts where their previous patronage has succeeded in making the high arts more widely accessible and popular. By continuing to sponsor art that is difficult, whether avant-garde or antique, such patrons encourage artists and audiences to greater mastery of complexity. Elitists who support both tastes believe that by helping to keep the sophisticated work of the past available in the present, they enable it to serve as stylistic template for substantive innovations that have some probability of outlasting faddishness. However, "classical lite's" succession to "new-age" music is not the answer: mere acquaintance, such as "lite" affords, is not enough to sustain the elitist principles.

Still, the "fascination of the difficult" and its long-term rewards are not usually obvious to nonelite conservatives with whom elitist patrons may be politically aligned. Their tastes are usually more comfortably traditional and trite, less attuned to "the difficult," than elitist art patrons can readily accept. Similarly, many populist and politically radical intellectuals have trouble dealing with the banality of the mass-mediated art forms that are popular among those groups whose interests they claim to advance.

To be sure, as individuals, both patrons and artists may be able to reduce these contradictions as they put their artistic and political ideologies into practice. This is particularly the case in the United States, where egalitarian charitable principles underlying public education have long been used to support art patronage, with art seen as a means of building a common culture across groups of great diversity. (We have seen this principle operating—with some bureaucratic difficulties—in the New York City Department of Cultural Affairs.) At the same time, elitist philanthropic principles support patronage of the "brightest and best," regardless of their original social location. Comparably mixed principles now underlie efforts of developing nations like India and international organizations like the European Community, which are trying to forge a collective yet distinctive identity through the arts.

Bach to Rock, Corelli to the Telly:
The Merger of Patronage Traditions

The dichotomy of elitist and populist ideologies and ideal types is of long standing in the social sciences. Sociologists will have recognized the ironically contradictory principles of *Gesellschaft* (Society) and *Gemeinschaft* (Community) that are at the heart of their discipline; political scientists and economists will have seen the ideal types of democracy and the open market versus the welfare state and the controlled socialist economy. As the twentieth century comes to a close, it appears that the American "mixed case" is becoming more universal, if no less problematic. Now the principles and practices conflict not because they are on opposite sides of the Pyrenees, so to speak, but because they must coexist in the same settings, both in the arts and the structures of their patronage and in other spheres of public life. Thus the frequent conflation of art *patronage* with art *support:* for the "politically correct," the former is inherently patronizing and thus bad, the latter inherently democratic and thus good. Yet freedom of artistic expression may be fostered more by the former than the latter, as we have seen. In any event, it is here that the logic of social science disinterestedness may be useful, in helping both patrons and artists focus on strategies to coordinate their own agendas with those of the larger society (even if control of the outcomes is likely to elude both analysts and practitioners).

Thus following established categories developed in social science, in addition to exploring cases of elitist and populist patronage the essays in this volume have been arranged in order of increasing units of scale of patronage (from individual to private institutions, from these to the public institutions of the city, the state and emerging transnational organizations). As scale and complexity have increased, direct patronage—whether elitist or populist in ideological justification—has given way to indirect forms. Let us reconsider these dimensions.

Private or Public Patronage

Private patronage of the arts has not always met with approval: certainly Plato was opposed, and various Savonarolas have appeared at intervals throughout history. Their argument asserts that society suffers when individual imagination is set free through the acts of private patrons, presumably without whom any distinctive creativity would remain unrecognized. Once released into society, it cannot again be fully controlled. More generally, however, such ecstatic release is not what bothers most contemporary critics of private patronage. To the contrary, on the assumption that "he who pays the piper calls the tune," critics have accused both individual and institutional private patrons of altering some presumably "natural" development of art, in their own class and commercial interests.

This charge is frequently directed at private corporations (Schiller 1989). Considering the importance of corporate patronage (especially in the United States), it has been given insufficient attention in this collection of case studies. However, recent studies of the field show that corporations and their directors (whether analyzed as institutions or as individuals) are like most other private patrons in their self-serving biases (Harris 1990;

Martorella 1990; Useem 1989; Whitt 1989). But while corporate taste is usually attacked for being consistently conservative, private individual patrons who support innovation and the avant-garde also have been criticized, accused of crass social-climbing and market manipulation (Hughes 1989; Moulin 1987). However justified these latter descriptive analyses may be, their ethical implications are clear: although apparently grounded in a purist "aesthetic ethic," these are actually late-twentieth-century versions of Platonic attacks against forms of selfish release from societal responsibility. Particularly problematic is the fact that in such cases, the "release" is obtained immediately and democratically through the open market, with new money, rather than through long processes of legitimation and purification that old money and traditional connoisseurship have undergone. Newcomers are trying to buy cheap what oldtimers have sweated blood to buy dear.

Inverting both the orthodox and the leftist arguments against private patronage, more libertarian/conservative critics have argued instead that it is public art patronage that is unwarranted, because it inevitably imposes some degree of "official" control. In this view, the thriving new-money commercial sphere of galleries, theater, dance, film, video, recording, and design reproduction demonstrates that the open market stimulates freedom of expression and thus enough artistic innovation and production to satisfy most people, as we have seen here in New York's East Village (Banfield 1984; Grampp 1989). Why then, such critics ask, should artists and their patrons continue to receive *any* indirect public subsidy through the tax structure of nonprofit organizations, as in the United States, let alone through direct public support via ministries of culture, as in France and other European states (Cummings and Katz 1987)?

Certainly, as various authors in the collection have noted, the American tradition has tended to oppose public art support (Feld, O'Hare, and Schuster 1983; Larson 1983; Mulcahy 1987; Netzer 1978). In recent decades, however, this view has been challenged if not totally overcome. Now, in reply to those who object to private *or* public patronage, some analysts argue that commercial culture is simply not good or innovative enough. Further, they note that those arts that are more innovative and difficult, less established, and produced by various subcultures need public subsidy as no open market and little private patronage yet exists for such work (Benedict 1991). Additionally, patronage is needed by the established high culture arts, both to preserve them and to expand their accessibility (DiMaggio 1986). Neither private nor public patronage alone can provide sufficient support; some of both are needed to mitigate each other's control as well as to enhance each other's legitimacy through the art they jointly sponsor. At the same time, as we have seen here in the case studies of New York City's Department of Cultural Affairs, the Chicago Art Institute, and the NEA peer panels, trying to satisfy the respective requirements of both private and public funders (for grant applications, evaluation, let alone for the nature of the artistic product) has so compounded the difficulties of artmaking that some artists are withdrawing from the field altogether (Zeigler 1991).

Despite arguments for continued patronage presented by arts advocates, given the counterarguments we must still ask why patrons continue to provide philanthropic support above what the market will bear. After all, in the United States and in most of the Western world, despite their obvious interrelationship the commercial sector of the arts has not been led to subsidize the nonprofit sector to any degree, even though the latter has been described as the "research and development" arm of commercial culture (Chartrand and McGaughey 1989).[6] It is probable that those who manage for-profit arts organizations, facing the bottom line as they do, see little need to invest in such "R&D" when public subsidy and free-lance artists themselves already provide it. But they may also see too much risk in direct patronage—for all the reasons we have detailed.

Direct or Indirect Patronage

Related to the issue of private or public patronage is the degree of direct control that the patron is able to assert. From the evidence presented here, if judged by the artistic consequences there is a crucial intervening variable: scale. From the perspective of artists, patrons, and subsequent audiences, whether elitist or populist in tradition, direct patronage appears most successful when carried on by private individuals and local institutions (although none of the latter, such as town councils, have been described in this volume). However, direct patronage appears to be far more problematic when provided by large public bureaucratic institutions, that is, by the state. On the other hand, indirect patronage appears most successful when carried on precisely by such large-scale public institutions. To be sure, such patronage typically relies upon the participation of various smaller private institutions as well as the mass media; it inevitably requires political and hence artistic compromise. Thereby—in the long run if not in the short—it is likely to result in broad consensus. (Of course, some argue that any such consensus is inherently anti-art: if a work does not offend the status quo, it doesn't speak to the future. But while some art is, at first, offensive, not all that offends is art.)

Paradoxically, art patronage at the middle level of scale, in cities, appears to present the greatest difficulties. Yet throughout history, cities have provided the social matrix out of which the fine arts have flourished and, in recent years, both popular and folk arts have been produced and preserved. Why, then, are both private and public, direct and indirect forms of art patronage so problematic in cities?

The polyglot and multiethnic cities of today provide common but limited turf for battles over power and the differing tastes that exemplify it, as vaster geographic entities do not. Urban political compromises (or standoffs) are personalized, despite the bureaucrats. Given national policies that largely determine any local government's obligations and the revenues at its disposal to meet them, urban officials have little control over any sphere of necessary action—even as they are held accountable by localized constituent groups. It can be argued that only the art formed under such conditions can express and address the personalized experience of these now near-universalized problems. If cities produce the conditions under which such serious art can be produced, inevitably they also produce the conditions of maximum complexity—of least likely success yet of greatest necessity—for public patronage.

For all traditions and forms of patronage—elitist or populist in perspective, private or public, direct or indirect, individual or institutional in structure, and of whatever scale—the current breakdown of virtually all ideologies results in pressure to replace either/or with both/and. Policies based on zero-sum or "win-lose" strategies have proved less effective in the long run than "win-win" strategies in which everyone benefits. However, hard choices must now be made as societal crises caused by the ancient evils of pestilence, famine, and war—to say nothing of more localized instances of pride, sloth, and greed—undermine the economic stability and growth necessary for all to share in any "winnings." Thus many who used to provide both private and public support for arts organizations now help the homeless, AIDS victims, or environmental causes.[7] As national and international needs for such charity increases, they compete with the evermore pressing demand for philanthropy to advance innovative solutions and address future possibilities. Yet elitist principles of noblesse oblige that have provided the foundation for most art patronage no longer hold in a world struggling to maintain populist principles of equality and the welfare state, along with the freedom of open-market competition among individuals, ethnic and subcultural groups, nation states and transnational consortia.

Paradoxes and ironies proliferate: the logic of "politically correct" liberals should oblige them to tolerate the open expression of provincial, sexist, racist, homophobic, or religious views they otherwise deplore, in the arts and elsewhere. Comparably, the logic of political conservatives should mandate governmental noninterference in the lives of artists and other people and communities whose values violate their own orthodoxies. (It was this logic that recently led conservative juries to acquit artists accused of obscenity [Dubin 1992].) Regardless of where they stand politically, individuals find that their "universal" rights to privacy have been invaded and undermined by the mass media of radio, film, and television. Comparably assaulted have been the "particular" rights of distinctive subcultural groups. Both literally and metaphorically, the "boom boxes" of commercial and politicized "public culture" are everywhere. At the same time, however, those media have been the channels through which both individual and group rights have been asserted and acknowledged, both at the city level, as in Chicago in 1988, and in the multinational European Community in 1992.

Through the media, the stars of rock music and television soap operas have reached contemporary audiences far larger and more diverse than those attracted over the centuries to the "live" presentation of works of recognized artistic genius. If one test of a masterpiece is its ability to transcend the social location of its creation, enabling those in its audience to enlarge their own vision with the realization that their particular social, economic, political, or spiritual boundaries are neither unique nor inevitable, then television and recorded music have carried the messages of human liberation everywhere. Without recordings and broadcasting, neither rock nor baroque music would have their current international followings, crossovers, combinations, or inclusions in the new "creoles" of world music—on NPR or elsewhere.

If another and contradictory purpose of great art is "to teach restraint" by demonstrating the difficulties of achievement and the inevitability of unanticipated consequences (Gombrich 1954, 268), these lessons too have been broadcast throughout the world. The price of my own freedom *from* (charity) and my freedom *to* (philanthropy) is the responsibility to make sure that others have access to those same freedoms. Of course, this means that they are likely to act as they choose, not necessarily as I wish them to act. Liberal parents and art patrons tend to discover this only after the fact; conservatives tend to anticipate it so strongly that they restrict themselves from the outset in order to restrain both progeny and protégés.

Conclusion

We return to the perennial problems and the specific lessons of contemporary art patronage, recognizing at the beginning that like the arts they sponsor, patronage is always particularized by its context. Generalizations are thus risky, and counterexamples can surely be found. Nonetheless, it appears that typically, when artists have been given support and new opportunities, they have taken their patrons—and the wider audience— in directions that none had foreseen. By using the respective logics of the elitist or populist models that have lain behind whatever patronage they have been able to attract, creative and performing artists (along with their collectors, agents, dealers, and unions) have pointed up the deficiencies of those logics. Thus it is within the "bottom line" logic of the atomized open market that an oppositional principle of "art for art's sake"—of purity and authenticity—has found support among a self-defined elite of artists, whether in nineteenth-century London, in the late-twentieth-century East Village, or in the European Community. It is within the "socialist" logic of the controlled economy that individualized expression has emerged to resist the hegemonistic tendencies of the collectivist state or simply the bureaucratized city, whether in East Berlin, New York, or New Delhi.

The principles of hierarchy that underlie the elitist position (whether it is based upon the qualitative distinctions of "blood" or upon the quantitative distinctions of money) inevitably provide the grounds for new forms of distinction and inequality—new ranks of status—which are "above" both heredity and the market. To be sure, in delegitimating the claims of prior elites, the new elitists may end up being merely particularistic, setting new status boundaries rather than reordering new status ranks. To the degree that this is the case, the very principle of hierarchy becomes suspect and all arts and tastes become equivalent as "postmodern texts" (Balfe 1990).

Comparably, those holding to the leveling principles of populism provide grounds for new assertions of equality among those individuals and subgroups who feel subordinated by the established egalitarianism—as in the Workers' Theatre movement, in East Germany, and in the European Community. Here too the principle can be used to undermine its own effects. In both cases, artists use the prevailing ideology of their patrons to adjust its application to themselves. Artists adhering to populism may help to perpetuate its belief while they subvert its practice; self-conscious "postmodernists" perpetuate the practice of elitism while subverting its accompanying ideology.

Without question, some forms of innovative art will survive without philanthropic or even commercial patronage, if only by artists serving as audiences to each other. The question remains whether the patrons— in original derivation, quite literally "the fathers"—could long survive without supporting the designs for the future that the arts of their "children" provide. Even if the odds of "success" in attaining *only* their desired purposes through their patronage are slight, some odds are better than none. From the evidence given here, in supporting the arts to enhance or merely to stabilize their own status among competitors, art patrons—like parents generally—have usually received something else than they have bargained for. If they "win" through any success in the art they have supported, they may "lose" in other ways, as the benefits come to others than themselves. But by thus "losing," they set in motion forces useful in the resolution of the contradictions and the social conflicts that they tried to exploit through their patronage in the first place. Obviously, there are other forces interested in those same conflicts, forces much less committed to a "win-win" strategy and much less benign in probable effects. If these forces and their established institutions—be they economic, political, ethnic, or religious—encounter no contesting and individualized voices of artists in the public arena, they will dominate it completely.

Should this occur, the artists will survive in some fashion, in private enclaves with their novels "in the drawer" or distributed in *samizdats*, their pictures taped to the refrigerator door, their music and dances performed alone on the beach in the moonlight. In such cases, it is the would-be patrons and their intended audiences who will be the losers—to say nothing of many who are outside the patrons' arena of intentionality altogether.

Charity to cope with today's vast social problems is not enough. Philanthropy is equally necessary to foster consensus on their public expression and definition, exploration of their resolution and suggestion for future directions. More than the objectivity and universality of science and its allied technology, the subjective personalization of the arts provides the ground for the sharing of meaning upon which collective action is based. That action may be divisive, as established groups and institutions become threatened; conflicts over taste provide expression of—and legitimacy to—more serious conflicts over status and power. By providing for the comparatively benign artistic expression of such rivalries, today's patrons provide as well the means of their transcendence. Why should anyone patronize the arts? The correct answer is not, "Why not?"; it is, "Because—or else!"

Notes

1. This appears in the American pattern of arts-in-education and for social service, following John Dewey. For the distinction between philanthropy and charity

and their ramifications for the arts, I am dependent upon the analysis of Margaret J. Wyszomirski (1987).

2. When such art is "discovered" by followers of the elitist and individualized Western tradition, it is usually decontextualized as "anonymous Primitive art" to remove any apparent taint of humanizing "anthropology" (Metcalf 1985; Price 1989).

3. Artists whose work is clearly following the principle of "art for art's sake" may be supported in any additional critique they may contribute. Those whose work seems to follow the principle of "critique for critique's sake" are unlikely to receive direct patronage, especially if little additional artistry is apparent, and even indirect support will be problematic (Dubin 1992).

4. "Folk" traditions may also depend upon rigorous hierarchical principles, perpetuated by such craftsmen as those named "National Treasures" in Japan who keep alive Zen Buddhist artistic traditions. Yet even here, such recognition is less for individualized and innovative talent; rather, such artist-craftsmen put superior form on what is regarded as a common "inside," in distinct contrast to the common Western "outside" (Hall 1984, 100).

5. Compare two American artists less than half a generation apart in age: Norman Rockwell and Jackson Pollock. Rockwell's realism and restraint appealed to conservative populist taste; Pollock's abstraction and exuberance to avant-garde elites. Both could find support from Deweyan principles of art-for-life's-sake, but only Pollock from the ethos of art-for-art's sake (Balfe 1979).

6. Indeed, in many respects the commercial arts are less successful than the nonprofits in seeking funding. In the United States, business investors can take a tax write-off for any losses incurred when their projects fail, similar to the deductions they can list as patrons of the nonprofit arts. However, the glory they may gain in the latter role may be enough to offset any potential profit they might gain as investors.

7. A 1992 survey by the National Assembly of Local Arts Agencies found that while 56 percent of LAAs are funding art projects designed as "solutions to social problems," among the fifty largest cities, fully 83 percent of the LAAs were doing this (Lynch 1992).

References

Balfe, Judith Huggins. 1979. "Two Faces of Modernity: Norman Rockwell and Jackson Pollock." Annual Meeting of the Association for Humanistic Sociology. Johnstown, Pa., Oct. 26.

——— . 1990. "Modernism and Postmodernism: Implications for Arts Policy." In *The Future of the Arts: Public Policy and Arts Research*, edited by David B. Pankratz and Valerie B. Morris, 189–98. New York: Praeger.

Balfe, Judith Huggins, and Margaret J. Wyszomirski, eds. 1985. *Art, Ideology and Politics*. New York: Praeger.

Banfield, Edward. 1984. *The Democratic Muse: Visual Art in the Public Interest*. New York: Basic Books.

Becker, Howard S. 1982. *Art Worlds.* Berkeley: University of California Press.

Benedict, Stephen. 1991. *Public Money and the Muse: Essays on Government Funding for the Arts.* New York: Norton.

Bourdieu, Pierre. 1984. *Distinction.* Translated by Richard Nice. Cambridge, Mass.: Harvard University Press.

Chartrand, Harry, and Claire McCaughey. 1989. "The Arm's Length Principle and the Arts." In *Who's to Pay for the Arts: The International Search for Models of Support,* edited by Milton C. Cummings, Jr., and J. Mark Davidson Schuster, 43–80. New York: ACA Books.

Cummings, Milton C., and Richard S. Katz, eds. 1987. *The Patron State: Government and the Arts in Europe, North America and Japan.* New York: Oxford University Press.

DiMaggio, Paul, ed. 1986. *Nonprofit Enterprise in the Arts: Studies in Mission and Constraint.* New Haven: Yale University Press.

Dubin, Steven C. 1992. *Arresting Images: Impolitic Art and Uncivil Actions.* New York: Routledge.

Feld, Alan, Michael O'Hare, and J. Mark Davidson Schuster. 1983. *Patrons Despite Themselves: Taxpayers and Arts Policy.* New York: New York University Press.

Gans, Herbert. 1985. "American Popular Culture and High Culture in a Changing Society." In *Art, Ideology, and Politics,* edited by Judith H. Balfe and Margaret J. Wyszomirski, 40–58. New York: Praeger.

Gombrich, Ernst. 1954. "Visual Metaphors of Value in the Arts." In *Symbols and Values: An Initial Study,* edited by Lyman Bryson, Louis Finkelstein, R. M. MacIver, and Richard McKeon, 255–81. New York: Harper's.

Grampp, William D. 1989. *Pricing the Priceless: Art, Artists, and Economics.* New York: Basic Books.

Hall, Edward T. 1976. *Beyond Culture.* Garden City, N.Y.: Doubleday.

———. 1984. *The Dance of Life: The Other Dimension of Time.* New York: Doubleday.

Harris, Neil. 1990 (1973). "Design on Demand: Art and the Modern Corporation." In *Cultural Excursions: Marketing Appetites and Cultural Tastes in Modern America,* 349–78. Chicago: University of Chicago Press.

Hughes, Robert. 1989. "Sold!" *Time,* Nov. 27, pp. 60–65.

Larson, Gary. 1983. *The Reluctant Patron: The United States Government and the Arts 1943–1965.* Philadelphia: University of Pennsylvania Press.

Lynch, Robert. Interview by author, Mar. 19, 1992.

Martorella, Rosanne. 1990. *Corporate Art.* New Brunswick, N.J.: Rutgers University Press.

Metcalf, Gene. 1985. "Black Folk Art and the Politics of Art." In *Art, Ideology, and Politics,* edited by Judith H. Balfe and Margaret J. Wyszomirski, 169–94. New York: Praeger.

Moulin, Raymond. 1987. *The French Art Market.* Translated by Arthur Goldhammer. New Brunswick, N.J.: Rutgers University Press.

Mulcahy, Kevin. 1987. "Government and the Arts in the United States." In *The Patron State: Government and the Arts in Europe, North America, and Japan,* edited by Milton C. Cummings and Richard S. Katz, 311–32. New York: Oxford University Press.

Netzer, Dick. 1978. *The Subsidized Muse: Public Support for the Arts in the United States*. New York: Cambridge University Press.

Price, Sally. 1989. *Primitive Art in Civilized Places*. Chicago: University of Chicago Press.

Schiller, Herbert I. 1989. *Culture, Inc.: The Corporate Takeover of Public Expression*. New York: Oxford University Press.

Useem, Michael. 1989. "Corporate Support for Culture and the Arts." In *The Cost of Culture: Patterns and Prospects of Private Art Patronage*, edited by Margaret Jane Wyszomirski and Pat Clubb, 45–62. New York: ACA Books.

Weber, Max. 1973 (1920). "The Sociology of Charismatic Authority and Religious Rejections of the World and Their Directions: The Aesthetic Sphere." In *From Max Weber*, edited by Hans Gerth and C. Wright Mills, 245–52, 333–39. New York: Oxford University Press.

Whitt, J. Allen. 1989. "The Art of Growth: Ties between Development Organizations and the Performing Arts." Annual Conference on Social Theory, Politics, and the Arts. Toronto, Ont.: York University. Oct. 12.

Wyszomirski, Margaret Jane. 1987. "Philanthropy, the Arts and Public Policy." *Journal of Arts Management and Law* 16(4): 5–30.

Zeigler, Joseph Wesley. 1991. "Collapse: A Seminar on a Crisis in the Arts." *Journal of Arts Management and Law* 21(3): 232–52.

✤ CONTRIBUTORS ✤

JUDITH HUGGINS BALFE is associate professor of sociology, City University of New York: Graduate Center and College of Staten Island. With a degree in art history, she spent a decade in art museum education, and then completed a Ph.D. in sociology at Rutgers University. She has chaired panels and conferences, both national and international, that have focused social science inquiry on the arts, and has published a number of articles in the field. She is coeditor of *Art, Ideology, and Politics* (1985) and *Arts Education beyond the Classroom* (1988), and is executive editor of the *Journal of Arts Management, Law, and Society.*

CLYDE W. BARROW is associate professor of political science, University of Massachusetts–Dartmouth, having completed his Ph.D. at the University of California at Los Angeles. He has published articles on the labor movement and twentieth-century political thought, and is the author of *Universities and the Capitalist State* (1990).

ANNE E. BOWLER is assistant professor of sociology at the University of Delaware. Her Ph.D. dissertation at the New School for Social Research earned the school's Alfred Schutz Prize. Her research has been focused on the relations of artistic and political avant-gardes.

THOMAS A. CASSILLY retired from a career in the United States Foreign Service and since completing a Ph.D. in political science at Columbia University has taught at several colleges, including Montclair (N.J.) State College. He has been cited by the French government for his work as chairman of the New York Chapter of the Friends of Vieilles Maisons Françaises.

KENNETH DAUBER is assistant professor of sociology at Northwestern University, having earned his doctorate in sociology from the University of Arizona. His article on the reception of Buddhist art in eighth-century Japan won the Graduate Student Prize from the Sociology of Culture Section of the American Sociological Association.

TIA DENORA earned a Ph.D. in sociology at the University of California–San Diego. She is a lecturer in sociology at the University of Exeter, England, and has published articles on the sociology of music and its interpretation.

STEVEN C. DUBIN holds a Ph.D. in sociology from the University of Chicago. He is associate professor of sociology, State University of New York–Purchase, where he directs the Social Science and the Arts Program. His extensive writings on culture include two books: *Bureaucratizing the Muse* (1987) and *Arresting Images: Impolitic Art and Uncivil Actions* (1992).

LINDA MARIE FRITSCHNER earned her Ph.D. in sociology at the University of California–Davis. She is associate professor and chair of the sociology department at the University of Indiana–South Bend, and has written on art and art audiences, on publishers' readers, on karate and off-road racing, and other topics.

ANN M. GALLIGAN is assistant professor and fine arts coordinator in cooperative education, Northeastern University, Boston. She holds a doctorate in communications and history from Teachers College, Columbia University. She has been consultant to a number of arts institutions and has written on the subject of arts policy and funding.

ESTHER GELABERT earned an M.A. in arts management from American University in Washington, D.C., as a Fulbright Scholar. She has done extensive international research on comparative support systems and arts management structures and is presently assisting the director of the National Catalonian Museum in Barcelona, Spain.

JUDY LEVINE has taught, written articles, and consulted with hundreds of New York City arts groups on all aspects of non-profit management. She entered arts administration after working as a professional dancer and musician, and is a doctoral candidate in performance studies at New York University.

BLAINE MC BURNEY completed his doctorate at the New School for Social Research in New York, where he continues to do research and program development in the Central European Program at the Graduate Faculty. He teaches at Eugene Lang College.

RICHARD A. PETERSON is professor of sociology at Vanderbilt University. With a Ph.D. in sociology from the University of Illinois, he is the author of many articles on the production of culture, especially in the field of jazz and popular music. He has edited *The Production of Culture* (1976) and has served as consultant to the National Endowment for the Arts and to National Public Radio.

MARILYN RUESCHEMEYER holds a Ph.D. in sociology from Brandeis University. She is associate professor of sociology at the Rhode Island School of Design, and research associate at the Center for European Studies and a fellow of the Russian Research Center, Harvard University. She is coauthor of *Soviet Emigré Artists* (1985) and several books on eastern Germany.

JAAP VAN DER TAS is research associate in the Department of Art and Cultural Studies, Erasmus University, in Rotterdam, Netherlands, where he earned his Ph.D. in the sociology of culture.

VERA ZOLBERG is senior lecturer in sociology and chair of the Committee on Liberal Studies, New School for Social Research, in New York. Having earned her Ph.D. from the University of Chicago, she has published a number of articles on the arts and is author of *Constructing a Sociology of the Arts* (1990).

✤ INDEX ✤